Mirror Lake, Formerly Bennet Pond

by Mary Monel Wait
(circa early 1870s)

Thou sweet reflection of the woods,
Framed by nature's regal hand,
Deep set in mountain solitude
That crowned this Adirondack land.

Those amethyst and sapphire heights,
Tho' far receding from thy shore,
Are sometimes seen reflected deep
Thy soft and crystal water o'er.

Not always is the vision shown
From out those lucid depths of thine,
'Tis rare and sweet as lovers' dreams
Round which all blessed memories twine.

But when the air is full of light,
And o'er thy waves no shadow darts,
Ah! then we see the images
That sleep within thy heart of hearts.

The Plains of Abraham

A History of North Elba and Lake Placid

Collected Writings of Mary MacKenzie

Edited by
Lee Manchester

Nicholas K. Burns Publishing
Utica, New York

Nicholas K. Burns Publishing
130 Proctor Boulevard
Utica, New York 13501
www.nkbpublishing.com

 Printed in the United States of America.

ISBN 13: 978-0-9755224-3-1

Frontispiece: Soon after the Lake Placid House opened, a significant event occurred. Among the guests in the early 1870s were a Mrs. Monel and her daughter, Mary, a young woman of considerable literary talent. Mary Monel fell deeply in love with the pristine little body of water at the foot of Lake Placid House. It had been known as Bennet's Pond for some seventy years in honor of North Elba's first settler, Elijah Bennet. Mary now christened it Mirror Lake and, to commemorate the occasion, meticulously wrote down in the hotel register a poem of her own creation, entitled "Mirror Lake, Formerly Bennet Pond." The name Mirror Lake immediately caught on with both summer and local people who almost overnight made it official. Mary Monel later married Judge Frederick Scott Wait, and the couple acquired Nytis Lodge on Lake Placid. Here the woman who named Mirror Lake spent her summers until her death on February 13, 1927, at Greenwich, Connecticut.
Mary MacKenzie

Cover photo: The Stevens House on Signal Hill reflected in Mirror Lake, circa 1900. Photographer unknown.
From the Mary MacKenzie Historic Slide Collection, curated by Lee Manchester

Library of Congress Cataloging-in-Publication Data
MacKenzie, Mary, 1914-2003.
The plains of Abraham : a history of North Elba and Lake Placid : collected writings of Mary MacKenzie ; edited by Lee Manchester.
p. cm.
ISBN 978-0-9755224-3-1 (pbk.)
1. North Elba (N.Y. : Town)--History--Anecdotes. 2. Lake Placid (N.Y.)--History--Anecdotes. 3. North Elba (N.Y. : Town)--Biography--Anecdotes. 4. Lake Placid (N.Y.)--Biography--Anecdotes. 5. North Elba (N.Y. : Town)--Social life and customs--Anecdotes. 6. Lake Placid (N.Y.)--Social life and customs--Anecdotes. 7. Historic buildings--New York (State)--North Elba (Town) 8. Historic buildings--New York (State)--Lake Placid. 9. North Elba (N.Y. : Town)--Buildings, structures, etc. 10. Lake Placid (N.Y.)--Buildings, structures, etc. I. Manchester, Lee, 1956- II. Title.
F129.N8M33 2007
974.7'53--dc22

2007012856

I have traveled a great deal—in the town of North Elba.

Mary MacKenzie

CONTENTS

PART ONE: THE PIONEERS

PART TWO: THE GOLDEN AGE OF HOTELS

PART THREE: LAKE PLACID

Preface

Editing Mary MacKenzie

In May 2000, when I came to Lake Placid and started working for a local newspaper, one of the first contacts I made was with the official town historian, Mary MacKenzie. She provided me with documentary material for a few stories—really good documentary material—but, frankly, I didn't give Mrs. MacKenzie a great deal of thought until the summer of 2002.

I had come to know the Beatties, proprietors of Lake Placid's Bookstore Plus, in the course of doing a few stories, and they had come to know a little bit about me, including my background in publishing. When they were getting close to finishing pre-press work that summer on a short illustrated history Chris Beattie's aunt, Mary MacKenzie, had written, they asked me if I would do a final proof on the pages before they went to the printer.

As I worked my way through those pages, I started to really get an appreciation for the depth of knowledge Mary had built up over the years about the Town of North Elba and the Village of Lake Placid. But I could also tell that the book I was reading was just a surface treatment, an outline that bespoke many more stories that could have been told in much greater depth, if only there had been time.

When I brought the proof pages of Mary's illustrated history back to Chris Beattie's wife, Nancy, I asked her where the book was that Mary had *really* wanted to write.

Nancy told me—and I later learned from reading Mary's correspondence—about Mary MacKenzie's old, old dream of researching and writing the complete history of the community in which she'd been raised. Since the 1960s, in fact, she'd been telling people about the history she was working on.

But Mary MacKenzie loved the detective work of historical research too much to sit herself down, gather her materials, and focus herself for a year or two on "scribbling." From her correspondence and the stories her friends and family members have told me, it was Mary's ongoing study of the history of North Elba and Lake Placid that prevented her from writing the book she *really* wanted to write about that history.

"Someone else will have to go through my files and put it all together," she said, according to Nancy Beattie, "but they'll have to do it after I'm gone." (The truth is that Mary would *never* have let someone get his or her hands on all those files while she was still alive!)

As soon as I heard Nancy say that, something in me suspected that I was going to be the one to compile and edit Mary MacKenzie's collected works—but I didn't think that the time for the job would come as quickly as it did.

As it turned out, Mary MacKenzie's little illustrated history made it into print in the nick of time, just a few months before her passing. *Lake Placid and North Elba: A History, 1800 to 2000*, was published in August 2002. Eight months later, she passed out of this life.

Mary's family viewed her death in April 2003, at the age of eighty-nine, as a release rather than a loss. During her final years, she had suffered excruciating pain from acute neuralgia. In the end, the pain just wore her out.

When I got together with Mary's family and friends to write her obituary profile, we started talking about the process of going through her files to compile her collected historical works for publication. For reasons that are still not entirely clear to me, everyone seemed to have already assumed that I was going to be Mary's literary executor. They knew that I could not bear to see Mary MacKenzie's lifetime of research and writing just sit in the file cabinets she had turned over to the Lake Placid Public Library, slowly turning to dust.

In those conversations with family and friends, I learned that Mary had left more writing behind than just her vast body of historical monographs, letters, and articles. Nancy Beattie told me that, when they were going through her belongings, they came across a packet of poems, carefully typed on notebook paper, wrapped in rubber bands, and put away in a drawer of her desk. Mary had been aware that the end was coming soon, and had thrown out everything she didn't want found after her death, Nancy said; this was clearly something she had wanted to be found and, presumably, to be read.

After committing Mary's ashes to the North Elba Cemetery in a plot next to her husband's grave, her family and friends were invited to the Beatties for an informal reception. Nancy brought out the poems she had found and invited people to look through them. As soon as I got my chance, I knew they were the real thing: a body of really good poetry, written when Mary was in her early twenties, nearly seventy years before. I decided right then that, if I was going to spend the time to ensure that Mary MacKenzie's historical research and writing were preserved for future generations, I was also going to do what I could to bring these hidden poems to light—and, hopefully, to a publisher.

I began that job first.

Before doing anything else with the poems, I scanned them into my computer so that I would not have to handle the aging pieces of paper on which the poems had been written any more than necessary. After that, I began the long, slow process of keying those poems into my computer's word-processing program, doing some minor editing, and formatting the material.

After about a year, Mary's poems were ready to show to a publisher. My only question then was, *which* publisher? Poetry is a pretty specialized field of publishing, and I really didn't know anything about who to contact or how to approach them.

Fortunately, just as I was finishing my work on the poems, I was also preparing to interview Roger Mitchell, an accomplished poet who had retired to Jay. Roger had just come out with a new book from which he was going to be reading at the Keene Valley Library, and I was writing a preview profile for my newspaper. From my research, I knew that Roger's wife, Dorian Gossy, had taught classes on how writers could find publishers for their work.

When Roger and I finished our interview and he introduced me to Dorian, I briefly told her about the poetry project and asked her if she had any ideas. Without hesitation, she came up with *Blueline,* the self-styled "literary magazine of the Adirondacks," published annually out of the State University of New York at Potsdam. Dorian suggested picking out a dozen of Mary's 150-or-so poems, sending them in to *Blueline* with a query, and seeing what happened. If *Blueline* ran them, she said, the reaction to their publication there might result in the entire book being picked up a few years down the line.

I sent my first query to *Blueline* editor Rick Henry on March 14, 2004.

Twelve days later, Rick wrote back, asking how much more such material I had.

On April 8, after looking at the entire body of work, Rick wrote again to ask if *Blueline* could publish the whole thing as a book-length supplement to the magazine's 2005 annual issue.

The next May, Mary Landon MacKenzie's *Collected Poetry 1931 to 1937* was mailed to *Blueline's* four-hundred-plus subscribers, and the Lake Placid Public Library—which had been given the copyright to the poems by Mary's family, at my suggestion—was given one hundred more copies as a "royalty." Those copies were offered for sale through a local bookshop.

By the end of the summer of 2006, Mary's book of poems had completely sold out.

The process of finding a publisher for Mary MacKenzie's "secret poetry" had been surprisingly simple, almost as if it had been "meant" to happen.

Finding a publisher for Mary's collected historical works was even simpler—in fact, the publisher actually called *me.* Nick Burns, who runs his own Utica publishing house—Nicholas K. Burns Publishing—was tipped off to the project by Adirondack historian Ted Comstock.

Nick called, I did a little research on his operation, and we made a deal—which meant that all I would have to worry about was compiling and editing Mary's work, not selling it. (Just to set matters straight, this is a volunteer project on my part; one hundred percent of the royalties are going to the Lake Placid Public Library, to which Mary MacKenzie transferred the copyrights to her historical material before her death.)

Compiling Mary MacKenzie's collected historic works was much more involved than the process of putting her poetry together. In her forty years as North Elba town historian, she had gathered material into hundreds and hundreds of files. That material completely filled two file cabinets, each holding four drawers, each drawer three feet deep.

At the beginning, I wanted to read all that material, every piece, every word. Before I had bushwhacked my way through the very first drawer, however, I came to the conclusion that working that way would take years, and I was simply not willing to commit that much time to the project.

I adjusted my work process: I looked quickly at each document to see if it was something Mary MacKenzie had written herself—whether it was a letter, a speech, a monograph, a research note, or a finished article—and whether it was ready, as it was, for publication. Each piece that met those criteria was photocopied and inventoried.

If the copy of a given item was typed clearly enough, I scanned it into my computer and used optical character recognition software to turn it into text that I could clean up in a word processor.

There were many items, however, where the quality of the copy I had was too poor to be scanned with the OCR software. I had to retype those documents, from start to finish, before I could start working on them.

Once all the material had been converted into word-processor documents that matched the documents I had copied from Mary's files, I started going through them as an editor.

First, I gave the material a thorough copyediting. The quality of Mary MacKenzie's prose was very strong but, like every writer, she still made her share of copy goofs that had to be cleaned up.

The hardest part was deciding what to do with the repetitions throughout the material, from item to item, and how to reconcile the various stories Mary had written in the course of her long career on the same topic.

In some cases, such as the twenty-five individual monographs Mary wrote on the individual settlers in Gerrit Smith's famous North Elba Black colony, I combined them into a single, comprehensive chapter, preserving virtually everything except the duplications from monograph to monograph.

In other cases, I combined them wherever I could, using the latest version wherever there was a conflict in factual material, but always preserving the lyrical elements of Mary MacKenzie's storytelling.

With as much as has been written about the Adirondacks, it may come as a surprise that there has never been a really comprehensive history written about Lake Placid, New York, a village that for many stands at the spiritual center of the Adirondack Mountains—but it's true.

In fact, until Mary MacKenzie became town historian of North Elba in 1964 (Lake Placid lies within North Elba township), there had been no one, really, who had studied Lake Placid history in a really rigorous, systematic way.

In the minds of many Adirondack scholars and lovers of history, Mary MacKenzie *created* the history of Lake Placid, researching it from scratch and starting at the very beginning—and by the beginning, I mean the *beginning*. Mary's studies took a look back not only to the start of the human settlement of North Elba, but to the beginning of Adirondack geologic history over a billion years ago.

Long before I had finished editing the entire body of Mary MacKenzie's collected historic work, the research she had done started finding its way into my own writing. I used Mary's work as the primary source for some very popular pictorial tours of Lake Placid's grand old tourist hotels, the village Main Street, and the township's nineteenth century network of one-room schoolhouses.

For other stories, Mary MacKenzie's research into a particular subject caught my interest, inspiring me to do my own story, albeit from a very different angle. For instance, Mary's careful, extensive research on the early Northwest Bay-Hopkinton Road led me to hike a very beautiful backwoods trail that had been made from an abandoned five-mile stretch of that old, old road. The same thing occurred in connection with Mary's writing about the original Wilmington-North Elba road, built high above the Wilmington Notch in the early 1800s.

Mary MacKenzie's research was also invaluable in providing me with the ammunition I needed to debunk some of the same myths that she had fought to correct. When a state agency started a grant program to fund interpretive programs surrounding Underground Railroad sites in the North Country, I used Mary's research as the starting place for an examination of each supposed site and each legendary reference to such activity in our neck of the woods. Every single one of them turned out to be incorrect.

Later, when the state started funding interpretive projects at some of these sites *anyway*—work that was written up uncritically on the news pages and applauded on the editorial page of a competing newspaper—Mary's material gave me more ammunition to use in blowing those stories apart.

And yet, the stories still come. Clearly, people want to believe there was an Underground Railroad line coming through North Elba, for some reason, as if the town's true history isn't sufficiently exciting for them. Now that the book containing Mary MacKenzie's collected work has made it into print, all we have to do is tell such people, "Just read it."

By August 2005, I had finished nearly all the work I intended to do on editing Mary's "Big History," which Nicholas K. Burns has now published as *The Plains of Abraham*—but only after Burns did another full round of copy and line editing himself.

(Nick Burns, by the way, deserves a medal for the way he edited the manuscript I delivered to him. Nick was especially skillful at eliminating many of the textual duplications within Mary's materials that I couldn't bear to touch. This book is significantly more readable because of Nick Burns' superlative editorial touch.)

There was, however, one final piece of Mary MacKenzie's legacy still missing. In her papers, I had seen many references to a set of slides she had made from historic photographs borrowed from dozens of local sources. I had not found those slides, however, in her files, and I couldn't find anyone who could tell me exactly what had happened to them. I hoped that they hadn't been tossed out wholesale when her family had gone through her belongings following her death, but I thought that was the most likely scenario.

Then, in November 2005, I learned that the slides had come into the possession of Mary's successor as town and village historian, Beverley Reid—which is exactly where they should have been in the first place! How long she'd had them, and where they had been in the meantime, I wasn't sure. All I knew was that, at last, I had found the final body of work that Mary MacKenzie had prepared for the benefit of her community.

I talked to Bev, and we arranged for me to borrow those slides for a couple of days so that I could scan them, one by one, on a special piece of equipment at my newspaper's production plant. The images on those slides were in pretty poor shape. It took me many an evening at the computer to digitally restore them—all 332 of them.

With the help of Bev Reid and former Lake Placid chief librarian Therese Patnode, we prepared interpretive captions for the slides, each of which has been used for a panel in a Power Point slide show. The slide show will be available for Bev to use in presentations to school classes or community groups, for screening at the Lake Placid Historical Museum, or for anyone else who wants to use it. The show will also be available for viewing on the Internet, we hope, courtesy of the Lake Placid Public Library.

There are probably more historic photographs of Lake Placid in circulation than of any other village of comparable size that I can think of, even in the Adirondacks, because of Placid's dual roles as a summer mountain resort and a winter sport center. Even with all the other photos floating around out there, I believe that the range of images preserved in the Mary MacKenzie collection is probably the broadest I've ever seen.

And now, Mary's last book is, at last, finished. Her historical essays are the product of a truly original intellect. That's why it seemed so important to give this collection a title that was just as original. *The Plains of Abraham* seemed just right: biblical, poetic, even a little romantic, it was the name the first settlers themselves gave to the land of woods and fields between the High Peaks, the Cascade Lakes, Whiteface Mountain, and the Saranac lakes, where they had come to make their new home.

Welcome to *The Plains of Abraham.*

Read it.

Criticize it.

Enjoy it.

And if you find that Mary has missed some crucial aspect of Lake Placid or North Elba history in her research, then do your own research! The job of writing a community's history, after all, is never really *finished*; there's always more to discover, errors to correct, new angles to explore, and history being made.

Acknowledgments

There are many people who have contributed to this project, not the least of whom are Mary MacKenzie's nephew and niece, Chris and Nancy Beattie, proprietors of the Bookstore Plus in Lake Placid. Not only did they take it upon themselves to publish Mary's wonderful little illustrated history just a year before her passing, but they have been constant sources of encouragement in my effort to ensure that Mary's larger body of work is preserved and made freely available to the community.

During her lifetime, there were several periodicals that helped Mary bring her work into public view: *Placid Pioneer*, a newsletter Mary edited for the Lake Placid-North Elba Historical Society; *Patches and Patterns Extended*, the journal of the Ticonderoga (New York) Historical Society; *Franklin Historical Review*, published by the Franklin County Historical and Museum Society, Malone, New York; *Adirondack Life* magazine, Jay, New York; the *Conservationist*, published by the New York State Department of Environmental Conservation; and the *Lake Placid* (New York) *News.*

Mary also wrote numerous public talks for presentation to various organizations as well as for broadcast. Mary MacKenzie considered the material she created as North Elba town historian and Lake Placid village historian to be the property of the community she served. Before her death, Mary conveyed the copyright to her entire body of historical writings—including her letters, notes, published articles, monographs, speeches, and genealogies—to the Lake Placid Public Library. All royalties for *The Plains of Abraham* will be paid directly to the library to help it continue fulfilling its mission, which includes the maintenance of historical archives for Lake Placid and North Elba.

I want to thank my wife, Jody Leavens, for her understanding as I worked on this project during my off hours. She appreciates as much as I do the importance of preserving the work that Mary did: recovering the history of Lake Placid and North Elba.

Lee Manchester
Lake Placid, New York

Mary MacKenzie

Over twenty years ago, a student wrote a letter to Mary MacKenzie, official historian for Lake Placid and the town of North Elba. MacKenzie had recently spoken to his school class.

Dear Ms. MacKenzie,
I'm glad you came to our school.
I want to know something. How do you know so much about Lake Placid?
Your friend,
Donny Hare

A couple weeks later MacKenzie wrote back:

Dear Donny,
You were nice to write me, and I'm answering your letter as you asked. You want to know how I know so much about Lake Placid and its history. Well, I guess it's like everything else. If you want to learn about a subject, you have to do a lot of studying, and that's what I have done for twenty-five years. I've also gone to a lot of places to find out about our past—the National Archives in Washington, D.C., all the state offices in Albany, our county clerk's office, and many museums. I have also studied old newspapers, books, and magazines. It is a lot of hard work, but a lot of fun, too.
Sincerely,
Mary MacKenzie

"A lot of hard work, but a lot of fun, too." That was how Mary MacKenzie approached her job of nearly four decades as local historian, first of the town of North Elba, then of the village of Lake Placid—a job she defined as she went, gathering the documentary and photographic traces of our past, cataloguing them, and making sense of the patterns they revealed to an ever-interested community.

Mary was born in Lake Placid on March 12, 1914.

No sooner had she graduated from Lake Placid High School in 1930, at the age of sixteen, than she went to work for Ernest Gamache, executive secretary of the local committee preparing for the 3rd Olympic Winter Games, scheduled here for 1932.

"I don't know how much time she actually put on the job, though," said niece Nancy Beattie, co-owner of Bookstore Plus on Main Street and publisher of Mary's first book, *Lake Placid and North Elba: A History, 1800–2000.*

"In her desk we found notebooks with page after page of truly astonishing poetry she wrote during that time," Beattie said, "some of it surprisingly deep."

Mary's work with the Olympic Committee decided her on a career as a secretary. Over the years, she worked as a legal secretary, as Lake Placid's acting village clerk, and for twenty-one years as Henry Uihlein's personal secretary and office manager at Heaven Hill Farm. She retired from secretarial work in 1976.

By that time, Mary had already been North Elba's official town historian for a dozen years, receiving her appointment in 1964. Three years earlier, she had been one of the founding members of the Lake Placid-North Elba Historical Society, created in 1961. She remained active in the society for the rest of her life, serving as an officer, a trustee, and editor of its quarterly bulletin.

Over the years, Mary joined at least eight more county, regional, state, and national historical associations, always using the expertise she gained to help her interpret local history for area civic and school groups. By the mid-1990s, she had given more than one hundred talks on Lake Placid history and had overseen the creation of more than one hundred slides of historic photographs for use in her interpretive lectures.

When the Mill Pond dam broke in April 1970, Mary was one of those who rallied the community behind the effort to rebuild the structure that had played such a key role in Lake Placid's history. She explained the importance of its restoration in a pamphlet she wrote for the project:

> Mill Pond was born about 1853...Two men laid a log dam across the Chubb River, impounding a picturesque body of water for the operation of a sawmill....The pond was steeped in the early history of Lake Placid....The village rose and grew and flourished

> on its shingle, saw and grist mills....A railroad station, blacksmith shop, slaughter house, the American House hotel, George White's Opera House, old-time country stores—all these lined the shores.

Today, thanks to Mary and the rest of her committee, the Mill Pond dam stands again on the Chubb River, across from the railroad station on Averyville Road at the foot of Mill Hill off Cascade Road.

Mary MacKenzie's unique position as both town historian and former secretary to the director of the 3rd Olympic Winter Games led ABC Television and other media outlets to draw on her as a key source before and during the 1980 Games in Lake Placid. Shortly after the conclusion of those Games, Lake Placid named Mary its official village historian.

For many years Mary MacKenzie had planned to write a book about Lake Placid and North Elba's history, dating back not merely to the creation of the village (1900), the township (1850) or the first local settlement (1800)—but to the area's geological formation, millions of years ago. Mary was, you see, not only a historian but also an avid amateur rock hound. She first joined the Northland Rock and Mineral Club in 1962, serving at different times as its program chairwoman and vice president.

And that wasn't all.

Mary was a long-time member of the Garden Club of Lake Placid, first joining in 1959. She was twice elected to the club's executive board, first in 1959 and again in 1967.

She also had an abiding interest in local partisan politics. In 1955, she joined the North Elba Women's Republican Club, serving as its president in 1961 and 1962. From 1962 to 1964, she also served on the Lake Placid Village Republican Committee.

Mary finally published her first book on local history in 2002, just a few months before her death, with the help of nephew Chris Beattie and his wife Nancy. That book, however, was by no means the only publication to result from Mary's historic scholarship. She wrote numerous articles for *Adirondack Life* magazine, the *Conservationist*, and *Encyclopedia Americana* as well as the two local newspapers, the *Adirondack Daily Enterprise* and the *Lake Placid News*.

Mary was also a frequent contributor to the newsletters of all the local historical societies. Two of her articles for the Lake Placid-North Elba society's newsletter were reprinted as pamphlets for sale at the society's museum. One of them, *History of the Village of Lake Placid, New York*, first published in 1970, is still probably the best short history of the community available.

Mary MacKenzie was recognized over and over again for her extraordinary work as a local historian:

- For ten years, she was listed in the *Who's Who of American Women* because of her contributions to Adirondack history.
- In 1992, she was inducted into the Lake Placid Hall of Fame.
- She won the Clinton County Historical Society's McMasters Prize.
- She was given the "Bessie" Award of the North Country Local Historians Association for community service above and beyond the call of duty.
- In 1997, the Association of Municipal Historians of New York State chose her as its Outstanding Historian of the Year.
- Finally, following the publication of her book in 2002, Mary won what she said was the award that meant the most to her, the Edmund J. Winslow Local Government Historian's Award for Excellence. The award, given jointly by the Office of the State Historian of New York and the Association of Public Historians of New York State, recognizes excellence in one or more public history projects or publications.

Mary began one of her many talks with a quote from Henry David Thoreau:

> Thoreau used to have a marvelous answer for people who asked him what the extent of his travels had been. He used to say, "I have traveled a *great deal* in Concord, Massachusetts." Well, if anyone were to ask me where I had traveled, I could very well answer, "I have traveled a *great deal* in the town of North Elba." I guess I'm luckier than most because, in my job as historian of North Elba, I've had to do a lot of research and snooping around, and I've been able to learn in a comparatively short time what the average resident would not learn in a lifetime.

Following Mary MacKenzie's death on April 15, 2003, Lee Manchester spent time compiling a pair of books out of the two bodies of work she had left behind.

One was a collection of poetry Mary had written as a young woman. First published by *Blueline* magazine in the spring of 2005 as *Collected Poetry, 1931 to 1937,* Nicholas K. Burns Publishing has re-issued the book under a new title, *The Secret Poems of Mary C. Landon.*

The second body of Mary MacKenzie's work collected and edited posthumously is the one you hold now in your hands, *The Plains of Abraham: A History of North Elba and Lake Placid.* It is the culmination of Mary's long love affair with her native town and village.

PART ONE

The Pioneers

ONE

Elijah Bennet: Lake Placid's First Settler

*This chapter was compiled from three sources: "All Stories Should Begin with Once Upon a Time" (date unknown), "The Patriot and Wanderer Who Was Lake Placid's First Settler" (*Lake Placid News, *March 29, 1979; reprinted in* Patches and Patterns Extended, *Winter-Spring 1992), and "Chapter 1: Lake Placid's First Settler, Elijah Bennet" (date unknown).*

Early in the morning and again at dusk, Mirror Lake, in the heart of Lake Placid village, holds in its shallows the calm reflex of mountain, tree, and sky. Sometimes at night, the spectacular full moon, rising over Cobble Hill, looks down upon itself.

This lovely little water gem was poetically, but aptly, christened Mirror Lake in the early 1870s by Miss Mary Monell (later Mrs. Frederick S. Wait), who was among the first guests at Benjamin Brewster's popular new hotel. From a rocking chair on Brewster's porch, she admired the view, then wrote in the hotel register for posterity four verses entitled "Mirror Lake." Happily, the "city slickers" and natives alike adopted the name at once.

Yet for seventy years and more before the advent of Miss Monell, the lake bore quite another name—Bennet's Pond—and was so designated on early maps of the region. For what intrepid pioneer it was named in the dim, forgotten past, no historian of the Adirondacks seems to have known. In only one published history touching on Lake Placid or its township, North Elba, has the mysterious Bennet been singled out for identity. A clue appears in an 1860 State Historical Gazetteer compiled by J.H. French. Included in his story of North Elba is the simple, unadorned statement, "Settlement was commenced about 1800 by Elijah Bennett."

Unfortunately, fire destroyed the early records of North Elba almost a hundred years ago, and there is no trace of Elijah Bennet anywhere in the annals of Essex County. Yet, by a strange set of circumstances, much of his personal life story has been preserved in a file in the National Archives at Washington, D.C., and from that and a few other scattered state records, a full-length likeness of Lake Placid and North Elba's elusive first citizen can now be sketched.

There has probably never been, anywhere, at any time, a more unlikely first settler.

To begin with, Elijah Bennet (his last name is properly spelled with only one "t") was not a young man when he arrived on the remote shores of the lake that was to bear his name for the better part of a century. Pioneering, by tradition and according to the "Gospel of Television," is a pursuit of the young. In 1800, Elijah was forty-six, having been born in 1754. For the modern teen-age TV fan, he was over the hill. For that particular era, he had one foot in the grave.

Secondly, Elijah was a cripple. A patriot of the American Revolution, he had served in the Continental Army as a private. A musket ball had fractured his left arm at the famous battle of Bunker Hill. The bones were so shattered that, in the words of one of his daughters, "a part of them were loose and never grew fast," and his arm was afterwards always weak and lame. Then, in his own words, he had "three breaches in his body, one nigh each groin at the bottom of his belly and one nigh his navel."

To complicate matters, his wife Rebecca was also past her youth, being thirty-six in the year 1800, and during their early years in North Elba, along with the severe hardships of pioneer life, they were burdened with seven young mouths to feed.

Finally, Elijah was poor. He was no Sir William Johnson, regally enthroned in a stately Georgian manor house in the Mohawk Valley, and no affluent William Gilliland of Essex, who carved out a wilderness barony on the shores of Lake Champlain. He was an unimportant man, as were almost all of North Elba's early settlers, a simple farmer who lived off the land by the sweat of his brow. He also followed the blacksmith's trade.

He brought to North Elba around 1800 little in worldly goods. He died in North Elba (then a part of the Town of Keene) in 1830, leaving an unmarked grave and nothing to his widow and children but the memory of a courageous spirit.

Before he earned the title of North Elba's first permanent resident, Elijah was one of the early settlers of Orwell, in Addison County, Vermont, just across Lake Champlain from Ticonderoga. Orwell today is still a sleepy village, off the main route of travel and brooding on its past. He arrived there after the Revolution, probably from Connecticut, where he had enlisted for military service.

At Horwich, Connecticut in April 1775, hot-blooded and adventurous at twenty-one, he joined Company 10, Putnum's Regiment, Connecticut

Troops, commanded by Captain Durkee. Enlisting for seven months, he served out his time at Roxbury and near Boston, and he was severely wounded, as already related, in the Bunker Hill battle. The army then discharged him and he returned home.

But mere battle wounds could not restrain our hero. Filled with the "Spirit of '76," in January 1776 he immediately reenlisted for one year in the company commanded by Captain Robinson, in Captain (later Colonel) Durkee's regiment. When his year expired, he was discharged near Philadelphia. But we find the dauntless Elijah again out for several short tours—three months at the taking of the British Army at Saratoga, and two months with General Greene of Rhode Island.

At war's end, the infant United State government granted him a pension of the huge sum of forty-eight dollars a year. By this time, he had taken a wife, but his life was marred by her early death and he was left a widower in 1790. There is no evidence of any children born to Elijah and his first wife.

At this period of his life, he lived alone on his own holdings in the thinly populated Town of Orwell. His sister—with the rather incredible, Dickensian name of Betsey Bottum—acted as his housekeeper, and he had the company of a number of close friends and neighbors, among them Clark Sanford and Samuel Griswold. Griswold was a carpenter by trade, and Elijah seems to have been somewhat of a carpentry buff, attending all of Griswold's house raisings.

Now, Elijah wasted no time in finding another young woman who suited his fancy. By the standards of her day, she was probably considered a spinster of advanced age, for she was twenty-eight when they married, having been born in 1764. Her name was Rebecca Baker, and she resided nearby with Lucy and Asa Parks. Elijah often boasted to his friend Sanford about the rapid progress of his courtship.

In 1792 at a religious meeting in Orwell, Rebecca and Elijah published their intention to marry. Whatever their reason, they vetoed a church wedding, and in November of that year "eloped" to Cornwall, Vermont, making the journey on a horse loaned by Elijah's old friend, Deacon Nathaniel Bacon. Esquire Joel Lindsley, acting justice of the peace, performed the ceremony, witnessed by three people of sound Yankee names, Eleanor and Daniel Foot and Roxalana Peet.

For eight years, Rebecca and Elijah continued to live in Orwell near Lucy and Asa Parks. It is strange, in light of the fact that they later produced a large family, that there is no sign of any children born to them in Vermont. It seems to have been alone, and without the impediment of offspring, that they embarked on the long and perilous journey that finally brought them to the present Town of North Elba. Before leaving Orwell, Elijah sold all his real estate, deeding fifty acres in 1799 and another small lot in 1800.

What could have prompted the removal of these two people to a remote, uninhabited tableland deep in the Adirondack wilderness? The answer is not too difficult. Quite likely, they were victims of what was then called "New York Fever," which was spreading like a contagion among the citizens of the New England states. Northern New York was then a western frontier of America. During the late eighteenth century and early nineteenth, a swarm of emigration from that prolific hive, New England, swept into the northern counties of New York.

These far northern lands in the Adirondack Mountains came into possession of New York State after the Revolutionary War. They were originally the hunting grounds of the Mohawk Indian tribe of the Iroquois confederacy and, by tradition, North Elba was for a long period the site of a Mohawk summer village. It was wild, rugged, forbidding country, the home of the panther, wolf, and wildcat, now largely owned by the state except for the shore of Lake Champlain. But tales of fabulous timber stocks and mineral deposits, rich, virgin lands and scenic wonders, traveled over Yankee soil like news of a gold rush, and the trek was on.

It was probably deep winter, not spring or summer, when Rebecca and Elijah started out. Winter was almost invariably the season for moving in the north. Ice bridged streams, lakes, and swamps, so primitive routes, which in warmer seasons were muddy, treacherous bogs, became passable. They must first have journeyed across to Ticonderoga. We can only guess at the complete route they followed, for it is not known whether North Elba was their original goal. In any event, the final phase of their journey would have taken them over the Northwest Bay (Westport)-Hopkinton Road, which became popularly known as the Old Military Road. Parts of it still bear the name today. This early road led westward from Westport through Elizabethtown and Keene village, to North Elba, continuing west to Hopkinton in St. Lawrence County.

History books to the contrary, there is plenty of evidence in old records that a road was in use all the way from Westport at least to Franklin County as early as 1800. Pioneer settlers had definitely extended the road from Westport to Keene village before 1800. The wealthy landowners of the great Macomb's Purchase in St. Lawrence and Franklin Counties had then continued the road—at their own expense and for access to Lake Champlain—from Keene village, through North Elba, bridging the Saranac River, and thence west. The year this occurred is uncertain. In any event, Stephen Thorn noted that the road was in existence to the border of Franklin County when he arrived in North Elba in 1804 to survey the Old Military Tracts for the state. It appears, then, that Elijah Bennet had no need to hack his way blindly through an uncharted wilderness.

Even today, over the abandoned, gloomy forest stretch of Old Military Road known as the "Old Mountain Road" hangs a mysterious and heavy silence. This was once the last leg of the journey to North Elba, and it has not changed much since Elijah Bennet's day. From Keene the road climbs up and up over Alstead Hill, hugs the north flank of Pitchoff Mountain, and finally plunges down to Cascade Road,[1] just west of the Freeman's Home motel.

Many a hair-raising tale was told in the old days of the hazards in negotiating this primitive mountain passageway to the west. One can picture Elijah and Rebecca plodding beside their span of oxen, under a canopy of towering maples, perhaps leading a cow or two, a pig, a goat or a sheep, Elijah cradling a rifle in the crook of his good arm, raising their heads in alarm at the far-off sound of a wolf's howl or the snarl of a panther crouched in a great, overhanging tree. While the lofty wagon pitched from side to side, threatening to overturn, the huge wooden wheels clanked over treacherous stones or churned a muddy track.

Then, suddenly, they were out on North Elba's wide, wooded, fertile plateau, the amphitheater ringed by splendid mountains. It is pleasant to believe that it was spring then—and quite probably it was—with no threat of the harsh winter ahead. Deer browsed in the beaver meadows, trout leaped in the shining brooks and rivers. Flocks of passenger pigeons were loud in the ancient beech trees. Ahead of them stretched untold miles of uninhabited land, virgin forest, the silver gleam of lakes and ponds and rushing streams, theirs alone for the choosing.

---

1 State Route 73.

Rebecca and Elijah chose well. They settled on Great Lots 279 and 280 of Township 11, Old Military Tract.

In 1804, Surveyor Stephen Thorn valued the 200 acres of Lot 279 at $1.20 an acre, total $240, and the ninety-two acres of Lot 280 at $1.50 an acre, total $138. Of Lot 279 he noted, "This lot in the occupancy of Elijah Bennett who has a log hut thereon & 10 acres of improvements worth $100—good lot." And of Lot 280, "Poor lot but has a good mill place thereon & a house—possession own'd by Elijah Bennet & worth $150." The "good mill place" was almost certainly what is now the Lower Mill Pond.

Today Great Lots 279 and 280 would fetch a king's ransom. Roughly, they include the south end of Mirror Lake, the village beach, all the main Lake Placid Club buildings and grounds and its upper golf course, all of Parkside Drive, all of residential Wilmington Road, Main Street and its environs from the Post Office down to Mill Hill, the lower Mill Pond, and much of Sentinel Road.

The Bennets were not long alone in their mountain home. From 1800 to 1810, the clop of horse and oxen hoof was a familiar sound on Old Military Road as family after family careened down the Old Mountain Road, took one look at the marvelous mountains, woods, and waters, and settled in. The dull thwack of the axe sounded in the forests as the farmers cleared their land—and later, the spank of the water wheel and the squeal of the bellows as the Elba Iron Works rose on the Chubb River, lending the settlement their name.

Much has been learned concerning North Elba's first colony and its fate, though scant evidence remains of the Bennet family life. But it was essentially the life of all the pioneers of Elba, which will be covered in later chapters. Elijah was a farmer. He built his cabin, cleared his land, raised his crops, and pastured his cattle. That he did so with a crippled arm and with no mature sons to help out is cause for wonder. He was also a blacksmith, and it is safe to assume he plied his trade among his neighbors or at the Iron Works, which had need of such skill.

There was work and worry now a' plenty for Elijah and Rebecca. The climate of North Elba proved salubrious. After so many years of childlessness, their offspring came swiftly, one after another, until there were seven of them in 1810, four sons and three daughters, all under the age of ten.

Yet in 1818, we find the Bennets back in Orwell, Vermont. On March 18, 1818, Congress had passed an act to provide augmented pensions to disabled veterans of the Revolution. On April 23, Elijah appeared before the Chief Judge of Rutland (Vermont) County Court to make the proper application. He gave Orwell as his residence.

It is not difficult to pinpoint the year he said goodbye to Elba. The little settlement had been dealt a two-edged blow. In the summer of 1816, an arctic cold wave destroyed all crops, and near starvation followed. In 1817, the Iron Works shut down, leaving many without work. In the wake of these two tragedies, there was a general exodus from the town, which probably included the Bennets.

But the lure of the Adirondacks was too great. By 1820, Elijah was back at Elba. He was sixty-six years old, and again he came as a pioneer to a lonely land. Gone was the hustling, thriving community of Elba. Most of the farmers had moved on. Already the forest was encroaching again on abandoned pastures. The Elba Iron Works was closed, and the water wheel was still. In the clearings, the bobcat screamed again. Deer grazed unmolested in the deserted fields, feeding on wild oats. Bears gorged themselves on the blackberries that crowded the cutover lands. Only ten families were left in the whole of what is now North Elba.

And here Elijah settled down to spend the remainder of his days. His good wife Rebecca was still at his side. She was fifty-six, "tolerably healthy for her age and able to do the common work in a family." Six children were with him: a tragic daughter, Laurillia, about twenty, "subject to frequent fits followed by derangement, and requires one person constantly to watch her"; son Oliver, nineteen, "tolerable healthy but of feeble constitution, able, however, to support himself"; three sturdy sons, Cromwell, seventeen, Aaron, fourteen, and Elias, thirteen; and little daughter Lois, age eleven. It will be noted that Elijah apparently was an admirer of Oliver Cromwell.

Even in that era, the mills of bureaucracy ground slowly. Elijah was still trying to obtain the increased pension promised by the government. He appeared at Elizabethtown on September 26, 1820, in the Court of Common Pleas of Essex County before Deputy Clerk Ashley Pond to make a further declaration. His signature on various papers is that of an educated man and one who had had more than a little schooling. He stated he was no longer able to work because of his old war injury.

In order to take advantage of the new pension, Elijah had to declare himself a pauper. There has been handed down to us his pitiful little list of assets. It seems obvious he purposely neglected to declare all of them. That a family of eight could eke out a living with so few household and farm effects is hard to believe. Perhaps Elijah, in 1820, was only doing what so many Americans do today on April 15. The list deserves publication, if only for its revelation of pioneer life in North Elba in the year 1820.

Real Estate - none
Personal Property:

1 span of old horses	1 pair tongs
2 cows	1 fire shovel
3 pigs	1 pair andirons
1 dog	1 trowel
1 plough	1 sad iron
2 chains	1 tea pot
1 set drag teeth	6 tea cups & saucers
3 hoes	5 plates
4 axes old and new	1 pewter platter
3 sickles	4 knives and forks
1 5-pail iron kettle	4 tin dishes
1 iron pot	

One debt due me of about $12, but the debtor is insolvent, and I owe in the whole $80.

His entire property was valued at $70 by Thomas Stower, clerk of the court.

It is good to relate that soon Elijah obtained his new pension of $96 a year, a handsome sum in that backwoods outpost.

By 1830, Oliver was married, had a daughter, and lived in a cabin of his own. Elijah still had four children with him, three sons and a daughter. Lois had married a man by the name of Mighell and lived in Vermont.

The site of the Bennet residence at that time is unknown. Elijah had always been a squatter in Elba—that is, he never bought the land he lived on. In the early days, he had erected a house on Lot 280 and a hut on

Lot 279. In 1813, the Elba Iron & Steel Company bought Lot 280, on which they had already located their works, from the State of New York. Elijah may have been allowed to continue occupying his house. We do know that in the 1850s, when Benjamin T. Brewster moved onto Lot 258, Township 11, on the west side of Mirror Lake, he found a rude log cabin on the place and was told it was the "old Bennet cabin." The dwelling was located at the head of the lake on the site of the so-called Maxwell or Packer house, now used as a beach by the Chalet hotel.[2] Whether it was Elijah's or his son, Oliver's, is not told. For many years, Mr. Brewster used the cabin to shelter his pigs.

On December 17, 1830, in Elba, our worthy old Revolutionary War pensioner died at the age of seventy-six. No cemetery here or in Keene contains Elijah's bones, but it was the custom in those days to bury family members on their own land, close to the home. The spot was sometimes marked with a simple cairn. Often a rude wooden cross was planted, soon falling prey to dry rot and the wintry gales. In time no traces of a grave remained. We will never know where Elijah was buried.

Rebecca and the children, including Oliver and his family, almost immediately returned to Vermont. Many years later Rebecca, living in Rutland with Lois and destitute in her old age, was appealing to the government for the pension of a veteran's widow. She was granted a pension of $80 a year.

Beyond this meager fact, all trace of the Bennets of a later day was lost until 1999. By a stroke of good luck, a direct descendant of Elijah Bennet through his son Oliver was found in March 1999 in Chelan, Washington—Mrs. Bettie Kenck. Fortunately, by an odd circumstance, a large file concerning Elijah Bennet was found in the National Archives at Washington, D.C., giving many details of his life and making possible this intimate acquaintance with Lake Placid's and North Elba's first family.

Mrs. Kenck, descendant of Elijah Bennet, came to Lake Placid during the summer of 2000 to join in our multiple celebration festivities of that year—the settlement bicentennial, the sesquicentennial of North Elba township, and the centennial of the village of Lake Placid.

---

2 At this writing, the Chalet buildings have been used for several years as the campus of the National Sports Academy.

TWO

First Pioneers in North Elba

This chapter draws primarily from an essay published in the October 1990 issue of Patches and Patterns Extended. *Some elements of an earlier version, published in 1982 in the* Lake Placid News, *have been included.*

The Revolution was over and the great Yankee exodus was on. Like wild bees to a bee tree, New England's restless farmers were swarming over Lake Champlain to the promised land of northern New York.

The men came first to that howling wilderness, felling trees, planting crops, and building the barn and home cabin. The wives and children arrived in time to pick and preserve wild berries and harvest the first vegetables.

By 1800, Westport, Elizabethtown, Jay, and Keene were colonized, and a primitive wagon track wandered the woods from Westport to St. Lawrence County. Traveling this road in the spring of 1800, Vermonter Elijah Bennet ventured into the wilds of North Elba.

If first settler Elijah craved fellowship, he was soon content. In a bustle of wagon wheels, family after family careened down the Old Mountain Road to his picturesque plateau laced with ponds and streams and ringed by rugged mountains. By 1810, the little outpost was harboring two hundred souls.

They called it "The Plains of Abraham"—sometimes just "The Plains" or "Keene Plains." Nobody knows exactly why. While an 1810 visitor remembered it as "a species of prairie land," documentary evidence is quite to the contrary. It was, in fact, initially a vast forest of antique hardwoods—mixed with a few stands of pine, spruce, and hemlock.

Such a name—and such a memory, evoking visions of a treeless expanse—were perhaps not so incongruous. That first settlement occupied the great tableland just south of Lake Placid village. Beaver meadows abounded where cattle could be pastured, and much of the forest had been hacked down by 1810.

Elijah Bennet's story has already been told. Not much is known of his fellow pioneers beyond their names.

Among them were Jonathan Jenkins, Iddo Osgood, Isaac Griswald and his son Isaac Jr., all from New Hampshire. (It was a time of biblical first names.) The Griswalds were reputedly the first settlers of nearby Keene, naming it for their old hometown. There Cynthia Griswald married

Thomas Dart Jr. The Griswalds moved up to the Plains in 1802, followed the next year by Cynthia and Thomas. Four other Darts—Josiah, Joshua, Justus, and Justus Jr., likely all related—showed up in 1803.

Jeremiah Needham Jr. and his brother Charles, born in Wales, Massachusetts, appeared on June 26, 1806. Jeremiah, farmer and shoemaker, brought his wife Ruth and a passel of offspring. His little daughter Eunice would not survive for long. She died January 2, 1810, at four years of age. Hers is the earliest grave in our North Elba Cemetery. But Arunah Taylor, buried in an unmarked spot, was the first of the fledgling colony to go. Arunah perished "by cold in the woods."

It has often been claimed that our pioneers, like Elijah Bennet, were squatters on the state's Old Military Tracts and never owned the lots they farmed. This was not entirely the case. Upon their arrival, the tracts were not yet surveyed into lots. Once they were, the settlers were supposed to obtain patents or signed contracts for purchase on the installment plan, though many contracts were unfulfilled and few patents were actually issued.

Surveyor Stephen Thorn came up from Albany in the summers of 1804 and 1805 and laid out the lots. His 1804 map of North Elba has an intriguing tale to tell. With the exception of Lake Placid, every stream, pond, and lake, and even the islands of Lake Placid, bear different names than they have today. Whether Thorn himself, or the pioneers before him, christened the waters of North Elba will probably never be discovered. In any case, only one appellation, Lake Placid, survives.

Equally undiscovered are the whereabouts of all the pioneer farms, because of the unfulfilled contracts and few patents issued. Enough is known to sustain the image of a sprawling and widely scattered community.

They were everywhere—Elijah Bennet close to Lower Mill Pond; Joshua Dart on the Adirondack Lodge Road; Justus Dart near the Uihlein Mercy Center; Thomas Dart Jr. on the Cornell potato farm.

On the old Ames farm and Craig Wood Golf Course were Allen and Daniel McArthur and Jonathan Dart, with Gilderoy McArthur across the way. On the Torrance farm lived Joshua Dart, and across Cascade Road,[3] Isaac Griswald Jr. and Samuel Bliss had homesteads (the saucer shapes of ancient cellar holes still pock the land).

---

3 State Route 73.

Isaac Griswald's three hundred acres on Riverside Drive commenced at the ski jumps. Daniel Wilson's great farm arched from Pinebrook Farm to the airport and his neighbor, James Porter.

Out Averyville way were Jonathan Thorndick, Samuel Rogers, Ebenezer Mack, Thomas Ryder, James and Josiah Wilson, and Jonathan Jenkins on the Wescott farm.

Far west on the Saranac Road[4] lived Moses Hazelton, David Fuller, and Daniel Ray. Almost two hundred years have passed, and the stream near Daniel's place is still Ray Brook.

Joseph Chubb had a great holding of four hundred acres on Old Military Road from River Street[5] to Carolyn Road, some of it later the Ruisseaumont golf links. By 1804, Chubb boasted a house and two barns and had cleared twenty-seven acres, but he abandoned the place before 1810. He, like Daniel Ray, left his name behind. Chubb River and Chubb Hill remind us that Joseph was here two centuries ago. And, for those who search carefully among the blueberries near Carolyn Road, there is added evidence of Joseph's stay—the outline of a cellar and the remnants of a well.

Numerous log houses and barns soon speckled the Plains of Abraham, and the colonists set about providing a school for their children. Fanny Dart was the first teacher. The Reverend Cyrus Comstock, a Congregational circuit rider, provided sustenance for the soul. "Father" Comstock, as people affectionately knew him, devoted a long and remarkable life to serving the remote, backwoods hamlets of Essex County. It was probably he who performed the first marriage at the Plains, that of Elijah McArthur and Electa Brooks.

Was life harsh and grueling then, a grim struggle for survival? No one can truly say. America was a nation of farmers, and hard labor was the universal lot. In the Adirondacks, bear, moose, wolves, and panthers had to be fended off and the long, cold winters endured. But the people of the Plains had a measure, at least, of security. The soil was rich and productive. No one could grow finer potatoes anywhere. Sheep and cattle thrived, fish and game abounded. There was butter, milk, meat, and wool, and maple sugar as a substitute for cane. And soon a captive market for surplus produce appeared on the Plains.

---

4 State Route 86.

5 Now called Mill Pond Drive.

In 1809, Archibald McIntyre of Albany, a man of large dreams, created Lower Mill Pond and erected the Elba Iron Works. A large industrial complex for the time and place, it comprised a forge, blacksmith shop, grist and sawmills, boarding houses, barracks, and charcoal houses. Foremen, wagoners, miners, ironsmiths, bloomers, and their families poured into town, swelling the population by a hundred or more. The works consumed tons of charcoal, and the farmers turned a hand to manufacturing the product, earning 3¢ for every bushel sold.

Now the settlement became "Elba," and so it would remain until the "North" was tacked on thirty years down the road.

Hard on the heels of Elba's prosperity, war came to the northland. The first hostilities of the War of 1812 occurred in Canada and on Lakes Ontario and Erie. By 1813, the Adirondack people were extremely apprehensive of Indian raids. They expanded the militia, and the state began to distribute arms and ammunition in the district. The state issued "fifty muskets and equipments, and 1,000 musket cartridges" to McIntyre at Elba.

In 1814, the action shifted to Lake Champlain, and by September, it was no secret that the British were massed before Plattsburgh for a huge invasion by land and water. A call to arms rang out, and down from the Adirondack hills poured the pioneer farmers, eager to defend their land and homes. If memoirs are any yardstick, half the men of Essex County, young and old, fought in the famed Battle of Plattsburgh that sent the British running for the Canadian border. Among the combatants from Elba were Malcolm McMartin, Benjamin Needham, Thomas Dart Jr., one of the Wilsons, and Elijah Bennet. This was the same Elijah, now frosty-haired, who had once fought in the Battle of Bunker Hill.

The Yankee victory at Plattsburgh sparked a wild celebration in the north. At Elba, the jubilation was tempered with gloom, for one of the Wilsons had been killed in action.

It was during this period, beginning with 1813, that something seemed to have gone wrong with the weather. For three years, the summers were short and cold and the crops poor to middling.

1816 came on with great promise, although the Elba Iron Works had deep financial woes. January was so mild that most let their fires die out and burned wood only for cooking. February was warm and spring-like. March and early April were balmy, too. Yet as the first pale shoots emerged in the nut-brown woods, the air grew strangely cold. All of May was bitter, with frosts retarding spring planting.

Warm weather finally arrived June 1, and the Elbans scrambled to plant their crops. Even as they plowed and tilled and seeded, disaster stood in the wings. Winter soon returned with a howling vengeance. From June 5 to 10, blizzards battered the countryside. When they were done, snow lay twenty inches deep. Every green thing was dead, along with thousands of birds newly arrived from the south. In the cabins, roaring fires were built and greatcoats and mittens were dug out of storage. A short period of good weather followed and the farmers replanted, praying for mature crops before the autumn frosts.

The Elbans were not alone. The entire northern hemisphere suffered from that dismal spring. There was worse to come. In July, the wind blew steadily from the north in blasts of snow and sleet. On Independence Day, ice as thick as window glass skimmed the ponds and lakes. To everyone's surprise, August proved the cruelest month. Frosts came as early as the 18th, tumbling temperatures forty degrees. Then autumn was at hand, and the farmers at last faced the enormity of their loss. There was little or nothing to harvest.

That dreadful time of 1816 has gone down in history as "the year without a summer," or "eighteen hundred and froze-to-death." The farmers would never know it, but their misery was hatched on the other side of the world. Three major volcanic eruptions had occurred—Soufriere on St. Vincent Island in 1812, Mayon in the Philippines in 1814, and Tambora on Sumbawa in 1815. Tambora remains the most catastrophic volcanic explosion in recorded history. The cold years, and notably 1816, were the byproduct of huge amounts of volcanic dust in the atmosphere, shutting off the sun's rays.

Winter came—a winter so glacial that the mercury froze in thermometers. There was little food. Often only the milk from a cow or two and the local fish and game spelled survival. It was Father Comstock's finest hour. Crisscrossing the Adirondack frontier without rest, he gave comfort and hope—and all his money and credit, as well—to save his flock from starvation.

The spring and summer of 1817 were no improvement. Gone was the cold, but there was little seed to sow. The few seed potatoes planted in spring were often dug up and eaten before summer arrived. On the Plains of Abraham, the plight of the farmers was acute, but that was not all. The beleaguered Elba Iron Works at last folded, leaving scores without work.

It was a time to leave. A great exodus from Elba began, with many a backward look at the beautiful Plains of Abraham. Down the Old Mountain Road filed the ironworkers and the husbandmen, hauling their puny possessions to greener pastures. They would soon merge into the great American trek westward that would end, decades later, on a Pacific beach.

Almost nothing is known of the fate of our first pioneers. Jonathan Jenkins went as far as Lewis and lived out his life there. His daughter Jane would come back to Elba in 1824 as the wife of Roswell Thompson. Jeremiah Needham returned to Vermont and died in Vergennes in 1846. His son Benjamin journeyed the few miles to Wilmington and later emigrated from there to Iowa.

A few clung to Elba for several years, eventually moving out. Eleazer Darrow operated the mills and blacksmith shop. Moses Hazelton and Samuel Rogers farmed, as did Dan Brooks Jr. who, in a sense, never did forsake his mountain home. He died on February 18, 1821 at thirty, and one can find his grave in the North Elba Cemetery. The Elijah Bennet family hung on until Elijah's death in 1830, and then returned to Vermont.

Elba was a ghost town, and a ghost town it would be for the next thirty years. A few new settlers occasionally drifted in, with no more than ten families in residence at any one time. Peter Smith of Utica, New York, a partner of John Jacob Aster in the fur trade and father of noted abolitionist Gerrit Smith, purchased extensive lands in the town from the state around this time, but he sold out few lots.

'Tis an ill wind that blows nobody good. One denizen of that first colony did remain permanently and, moreover, flourished like the green bay tree. He was Iddo Osgood.

Squire Osgood, as he was always known, was a Renaissance man. He arrived in Elba from New Hampshire on March 4, 1808 with his wife Clarista, two sons, and a daughter. The squire was then twenty-eight, in the prime of life, and sharp as a steel tack. If anyone could turn a dollar, it was Iddo Osgood.

The exodus of 1817 presented a bonanza. Forthwith helping himself to the abandoned fields and pastures, Iddo became, if not exactly a cattle baron, something close. He maple-sugared on a grandiose scale, and his crops were biblically abundant.

He had, besides, a large farm of his own, 320 acres along Old Military Road, purchased from the state. Roughly, it spread from Bear Cub Road[6]

6 Now called Bear Cub Lane, County Route 26.

to Peter Moreau's inn, and in depth embraced Bob Wikoff's lot, the entire Sentinel Heights district, the hospital, and a large tract off Bear Cub Road.

Iddo was a lay deacon, often pinch-hitting for Father Comstock. Sunday worship at Osgood's house just west of the Uihlein Mercy Center was the rule. There, before 1833, he also inaugurated the town's first inn for travelers. The earliest mention I have found of this is of Archibald McIntyre and party stopping there in 1833 while visiting Cascade Lakes. Many an early Adirondack wayfarer put up at "Osgood's" for the night, among them Richard Henry Dana Jr., famed American author of *Two Years Before the Mast,* who stopped off in 1849.

The squire had his thumb in every political pie, and always pulled out a plum. Appointed commissioner of the Old Military Road in 1816 and of the Cedar Point Road in 1828, he reeled in $2 a day at each job. He was, during his lifetime, a five-term supervisor, justice of the peace, town road commissioner, and overseer of the poor.

Sons Daniel and Dillon, both born in Elba, got into the act, too. Daniel was supervisor, town clerk, tax collector, constable, justice of the peace, and overseer of the poor. Dillon, a Congregational minister, was North Elba's first postmaster in 1849, with headquarters at his father's inn, and moonlighted as superintendent of common schools and justice of the peace. The Osgoods, it seems, had sewed up the town.

Furthermore, Iddo Osgood was in charge of lumbering, guiding, and other jobs at Archibald McIntyre's iron mines at Adirondac, beyond the south range. He commuted on foot by way of Indian Pass—and this is probably one reason why he was chosen as a Cedar Point Road commissioner. And he was, in his spare time, a wolf slayer, augmenting his many-splendored income by collecting bounties on wolves he trapped or shot. For instance, in the year 1831 it is recorded he collected $20 in bounties from the county of Essex, a handsome sum for that era.

Prosper he did as a farmer, politician, innkeeper, and nobody knows what else. But as a husband, he fared only half as well. Clarista died in 1816. He then married Prudence and fathered a second brood. Prudence died in 1831. He then married Mary P. and, it is hoped, lived happily ever after.

All of his children and his third wife moved from North Elba well over a century ago. Iddo himself died in 1861 at eighty-two, having witnessed over a span of fifty-three years the birth of a town, the death of a town, its long sleep, its rebirth in the 1840s, and its first stirrings as a summer resort. He lies in the North Elba Cemetery beside Clarista and Prudence and his son Dillon.

"Life's labor done, as sinks the day," proclaims his tombstone, "light from its load the spirit flies."

With the passing of Iddo Osgood, the curtain at last rang down on North Elba's first and long-forgotten colony on the Plains of Abraham.

THREE
Save Chubb Hill!

This appeared as an editorial in the Spring 1969 issue of Placid Pioneer, *the newsletter of the Lake Placid-North Elba Historical Society, which Mary MacKenzie edited.*

Your editor, of late, has noted with alarm a growing tendency on the part of many to change the name of Chubb Hill on Old Military Road to Riki Hill. Not only our summer residents, but even our hard-core natives, have fallen into this—to our mind—most grievous error, apparently influenced by the sign "Riki Hill" at the entrance to the hilltop estate of our member, Mrs. Artur Rodzinski.

We admit that Riki Hill is a charming name for the Rodzinski property. And we agree that under any other circumstances it would be most fitting for the hill itself, honoring, as we understand it, the son of the late, great and highly admired symphony conductor, Artur Rodzinski, who made Lake Placid his second home. Yet we must deplore the loss of a name as ancient and traditional as Chubb Hill.

Chubb Hill and Chubb River were named in the first decade of the 1800s for Joseph Chubb, one of North Elba's very earliest settlers. Joseph, with his family, arrived on the beautiful "Great Plains" (now North Elba) probably in 1800 or 1801. He immediately took possession of Great Lots 199 and 219, Township 11, Old Military Tract, a total of four hundred acres, at that time valued at $1 an acre. The lots, even then well situated on the Old Military Road, were to be the site of the old Ruisseaumont golf links a hundred years later. Today Mrs. Rodzinski, Fred Fortune Jr., and Ronald Allwork own parts of these old Chubb lands.

By 1804, Joseph had hewn a substantial farm out of his primeval forests of hemlock, spruce, tamarack, beech, and maple. On Lot 199, on the south side of Old Military Road, he had cleared and was farming fifteen acres. Here were located his house and main barn, valued at $180. On Lot 219, across the road, he was farming twelve cleared acres on which stood a log barn valued at $65.

The Chubb River did not flow through Joseph's lands, but one can understand why and how it was named for him. He was the only one of our first settlers to locate so far out on Old Military Road, and we can well imagine the pioneers saying among themselves, "that river out toward Joe Chubb's" and "that big hill before you get to Joe Chubb's farm." And then, soon, in the way such things happen, the river became Chubb's River and the hill became Chubb's Hill.

Ancient cellar and well holes (the well marvelously preserved) can be found today, for those who search carefully among the blueberries, on the south side of Old Military Road, just past Fred Fortune Jr.'s house at the junction of Carolyn Road. We strongly suspect they are the last remaining evidence of Joseph Chubb's tenure in North Elba. To our knowledge, no other person has ever lived on that particular site.

Joseph moved on before 1810, but he left the legacy of his name to the river and the hill. Yes, Chubb Hill has been Chubb Hill for 165 years. Help preserve a picturesque bit of our heritage and history. Save Chubb Hill!

FOUR
Farming in the Adirondacks

Mary MacKenzie was adamant that North Elba never suffered for lack of fertile soil and that farming there was good. She wrote often of "the great success story of Adirondack agriculture in the nineteenth century." She took any opportunity she could to debunk the persistent myth that the soil was poor in Lake Placid, "and that farming in the Adirondacks has always been a bust." In a letter to the author of an article about a North Elba farm, written on April 7, 2000, Mary's defense of farming is passionate. The author to whom she is writing is the "you" in the letter. She starts out decrying one of the sources of the myth, a forest commissioner of New York State.

When I came to your quote of the New York State forest commissioner, in 1885, I actually groaned aloud, "Oh, dear God, not again!" Writers have used this quote ad nauseam, and every time I encounter it, I go berserk. A lot of stupid remarks have come out of the mouths of bureaucrats (who are superbly uninformed about almost everything) but this one deserves a special prize. This dumbhead must have gone about wearing blinders. At the time he made this screwball observation, a great many tidy farms were in existence throughout the Adirondacks, and many of them had been in existence for almost a century! Very few areas were unsuitable for farming.

You use the word "thin" for Adirondack soil, but it was anything but, except on mountainsides. It certainly was not hard and infertile soil, as almost always described. It was rich, deep, and organic for the simple reason that the area was originally a vast antique hardwood forest. Essex County appears to have had the best soil [in the Adirondacks], and North Elba soil was the most fertile in the county and described as "equal to the flats of the Mohawk."

And it is upsetting to me that you used the word "fail" so many times. Adirondack farms seldom "failed" in the old days. They went out of existence, yes, for a number of reasons we shall examine. Farms went out of existence all over the country for one reason or another.

You describe the Estes farm as "thriving." What makes you think the other farms in Keene Valley (and for that matter, in other sections of the Adirondacks) did not thrive?

Of course, farming was not an easy task in the old days. It is hard farming anywhere and at any time when you have to use primitive methods.

And, of course, farming in the Adirondacks cannot be much of a success today except as a hobby. Farms today have to be geared to production and not to family subsistence, and practically none of the farm acreage is extensive enough to sustain large operations.

One success, of course, has been potato growing in North Elba. Incidentally, the Cornell potato farm is part of one of our great old pioneer farms that has been in existence since 1840. In spite of its high altitude, short growing season, early frosts, and long winters, North Elba had a most successful farming history because of its wonderful soil. Farms persisted here right up until World War II, and our last dairy farm did not go out of existence until about twenty years ago.

The history of Adirondack farming is very dear to my heart, and I have devoted a lot of time and effort to the study of it. There is much to be learned in old county histories. The excerpt I sent you from *Geographical History of the State of New York* (1848) clearly indicates, "a majority of the inhabitants devoted to agriculture" in Essex County. For all the other nine counties now within the Blue Line, it also clearly states under Pursuits, "The people are chiefly engaged in agriculture."

Unfortunately, early writers on the Adirondacks ignored the farms and depicted only wilderness. Early Adirondack artists also ignored the farms. And even more unfortunately, later writers have also ignored this wonderful history of agriculture.

Thank heaven, at last something is being done about educating the public about our wonderful history of farming. A great article was published last year in *New York History.* And last year Glenn Harris, of the Environmental Studies Program at St. Lawrence University, contacted me. He has totally immersed himself in the study of our agricultural history and asked my help as he had heard of my interest. He has compiled some incredible statistics and plans some articles.

Farming died out in the Adirondacks for several reasons. The obvious one, of course, is the dying out of the family farm all over America as a way of life, with the change in the economy. Adirondack farms were never "production" farms but were meant only for family sustenance. Farms began to disappear quite rapidly, of course, with the rise of tourism and other industries—TB, etc.

You seem to indicate that the farmers moved west because they failed at farming in the Adirondacks. This is an inaccurate assessment. There was indeed a great westward movement after the Civil War. Farmers were moving west because Americans have always moved west. Many left thriving farms for the wild unknown because Americans have always sought the wild unknown. Many of the early North Elba farmers moved west, too, but newcomers immediately took up their farms.

FIVE
Boozing

This item consists of several fragments found in Mary MacKenzie's files; the date or dates when she composed them are unknown. The first page obviously had at least one more attached to it, completing a story she started, but no succeeding pages were found that were directly connected to the first.

But there was one thing going on in Essex County in those early days—and, in fact, in the whole of this new democracy—that is never mentioned in the history books and is very, very seldom talked about. It had a great deal to do with the customs and social life of the time, but historians seem reluctant to mention it. I have pieced together quite a tale from bits here and there in old newspapers and gazetteers.

The people of Essex County in the early days, my friends—and there is only one way to put it—were boozers. The amount of hard liquor consumed was astronomical. They drank at barn raisings and church socials and quilting bees and on any and every occasion whatsoever. One reporter of the social scene[7] put it this way:

> In 1810, the population of Essex County was 9,500 souls, and as nearly as I can discover, there were at least 10 distilleries in operation:
>
> - 5 in Jay
> - 1 in Keene
> - 1 in Elizabethtown
> - 1 in Schroon
> - 1 in Essex
> - 1 in Willsborough

There were a great many more in the years following. It is said that the Town of Keene and Jay supplied all the whiskey for the soldiers on Lake Champlain during the War of 1812.

Whiskey was made from rye and potatoes, and rum from maple syrup. As Burton Bernstein has said, "At the going price of only 20¢ a gallon, liquor was as available as birch beer and drunk as copiously. This particular

7 MacKenzie's source is not named.

home industry lasted in Essex County right down through Prohibition, and some say it's still thriving in a few backwoods quarters." Most every household had variations of "the recipe" that has achieved so much fame in "The Waltons" television series.[8]

During this period, there was in the Town of Jay a Baptist minister who was addicted to the bottle. His parishioners accused him of continual drunkenness, and there was much dissension in the church. A council of county church deacons was called to resolve the matter. Among them was our old friend Father Comstock. They met at the home of Deacon John Purmont, of Jay, who ran a local store that sold whiskey by the barrel. When the deacons had taken their seats around the dining room table, as was the custom, Purmont placed mugs in front of all of them, filled them from a whiskey decanter, and they all started to sip. Suddenly Father Comstock arose and said, "Are we our brother's keeper? We ought to start with ourselves." Thereupon, Deacon Purmont emptied the entire liquor stock in his store into the gutter. Down it swirled.

But my favorite story is about the good lady of North Elba who was a bit too fond of alcoholic beverages. Her husband was a very substantial citizen who often had to travel on the road,... [fragment ends.]

SIX
The Early Roads to Lake Placid
Date unknown

By birch-bark canoe, stagecoach, steam locomotive, Model T, and Mercedes, pioneers, vacationists, and tourists have poured into the Lake Placid area over a span of some three hundred years.

Historians say the Iroquois were the first tourists at Lake Placid. For untold summers, on this ancient beaver-hunting site, they powwowed in large numbers until the biting cold drove them back to their Mohawk Valley home for the winter. Indian relics found on the plateau east of the ski jumps confirm the legend. By what routes they traveled is lost in the mists of time, but a known western trail up to the Adirondacks followed the Fulton Chain of Lakes and the Saranac River. On the east, they probably came by way of Lake George and Indian Pass.

8 "The Waltons" aired from September 1972 through August 1981.

But how, in 1800, did Placid's first white settlers from Vermont and New Hampshire find a passage over the rugged mountains? They were in luck. Crossing the Champlain ice to Westport in early spring, they discovered a primitive wagon track already in place from Westport to St. Lawrence County. Built by early landowners in St. Lawrence and known as the Northwest Bay Road, it wandered the howling wilderness via present-day Elizabethtown, Keene, Lake Placid, Saranac Lake, and Santa Clara. The state took over the job of maintenance and repair in 1810. It later became known as Old Military Road, after the military land tracts through which it passed. Today's motorists know it under various bureaucratic numbers.

No superhighway—at its very best, it was stony, rutty, boggy, hair-raising. The reach between Keene and Lake Placid, threading a gorge north of Pitchoff Mountain and known as the Old Mountain Road, was said to be "six miles, six hours." Old Mountain was, in fact, so lamentable a road that, in 1858, the state built the present Route 73 from Keene through the romantic fault valley of the Cascade Lakes.

The Cascade bypass was not much of an improvement, labeled downright dangerous by many an early tourist. One wayfarer said it was "ten miles of rocks and mudholes," and the stretch past the lakes, wedged between precipitous mountains, "so narrow that the hubs of the wheels almost impended over the water." A peddler and his wagon actually did go over the bank, but whether that gentleman drowned no one now can say.

Until 1893, when the railroad came to Lake Placid, the stagecoach was king on the Northwest Bay Road all the way from Lake Champlain to the Adirondack resorts. The famous "stagecoach rock" in Cascade Pass is an affectionate reminder of the rumbling wheels of yesteryear.

The original Northwest Bay Road was a pretty good job of location. Today, almost two hundred years later, a modern highway runs on the same "as the crow flies" course, barring a few segments. The state has erected historical markers along its length. Old Mountain Road, long impassable for automobiles, is worth a hike or a cross-country ski for its scenic views.

In 1814, Archibald McIntyre built a second access road, from Lake Placid to Wilmington, over the Sentinel Range, to haul iron ore for his Elba Iron Works forge. Though lumbering long ago obliterated its course, an old map shows it high in the hills above the Au Sable River, skirting the mountain ponds Copperas and Winch. It was abandoned in 1854 when the lower and picturesque Wilmington Notch road, now known as Route 86, was built along the river.

The coming of the automobile changed forever the character of those two antique gateways to Lake Placid. Macadam strips overlie the tracks of the pioneers, but a high sense of adventure and discovery is still there for the Adirondack tourist.

SEVEN

The Northwest Bay-Hopkinton Road

From the Franklin Historical Review, *Vol. 29, 1992-93-94.*

To begin with, it was the Northwest Bay-Hopkinton Road. Soon it came to be called Old Military Road. Today it goes by a miscellany of bureaucratic numbers, but for North Country people it is still and will always be Old Military Road.

All old roads are romantic—their very names summon ghosts from the past. Yet no other highway in Adirondack country can rival the romance and lore of the Northwest Bay or Old Military Road. It began its meanderings as a primitive wagon track in the late 1790s. It was the first track to penetrate and cross the vast, unexplored Adirondacks. Amazingly, it is still in use today along much of its final course, laid out by the state in 1810.

The Revolution was over and Americans began their great trek westward. Yankee farmers of New England swarmed over Lake Champlain to the howling wilderness of northern New York. Untold acres were for sale in the state's Old Military Tracts of Essex County and the mighty Macomb's Purchase of the counties of Franklin and St. Lawrence. Shortly before 1800, a little clutch of log cabins had made an appearance on Champlain's Northwest Bay, now known as Westport. Pioneers had already struggled inland twenty miles to Elizabethtown and Keene, furrowing out a rude wagon track followed fairly closely today by Routes 9N and 73. By 1800, the Yankee settlers had extended the track over the hills to the Lake Placid area, another sixteen miles. Beyond lay the brooding primeval forest, trackless to St. Lawrence County. The proprietors of Macomb's Purchase soon remedied that. To lure prospective buyers, they blazed a trail from Placid some fifty-five miles to the fertile reaches of the St. Regis River.

Nobody knows how many hundreds of stalwarts took the trail from Westport to the St. Regis in the first decade of the nineteenth century.

Only one journey has been profiled, that of Dr. Roswell Hopkins, former secretary of state of Vermont and surgeon in the Continental Army, his son Benjamin, and a few of his neighbors in June 1802. Interested in a tract bordering the east branch of the St. Regis, Hopkins aimed to inspect it first-hand.

Leaving Vermont, the little party of horsemen crossed Champlain by ferry from Basin Harbor to Northwest Bay, fed their horses at Westport, and rode west to the next clearing, Elizabethtown. There, they forded the Boquet River and followed the beaten track to Keene. At Keene, they forded the east branch of the Au Sable and took the long haul up Alstead Hill and through a mountain pass on the north side of Pitchoff, up to the lofty North Elba plateau near Lake Placid. Then the little band forded the turbulent west branch of the Au Sable and left civilization behind.

Marked trees guided them across the sandy plains of Ray Brook and along a course approximating the present McKenzie Pond Road to the Saranac River, where the settlement of Saranac Lake would make its debut twenty years later. Fording the Saranac and veering ever north of west, they passed through the future sites of Gabriels, Easy Street, Paul Smiths, and McColloms, skirting Barnum, Osgood, and Mountain Ponds. At a point about a half-mile southwest of Meacham Lake, the blaze abruptly beckoned west. The fork would be known one day as Meacham's Corners for that mighty nimrod of the Adirondacks, Tom Meacham, and his cabin close by.

The company now entered the wild and woolly "fifty-mile woods," future home of Santa Clara and St. Regis Falls, and at length came to the fertile land of the east branch of the St. Regis. To this spot, Roswell returned the next year and founded the hamlet of Hopkinton, now at the extreme northwestern edge of the Adirondack Blue Line.

Modern highways are, in the main, faithful to the essence of that route traveled by Roswell Hopkins and his little band almost two hundred years ago. For the serious researcher, maps old and new from 1804 to the present, as well as historical markers, will illuminate the original course and the inevitable modifications of two centuries of progress. A street on Highland Park hill in Saranac Lake perpetuates the name Old Military Road, as does an outlying road at Lake Placid.

After Hopkins traveled it, the track began to resemble a road. Each horse and ox, each wagon wheel marked the trail and the river fords more plainly for the next comer. The St. Lawrence proprietors soon built a substantial bridge at the difficult ford of the Saranac, spanned today by Baker Bridge. In 1809, a spring flood carried away that early bridge, setting in motion a series of events down at the Capitol in Albany.

The political climate in Albany does not change. Powerful people and lobbies often persuade lawgivers, and that is just what they did two hundred years ago. In 1810, Roswell Hopkins was a member of the state Legislature and needed a good path from Hopkinton to Albany. His friend, Archibald McIntyre, state comptroller and potent political force, was building his Elba Iron Works at Lake Placid and needed a good trade route to markets. The bridge was out and the Northwest Bay wagon track was awful anyhow—narrow, stony, boggy, treacherous, and blocked by fallen trees.

Hopkins and McIntyre lost no time in shaking things up. In 1810, the Legislature passed an act for the repair and improvement of the Northwest Bay-Hopkinton Road. It optimistically appropriated $1,000. Benjamin Hopkins, Roswell's son, of St. Lawrence County, and Benjamin Pond, of Essex County, were appointed commissioners to oversee the work. The money soon proved a drop in the bucket, and in 1812, the Legislature appropriated another $3,000 and taxed adjacent private lands from 2¢ to 5¢ an acre.

Two years later, in 1814, the road was still unfinished. At the eastern end, overseen by Pond, work had progressed well, but at the western end, the Hopkinses were dragging their feet. Roswell had completed his stint as state legislator in 1813 and was immersed in new projects—real estate, a general store, and a gristmill. The road was now less than a major concern. For Archibald McIntyre, a good road was still vital—and, besides, as comptroller, he kept a sharp eye on construction funds. Lacking an accounting from Hopkins, he dispatched his scouts at Lake Placid, Malcolm McMartin and Iddo Osgood, to Hopkinton to assess matters.

McMartin and Osgood went through the woods in June 1814. They found some of the road cleared and bridged from the forty-one-mile tree westward, but much remained in a sad state. Roswell was in ill humor and refused to give an accounting. At the last, he and Benjamin promised to complete another thirteen miles.

Nothing much happened until the Legislature acted again in 1816, most certainly spurred on by the McIntyre camp. Benjamin lost his job and was replaced by Iddo Osgood, Malcolm McMartin, and James McIntyre, at Lake Placid, the latter two relatives of Archibald. Benjamin Pond having died, Boughton Lobdell of Westport, John Calkins of Elizabethtown, and David Graves of Keene were appointed to superintend the eastern end. Another $4,000 was appropriated.

No further construction acts were passed. At long last, most probably by 1817, after years of alternate progress and procrastination, the Northwest Bay-Hopkinton Road, though still a primitive affair by today's standards, was a full-fledged public highway. Ninety miles long and four rods wide, it had been a colossal undertaking, accomplished solely by horse, ox, man, and muscle.

Oddly, failure and tragedy stalked both of the main backers, McIntyre and Hopkins, and they did not long enjoy the benefits of the new road. McIntyre's iron works at Lake Placid foundered in 1817 and was shut down. On top of financial ruin in 1819, Dr. Hopkins was thrown from his wagon at Chazy in 1829 and died from injuries. His son Benjamin had faded from the picture years before. Ousted from his job as commissioner, he in any event soon met an untimely end. In 1819, he was aboard the schooner Halifax on a business voyage when a storm drove the boat into Cuba's Havana harbor. There he contracted yellow fever, dying on August 13.

* * *

For years, it was customary to keep the road clear by occasionally dispatching workmen from both ends. In 1896, Squire Lee, then eighty-nine years of age, recounted his personal memory of one such contingent of 1826. Led by Captain John Lobdell and Alonson Mitchell of Elizabethtown, a crew of forty-seven men from the eastern end repaired the road up to Meacham's Corners and turned west through the infamous "fifty-mile woods." Seventeen teams carried food and provisions. Rendezvousing with the western crew at the St. Regis, all camped together for the night after consuming twenty gallons of potatoes and six pails of fried mutton.

* * *

The road played an important part in the development of the region. Great farms were hacked out of the wilderness. Settlements grew and industry flourished—mills and distilleries, iron mines, forges, and country stores. Local travel, though slow as a snail's pace, was intense between the burgeoning communities. Travelers found small inns and taverns—Abel's at Elizabethtown, the Graves place at Keene, Iddo Osgood's at Lake Placid. Settlers began to filter into Saranac Lake and the country beyond, as far as McColloms.

But at the far western end, the fearsome "fifty-mile woods" up Hopkinton way remained virtually uninhabited. Santa Clara, St. Regis Falls and their mills lay years in the future. With the construction of a new road to Hopkinton from Port Kent on Lake Champlain, begun in the late 1820s, pioneer commerce between the lake and St. Lawrence turned to that more direct and shorter route. By the 1840s, much of the road from Meacham's Corners to Hopkinton had fallen into neglect and disuse. By the 1870s, the large segment up to Santa Clara had all but disappeared, a narrow grass-grown alley wandering among towering trees.

Gradually the outside world discovered the Adirondacks as playground and retreat. What began as a trickle of tourists before the Civil War became a freshet, and the freshet a stream. Resort hotels appeared along the margins of Old Military Road, and the burly Adirondack stagecoach was king. The names of the great old hostelries, vanished now, echo down the years—the Weed House at Westport, the Windsor and Mansion House at Elizabethtown, the Stevens House and the Adirondack Lodge at Lake Placid, Martin's near Saranac Lake, and Paul Smiths and McColloms.

Just before the turn of the twentieth century, with the mills in Santa Clara and St. Regis Falls in full throttle, the old byway from Meacham's Corners was revived. A rough dirt road was scratched out of the ancient bed. That new invention, the automobile, found it a sorry stretch. In 1922, the state constructed a paved road of sorts over the route and finally, in the 1960s, built a completely modern highway, moving the entrance a few hundred feet north of Meacham's Corners and straightening out the twists and turns up to Santa Clara. The original entrance is still in evidence at the Meacham General Store, and so, too, are fragments of the old 1920s road in the woods along the way. In 1929, the state laid a new concrete road from Santa Clara to St. Regis Falls.

Old Military Road was whole again.

* * *

Today there is only one significant abandoned segment. It lies between Keene and the outskirts of Lake Placid and was given a name of its own, Old

Mountain Road, a century ago. Slipping into the woods beyond Jossey Bilan's former studio barn on the brow of Alstead Hill, it threads the picturesque gorge between the north cliffs of Pitchoff and the escarpments of the Sentinel Range, emerging on Route 73 just west of the Olympic bobsled run road.

Old Mountain, along with its approach up Alstead Hill, was precipitous, hazardous, and hair-raising. In 1858, it was bypassed by the present Route 73 from Keene through the romantic fault valley of Cascade Lakes. Regardless, Old Mountain saw use for many more years by the wagons of local farmers and some of the early resort stagecoaches, and later by an occasional maverick automobile, mostly because it was two miles shorter.

The abolitionist John Brown of Harper's Ferry fame was almost lost to history on Old Mountain. Then farming in North Elba, two miles from Lake Placid, he came near to death by freezing while walking home alone in mid-winter of 1850. He had hired a rig from Westport to Keene but could find no transport over the mountain. Carrying a heavy satchel, he set off on foot. Again and again he collapsed in the snow, exhausted and half-frozen. Again and again he rallied. With a last mighty endeavor, he gained the first house at North Elba, Robert Scott's, and was hauled home by ox team.

Though it is not recorded by which route from Keene the fanatical old warrior was borne home for burial in 1859, one must hope he made his last journey over Old Mountain, like himself steeped in history.[9]

Old Mountain, too, is the true locale of Anson Allen's legendary "bear fight up in Keene" while he was traveling on foot through Essex County and taking the federal census in 1840.

Save for a mile at the Lake Placid end still open to traffic, Old Mountain has not seen an automobile for over fifty years and is little more than a forest trail. As they have always been, the woods are uninhabited by

---

9 The abolitionist Wendell Phillips, who accompanied John Brown's funeral cortege, left an account of their journey that clearly identifies the route they traveled from Keene to North Elba: the Old Mountain Road. "Two miles beyond Keene we began to ascend the mountain in good earnest," Phillips wrote. "When we got to the steepest part, mercy to the horses induced us to alight; nor did we reenter the vehicle until we had passed the crest of the mountain. Near the top we came to a lily pond, from whose southern border Pitch-Off Mountain raises almost perpendicularly several hundred feet in height; the scenery is here truly majestic, the gorge is narrow, that the really towering mountains on either side seem more overshadowing than they really are." To have seen along their way "a lily pond from whose southern border Pitch-Off Mountain raises," the Brown funeral cortege must have traveled by a route that went north of Pitchoff: the Old Mountain Road.

man, hushed and secret. The intruder half expects to see an ox-drawn cart coming around each bend. Old Mountain is the haunt of hikers and lovers of solitary places. The children of nearby North Country School and Camp Treetops ride it on horseback and picnic on its ice-age boulder, Shelter Rock. Now a segment of the great Jack Rabbit Trail, cross-country skiers frequent it in winter.

* * *

Still, for all the witchery of Old Mountain, one other spot along Old Military is just as compelling: the now-extinct Jennings Clearing, six miles east of Santa Clara, eternalized by a state historical marker on Route 458.

Jennings Clearing was bad news for almost everybody who chanced to live or visit there. What befell the gentleman who presumably settled that lonesome patch of the "fifty-mile woods" in the early 1800s, building a cabin and giving it a name, is unknown. Mr. Jennings slipped in and out of the pages of history without leaving a footprint.

The first identifiable resident was Alvah Rice, from Elizabethtown. Mr. Rice liked to tell of his first night in the one-room cabin. He had taken in a group of travelers, one of whom was a woman, and all slept on the floor—fitfully, it would seem, for during the night the woman gave birth to a child. In 1837, Rice purchased land on the Port Kent-Hopkinton highway four miles to the north (now known as Red Tavern Road) and built a road to it from Jennings Clearing. There he raised a hotel and tavern, later acquired by Calvin Waite.

One casualty, Chapman Olmstead, lived in the cabin but a few years. On a bone-chilling winter's day, he ran short of provisions and set off down Jennings Road for the Waite Hotel. Chapman never made it. Found frozen to death on the road, he was buried in the clearing.

Chris Crandall, the legendary one-legged, hare-lipped guide of the region, was a loser both before and after he inhabited the cabin during the Civil War. Years back, while still-hunting in the dead of winter, he was accidentally shot and a leg was amputated. Chris carried the Jennings Clearing curse to a later home. He blew out his brains with a rifle, pulling the trigger with the toes of his one foot.

But the two dozen ancient and unmarked grave mounds once in evidence in Jennings Clearing, and antedating by almost half a century the settlement of Santa Clara, pose the larger questions. Who were the occupants, from whence did they come, and from what shared calamity did they die? Many historians came to believe the answer would resolve the riddle of the popular name, Old Military Road, soon after the War of 1812 supplanting the state's original title of Northwest Bay-Hopkinton Road.

Historical sources at Washington have reported no evidence, and past historians have rejected the concept, that American soldiers tramped Old Military in the War of 1812. Historian Alfred Donaldson dismissed the notion out of hand, contending the road was renamed for the Old Military Tracts through which it passed. It has simply been assumed that only the old road from Plattsburgh through Chateaugay and Hopkinton served as a military route between Lakes Champlain and Ontario.

One vital piece of evidence to the contrary has gone unremarked. Early in 1813, Secretary of War John Armstrong drew up orders to Major General Henry Dearborn for the massing of U.S. troops on Lake Ontario. Among his directions was this: "The two brigades on Lake Champlain you will move so as to give them full time to reach their destination on the 25th of March. The route by Elizabeth will, I think, be the shortest and the best. You will put into your movements as much privacy as may be compatible with their execution." "Elizabeth" was, of course, Elizabethtown, and the most secluded, as well as the shortest, route from there to Sackets Harbor via Hopkinton was none other than the Northwest Bay-Hopkinton Road.

There is more. Local tradition has always linked the graves in Jennings Clearing to soldiers of the War of 1812, who are claimed to have bivouacked there. Hopkinton, the terminus of the Northwest Bay Road, was certainly a hotbed of military activity at the time and, historically, a virulent measles epidemic snuffed out the lives of many transient soldiers in the neighborhood. Local tradition is buttressed by military relics in the form of gun barrels, buttons, bayonets, canteens, and canister shot unearthed over the years at several points in the Town of Santa Clara. In 1939 the state erected the historical marker on the spot—"Jennings Road, used by U.S. Troops, War of 1812, marching from Lake Champlain to Lake Ontario." Surely Old Military Road was exactly that.

Jennings Clearing and its mysterious graves, though still in evidence well into the twentieth century, have vanished, erased either by road construction or the relentless march of the Adirondack forest. Jennings

Road survives in part, ending suddenly only a mile into the woods of what is now the William Bolton estate.

* * *

The coming of the automobile altered forever the backwoods character of this antique avenue to the wilds of Essex, Franklin, and St. Lawrence Counties. The environment of its countryside has changed and yet has not changed. Past and present collide. Villages with modern motels are sandwiched between long miles of existing wilderness and extravagant lake and mountain views. Some of the smaller villages hold fast to a rural charm, encased in a bygone era like a fly in amber. Others, such as Saranac Lake and Lake Placid, have ballooned far beyond recognition. A few farms and historical landmarks survive. Here is the home of old John Brown, and here the cottage where Robert Louis Stevenson composed his *Master of Ballantrae.* Here and there stands a stately Victorian mansion, an abandoned farmhouse with vacant windows and ancient lilac trees. Paul Smith's College occupies the site of the grand old hotel, and where the McColloms proudly presided is a cemetery of forgotten names. The "fifty-mile woods" are not entirely intact, but in no other place do the leaves blaze as bright in October.

Blacktop overlies the tracks of the pioneers and the boys of 1812 on the Old Military Road. No matter. Adventure and discovery still beckon around each bend, from Indian-haunted Lake Champlain to sleepy Hopkinton.

EIGHT
Donaldson's "Biddlecome Road"

On March 25, 1990, Mary MacKenzie wrote to James Bailey debunking historian Alfred L. Donaldson's account of events on the so-called "Biddlecome Road" in his book, A History of the Adirondacks *(Century Publishing Co., 1921, reprinted Purple Mountain Press, 1996).*

As far as I'm concerned, you have not been able to find the so-called "Biddlecome Road" or "Tight Nipping" on very old maps such as Burr, Gray, 1858 French, etc., because there never was any such road.

Let's begin with Donaldson. You would have no particular reason to know this, because hard-core Adirondack history is not your game. But

Donaldson's history is riddled with errors, misconceptions, and fantasies. His sins of omission are even greater than his sins of commission. Today no Adirondack historians worth their salt accept anything in Donaldson as gospel. I don't mean to imply there is nothing at all worthwhile in Donaldson. Of course there is. It's just that you never know what is correct unless, with great effort, you check it out yourself.

There are a number of reasons for what I call "the Donaldson mess." In the first place, he was a very amateur historian who never did learn how to research properly. Then he was a sick man when he compiled the history, curing for TB in Saranac Lake and mostly bedridden. He could not travel around and he depended heavily on old-timers to come to his bedside and recount their (dubious) tales. Horrendous! We all know better today than to take the word of old-timers. Modern research methods and the wealth of source material now and not formerly available are constantly revising old texts, with their fables and foibles. Mind you, I am not against a good tale, and enjoy one as much as the next person. But a responsible historian has to learn where to draw the line.

If there was anything Donaldson loved to hear, it was a colorful yarn, no matter how suspect, and he unabashedly reported dozens of them as history without a single attempt at authentication, and with embellishments of his own besides. I have hunted down some of them and dug out the truth, which is sometimes more interesting than the fiction. But let me add here that I admire him tremendously for one thing—his writing style. Oh, could I only employ the English language as elegantly and as engagingly as Donaldson did.

In my estimation, Donaldson's "Biddlecome Road," his designation of it as the locale of the famous "Allen's bear fight up in Keene," and his story of the lady who supposedly traveled it in 1840, are hogwash. Let me try to present a coherent summary of my findings.

Donaldson says that Biddlecome was an early settler of Keene Valley and was living on Lot 23 of Mallory's Grant in 1797. This is probably true. Smith's History of Essex County also labels him an early settler.

But Biddlecome never bought Lot 23. In 1800, it was purchased and occupied by Stephen Estes, whose family continued to farm it for generations. Biddlecome does not appear on a single Keene census, from 1800 on. He is a shadowy figure. He walked in and out of the pages of

Keene history, scarcely leaving a footprint. He was just plain gone by 1800, and there is no record ever of any Biddlecome house in Keene Valley.

And what would he or anybody else be doing building a road to South Meadows at the turn of the century? I could write paragraphs about the absurdity of such a road, with emphasis upon its unfavorable location.

But the main point is, there was no need anyway for that Biddlecome Road through the panther-infested wilds. Even before 1800, the Old Military Road from Westport to Hopkinton, in St. Lawrence County, had already evolved. By 1800, it was a well-worn wagon track from Westport to Keene, and beyond that a blazed trail all the way to Hopkinton. As settlers moved ever further west, it gradually became a real road, and in 1810, the state took it over and did a lot of work on its entire length. There was also a road from Keene Valley to Keene in those earliest years, and Keene Valley people could reach North Elba with little trouble.

The segment of the Old Military Road that you skied in February, running from Alstead Hill Road[10] through Pitchoff Pass to Route 86 in North Elba, was always called—and, for that matter, is still called—Old Mountain Road by the locals. It is, of course, now part of the Jackrabbit Trail. I will be referring to that segment as Old Mountain Road hereafter.

Moreover, Donaldson's tale of the lady who rode with her baby over the Biddlecome Road in 1840 (when it had dwindled down to a bridle path) is as corny as the bag of kernels she was carrying. It scarcely deserves dissection, but here goes anyway. Why in the name of heaven would anybody with all their marbles have taken such a lonesome, lamentable trail on their way to Westport? Suppose she really did. She rode several miles out to South Meadows—no trail to it then from the Elba settlement, and the Adirondack Loj road wasn't even in existence until 1880, when Henry Van Hoevenberg built his log hotel. Then she took off on an eight-mile ride to Keene Valley through a wild, lonely, uninhabited, and hazardous wilderness, and another three miles over to the Elizabethtown road. When all the time she could have saved a few miles and some hairy situations by taking the long-existing, publicly maintained and fairly well-travelled road from North Elba through Keene to the Elizabethtown road, and thence to Westport. (If this story has any basic truth in it, I would wager that's the road she took anyway.) We won't touch on the other nutty aspects of the tale.

---

10 Now Alstead Hill Lane.

I know all the names and biographies of the handful of people living in the North Elba part of Keene in 1840. Only nine families—and, at that, one was living in the Saranac Lake end, two in Ray Brook, and one in Averyville. Only five in the Elba settlement proper. But they are of no interest to you if you accept my version of the Anson Allen story. And we do now come to Anson Allen and his spectacular bear fight.[11]

Allen himself never pinpointed the exact locale of that stirring adventure, and neither did anybody else (except Donaldson). All the old and original accounts simply say it took place "in the wilds of Keene."

Years ago, I personally worked out Allen's true itinerary from my Xerox of his original Keene census of 1840 in his own handwriting—I got this from the National Archives some thirty years ago.

I will digress a moment and speak of these old censuses of the nineteenth century. You already know this. They are especially valuable to researchers in that the inhabitants were not listed alphabetically. While this makes for a lot of work when you are searching for a specific individual and have to wade through all those names, it has one great reward: The census taker didn't skip around haphazardly; he went through a town methodically, listing inhabitants in the order in which they lived. This tells a researcher exactly where each person lived in relation to his neighbors, and in which specific area.

I happen to be quite familiar with most of the Keene names in 1840 because I've done a lot of genealogical work down there. Anson Allen's route through the Town of Keene in 1840, as reflected in his census, was a very orderly one. He started in the north at the Jay border, proceeded down to Keene village, and then did the side roads to the east. He then went down the road toward Keene Valley until he came to the junction with the Elizabethtown road. He went up the Elizabethtown road to the Keene-Elizabethtown border. Backtracking to the road junction, he walked down to Keene Valley and covered the entire settlement. He then returned to Keene village via the Hull's Falls Road, censusing as he went. He then proceeded up Alstead Hill toward what is now North Elba, covering all of Alstead Hill, until he came to the last house before you plunge into the uninhabited woods of the Old Mountain Road: that of Reuben Davis. The

---

11 While taking the 1840 census of Keene township, census-taker Anson Allen fought off a bear he encountered on a lonely stretch of trail. The fight was memorialized in a poem that became part of Adirondack lore.

last house today is of course the Jossey Bilan place (just beyond the old Davis house, which burned down several years ago), but that wasn't there in 1840.

The very next house on Allen's census is that of Oliver Bartlett, who lived in what is now North Elba. I have an old letter that says Oliver Bartlett's cabin was the first place you reached in North Elba after emerging from the woods of the Old Mountain Road. After Bartlett, Allen lists all in one bunch that handful of residents then living in North Elba.

However much it will disappoint you (and I weep for you), the evidence is crystal-clear: Allen journeyed to "Abram's Plain" not on any trail, real or fictitious, from Keene Valley, but from the end of Alstead Hill over the Old Mountain Road many miles to the north. And it was surely on that road that he encountered the legendary bear.

Where Donaldson got his information that the bear fight took place on "Biddlecome Road" is beyond me. This was a Donaldson exclusive and did not appear in any preceding Adirondack literature. I can usually identify the culprit who provided him with a certain piece of nonsense because I have read all his correspondence housed in the Saranac Lake Library. But not this time. My own mean-spirited suspicion is that he chose the locus himself because he was so enamored of that Biddlecome folderol.

And all this brings up the question: In what area does "Tight Nipping" really belong?

Everybody and his brother, innocently and trustfully, has lifted this locale out of Donaldson, and there has been more than one published article perpetuating the error—at least a couple have appeared in *High Spots.* I suppose it is now time this misconception was thoroughly examined and corrected, and the bear fight publicly moved to its rightful and legal setting. I have never done anything about it.

Over the years other area historians—and Harry MacDougal was one of them—became highly suspicious of that Biddlecome Road, and felt that if a man named Biddlecome had anything at all to do with road-building, the road had to be Old Mountain. In fact, back in 1963, there was a huge map hanging in your Adirondack Center Museum at Elizabethtown showing the Old Military Road, among others. It was hand-drawn and of rather modern vintage—probably a Museum project. It erroneously showed Old Mountain Road going past Cascade Lakes, and the Old

Mountain Road segment was labeled—can you believe it?—"Biddlecomb Road." I questioned Harry MacDougal about that map, and that was when he told me he believed Old Mountain Road and Biddlecome Road were one and the same.

Well, now, if there wasn't any ancient road from Keene Valley to South Meadows, when was the trail constructed—the trail that shows up on the maps of a hundred years ago? You sent me the 1895 U.S. Geological Survey Mount Marcy sheet indicating such a trail in its entire length. I know of no earlier map depicting it. I have in my collection Geologic Map of New York, Adirondack Sheet, of 1901, and the USGS Mount Marcy Quadrangle topographical map of 1902, reprinted 1940, and both show the South Meadows-Keene Valley trail following exactly the same course as your 1895 map. This trail is also shown on a map in the Lake Placid Club's Wilderness Ski Trails at Adirondack Loj, undated but undoubtedly early 1930s. It is labeled "unmarked trail."

This trail had reached a real state of deterioration by 1934. The ADK's Guide to Adirondack Trails, Northeastern Section, published in 1934, has this to say about it:

> **Keene Valley to South Meadows**
>
> This is not a maintained trail, but an old logging road, and should be attempted only as an exploratory trip. The trail may be difficult to follow in places due to rapid growth of underbrush. The condition of the trail, windfalls and bridges, is undetermined.
>
> Out of Keene Valley village follow the Marcy Trail on the N. side of Johns Brook for 2 m., to the point where the ADK trail to Johns Brook Lodge turns left and enters the woods.
>
> Keep straight ahead on the old wood road. This climbs for 2½ m. along the S. bank of Slide Brook (not to be confused with Slide Mountain Brook). The descent is more gradual and follows the general course of South Meadow Brook along its S. bank.
>
> About 6+ m. from Keene Valley this trail meets the South Meadow-Cascade Lakes Trail. Turn right for Cascade Lakes road; turn left for South Meadows. Trail continues W. 1+ m. on high ground above the swamp caused by beaver dams, along South Meadow Brook. From the junction just mentioned the trail is maintained. The last half

mile is through the clearing and brings one to the dam where it joins the Johns Brook-South Meadows Trail.

Distance: Keene Valley to South Meadows, about 8 mi.

Note that the ADK calls this trail "an old logging road." That is precisely what I believe it was.

Commercial lumbering began about the mid 1890s in the Adirondack Loj-South Meadows-Klondike-Marcy-Indian Pass-McIntyre sector. I think it started a few years before up around Johns Brook. The logging operations in the South Meadows and Klondike area were very extensive and of particularly long duration—so much so that a little village sprang up at South Meadows, where wives and children could be with their men. There were quite a number of houses and other buildings, and even a schoolhouse, probably existing for some ten years. Cellar holes, foundations, etc., were in evidence a long time after the settlement was abandoned and buildings dismantled, but today no trace remains except the ruins of the old dam. South Meadows today is not the great clearing it once was, even as recently as thirty years ago. Tree growth has been rapid, and the clearing has shrunk considerably.

It is my opinion, based on the above, that a trail from South Meadows to Keene Valley did not come into existence until the time of those protracted lumbering operations, and that is the trail shown on the USGS maps of a hundred years ago. This is the only explanation that makes any sense to me: Like all old logging roads of that era, it gradually was obliterated by tree and undergrowth rebirth.

I do hope that on your next reconnaissance trip into this region, when the snow goes, you will be able to discover some remnants of the trail, and maybe the 1934 ADK description will be of some help.

Just one more comment (your patience must be exhausted):

When I saw the printed words "Railroad Notch" on the 1979 USGS Metric Topo you sent, I was reminded that behind the name "Railroad Notch" lies an enigma. While it is applied today to the area as marked on the 1979 map, the name Railroad Notch was originally applied to what is known today as Klondike Notch on the trail from South Meadows to Johns Brook Lodge. Klondike Notch was called Railroad Notch at least up into the 1930s. In fact, the entire Johns Brook Lodge-South Meadows trail was called "The Railroad Notch Trail." If you want, I can furnish documentation. When and why the name Railroad Notch was booted over to the present location, and whodunit, is something I've never tried to track down.

Maybe one of your puzzle-addicted ADKers would like to tackle the problem.

Well, Jim, this is my report, and I certainly am not going to advise you what you should do about it. I have no documented proof one way or the other—only an educated surmise—as to whether or not there ever was a Biddlecome Road. But I am darned sure, and will stake my reputation on it, that "Allen's bear fight up in Keene" never took place in that hallowed region between Keene Valley and South Meadows, but rather in the wild and woolly woods of the Old Mountain Road on the way to North Elba from Keene village.

NINE
Chapel Pond Road

In a letter dated June 24, 2001, Mary MacKenzie answers an inquiry into the history of the Chapel Pond Road. She defines the road as "that part of Route 73 beginning at the site of the old Beede farm in St. Hubert's and proceeding all the way to the Northway."

A very early road was built from Albany by way of Schroon Lake, North Hudson, New Russia, and Elizabethtown to the Au Sable River and thence through Clinton County to Canada. I am not sure who laid out the road up to Schroon Lake, but I do know that Capt. Platt Rogers in 1789 laid out the section from Schroon Lake to Elizabethtown. For this work, he received a grant of land in Essex County. This road was known for a great many years as the Old State Road. Today, from the intersection where it branches off from the Chapel Pond Road to Elizabethtown, it is called the Poke-O-Moonshine Road. This intersection is known locally and by state troopers as "Crazy Corners" because the state laid out a ridiculous, complicated, and unnecessary maze of traffic lanes that nobody has ever paid any attention to anyway.

There is the old story, mentioned in a 1967 article in the *Tupper Lake Free Press,* that in the War of 1812, American troops used this Old State Road in marching from Plattsburgh to Albany after the Battle of Plattsburgh. This may be true, as I have found another reference, apparently authentic, that following the Battle of Plattsburgh, General George Izard and his troops travelled down the Old State Road in the late summer of 1814 and camped for a night in Elizabethtown "where the Methodist Church now stands."

In the early years, the people living in Keene township who wanted to go south had to go all the way over to Elizabethtown to gain access to the Old State Road. But somebody in Keene must have had political pull, because in 1811 the Legislature passed an Act authorizing the construction of a road from the south line of the Mallory Tract (i.e., the old Smith Beede farm at St. Hubert's) to the house of Levi Farr in the Town of Schroon. This road, of course, would merge with the Old State Road.

The article in the *Tupper Lake Free Press* erroneously suggests that this first Chapel Pond Road was built for the use of soldiers in the War of 1812. The road was, of course, proposed and built before the war. The *Free Press* article also suggests that after the defeat of the British at York (Toronto) and Ogdensburg, American troops used the Chapel Pond Road in traveling to Albany. I find this preposterous, and there is no evidence to sustain it.

Incidentally, the new Keene book[12] tells about the 1811 Act but says the Act indicates there was already a road there. In fact, it indicates no such thing.

What baffles me the most in the *Free Press* article is the reference to that "old log barracks" built by the army for winter quarters when they were "overtaken" by winter in their march. I find it very hard to follow the descriptions given in the *Free Press,* but it appears to me that this barracks was supposed to have been located somewhere between Crazy Corners and Underwood. One of the big problems with the story is that it uses the names of ponds, streams, etc., that do not appear on modern maps. The only ones I can locate are Lower and Upper Moss Ponds, down near Underwood.

What about that log barracks? I find such an account sheer nonsense and totally unbelievable. It is probably one of those old, fanciful myths that find a firm lodging place in the public domain and remain there forever. The "bottom logs of the structure still visible" in 1900 could have belonged to many another building.

---

12 *Two Adirondack Hamlets in History: Keene and Keene Valley,* ed. Richard Plunz (Fleischmanns, NY: Purple Mountain Press, 1999).

If the army was overtaken by winter, why on earth would it have stopped at such a godforsaken spot in the wilderness? A couple of days' march backward or forward would have landed them in an inhabited neighborhood. And if winter was so near, why would they have left Plattsburgh when they did? Where would they have gotten building supplies for such a structure? (And it would have been pretty big.) Where would they have procured food and provisions to carry them through the winter? The idea of this barracks somewhere on the Chapel Pond Road, in my opinion, is so absurd that it should be discarded completely.

It is certainly made obvious in the *Free Press* article that the original road built in 1811 followed a somewhat different course than the next road to be built, certainly from Crazy Corners over almost to Chapel Pond, and probably also from Crazy Corners down to the Northway.

The *Free Press* story says that, in 1900, remnants of this original road were plainly visible. I have another article in my files from the *Elizabethtown Post* of March 1, 1906, which mentions "a piece of road still visible in the woods in the southeasterly part of Keene and in portions of North Hudson." Now, after the passage of so many years, could these same abandoned stretches—such as a few woodsmen say they have come across from time to time—still be visible today? It seems unlikely, but we cannot rule it out.

I do not know when the first Chapel Pond Road was abandoned, and it appears nobody else does either. Deep digging on my part has failed to unearth the answer. But the road certainly was abandoned. Obviously, it was allowed to deteriorate, fall into disrepair, and become impassable. Maybe it existed for only a short time. It is not shown on early nineteenth century maps, and it is not on the comprehensive 1858 French map.

In 1863, the Legislature passed an Act for the construction of a new road from the old Beede farm at St. Hubert's to North Hudson, "a distance of about nine miles." Nothing happened, however, and in 1867 the Legislature passed another Act repealing the 1863 law and allowing the construction of a road "by the nearest and most feasible route...from the Beede farm to some point on the state road in or near Lot 96 in the North River Tract, a distance of about five miles." This means it was to go down as far as Crazy Corners, because the latter is close to Lot 98 and is just about five miles from the old Beede farm. We know that the new road followed a somewhat different course than the original, and it must have been built shortly after the Act was passed—although, strangely, it does not appear on the 1876 Gray township map of Essex County. It does, however, appear on later maps of the nineteenth century.

The new Keene book, I believe, completely ignores this Act of 1867 and the building of a new road. However, it does mention a Chapel Pond Road being there in the 1870s and 1880s. The reader is, therefore, left with the impression that the original 1811 road continued on the same course throughout the century.

I have not attempted research beyond 1900, but the new Keene book supplies some material. It says that by the 1920s the Chapel Pond Road was in very poor condition but was still being used, but became almost impassable until the 1930s in spite of numerous state attempts to improve it. Then it says that a new road was built through Chapel Pond Pass in 1935.

I wonder if that new road in 1935 followed the same course as the road built in the 1860s? If it did not, the remnants of an old road that people report finding could very well be abandoned stretches of the 1860s road and not of the original road built in 1811.

TEN
Stagecoach Rock

In a letter dated January 16, 1986 to Jeffrey G. Kelley, editor of Adirondack Life *magazine, Mary MacKenzie comments on a February 1986 article about the popular tourist attraction, Stagecoach Rock. She says that "the present highway 73 from Keene to North Elba through Cascade Pass and along the lakes was probably one of the most traveled stagecoach routes in the Adirondacks, and a stagecoach rock could find no more appropriate niche to memorialize that picturesque era of our history."*

She goes on to say that some inaccuracies in the article arise from a misunderstanding of the histories of Old Military Road and the Cascade Road relative to the time of the stagecoach era—specifically, that the Cascade Lakes stretch of road was constructed in 1858–59, before the advent of stagecoach travel.

She continues with the history of Stagecoach Rock:

The story goes like this. In the beginning, there was Old Military Road, originally called Northwest Bay-Hopkinton Road. It appears to have been in existence before 1800 and ran all the way from Westport on Lake Champlain to Hopkinton in St. Lawrence County—Westport to Elizabethtown, Keene, North Elba, Harrietstown, and so on. It never touched Keene Valley; Shackett Road is in Keene, not Keene Valley. From Keene it ran up Alstead Hill Road (now Shackett Road, more's the pity)[13] past Jossey Bilan's, threaded a gorge on the north side of Pitchoff and so into North Elba. The stretch from Bilan's to North Elba became known as Old Mountain Road. In other words, Shackett Road and Old Mountain Road were not separate entities, but both were just a part of Old Military Road. The Bilan end became obliterated by beaver ponds in modern times, but otherwise the road is still there as a woods trail.

Old Mountain Road was just about the most deplorable segment of Old Military—the pioneers used to say of it, "six miles, six hours." In the late 1850s, the Keene and North Elba folks got together and petitioned the state for a new bypass highway through Cascade Pass. In 1858, the Legislature authorized construction, the new route was surveyed and roughly laid out, and in 1859, it was completed. It was primitive and hair-raising, sure enough, but still an improvement over Old Mountain. The latter continued to be used for a long time, but mostly by farm wagons and buckboards.

Old Military Road—i.e., Old Mountain Road—did not antedate Cascade Road in stagecoach travel. The stagecoach era in the Adirondacks did not begin until after the Civil War with the advent of places of accommodation for tourists. Before that, it was all buckboards, wagons, and the like. Regular coach travel from Westport to Lake Placid, and on to Harrietstown, was then inaugurated. Coach drivers rarely used Old Military Road from Keene to North Elba—they chose Cascade Road, even though it was two miles longer, simply because it was a less hazardous route.

Yes, the Cascade House did draw coaches that way, because it was a regular refreshment stop. But there were many other hotels on the run. The Golden Age of Hotels began at Lake Placid in the 1870s, and by the 1880s, when stagecoach travel was in its heyday but before the arrival of the railroad, Placid was well on its way to becoming a premier summer

13 The name has been changed back, more or less, to Alstead Hill Lane.

resort of America. All of these Lake Placid hotels were in existence before the railroad came in 1893: Mountain View House, Stevens House, Adirondack Lodge, Mirror Lake House, Allen House, Grand View, Westside, Brewster's, Lakeside, Placid Heights, Lyon's Inn, Castle Rustico, Nash's, Undercliff, and Hanmer's—Ruisseaumont, too—to say nothing of summer camps. Lyon's Inn, still standing, was well known as the "stagecoach inn" because it was a regular stop on the Elizabethtown-Harrietstown run. When you consider that the clientele of all these great hotels had to arrive by stagecoach, you can well imagine the heavy traffic through Cascade Pass. True, some coaches did come via the Wilmington Road, but the preferred route was Cascades.

ELEVEN
The Iron Works Road
August–October 1996

The Elba Iron Works constructed the first road to Wilmington in 1814 to lessen the distance from North Elba to Arnold Hill near Clintonville, where it was then purchasing its iron ore. The road started at the Elba Works (site of Lake Placid village power dam on Lower Mill Pond) and went up past the former Gordon Pratt house to the present Wilmington Road. That old dirt road is still in existence. From there, it followed a slightly different course than the present Route 86, crossed the Au Sable River where the State Conservation monument is located, and went up over the Sentinel Range behind Owen and Winch Ponds. It came down to the river again at the Flume, crossed the present Route 86, and went up the dirt road still in existence to the heights above present Route 86 and then along the heights to Wilmington hamlet. This road can be found almost in its entirety on Surveyor John Richards' map of the Jay and Whiteface Mountain tracts of March 1815.

This was the only road from Lake Placid to Wilmington until 1854. Apparently by 1839, it had become impassable for wagons or carriages and was used only as a footpath, according to a letter from early settler Timothy Nash to his niece Fannie Nash, dated March 26, 1891. In that letter, Nash recounts a trip over this old road in the spring of 1839:

In March 1839 my father went from Willsborough Essex Co. to what was then known as Abrahams Plains, now North Elba, and bought a farm from Roswell Thompson. In June of that same year your father and I, then were boys, went from Willsborough and drove some young cattle to the farm to pasture. We went by way of E'town and Keene crossing the Keene Mountain from Alstead Hill.

We stopped at Mr. Thompson's until the next morning, and he recommended a new road for us to return that he thought would shorten the distance.

On June 12 we started on our return trip over the new proposed road. The morning was cool and cloudy and it had been raining through the night and the ground was soft and muddy. The first nine miles was through the woods towards Wilmington, was an old winter road, but impassable for wagons or carriages. After traveling three or four miles we discovered a new fresh bear track in the mud going the same direction we were, but we did not know how soon we should overtake the animal. We had no weapons of defense, but armed ourselves with clubs ready for a fight, and walked along in silence. We had walked about ½ mile with nothing in our mind but "bear," when a big rustling in the leaves was heard together with a strong noise that sounded to us, at that time, very loud. It was on the side your father was walking and near the road, but the subject of the commotion was hid from view by thick underbrush, We squared ourselves with clubs drawn ready for fight with our face to the enemy, but as it became visible, lo and behold! instead of being a bear, it was only a partridge with her young brood. Your father told me years after that that partridge looked as large to him as an ox. The balance of the nine miles was made with no unusual excitement.

Famous North Elba guide Bill Nye and Robert G. Scott of North Elba built the present road along the river, Route 86, in 1854. Peter Comstock built the Wilmington end of it. They built it by extending Riverside Drive along the present course along the river and through Wilmington Notch. After that, the old road over the mountain was practically abandoned. I did find an article[14] over at the Feinberg Library that said the last known trip over this road was in March of 1871, when Peter Comstock, Norman Kilburn, and Millard Hayes drove over it because the Notch Road was impassable.

The section from the bridge at the intersection of Riverside Drive to Lake Placid village, through the woods and the Lake Placid Club golf links to the traffic light at the top of Mill Hill, was built in 1885–86, according to the following statement appearing in the *First Annual Report of the Forest Commission of the State of New York* for the year 1885 (Albany: Argus Company, 1886), p. 101:

> A new road is being opened this winter from Lake Placid to intersect the road leading through Wilmington Pass on the Au Sable River near Wilmington Notch. This road passes through state Lots 317, 337, 357, using an old road which was built by the MacEnteries [i.e., Archibald McIntyre, proprietor of the Elba Iron Works] to their forge.... This road lessens the distance from Au Sable Station to Lake Placid six miles.

In 1985, the original Iron Works road was still in existence, at least as far as the old Roswell Thompson farmhouse, which became the Lake Placid Club's Mohawk clubhouse, situated next to the present Theanoguen.[15]

North Elba Roads
[1985]
Riverside Drive

This road, known locally as "River Road," extends from the ski jumps on Route 73 to the Wilmington Road, Route 86. The first part of this road must have been in existence very early in the nineteenth century, as some of the pioneer farms of North Elba's first colony were in the area.

14 From the *Essex County Republican*, April 18, 1924, titled "An Abandoned Road: The Last Man to Drive Over It."—"March 1871, the last man was Peter Comstock, with him were two other men, Norman Kilburn & Millard Hayes of Wilmington. Employed by Comstock to run lines of lots 5 & 6 of the Whiteface Mt. Tract. Ice piled up in the Notch and they could not use the road, so they went on the old road east of the Notch. Comstock went to Henry Congers and Owens cabin. They went from the North Elba side and came out above the Flume."

15 Theanoguen burned in a wave of arson fires on former Lake Placid Club buildings in November 1991.

It was extended gradually later in the century as new farms came into being. In 1854, it was extended all the way to Wilmington Road, Route 86, when the latter road was constructed along the river, the only route to Wilmington until 1885, when the bypass was constructed from Lake Placid village through the Club golf links and the woods down to the state bridge at the intersection of Riverside Drive and Route 86.

TWELVE
Averyville-Adirondac Road
June 12, 1999

There was indeed an old road from Averyville, in North Elba, to McIntyre's Adirondac Iron Works, in Newcomb. Anecdotal reports of this road have always abounded in North Elba. When I became town historian thirty-five years ago, I think a descendant of every one of our extant pioneer families told me about it, bragging that his forebear had had a hand in building it.

The Adirondac Iron Works was in full throttle in the late 1840s and provided a ready market for North Elba farm produce. The problem was, how to transport it? It was a long trek from North Elba to McIntyre's Newcomb iron plantation, called Adirondac (spelled without the usual "k" at the end), via established highways, and wagons and sleds could scarcely negotiate the trail through Indian Pass. A group of North Elba men therefore banded together, laid out, built, and maintained a toll road from the end of so-called Averyville Road[16] down through the wilderness to Lake Henderson and the iron works.

I have always wondered if and from whom permission was obtained to build such a road, especially a toll road, but permission was probably never sought or obtained. Gerrit Smith owned some of the northern lots, but most of the territory was untrammeled, primeval wilderness owned by the State of New York.

Of course, the Adirondac Iron Works closed down just a few years later, so the road served its original purpose for a very short time. It seems to have continued as a trail ever afterward.

The road started at the end of the so-called Averyville Road in North Elba (the same back then as it is today) and went south to Moose Pond,

16 Now Averyville Lane, County Route 23.

then southeast to Preston Ponds, and thence down to Lake Henderson and the Upper Works.

Today, of course, much, if not all, of this old route is still in existence. From Averyville down to Preston Ponds, it is the first leg of the Northville-Placid Trail, and probably follows the original track pretty closely.[17] There is still a trail from Preston Ponds to Henderson, but I have been told it does not exactly follow the original route.

I have, after much searching, been able to find three published accounts that note the road. However brief, they do definitely corroborate its existence. Winslow Watson mentions it in his important 1869 *History of Essex County.*[18] The article "Averyville so-called" in the *Elizabethtown Post* of October 31, 1907, gives a very interesting little account of it, and G.A. Alford covered it in the February 29, 1952 *Lake Placid News* as part of his "Early Days" series.

It is very true that mining towns provided local markets for Adirondack farmers in the early history of these mountains. North Elba is a good example. Our first settlers came here in 1800, and by 1810 we had forty families, all engaged in farming. The colony had hard going initially, but when Archibald McIntyre established his rather substantial Elba Iron Works here in 1810, things began to look up. The farmers not only now had a ready market for produce, but also manufactured charcoal for the Works, receiving 3¢ per bushel.

THIRTEEN
Mining and Minerals in Essex County: A Short History

This is part of Mary MacKenzie's speech to the Northland Rock & Mineral Club. The date of the speech is February 1965.

17 The Averyville end of the trail was moved in 1978. The trail originally followed the left bank of the Chubb River above Wanika Falls (located about halfway between Duck Hole and the Averyville Road) northward to Wescott Farm. In 1978, the state moved the Northville-Placid Trail across the Chubb to the right bank of the Chubb above Wanika, from which point it now veers off toward the northeast.

18 The proper title is *The Military and Civil History of the County of Essex, New York,* by Winslow C. Watson (Albany, NY: J. Munsell, 1869).

Then the history of people began in our mountain region. The Indians knew our area for five thousand years, and then the stage was set for the first white man to scale the natural barriers that sealed this region off from the rest of the world. The first white man was probably a trapper pursuing the beaver, shortly after the Revolution, because everyone in Europe wanted a beaver hat. It was about 1795 when the first white farmers began to filter in to Elizabethtown, Jay, and Keene Valley, and then in 1800 the first settler came to Lake Placid.

Our Adirondack region had been settled for some forty years before the state finally decided to make a geologic reconnaissance of this vast wilderness, which was completely unknown to the outside world. They sent Professor Ebenezer Emmons up to make a geologic survey in 1837. We smile a little today at some of Professor Emmons' notions—that our primitive limestone was of igneous origin, and that the mountains of New England were far older than the Adirondacks. But let us remember that the geologist of 125 years ago was not as well informed as he is today—and, after all, Emmons was dealing with a geologic puzzle the like of which he had never encountered before. We are indebted to him for publicizing the Adirondacks and thus opening them up for further exploration, and above all for bestowing the actual name of Adirondacks upon our mountains.

The first settlers, of course, were always on the lookout for precious metals, because the region was reputed to be one of great mineral wealth. Indeed, the very first name of our mountains was the Peru Mountains, given by the early French, who saw them from Lake Champlain and believed they held the treasures of South America.

But it was not gold or silver that the pioneers found. It was iron ore.

We do not know who the first man was to discover Adirondack iron, but early settlers William Gilliland and Phillip Skene knew the wealth of ore in the hills behind Port Henry before the Revolution. The British at Ticonderoga may have worked these deposits. The Americans certainly did, for Arnold wrote in his diary in June 1775, "Sent a boat with Skene's negroes to dig ore."

It was suggested that I tell you tonight the history and location of all the mines and forges in Essex County, but I found to my dismay that there were actually over two hundred iron mines and forges worked during the nineteenth century.

At any rate, knowledge of the great Cheever ore bed at Port Henry existed just after the Revolution. The ore cropped out on the surface of the ground to such an extent that the early settlers could not fail to notice it. Ore is known to have been taken from the bed as early as 1804. Iron ore beds in Elizabethtown were worked to some extent about 1800, and some of the great beds near Clintonville were opened early in the nineteenth century.

There were three very early iron works in the county. The Willsboro forge was erected in 1800 and manufactured anchors. The New Russia forge, south of Elizabethtown, was erected about 1802. The third oldest was the iron works here in North Elba, which began operations about 1809.

Ore was discovered in the usual manner in those days: quite by accident. One young boy found a bed in Crown Point in 1826 while hunting. He took hold of a bush to help him up the mountain; the bush broke from the rock, and there lay the shining ore. Another Crown Point resident's find proved not very lucky for himself. He was hunting for bees in 1821 and found ore instead. He put some small specimens in his pocket, which he later exhibited to his friends. They kept the secret for two years; then it leaked out, and the location became generally known—but the bee hunter lived and died a poor man.

The immense graphite deposits at Ticonderoga were discovered by one Mrs. Zuba Pearl while driving her cows home down the slopes of a mountain. One of them slipped and broke the wet moss off a sloping rock, and there lay the graphite, pure and unmixed.

In the early and middle 1800s, Essex County was a vast beehive of activity in mining iron ore and forging it. On almost every river and stream, no matter how small, in almost every hamlet and town, the fires of small bloomeries and forges winked in the night. Most of them used the old Vulcan forge method, as old as the Phoenicians. And in almost every hamlet and town, iron mines were being worked, sometimes two and three to a town, and splendid were the dreams of the great fortunes to be wrested from the earth.

Only a few of these mines are being worked today.[19] Sometimes money ran out, and the owner went bankrupt. Sometimes the magnetite was not found in true veins but only in pockets that were soon worked out. Other

---

19 The last major iron mine in Essex County, in Moriah township, closed in 1971. National Lead's titanium mine at Tahawus, in Newcomb township, was open until 1989.

beds contained enough sulphur or titanium to make the iron unprofitable. The value of titanium for commercial use, of course, was not known then. It is amusing that Professor Emmons in his geological report mentions it as being found in small quantities only, and that its sole use was for coloring artificial teeth! The great Arnold Hill mine, which was worked for over a century, finally shut down in the first part of the twentieth century, not because the ore ran out but because the ore was finally too far down to be mined profitably.

Not much remains of the little forges and iron works; most have been closed for a century or more, but even today traces can be seen. There is scarcely a stream anywhere that is not marked with the remains of old dams, and nearby the old cinder pile and what is left of the kilns where the ore was roasted. Many woods are not merely second growth, but third or fourth or fifth growth. All through them are spots where kilns or pits stood for making the charcoal that supplied the forges located on the streams. It seems that charcoal never decays, and often bits of it can be found in the woods, as sound as the day it was burned.

The belief that the early lumber barons and forest fires were the culprits that destroyed much of our primeval forest is only a myth. The truth is that thousands upon thousands of acres were cut down for the charcoal industry. In fact, to encourage the manufacturing of iron, the state in 1808 set aside vast unsold forest lands in Essex County to furnish fuel for the forges. As late as 1877, charcoal was still being used in the iron forges of Essex County. In that year, twenty-four thousand tons of forge iron were produced in the Adirondack region—and only about three thousand or four thousand tons in all the rest of the United States. When you realize that it took timber from about six thousand acres of land in that year alone to make charcoal, you can begin to understand how rapidly the forest resources were being depleted.

Here in North Elba, for almost fifty years, the Peru Iron and Ore Company of Clinton County owned the dam at Lake Placid's outlet and all the land within a circuit of fourteen miles, from which were drawn their immense supplies of charcoal. They used about five thousand bushels a day. The very earliest lumber operations of all in our town took place during the years 1809 to 1816, when large areas of what is now the lower village and the outskirts along Old Military Road were cut over to supply the Elba Iron Works with fuel. The town at that time was dotted with charcoal pits, and the iron works bought the charcoal for 3¢ per bushel.

As we have noted earlier, the first white settler came into North Elba in 1800. His name was Elijah Bennet. He was a farmer and a veteran of the Revolutionary War. Between 1800 and 1810, many more families came down the Old Military Road and settled on our secluded plateau. By 1810, there were two hundred souls living in North Elba, almost all engaged in farming. There was a gristmill, a sawmill, a school, and finally, in 1809, an iron works.

Archibald McIntyre and his associates had come into the town prospecting for minerals and, discovering several ore beds, erected a forge of four to six fires on the present lower millpond. They formed the Elba Iron and Steel Company, with a capital of $100,000—a lot of money in those days—and planned the manufacture of iron, steel, hollowware, nail rods, and sheet iron. The ore was at first drawn mostly from their Cascade Lakes bed, but was found to be so highly charged with pyrites that it proved almost worthless.

Then it became necessary to bring in ore by ox cart from the Arnold Hill bed near Clintonville, a long distance away, over roads passable only on snow. A road was cut out over the Sentinel Range, which has long since disappeared, and over this for a number of years passed the oxen sleds in winter. The expense and labor of this operation proved so great that the works were abandoned in 1817. Today, no outward trace remains of these once-busy iron works, which were located just below our present electric power dam—but in the little pine woods that has grown up there, if you will dig carefully under the carpet of needles, you will find huge chunks of the old slag.

There is a mystery that surrounds this old Elba Iron Works, from which our town derived its name, which has always intrigued me. Winslow Watson, who wrote a history of Essex County in 1869, said, "I examined in North Elba several large deposits, apparently of a high grade of ore. These were strangely overlooked when the original beds owned by the Elba Company were abandoned, and it was judged necessary to export the raw material from the Arnold bed." There is a puzzle for all of you to solve. Where are these ore beds that Watson claimed to have seen? Perhaps some of you already know the answer. Professor Emmons gives a clue in his report, saying, "Another vein of ore has been discovered on Chub

River." Another clue lies in the fact that, when the Elba Works purchased the Mill Pond site from the state, they also purchased Lots 75 and 76 at Ray Brook, about where the Conservation building stands. It seems logical to suppose that those lots, then standing in the middle of the wilderness, were purchased for their iron ore content. At any rate, somewhere in the Town of North Elba are said to be large deposits of magnetite.

The Adirondack region, as does almost every community in the state, has its quota of tales of lost silver deposits, of men who came upon them in the deep forests, returned home to get a shovel, and never again could locate the spot. There is a similar tradition about lead mines. Nearly all stories are to the effect that there is, near some village, an Indian lead mine that cannot be located, and that at one time the Indians brought in the lead and traded it for powder and firewater.

The most famous of the lost silver deposits lies right here in the Town of North Elba. Shortly after 1840 Robert Scott,[20] who owned what we know as the old Ames Farm at the base of Scott's Cobble, was hunting in the hills and became lost in the intricate mazes of the forest. He wandered a day or two, totally bewildered and uncertain of his position, and suddenly came upon the ore. Attracted by its remarkable appearance, he broke off some of the mass, which was large and compact and embedded in the rock, and carried it home in his pockets. As could be expected, in his confusion he lost all trace of the locality or direction of the deposit and could never find it again.

What gives the story added interest is that he afterwards displayed spoons of pure silver that he said had been made from the ore. These were handed down to his descendants and were shown to Alfred Donaldson, whose *History of the Adirondacks* (Century Publishing Co., 1921, reprinted Purple Mountain Press, 1996) was published in 1921.

To further strengthen the story, I might add that even after our iron works closed, Archibald McIntyre's associates continued to come here on prospecting trips, and they were here in 1826 to investigate rumors of a silver mine nearby. They did not find the silver, but it was at that time they were guided by a St. Francis [Abenaki] Indian to the great Adirondac iron ore deposits, which now contain the largest titanium mines in the world.[21]

---

20 Later, MacKenzie revised this tale. See the "Aftermath" segment at the end of Chapter 14.

21 Those mines closed in 1989.

Silver, of course, has been mined near Gouverneur as a by-product of zinc, but it is not known to occur in New York State in any other mineral combination than zinc-lead ore.

But there is your challenge. Find the lost silver vein of North Elba. Just don't go home for a pick and shovel, because you will never find your way back to the silver again. Better to bring a bag of white beans with you and drop them along the way. But be a bit more careful than the two prospectors over Rainbow Lake way in Franklin County one hundred years ago. They stealthily followed into the woods an Indian who, they had reason to suspect, was about to visit his secret lead mine. They had conceived the clever idea of filling their pockets with white beans and dropping them as they went along. After about an hour of trailing the Indian through the woods at an exhausting pace, he suddenly turned on them and announced that he would shoot any one who attempted to follow him further. The prospectors were quite ready to desist, but as they started to turn back, they were surprised to find that the old Indian's squaw had been trailing them: She silently handed them all the beans they had dropped and offered to conduct them back to Rainbow Lake.

A nugget of platinum was found some years ago near Plattsburgh. It was probably a stray brought along in glacial debris from Quebec. No gold has been found anywhere in the Adirondacks in any more than bare traces. It normally occurs in quartz veins or other hard rock. There is a remote possibility, of course, that some favorable circumstance may exist in local geology that has been overlooked.

In almost all the Adirondack books I have read, there is one spot mentioned, time and time again, as the location of a fabulous collection of rocks and minerals. That spot is the Cascade Lakes. These were first known as Long Pond, and also as Edmond's Ponds, and that is how they are designated in the following little stories. In 1869, Winslow Watson wrote:

> A long and attractive list of rare and beautiful minerals might be exhibited which are incorporated with the rocks of Essex county, or imbedded in its earth. Particular localities are peculiarly rich in these deposits. The avalanches at Long Pond in Keene

present a site lavishly supplied with brilliant gems and minerals. Augite, garnet, zircon, sahlite, sphene, coccolite, adularia (which is moonstone), rose-colored quartz spar, epidote, chlorite, jasper, cornelian, are among the minerals yielded by these remarkable deposits. I have been favored by the Rev. Mr. Pattee with a more particular and highly interesting description of the latter locality. It is situated near Edmond's Pond, at a precipice laid bare by an avalanche in 1830. In the bed of a little brook, which leaps down the slide, innumerable minerals sparkle and are strewn about the vicinity in every direction. High up the precipice a series of caves occur, which are the peculiar deposits of the gems and minerals, and almost rival in beauty and variety the caverns of eastern story. Here are found large boulders, and even ledges, of calcareous spar, blue, white, and sometimes beautifully variegated by crystals of epidote, coccolite and hornblende. They are occasionally found in stalactitic and crystalline forms, but more generally in amorphous masses.

In 1885 H.P. Smith wrote:

At Edmond's Ponds the primitive limestone has been bared by a slide on the southwest side of the ponds. It lies in the upper part of the slide in a vein from 20 to 40 feet in width. The limestone contains pyroxene in crystals, feldspar, rose quartz, asbestos, the red mica, calcareous spar, zircon, graphite, yellow chondrodite, yellow, brown and green tourmalin[e], pink spinelle, hornblende and scapolite.

Moreover, Russell Carson wrote in 1927:

The richest specimens of Grenville rock to be found in the Adirondack region are in the bed of the stream from whose cascade the mountain takes its name. In Indian Pass, one finds fragments, but in the bed of this cascade stream there are blocks of this earliest rock formation that are four or five feet square. Watson's *History of Essex County* mentions rich mineral caves high up on the slide on

> Cascade Mountain, but no one can be found now who knows of their existence.

And what, if anything, did Professor Emmons have to say about Cascade Lakes in his report of 1842? Quite a good deal. He describes the locality thus:

> Found a bed of primitive limestone twenty to forty feet wide, brought to light by a slide from the mountain nearly half a mile up from the pond. The mineralogist will find at this place a rich locality of pyroxene in all its forms and varieties. In color it varies from the darkest green to nearly white. It is in fine glossy crystals in perfect forms, and easily obtained by blasting the limestone. Phosphate of lime, in tolerable good crystals, may also be obtained. Another mineral which resembles idocrase is quite common; it is in very small crystals, but it has not been particularly examined.

The minerals observed at Cascade Lakes by Emmons and described in his words were calcareous spar or carbonite of lime. One of the most interesting varieties is the blue; pyroxene, the most perfect crystals as well as best of the coccolites; scapolite in large crystals; idocrase in very small crystals; sphene; phosphate of lime.

If you are not aware of this region of apparently fine specimens, you may want to plan a field trip there one day.

Incidentally, on the opposite side of the lakes, on Pitchoff Mountain, extensive caves were discovered in 1949, with an amazing number of passages. There is a thrilling account of their exploration in the *Ad-I-Ron-Dac* bulletin of May–June 1951. I would imagine that on Pitchoff would be found the same rock formations as on the other side of the lake.

I was pleasantly surprised to find in the current *Conservationist* magazine,[22] which I received over this past weekend, a wonderful article on gemstones of New York. Many of the stones shown in the article are those I've described as being at Cascade Lakes. It's disappointing that this article gives no locations where these gemstones might be found in our High Peaks area. It's up to you to go out, find them, and compile your own list.

22 February 1965 issue.

FOURTEEN

The Elba Iron Works

This is the earlier, more extensive draft of the Elba Iron Works story (date unknown). A very few details were edited for consistency with a much shorter piece published in the Lake Placid News *of April 14, 2000.*

Mackenzie refers to McIntyre's mine on the edge of the future village of Lake Placid by its proper corporate name, the Elba Iron and Steel Manufacturing Company and by Elba Iron Works, Iron Works, and Elba Iron and Steel Company. She refers to his mine in Newcomb township on Henderson Lake as Adirondack Iron and Steel Company, Adirondack Iron Mines, and Adirondack Mines.

In 1806, there was, down in Albany at the Capitol, a man with a dream. His name was Archibald McIntyre, and he dreamed of the vast wilderness of northern New York and fortunes to be made from its lodes of iron ore. Even to a canny Scot, the dream seemed practical enough: He would discover a rich vein of ore and, with a select group of backers, reap huge profits as a miner and refiner in the North Country. Though it was to bring him untold misery and financial loss—and this more than once —the dream was never to be relinquished.

Long before the Revolution, French voyageurs and trappers traveling down Lake Champlain from Canada speculated about the unexplored Adirondacks they saw to the west, far away and misty blue. They called them the Peruvian Mountains, believing fabulous treasures of gold and silver lay in their fastnesses. (The village and township of Peru, and Peru Bay on Lake Champlain, carry the last remnants of this romantic notion.) But it was not gold or silver the early settlers found. It was iron ore.

We do not know who the first man to discover Adirondack iron was, but we do know that William Gilliland and Philip Skene knew the wealth of ore in the hills behind Port Henry before the Revolution and that the British at Ticonderoga may have worked these deposits. Knowledge of the great Cheever bed at Port Henry existed just after the Revolution. The ore, cropping out of the ground to such an extent that the pioneers could not fail to notice it, was mined as early as 1804. Beds in Elizabethtown were worked to a degree about 1800, and some of the remarkable deposits near Clintonville were opened up early in the nineteenth century.

Encouraged by rumbles and rumors of mineral discoveries seeping down from the north, McIntyre began to send out scouting parties from Albany. Their make-up was chiefly relatives and friends, and friends of friends who had some knowledge of North Country geography. It was not long before one party stumbled upon what appeared to be large deposits of fine iron ore in the present Town of North Elba. All were on unsold state lands. With this discovery of iron, McIntyre was hooked for life—and the little settlement at the Plains of Abraham was in for a vast sea change.

Who was this man Archibald McIntyre? A leading political figure of the day, he was born in Kenmore, Perthshire, Scotland, on June l, 1772, to the parish schoolmaster. In 1774, when he was two, the McIntyre family emigrated to America. One of the first sights to greet them in New York City was the tarring and feathering of a Tory at a house directly opposite their first stopping place. Almost immediately, with four or five other Scottish families, they went up the Hudson to Haverstraw, and from there to Broadalbin (just outside the Adirondack Blue Line). The Revolution encroached upon this region, and in one instance, the McIntyre family barely escaped death at the hands of marauding Indians. Moving to Albany, where the young Archibald became a schoolmaster and surveyor, they later returned to Broadalbin, and it was from here that Archibald, at age twenty-six, was chosen a member of the state Assembly, serving from 1799 to 1802. He was then appointed deputy secretary of state, and in 1806 state comptroller, the fourth to hold the office. He continued as comptroller until 1821, a period of fifteen years. No other comptroller in state history has held the office as long, with the exception of Arthur Levitt, and at no time has it been more ably filled.

President Kennedy's *Profiles in Courage* might well have included Archibald McIntyre. His quarrel with Governor Daniel D. Tompkins reveals his complete integrity and moral courage. During the War of 1812, both Albany and Washington entrusted Governor Tompkins with very large sums for disbursement. At war's end, he was unable to produce vouchers for a great deal of money. McIntyre claimed that Tompkins had a shortage of $120,000, whereupon the governor indignantly countered that the state owed him $250,000! McIntyre refused to pay a penny of this claim without supporting documents and was given a tongue-lashing by Tompkins' friends.

His reply to them can stand today as a credo of every guardian of the public purse: "I am not to be intimidated from performing the duty I owe to the Public and to myself by the calumnies or denunciations of any man or set of men; and for support in the discharge of this duty, I rely with confidence on an enlightened and candid people."

The Legislature finally settled the matter in 1820 when it directed McIntyre to balance the accounts on the filing of a release from Governor Tompkins of all his claims against the state. McIntyre had stuck to his guns—and he lost his job. His stand, in part, led to Tompkins' resignation, and although McIntyre's first and dearest friend, DeWitt Clinton, was elected governor, there were those in power decidedly hostile to both. On February 12, 1821, the Council of Appointments removed McIntyre as comptroller. His second successor was none other than William Marcy, later governor, for whom Mount Marcy was named.

In 1822, McIntyre was appointed an agent for the state lottery, then in high regard as a source of revenue for schools, new roads, and other political projects. The infant republic, in fact, was largely financed through such state lotteries. Discontinued for many generations as abhorrent to the high moral standards of York staters, the lottery, as we know, is again in public favor. McIntyre ended his political career with a short term in the state Senate.

As comptroller, McIntyre figured in another piece of fiscal history. By 1800, the state had more than enough revenue to finance government services for its two hundred thousand citizens, and by 1814, the General Fund reached a high point: $4.4 million. With government expenses only $1.3 million and debts $1.5 million, it appeared that financial Utopia had come to roost. The Legislature promptly did away with general taxes. In vain, McIntyre and his successors argued that the state should only use the income from the fund and levy taxes to make up the difference. The Legislature continued to draw on the fund to finance government and, finally, in 1834, the bubble burst with the dissipation of the last of it.

This, then, was the Archibald McIntyre who came to be so closely associated with the great iron industry of Essex County, and whose dream shuttled the fortunes of North Elba.

As a state official, McIntyre was in an advantageous position to act quickly. He obtained the desired lands and water rights in North Elba from the state in 1811, though formal patents were not issued until 1813. These included:

- Lot 280, Township 11, Old Military Tract, 92 acres. (Today the site of Lower Mill Pond, Chubb River, parts of the village below Mill Hill, the village power plant, and part of the lower Lake Placid Club golf links.) Here were to rise the mills, forges, and related buildings of McIntyre's iron works.

- Adjoining Lot 92, Township 12, Old Military Tract, 160 acres. (Today the site of the town dump and part of the airport.) Used as pastureland for horses and cattle by the iron works.

- Lots 75 and 76, Township 11, Old Military Tract, 360 acres. Iron ore beds. (Exact location of the beds unknown, but in the vicinity of the state Conservation Department buildings on the old road to Ray Brook Sanitarium.) McIntyre later sold these lots to Daniel Ames.

A little later, the McIntyre interests acquired:

- Lot 94, Township 1, Old Military Tract, 67 plus acres. An ore bed lot at the foot of Cascade Mountain on Cascade Lakes.

- Lots 60 and 64 of the same township, totaling 1,098 acres. Ore bed and timber lots near the Cascade Lakes.

- Lot 234 of Henry's Survey in the Town of Jay, 59½ acres. Purpose and use unknown, but probably an ore bed lot.

With financial backing assured, a corporation was formed for "making Bar Iron, Steel and Anchors from Ore, nail rods, hoop iron and every kind of Iron Mongery at the Town of Keene[23] in the County of Essex." The capital stock was set at $100,000, and the main stockholders were Archibald McIntyre, his brother James McIntyre, John McDonald, and none other than Simeon DeWitt, Surveyor General; Archibald Campbell, Deputy Secretary of State; and John Richards, State Surveyor, of the state of New York. (Richards surveyed North Elba for the state in 1813, 1814, and 1833.)

The name of the infant corporation was the Elba Iron and Steel Manufacturing Company. The name, "Elba," originated, of course, from the island of Elba,

---

23 Note that, until 1808, the area now contained within North Elba township was part of the Town of Elizabethtown. From 1808 until 1850, North Elba was part of Keene township.

then celebrated as the locale of great iron ore deposits worked by the ancients, and a few years later equally noted as the scene of Napoleon's exile.

The first order of business was the building of a dam and the impounding of the Chubb River. An excellent site was found—in fact, the same site noted by state Surveyor Stephen Thorne in 1803 when he described Lot 280 as a "poor lot but has a good mill place thereon." The pond formed by the damming of the Chubb, probably in 1811, is today's Lower Mill Pond. The wooden dam erected by the Iron Works occupied the same site as the present village electric power dam.

A quorum of sidewalk superintendents must have been on hand when the buildings of the Elba Company began to rise on the shores of Lower Mill Pond. A fantastic industrial complex it was to the simple farmers whose rude cabins and barns dotted the Plains of Abraham. When all was done, thirteen buildings were reflected in the deep, black waters of the pond:

- Two forges under one roof, with two fires and one hammer each.
- A dwelling house for agents, one-plus story, two large rooms, kitchen, and two bedrooms.
- A boarding house, one story, forty-by-eighteen feet, two large rooms, and two bedrooms.
- A dwelling house for bloomers, one story, twenty feet square.
- A store with two rooms, one for dry-goods, one for storing iron, cellar below, forty-by-twenty feet.
- Two barns about thirty-by-forty feet, with barracks for workmen in one.
- A blacksmith shop.
- A gristmill with one run of stones.
- A sawmill with one saw, one set of running gears. Both the sawmill and the gristmill ran on the same dam with the forges.
- Three charcoal houses, two thirty-by-forty feet, the other forty-by-twenty-five.

Axemen arrived to begin felling trees on the Plains for the making of charcoal. The face of the town was to be altered for a generation or two as the resident farmers also took to lumbering the virgin stands on their own acres and manufacturing charcoal, for which the Works paid the princely sum of 3¢ a bushel. Access roads leading from Old Military Road to both the Cascade Lakes and Ray Brook ore beds were hacked out of the forests. The forges were fired, and the mill wheels began to spank the waters of the Chubb. Agents, managers, bloomers, and miscellaneous workmen poured into town with their families. The Elba Iron Works was in business and the settlement acquired a new name. Henceforth, it would be known and shown on maps as Elba, though the names Keene Plains and Plains of Abraham were long in dying (in the late 1850s they were still in use by old-timers).

All seemed to go well enough at first. There were, to be sure, the usual difficulties of a new enterprise, but it readily found markets in New York, Albany, and on the Great Lakes. With the advent of the War of 1812 and its government contracts, the business prospered.

In these early years, McIntyre referred to the Works fondly as "my New Jerusalem," after the nickname of the Massachusetts Bay Colony, the Puritans having compared their flight to America with the Jews' escape to Egypt.

McIntyre was not often at Elba. The affairs of the Comptroller's Office were demanding, and he left on-the-spot management largely to his brother-in-law Malcolm McMartin, his brother James, his son Jamie, and his nephew Dyer Thompson, all of whom made Elba their home. Many letters of an affectionate and homely nature passed between these family members during the years of the Elba Iron Works.

From Malcolm to Archibald:

> Jean requests me to inform you that she has filled one firkin of butter for you and now filling another as fast as she can, which two firkins will be as much as she can possibly spare. They will contain about 60 lbs. each, which I will send or bring to you as early in the winter as possible.

I have had the pleasure of exchanging a few shots with the British forces at Plattsburgh in the late contest there. Esq. Wilson our neighbor unfortunately got shot through the body of which wound he died at 2 o'clock next morning. Major Pangborn was slitely wounded in the leg who is likewise in our company. No other man belonging in this town was hurt. The particulars of that affair you no doubt had long ago.

And again:

> Jean wishes you to send her 3# Hyson Tea if you can conveniently. The overplus after pay for said tea and freightage you will please pay on my land.
>
> The bearer will hand you or your wife a few balls of homespun woolen yarn to make stockins [sic] for your children from your sister Jean as a token of love and friendship to you & family.

And from Archibald to brother James at Elba:

> Now that I have got the folks to bed, let me spend an hour with you. I was so employed all day that I could not devote a moment to you, nor yet in the evening, until now at 11 at night. Your two kind letters, of the 6th instant, were handed to me this morning by Mr. Beach.
>
> I hope the Hammer will prove better than what you suspect. Mr. Ely will find you a bill of it and of the Ledger the next opportunity that offers. The Hammer is not yet paid and he has no bill of it, and could not find time today to go for it.
>
> I will, if possible, be with you in May. Remember me most affectionately to your wife and my friend Donald. Remember me also to Jean, to Malcolm, & to Mr. Thompson. I hope Anny has done well enough notwithstanding her father's rage.

As time progressed, there was increasing cause for alarm. The deeper the ore was mined at Ray Brook and Cascade Lakes, the more highly charged it was with iron disulfide, or pyrite. In short, there was gold aplenty in those hills of ore, but it was fool's gold and a nuisance. The cost of refining spiraled, but McIntyre was far from ready to throw in the sponge. A solution had to be found, and quickly.

It was determined that the Elba mines would be abandoned and high-grade ore purchased from the great Arnold bed near Clintonville, some miles to the northeast. One drawback to such a solution was transportation. To be sure, there was a road from Elba to Clintonville, but long and roundabout—Elba to Keene Center, to Upper Jay and Jay, to Au Sable Forks, to Clintonville. A more direct route was mandatory. Within a year, the Elba Company had built a road over the Sentinel Range to Wilmington, at no small expense. Apparently it was financed from the proceeds of two two-year mortgages from Elba to the State of New York given in April 1814, each in the sum of $1,000. The moneys were spun off from the School Fund. Here it should be stated that no political hanky-panky was involved. It was common state practice at the time to loan funds for the development of land and resources. As a matter of fact, the state had, in 1808, set aside vast unsold forest lands in Essex County to encourage exploration for and manufacture of iron.

The new road to Wilmington, long since obliterated, is shown in detail on a map of the Jay and Whiteface Mountain tracts made by John Richards in 1815. It did not follow in any part the present Wilmington Road. From a bridge over the Chubb at the dam site, the road led up through the Gordon Pratt (Benham) property to the present Wilmington Road,[24] over the Lake Placid Club golf links and through the woods to the Au Sable, crossing the river just below the new bridge at the intersection of River and Wilmington Roads. Arrowing up into the mountains along the trail opposite the Conservation monument[s],[25] it circled in back of Owens, Copperas, and Winch ponds, dipping back down to the river at the state camp site. It crossed the Au Sable at the site of the new bridge, just above the Wilmington Flume, and mounted the bank on the west side. Traces of the old road still remain along the heights to Wilmington, west of the present road. This track was to be the main route to Wilmington until Robert Scott, William Nye, and Peter Comstock built the Notch Road along the river in 1854. (It is interesting to note on the Richards 1815 map that all present roads from Wilmington to Jay and Upper Jay, as well as side roads, were even then in existence.)

The ore could be drawn only in the winter, by sled, for the mucky forest soil of summer spelled disaster for heavily laden wagons. "I regret

24 This segment still exists. It winds around the east side of Power Pond, then angles up toward the Wilmington Road. Today, it is called Alpine Lane.

25 MacKenzie evidently wrote this version prior to 1985, when a second monument was added to the site.

the weather did not permit your getting more Ore home," wrote Archibald to brother James in Elba in March 1815, "but hope that even yet you may get some addition to your 260 tons. I observe the weather is getting cold within a few hours past."

Transportation costs proved horrendous, and there were other troubles as well, small and large. Eleazer Darrow, agent for the Works, quit in a dispute over salary and was lured back only with a promise of $450 a year. Mr. McLean, of Troy, a machine maker hired for vital work at the forge, had hocked his tools to secure the payment of a debt, and could not proceed to Elba until McIntyre had bailed him out.

A more serious matter was the stiff competition offered by top-grade foreign [iron] imports, as McIntyre mentioned in his letter of March 1815:

> I have heard that Malcolm sold the Iron he took to Sackets Harbor on a credit, payable next fall, but at what rate he sold, I have not heard. That sent here I fear we shall have to sell low enough, except that contracted for by T. McCann & Co. and James Rogers, which was sold for $8.50. It arrived too late in the season to answer well, even if the war had continued. I fear we may have to sell here as low as you sold at the works.

A year later the situation with foreign competition had worsened, and we find McIntyre writing to brother James at Elba on September 16, 1816:

> I have just received a letter from John McIntyre in which he informs me that the Engineer will not purchase any of our iron, or contract for any iron or nails or spikes—and what is still worse he says that the iron we have there does not sell and that he thinks that plan will be a bad market for it. He says the size of the barrs is against it, and that some small barrs would sell. This is most discouraging news. I really thought there could be no doubt but the Iron at Niagara would have been all sold before now, and that we would soon realize the money for it. He writes that Sweden iron sells for [$8.50] per C and that he offered ours for $8 but could not succeed—but he states also, what surprises me, that cut nails of almost all sizes sell for 25¢ per pound. That would, therefore, I

> should think be a good market for your nails, if not for your Iron. I presume the places must be glutted with Iron from Canada.

McIntyre and his associates were pouring sand into a sieve. The Works were operating one jump ahead of the sheriff, until the sheriff actually did arrive at Elba one fine day with the intent to foreclose on a lien. The mortgages to the state were in default, and a number of other loans were outstanding, including one to land speculator Peter Smith from Peterboro, New York, who had recently invested in Elba real estate. McIntyre complained to brother James in a letter of September 28, 1816:

> What scenes of trouble and vexation and distress are you not subjected to with that unfortunate business in which we are so deeply involved. I wish to Heaven we were all out of it some way or other that should not be absolutely ruinous.
>
> I have this very day received a letter from Smith in answer to one which I wrote to him about our Note to him. He consents to wait until his next payment becomes due in December on his lands purchased in Township No. 12. But how we are to pay him then or to pay any other of our debts I cannot conceive, unless the Legislature aid us. By your account nothing is to be calculated upon from sales of iron. You must not fail in coming down with Mr. Sanford [Reuben Sanford, member of the Legislature, from Wilmington], when the Legislature meets the first of November, to see what can be done. If they will attend to our Petition then, they will be more apt to grant us relief than in the Winter, when hundreds more will be pressing them for aid. If we do not get aid then I am afraid we shall be prosecuted.
>
> With all your troubles, incessant labors, fatigues, perplexities, and vexations, do not my dear Brother neglect the one thing needful. Search the Scriptures daily for his treasure and be earnestly importunate at the throne of Grace. In that there will be comfort when all the comforts fail. Remember me in your Prayers as I do you daily.

Despite his earnest prayers, no relief came, and the stubborn Scot was at last obliged to acknowledge defeat. The Elba Company terminated business in 1817. The Works buildings, however, were not completely shut down. Former agent Eleazer Darrow remained in residence for another ten years, operating the forge and mills for his own personal use.

The Elba Company was out of business, but its debts remained to plague the investors for many years. On May 12, 1820, McIntyre wrote brother James at Broadalbin:

> Our horrid Elba business keeps me in constant torment. July will soon be upon us, and I do not believe that Donors will do a single thing for us, unless some of us go up. If you can, it will be best, but if you cannot, I must go myself—in which event I shall want you to lend me a horse.

On December 18, 1823, the Elba Company at last discharged its major debts to the state and others by a loan of $4,000 from the Farmers Fire Insurance & Loan Company of New York City. The loan was secured by a new mortgage, after Major Isaac Finch had come up from Jay and appraised the land and buildings at some $12,000. This final debt was at last satisfied in March of 1833.

Aftermath

There are several interesting footnotes to the Elba Iron Works story.

Far from being put down by that abortive enterprise, McIntyre had only banked the fires of his dream. In the 1820s, his scouting parties were still beating the Adirondack bush for iron ore, using the old Works buildings as headquarters. They examined a new vein near Elba discovered by an Indian, only to find the ore of poor quality. On October 2, 1822, we find McIntyre writing brother-in-law Duncan McMartin Jr., a land surveyor who often worked in the Adirondacks:

> You do not say whether you propose to visit the woods this year. If you go, you will have a cold, uncomfortable time of it, I fear. Do you find no Iron Ore or other mineral in your long journeys through those northern woods? If you find anything new, do take specimens home and note the location.

Now a new element sparked McIntyre's dream: silver. McIntyre heard of William Scott's supposed discovery of silver somewhere in the foothills of Nye Mountain. William died in 1825, but not before he had imparted his secret to McIntyre or one of his men. The hunt was on.

Early in October 1826, a rather motley crew of McIntyre associates arrived at Elba from Albany. Their mission: find the "lost" silver mine discovered by William Scott. Much in the limelight were a garrulous and jittery Negro manservant, Enoch, and a dog of unknown ancestry answering to the name of Wallace. The balance of the party consisted of McIntyre's son, John, his nephew, Dyer Thompson, his two brothers-in-law, Duncan and Malcolm McMartin, and his future son-in-law, David Henderson. Henderson was in the pottery business and had introduced to America the British method of making earthenware from molds instead of on the potter's wheel.[26]

In a remarkable letter written in Elba by that bright young Scot, David Henderson, and sent to McIntyre in New York, is the full story of their ensuing adventure. Witty, poetic, offering rare glimpses of life at Elba, vividly descriptive of the largely unexplored Great North Woods, Henderson's letter should be read in its entirety. First published in Wallace's 1894 *Descriptive Guide to the Adirondacks,* it is also reproduced in Masten's 1923 *Story of Adirondac.* It is one of the most valuable documents of early Adirondack history, and contains what may well be the first descriptions of camping out and the first "deer story" ever to come out of these mountains.

The men put up at the half-abandoned Works, then occupied by Eleazer Darrow. Here at Elba they joined a community deer hunt—they saw several deer, but killed none—and attended Sunday services at Iddo Osgood's.

Next day, as they were preparing to enter the woods, a strapping young Abenaki Indian, Lewis Elijah Benedict, appeared at Darrow's gate, the first red man seen in the settlement for three years. Opening his blanket, he took out a small piece of iron ore about the size of a nut, and with the famous words recalled by Henderson, "You want see 'em ore—me know 'em bed, all same," offered to conduct them to a vein he had discovered

26 MacKenzie's note: Henderson, on the way to Elba, purchased a Vermont lottery ticket from Postmaster Graves at Keene. On the return trip from Elba, he again stopped in to chat with Graves, who tried to wheedle the ticket back. His suspicions aroused, Henderson refused to relinquish it, and shortly learned at Whitehall that it had won him a $500 prize.

beyond Indian Pass while trapping beaver the previous spring. Hesitant, skeptical, they nonetheless hired him as guide (for a dollar and a half and a plug of tobacco) and set off to the south down Old Military Road. Making their way to the Au Sable through a clearing, they wandered up its banks to a mile above the bow of it. Darkness came, and they encamped for the night. Dyer cut an ancient birch for back-and-fore logs; they procured the middle firewood from a huge pine splintered by lightning.

"Who could on that night boast of so sublime a fire?" Henderson wrote. "It was indeed a tremendous one, throwing a broad glare of light into the dark bosom of the wood—the very owls screech'd as if in wonder what it meant."

The next three days were spent in fruitlessly combing the Elba woods and cobbles for William Scott's silver, running lines, and examining every ledge from the Au Sable to the top of the largest burnt cobble. They then proceeded on their forest journey, passed between the giant walls of Indian Pass and, to their astonishment, came upon the remarkable iron ore deposits near the lake they named Henderson, the eventual site of McIntyre's second ill-fated venture, Adirondack Iron Mines. It was not learned for many years that the fabulous vein was "contaminated" by an unpopular element, titanium. Titanium, geologist Ebenezer Emmons declared in 1842, was useful only for whitening false teeth! Today, of course, the resurrected mines, owned by National Lead Company, are a major world source of titanium, that modern wonder-metal.[27]

An adventurous return through the Pass in the teeth of a wild northern storm, dining on partridge and pigeon, drinking raw rum to keep warm, and the men were back at Elba after eight days in the woods. Enoch, temperamentally ill-suited to the wilds and always a bundle of nerves, was in a state of virtual mental and physical collapse, but the canine Wallace was in rare spirits, having distinguished himself as a partridge dog.

Next day, the settlement staged a second deer hunt. Henderson wrote:

> I was on the opposite bank of the River from the deer.
>
> He came running toward me—I waited, expecting him to come into the river—but on his reaching the bank, he discovered me & turned. When I fired—the ball broke his hind leg—he

27 In 1989, National Lead closed its titanium mine.

> bleated piteously—gave a spring—and fell into the River head first. Thompson endeavored to get at him, but he turned about and got to the opposite side of the River out of his reach—poor creature! He hirpled up the hill towards the wood—his leg trailing behind him by the skin—and he looked behind him, lay down twice or thrice, before he made the woods—the dogs followed him in—brought him out again—the poor mangled animal lacerated behind by the ravenous dogs—caught at last—throat cut! Confound the sport say I if it is to be managed in this way.

Next morning they were off again for the Elba woods, and for several days continued their futile search for silver. But now, no longer able to contain the excitement of their stupendous iron ore discovery, they left Elba posthaste for Albany to buy up the land from the state. To safeguard their secret, they took the Indian with them.

The full story of the rise, the fame, and then the failure of McIntyre's great Adirondack Iron Mines has been told in many an excellent history and will not be repeated here. David Henderson, our articulate and talented penman, died tragically near Lake Colden in 1845, having shot himself by accident while hunting. At tiny, remote Calamity Pond, where he died, the occasional hiker is startled to find a beautifully carved stone monument in the heart of the wilderness, hauled up there in his memory at the direction of his children.

As the years passed, McIntyre did not completely forget Elba, despite his deep involvement in the new venture. In June 1832, he instructed Duncan McMartin, then at the Adirondack Iron Mines, to salvage some of the equipment at Elba, and McMartin duly reported in a letter to his wife:

> West Moriah, June 28th, 1832
>
> Came to Moriah 4 Corners on Sabbath where I heard three discourses by 3 different Presbyterian & Congregational Preachers....On Monday after having engaged castings and other irons made for a Sawmill I left there for Pleasant Valley [Elizabethtown] & got at 10 p.m. to Graves in Keene where the next day on Tuesday I contracted for bringing 2 or 3 loads of

> the irons from the Elba Works to this place, engaged a couple of common laborers & returned at 9 P.M. to Pleasant Valley.

In October 1833, McIntyre himself paid a visit to Elba and the old ore beds at Cascade Lakes (then called Square Pond and Long Pond), accompanied by several associates and guides Holt, Carson, and Scott, three able woodsmen of Keene. The journey seems to have been a sentimental one, with no particular purpose in mind.

Leaving the settlement called McIntyre at the Adirondack Mines on October 21, 1833, they traversed Indian Pass and camped a mile north of the notch. On the 22nd, they arrived in Elba and put up at Iddo Osgood's inn. On the 23rd, they proceeded on the Old Military Road to Round Pond, near the present North Country School, and obtained a boat there, portaging two miles to Cascade Lakes. Evidence of the tremendous landslide of 1830 was still fresh, and McIntyre's description is well worth quoting:

> Wednesday the 23d
>
> Proceeded to the Long Pond ore bed. Our hands carried from the Round Pond, so called, a boat to the Square Pond, so called, about 2 miles. Arrived at the Square Pond at 3 p.m. Concluded to encamp at the west end of this Pond—Carson remained and prepared the Camp whilst we crossed the Pond in our Boat to the slide and ore bed. There are several slides from the mountains on either side of this Pond, but that on the south at the foot of the Pond, which passes over the Elba ore bed, is the largest and is very remarkable from its having passed over a great ledge of Primitive Limestone bringing with it an infinite variety of Limestone, and various other Minerals connected with it.
>
> Thursday the 24
>
> Visited again the slide and collected a large number of specimens of the rocks and minerals. Within three or four rods above the old Elba Iron ore bed the slide exhibited three other veins of Iron Ore, one 4+ feet, another two and another one foot wide, having rock of about one foot between. Took specimens of the ore from each vein.

Friday the 25

Returned to Osgoods. Left at Ester's large duplicates of our collection of minerals, with directions to box them & forward them to Mr. Myers at White Hall. Paid him $2 for the service. Hire Scott left us & returned home.

Saturday the 26

Left Mr. Osgoods for McIntyre at 8 a.m. In passing on Osgood's line for home over the second brook from the Packard place [Packard was in possession of Great Lots 73 and 80, Township 12], we picked up from the stream two pieces of rock supposed to contain some metal, which we propose to have examined on getting home. This stream is in the region where Mr. Scott (now dead) found the ore which produced silver, and ought to be followed up & thoroughly examined. Put up at night at the camp which we occupied on our way out on Monday.

Sunday the 27

Arrived at McIntyre the ½ past 1 p.m.

There are two matters of interest in this account. First, McIntyre refutes once and for all the erroneous statement, found in early Adirondack travel books, that the two Cascade Lakes were created by an 1860 avalanche, having once been one body of water known as Long Pond. McIntyre clearly describes the two lakes as existing in 1833. Moreover, the 1812 patent from the state of New York to the Elba Iron and Steel Company for the Cascade Lakes ore bed also describes the two lakes precisely as they appear today:

> Beginning at a rock about four feet high above ground and nine links wide on the top and a heap of stones placed thereon, this rock stands partly in the water on the north side of the brook, just where the water empties out of the pond lying a very small distance westerly from another pond commonly called the Long Pond, the said brook runs easterly from the said rock across a narrow neck of land into the Long Pond.

So much for the legend of two lakes created from one. Such a cataclysm may have occurred back in the mists of antiquity, but certainly not as late as the nineteenth century.

Secondly, it will be noted that McIntyre's interest in silver had not been completely eclipsed by his brave new enterprise on the other side of Indian Pass. We also find him writing in his journal while at the Adirondack Mines:

> Sunday Morning Nov. 11
>
> Did John Steele Jr. find the piece of Quartz containing native silver at the place which he showed to us in the swamp below Lake Sanford, east of the river? I can scarcely believe it. Why? Because it was with manifest reluctance he wd. speak on the subject when we first came to the ore bed. Because the place he showed us had to my view, the appearance of never having been touched by hands before we began to dig of earth. Because he told Mr. McMartin last summer (when he (McM.) accidentally discovered his having the ore) that if it was silver, the mine could readily be found— when the truth is, if he has no other indication of the mine than what he now professes of finding a solitary piece of ore below the root of a fallen tree in an exclusive swamp, there is not the slightest probability of his ever finding the mine. Because also the man's whole conduct is misterious, cold and selfish.
>
> It is possible that I do the man injustice—time will show whether I do or not. I am inclined to the belief that he found the ore in some very different situation, and that he has probably found the very Vein—that he will endeavor to purchase the land and appropriate all to himself and his family. Will his father sanction such conduct towards his friends & his son's friends' employees? I hardly think he will, and yet he may.

If William Scott's silver has ever been rediscovered in the hills of North Elba, there has been no one willing to come forth and admit it. The treasure hunt has gone on for 150 years, and may well continue for another century or so.

There is no indication, either, that McIntyre ever again revisited the scenes of his early misfortunes following the Cascade Lakes expedition.

Though in close touch with the Adirondack Mines, he was never in active management and seldom visited there. Business interests kept him in Philadelphia and New York City for some years. The last of his life was spent in Albany. His death in May 1858 at the age of eighty-six at last snuffed out the dream that had brought him little but financial loss and disappointment. It is evident he was mentally as well as physically diminished at the end, for his will, dated April 7, 1857, was disallowed by the Court. Archibald McIntyre, said the Surrogate, was not competent to execute a will or devise real estate.

The Adirondack Iron and Steel Company drew its last gasp along with Archibald McIntyre. For the Elba Iron Works, the course had been downhill to the bone yard many years before. The buildings gradually fell into decay or were dismantled, and by 1850 little evidence of Lake Placid's first industry remained but the pond, a decaying dam, fragments of broken wheels and shafts, and a heap of slag.

Legend has it that up until World War I, one Lake Placid citizen jealously guarded a bar of iron forged at the old Works. In a fit of patriotism, he donated it to a war scrap drive. Thus, one hundred years after its demise, the Elba Iron Works—having supplied a goodly share of iron to the government in the War of 1812—made a contribution to yet another war.

In 1924, by proclamation of the governor, the Elba Iron and Steel Company was dissolved for lack of any corporate action in over a century.

FIFTEEN
The Year Without a Summer

It is thought that the "year without a summer" was caused by ash rocketed into the upper atmosphere by a series of three massive volcanic eruptions in the Caribbean in 1812, the Philippines in 1814, and Indonesia in 1815. Severe summer climate abnormalities destroyed crops in Northern Europe, the American Northeast, and Eastern Canada. Mary MacKenzie wrote this piece in the summer of 1972.

It began innocently enough. January of 1816 was so mild in northern New York that most people let their fires die out and burned wood only for cooking. Wintry days were few and far between.

February was not cold, either—a little more so than January, perhaps, but on the whole, warm and spring-like. March came in like a cowardly lion—only a token wind from the first to the sixth—and went out like the proverbial lamb. Early April was lazy, balmy. Yet as the days lengthened and the first pale shoots emerged in the nut-brown woods, the air began to grow strangely cold.

By May 1, winter had arrived, with snow cloaking the fields and pastures and inch-thick ice locking the ponds and streams. In late May, trees were usually in leaf, migratory birds calling their leasehold rights, and children picking arbutus in the Adirondack woods. But as the month advanced, delicate buds were frozen black. Fresh green sprouts of young corn withered. As the last days of May 1816 faded, almost all new growth had been killed by the polar air.

June, month of dandelion and foamflower, was the coldest ever experienced in this latitude. Frost and ice were as common as the wild strawberry blooms of other years. Along Lake Champlain, from Willsboro to Crown Point, snow settled to a depth of half an inch, while in neighboring mountain townships blizzards raged. Apple blossoms were blasted, and with them all hopes of a fall crop. Almost every green thing that had survived the month of May died. The pioneers, lately come to this new country from New England, began to watch the sky in fear and foreboding. Simple farmers all, their only hope of life was in the soil, for the evolution of the Adirondacks as a playground lay fifty years in the future.

They were not alone. Many other parts of the northern hemisphere were suffering from that bitter spring. In early June, seven inches of snow fell in Maine, three inches in the interior of New York, the same in Massachusetts. In northern Vermont, on June 5 and 6, a violent storm battered the countryside. When it was finished, snow lay twenty inches deep at Williston, eighteen at Cabot, and Montpelier was mantled in white. There was worse to come. One farmer sent his sheep to pasture on June 16. The morning of the 17th dawned with the thermometer below freezing, and at 9 o'clock the farmer set out to round up his flock. "Better start to the neighbors soon!" he called back jokingly to his wife. "It's the middle of June, and I may get lost in the snow!" An hour later, the sky darkened ominously. Flakes began to fall thick and fast, and before the day closed, a howling wind piled fleecy masses in great drifts along the windward side of fences and outbuildings.

Night fell and the farmer had not come home. Now thoroughly frightened, the wife alerted her neighbors, and a search party went out through the driving storm. On the third day, they found him. Lying in a hollow on a side hill, half buried in snow, both feet frozen, he was miraculously still alive. His sheep, however, were lost.

So ended the spring of 1816, that fearsome "year without a summer," known to succeeding generations of Adirondackers as "eighteen-hundred-and-froze-to-death."

All summer long, the wind blew steady from the north in blasts of snow and ice. Mothers knitted wooly-warm mittens and socks of double thickness for their children. Farmers who worked out their taxes on the country roads wore greatcoats, and hearth fires were indispensable. July came in with winter ferocity. On Independence Day, ice as thick as window glass formed throughout New England, New York, and parts of Pennsylvania. Crops that in some areas had struggled through May and June gave up the ghost. And, to the surprise of all, August proved the cruelest month. Icy fingers of blight and bane spread as far as England. Newspapers from overseas reported a snowfall at Barnet, thirty miles from London, on August 30.

Now autumn came to the northland, and the inhabitants began to sense the depth of the tragedy. There were few leaves to blaze in brilliant jewel tones—they had fallen weeks before. There were fewer crops to harvest. Here and there, in isolated pockets, by some strange local whim of the weather, stands had gone unharmed, and farmers brought in a plentiful yield. One wise husbandman who, night after night, built fires about his fields to ward off frost was repaid by having the only crop in the region. Over in St. Lawrence County, more corn was raised on Gallop Island and Livingston's Point than in all the rest of the county combined.

Winter came, and the wolf sidled very near the door of many an Adirondack cabin. There was little grain for food; the scanty hoard must be held for next year's planting. From many miles, families gathered about a mill, begging the privilege of collecting its sweepings to save their lives. Those who had were seldom willing to share with those who had not. Often only the milk from a cow or two and the local fish and game spelled survival for the poor.

During the spring and summer of 1817, wheat rose to $3 a bushel, rye flour to $11 a barrel, and both were hard to obtain, even at those prices. Seed potatoes planted in spring were often dug up again and eaten before summer arrived. Many Willsboro families were reported without bread for weeks. A Moriah carpenter, one of the best workmen in town, was willing to work seven days for a bushel of wheat.

During the bitter season, the men leached ashes in the woods, transporting the lye twelve to fifty miles to trade for seed and grain. Over at Lake Placid, hunger pangs were so keen that most of the early settlers abandoned the place, leaving a ghost town of ten families—and a ghost town it remained for the next twenty-five years. It was not until 1818 that the North Country people knew the meaning of security again.

That infamous northeast summer of 1816 has gone down in history. Cited by President James Madison in his annual message to Congress, unchallenged in the annals of the Weather Bureau, it remains the only instance in the chronicles of northern New York of extreme want and suffering. Could such a summer again bedevil the Adirondacks? Of course, but with a feeble impact. The old farms have faded into the tapestry of the past, and with them the need to grub a living from the stony mountain soil. The economic base of the area has shifted to recreation. For a season or two, only the voices of motel owners would be heard crying in the wilderness.

SIXTEEN
How Averyville Got its Name

Two stories on the Avery family's settlement in North Elba were found in Mary MacKenzie's files: an article that was written in 2000 for a series commemorating the 200th anniversary of North Elba's first settlement, and a combination family history and genealogy compiled in March 1989. The two are combined here.

We have seen that in 1800 our first settlers, Elijah and Rebecca Bennett, arrived from Vermont. By 1810, two hundred souls resided in our little farming outpost, known as the Plains of Abraham, and in 1811, Archibald McIntyre built the Elba Iron Works on the Chubb River.

Growth continued until two misfortunes caused a general exodus. The year 1816, that infamous "year without a summer," brought ruined crops and near-starvation; and in 1817, the iron works closed down, leaving many without work. A great departure from the Plains began, and by 1820, North Elba was virtually a ghost town. A ghost town it would remain for the next quarter of a century, with no more than ten families in residence at any one time.

New families occasionally drifted in and, in a few years, out again. Four of the newcomers did put down roots and remain permanently. One of them was the Avery family.

Simeon Shipman Avery came to North Elba from Vermont in 1819 with his wife, Polly Clark Avery, six children, and an older woman, probably his or his wife's mother. Simeon was born in Brandon, Vermont in 1788. His ancestor, Christopher Avery, a weaver from Devonshire, England, had arrived in Gloucester, Massachusetts in 1630 aboard the good ship Arabella. The Averys had originally come to England with William the Conqueror in 1066. Polly Clark, born in Vermont in 1790, married Simeon in 1809.

Simeon had purchased from the state of New York Great Lot 52 in Township 12, Old Military Tract, which contained 160 acres. The lot was about three miles southwest of Old Military Road. Some of our first colonists had previously lived in this isolated area, and an access road of sorts was in place. Simeon at once built a log cabin and started a farm. It is not known whether the Averys ever constructed a frame farmhouse on the farm. The census as late as 1865 shows the dwelling place as made of logs. Any farm buildings constructed by the Averys have long since disappeared.

Today a number of houses occupy the old Avery farmland, located on the east side of Averyville Road.[28] The oldest are those of Alan McNab,[29] built by Ruel Alford about 1885, and Andre Russo. It is believed the Russo house stands on or near the site of the original Avery log cabin.

Predictably, this section of North Elba soon became known as Averyville, and the access road as Averyville Road. They are still known as such today. Simeon's name has endured here for 181 years, but was almost lost to us seventy-five years ago.

28 Now Averyville Lane, County Route 23.

29 Alan McNab died in 2006.

In 1923, the noted concert pianist, Clarence Adler, established a summer music camp on land across the road from the McNab residence. The camp soon attracted many students and was visited by world-famous musicians. In 1924, a few residents of Averyville petitioned the Town Board to change the name of Averyville to Adlerville, and the name of Averyville Road to Adlerville Road, as a token of appreciation for Adler's enhancement of the area's image. The town granted the request early in 1925. Whereupon another group of citizens—residents and former residents of Averyville—rose up in fury to protest an act so outrageous and so disrespectful of one of North Elba's great and courageous pioneers. The name of Averyville was quickly restored.

Polly Avery died in October of 1846 at the age of fifty-seven and, as legend has it, in a rather mysterious way. In those early years the Averyville people regularly traveled to Ray Brook on foot by way of a trail through the forest starting at what is known today as Alford Pond (this pond has been known at various times as Round Pond, White Lily Pond, and Frazier Pond). Polly set out alone for Ray Brook on an October day, carrying her knitting bag. She never reached Ray Brook and never returned home. A search party discovered her knitting bag on the trail, and her body was finally found the following spring in the woods off the trail. (One version of the legend has it that only her knitting bag was found and her body was never recovered.) The cause of her death was never told. A trail still exists from Averyville to Ray Brook and possibly follows the original course.

Within a few years, Simeon married again. He and Polly seem to have had ten children, five sons and five daughters—Earl, Royal Alonzo, Julius, Simeon Fayette, Philip, Sophronia, Jane, and three daughters whose names are unknown.

County records reveal that fifty acres on the west side of the farm were deeded to Charles H. Rollins before the 1850s. About 1851, son Earl built a house on Old Military Road that later evolved into the noted Lyon's Inn or North Elba House. The building still stands and serves as Peter Moreau's bed-and-breakfast, called the Stagecoach Inn. It is one of North Elba's important historical landmarks.

Simeon S. deeded another twenty acres to his son, Julius Augustus, in 1853, leaving to himself a ninety-acre farm. Before 1850, Simeon S.'s son, Royal Alonzo (apparently always called Alonzo), left North Elba and acquired a farm in the neighboring Town of Keene. In 1854, his father persuaded him to return to North Elba and take over the family farm. On November 4 of that year, Simeon S. deeded over his remaining ninety acres to Alonzo, with the proviso that Alonzo support his father and stepmother for the remainder of their natural lives. This arrangement apparently did not work out to everyone's satisfaction. Alonzo deeded the property back to his father on April 17, 1856.

During this period Simeon S.'s son, Simeon Fayette (always called Fayette), had gone to work at Timothy Nash's sawmill in North Elba as a sawyer, and was living in the Nash household. At the same time Alonzo deeded the farm back to his father, Simeon S. persuaded Fayette to take over. On April 14, 1856, the farm was deeded to Fayette on the same condition, that he support his father and stepmother for the remainder of their lives. This Fayette did until his father's death in 1872, and he stayed on the farm along with his wife and children until shortly after that.

There are only two Avery graves in the North Elba Cemetery, those of Earl's children. The other Averys who died here are buried in the little family cemetery Simeon Avery established on land adjacent to his log cabin. This only vestige of the Avery family is still in existence, but is not easily found. Untended for well over a century, it is almost lost in tree growth. Small Adirondack boulders mark the several graves with no formal inscriptions. Almost certainly the graves of Simeon S. and his first wife Polly Clark are there, and since there are a number of boulders, probably those of some children. Sadly, in recent years, vandals have dislodged some of the stones. This little cemetery is on the right side of an old dirt road going in from Averyville Road.

By 1875, there were no Averys left in Averyville, but, after a lapse of some 113 years, an Avery came back—Richard Wyman, a descendant of Simeon Avery through his daughter Jane, who married Jacob Smith B. Moody of Saranac Lake.

The Moody family had settled in the Saranac Lake end of North Elba in 1819, the same year the Averys arrived in Averyville.

In 1988, Dick Wyman, of Tarrytown, with his wife, Jean, moved into his new house just down the road from his great-great-grandfather's pioneer farm. He remained there for ten years, until 1998. The Wymans now live in Jay.

Perhaps one day another Avery will return to the place where a young Simeon and Polly Avery made a home in the wilderness, 181 years ago.

The following is what we know, to date, concerning the Avery descendants:

Royal Alonzo, born in 1817, moved back to his farm in Keene in 1856. On March 2, 1865, he sold the farm to Alonzo Goodspeed. In that deed to Goodspeed he is described as "living in the Town of Harrietstown," so he must have moved to the Saranac Lake area. There the trail ends.

Alonzo's wife was Electa, maiden name unknown. In 1860, they had five children: Cornelia, born 1843; Royal Elijah, born February 27, 1847 (exact date is from an Essex County newspaper); Clara, born 1850; Simeon, born 1853; and Mary, born 1856. It is not presently known how long Alonzo and his family remained in the Saranac Lake area. No members of this family are buried in the Pine Ridge Cemetery in Saranac Lake, so all must have moved on to other parts.

Earl W., born 1824, lived and worked on his father's farm in Averyville until 1851, when he purchased two tracts of land on Old Military Road in North Elba totaling eighty-four acres and began to farm for himself. His farmhouse was located on the four-acre tract he purchased from Iddo Osgood.

Earl married Cordelia, maiden name unknown, born in Vermont. Four children are known: Daniel H., born 1850; Francelia A., born 1853; Almira, born 1855; and Dillon F., born 1857. Both daughters, Francelia and Almira, died in childhood in 1863 and are buried in North Elba Cemetery.

On December 7, 1864, Earl sold his farm to the Martin Lyon family and is said to have "moved west," meaning the western United States. Nothing more is known of Earl and his family.

The Lyons put a large addition on Earl's house, and it became the famous Lyon's Inn or North Elba Hotel, for many years a stagecoach stop on the old Elizabethtown-Saranac Lake mail and stage route. It is still standing, one of North Elba's oldest landmarks, and is now owned by Peter Moreau.

Where Julius moved after leaving North Elba shortly after 1860 has not been discovered. In 1854 or 1855, he married Lurency P., maiden name unknown, born in Essex County, New York. In 1860, they had one son, Lorin E. An Almeda M. Fuller, age nine, was also living in the household that year, relationship unknown. Julius may have had other children. No trace of him or his family has been found.

Simeon Fayette, born November 25, 1833, apparently moved to Keene, New York, after 1870. A deed dated September 21, 1872 (Essex County Deed Book 68, page 596) from Henry Fuller to Simeon F. Avery is for land in Keene. On September 23, 1893, Fayette deeded his land to his son, Leslie J. Avery, who had become a doctor and was residing in Au Sable Forks. In this deed, Fayette is described as "a farmer of the Town of Keene."

By 1894, Fayette was living in the North Elba township part of Saranac Lake. On March 10, 1894, he purchased Lot 13, Township 11, Old Military Tract, at Saranac Lake, described as "of the Town of North Elba." Fayette spent the rest of his life there. He died February 10, 1919 (his headstone reads "Simeon F. Avery") and is buried in Pine Ridge cemetery in Saranac Lake.

Fayette married Maryette F. Fuller, born August 20, 1833, who died January 4, 1897, and is buried in Pine Ridge Cemetery. Their known children are: Leslie Jason, born October 10, 1858; Lillian F.M., born 1860; Jasper A., born 1863; and Wilber F., born 1865.

Fayette's children:

Leslie Jason L. Avery became a doctor. According to G. A. Alford's "Early Days" in the *Lake Placid News* of February 15, 1956, he received his medical education at the University of Vermont and his early tutelage under Dr. F. J. D'Avignon of Au Sable Forks. Leslie took up practice in Au Sable Forks. His home and office burned in the big Au Sable Forks fire of 1925, and he rebuilt on the corner of Main and Forge Streets. Leslie never married. He died in Au Sable Forks on July 11, 1931, and is buried in the family plot in Pine Ridge Cemetery, Saranac Lake.

Lillian never married, and lived out her life in Saranac Lake. She died in 1926 and is buried in the family plot in Pine Ridge Cemetery.

Jasper A. may also have lived out his life in Saranac Lake. He died in 1940 and is also buried in the family plot in Pine Ridge. He married Belle M. Mihill, who died in 1935 and is buried beside him.

Nothing is known of Wilber F. His name and birth year are inscribed on the main Avery headstone in Pine Ridge, but no death date appears. Apparently he is not buried there.

The rest of Simeon S.'s children:

Sophronia, born July 9, 1828, married Joseph Wilson of Lewis, New York, on September 4, 1856. They settled in Elizabethtown on the old Bill Root place, where they lived about a year, and then removed to Lewis, where they became the proprietors of the Lewis House hotel. Sophronia was still living in the Lewis House when she died on December 23, 1904, her husband having predeceased her. The names of two children are known, Ada E. and Henry C., still living in 1885. Her obituary of January 19, 1905, states she was survived by one daughter, Mrs. Charles Bullis. Her son Henry evidently predeceased her. Nothing is known of any descendants. Another daughter, name unknown, married an M.L. Thompson, according to Sophronia's obituary, and in 1904 was living in McMineville, Oregon. Nothing else is known.

Jane, born 1823, married Jacob Smith H. Moody of Saranac Lake, always known as Smith Moody, who became a well-known hunter, trapper, and guide of his time. He was a son of Saranac Lake's first settlers, Jacob S. and Sally Brown Moody, of New Hampshire, who moved to Keene, New York, shortly before 1810, where Smith was born in 1812. The Moodys moved to the North Elba part of Saranac Lake in 1819. Smith died at Saranac Lake on March 22, 1890. Jane died at Saranac Lake on…[MacKenzie's typescript provides no date].

Jane and Smith Moody had the following children: Almeda Jane, born 1841 (she has been called Armelia by some historians); Benjamin R., born 1843; Sally A., born 1848; Hiram ("Ted"), born 1856; and James W., born 1860.

Philip. It has been reported that there is a stone in the old Avery cemetery in Averyville marked "Philip, 1816-." This is probably the fifth son of Simeon S. and Polly Clark Avery, who may have died in infancy.

SEVENTEEN
The Moody Family of Saranac Lake

As was the case with the Avery family, several pieces were found in the MacKenzie files that covered the Moody family, Saranac Lake's first settlers. The following is a combination of three pieces. Mary wrote one in October 1998 telling the whole story of the family and its settlement in the North Elba section of Saranac Lake. An addendum written the following month acknowledges Alfred Moody's description of his family's descent, beginning with the first Moody to settle in the New World. Finally, a third piece with various notes on the Moody story was written May 10, 1989, for Dick Wyman, an Avery descendant who had returned to North Elba, and his wife Jean Wyman.

The generally accepted version of the Moody family history has always been that contained in Alfred Donaldson's *History of the Adirondacks* (Century Publishing Co., 1921, reprinted Purple Mountain Press, 1996), due to the absence of any other published documentation.

Donaldson states that Jacob S. Moody was born in Keene, New Hampshire in 1787 and moved from there to Saranac Lake in the Adirondacks in 1819. Squatting at first on what is now called Highland Park in Saranac Lake, in the Town of St. Armand, he soon moved to "the pines" in the Town of North Elba, east of River Street in Saranac Lake, near the present Pine Ridge Cemetery. Donaldson fails to mention that Moody first moved to Keene, New York, in the Adirondacks, shortly after 1805.

Donaldson's account, and his family genealogy, contain a number of inaccuracies and omit many important facts. This researcher's investigation of public records and private sources reveals a story significantly different in many details, as follows:

Jacob S. Moody was born in 1787 in Unity, New Hampshire, a small town about twenty-five miles north of Keene. His father was Richard Moody, born in New Hampshire in 1750.

Jacob S. Moody moved from New Hampshire to Keene, Essex County, New York, in the Adirondacks, with his wife Sally Brown Moody, shortly after 1805. There, his first child Harvey was born in 1808. While living in Keene, Jacob served in the state militia in the War of 1812, from August l, 1813, to August 6, 1813, and again, as a fifer, from September 2, 1814, to September 15, 1814 (Battle of Plattsburgh), in Lieutenant Zadok Hurd's Company, part of an unregimented battalion of the 40th Brigade.

On October 3, 1810, Jacob received a deed from Asa A. Andrews for his small farm in Keene, located in Great Lot No. 1 of Township 1 of the Old Military Tract. He perhaps also worked in a sawmill in Keene. Donaldson says Jacob was injured in a sawmill at "Keene" (which he erroneously believed to be in New Hampshire), an injury that incapacitated him from further work there, but no mention of this has been found elsewhere. In any event, Jacob moved from Keene, New York, to Saranac Lake in 1819, and was the first settler in that area.

Donaldson states that Jacob first settled in what became known as the Highland Park section of Saranac Lake, apparently on land that later became part of the Trudeau Sanitarium. If this is correct, he did not remain there long, but very soon moved down to "the pines" in what is now North Elba, just east of River Street and next to the present Pine Ridge Cemetery. He built a log cabin on the Northwest Bay-Hopkinton Road (a.k.a. Old Military Road) as Donaldson correctly states, "at the foot of the steep hillside of pines where the upper road to Lake Placid crosses the railroad tracks"—in other words, at the end of the present McKenzie Pond Road where it merges with Pine Street. He lived in the cabin for many years but later built a frame house, reported on the 1855 North Elba census. This must have been "the red farmhouse" described as the Jacob Moody residence in Alfred B. Street's *Woods and Waters* (M. Doolady, New York, NY, 1860).

The Moody farm and residence were located in Great Lot 12 of Township 11, Old Military Tract. Jacob owned the whole of Lot 12, with a total of 160 acres. A map showing the bounds of Lot 12 is attached to this report. This map also pinpoints the location of the original log cabin, as designated on J. H. French's 1858 map of North Elba.

A most interesting article by Alfred Moody, entitled "Genealogy and Historical Sketches of Daniel Moody and His Father, Jacob Smith Moody," lodged in the Adirondack Collection of Saranac Lake Free Library, states the following: "On July 24, 1855, at age 57, he [Jacob S. Moody] applied for acreage under the Land Grant Act of March 3, 1855 (VA letter), and was given Lot 12 of Richards' Survey, consisting of 160 acres bordered by the present East Pine Street, Shepard Avenue, half of Moody Pond, and a corner of River Street. (Interview with Alfred Moody.)"

This is decidedly incorrect. Jacob S. Moody may possibly have applied for and even received acreage under the Land Grant Act of 1855 (this researcher has not found a recorded deed or patent for any such grant), but Lot 12 could not possibly have been the acreage involved. Records in the Essex County Clerk's Office tell an entirely different story, and an interesting one, about Lot 12, as follows:

It is clear that Jacob S. Moody acquired Lot 12 either shortly before or shortly after his arrival in Saranac Lake in 1819. He must have purchased it with his own money, as land grants for service in the War of 1812 do not seem to have been awarded that early. (Research in the National Archives might resolve this question.) Under any circumstances, he would have received a patent from the state of New York. His patent is not filed in the Essex County Clerk's Office, but this is not surprising. This researcher has noted over many years that, in the early nineteenth century, scarcely anyone ever filed his state patent with the county clerk, evidently believing it was not necessary.

The first indication in the Essex County Clerk's Office of Jacob S. Moody's ownership of Lot 12 of 160 acres appears in 1836. On November 7, 1836, Jacob deeded to his son Harvey Moody ("now on premises") fifty acres of Lot 12, being the northern sector and extending from the Essex/Franklin County line on the west over to the east line of Lot 12. The deed was recorded on January 29, 1841. Harvey built a cabin on the land. In *Woods and Waters,* Street stated that the cabin was half log and half clapboard, and that Harvey also had "a little log smithy."

Jacob retained for himself the remaining 110 acres, containing a small part of present Lake Flower. Unfortunately, it was not long before he lost those 110 acres. Prior to 1841, he had become indebted to Newell Reynolds for an undisclosed sum of money that would probably seem of little account today. Reynolds had died, and the administrators of his estate—Phineas Norton, Chester Bruce, and Hannah Reynolds—attempted to collect the debt from Moody, without success. The Court of Common Pleas directed the Essex County Sheriff, S. Alonson Wilder, to seize such goods and chattels of Jacob S. Moody as would satisfy the debt. The sheriff was not able to find sufficient goods and chattels, and the court then directed that the real property of Jacob S. Moody be sold at public auction to pay off the debt.

The auction was held October 25, 1841, and the 110 acres of Lot 12 went to Phineas Norton, the highest bidder, for $71.38. Sheriff Wilder gave a certificate of sale to Phineas Norton, subject to a redemption period of fifteen months. On October 20, 1843, Norton transferred his certificate of sale to Jacob S. Moody's son, Jacob S. B. Moody (Smith Moody), upon receiving from him two promissory notes signed by Leonard S. Green for

$55 and interest, and what appears to be a Colt revolver. (The handwriting in these old records is often almost impossible to decipher.) On October 12, 1849, Sheriff Wilder conveyed title to the 110 acres to Jacob S. B. Moody.

While old Jacob had lost title to his land, he had lost it to his son, and of course continued living in his old farmhouse until his death. The 1855 census reveals that son Jacob S. B. had his own log house somewhere on the land.

Jacob S. B. Moody was always known as Smith Moody. On February 14, 1863, for the sum of $100, he and his wife Amelia deeded to his brother Martin M. Moody fifty acres of Lot 12. This parcel was located to the south of Harvey's fifty acres and extended entirely across Lot 12 from east to west. On March 21, 1868, Jacob S. B. Moody deeded the remaining sixty acres of Lot 12 to his son Benjamin R. Moody. Benjamin lived on this parcel all his life, maintaining a house at 154 River Street.

Jacob S. Moody's first wife Sally Brown died in October 1852. She was buried near the farmhouse, next to the grave of her grandson, Jacob S. (son of Cortis and Martha Moody), who predeceased her on July 5, 1852, at five years of age. On July 25, 1855, Jacob married Polly Dudley, widow of Levi Dudley. She died June 27, 1883 at Bloomingdale, New York. The old pioneer Jacob S. Moody, head of Saranac Lake's first family, died April l, 1862, and was buried beside Sally. His grave bears a War of 1812 marker.

This burial ground became the Moody family cemetery, but the family offered free use to anyone who wanted a burial plot. A number of Saranac Lake's early settlers are buried there. In 1916, Pine Ridge Cemetery Inc. was formed and was deeded the old Moody cemetery—which had come to be known as "the old Protestant cemetery"—by Benjamin R. Moody and wife.

We now come to the matter of Jacob S. Moody's children. This researcher has attempted to make a thorough investigation, but there are still unanswered questions that quite likely will never be resolved. Donaldson's genealogical chart contains numerous errors and omissions that will be pointed out in this report.

Five of Jacob's sons—Harvey, Smith, Cortis (Cortez), Daniel, and Martin—became well-known trappers, hunters, and guides. Indeed, Harvey, Cortis, and Martin achieved considerable fame through extensive reporting of their exploits and colorful yarns in Adirondack literature, particularly Street's *Woods and Waters.* Maitland C. DeSormo's *The Heydays of the Adirondacks* (North Country Books, Utica, NY) has an excellent chapter on the Moody boys, and there is a wealth of material available elsewhere. Smith and Daniel were the quiet kind and not storytellers and did not receive the publicity accorded to their three brothers. Much information about them can be found in Alfred Moody's "Genealogy and Historical Sketches" heretofore cited.

Donaldson is said to have received his genealogical information from a Moody descendant. If that is so, the descendant was unaware of much of the family history. In cases such as this, the only source of authentic and dependable information is censuses.

Trying to trace the Moody family in old censuses is confusing and mystifying. In 1810, they appear under the Town of Keene. They are not listed on any 1820 census of the Adirondack area. Their recent arrival in the unsettled wilderness of Saranac Lake was evidently unremarked, and the census taker overlooked them. In 1830 and 1840, they appear under the Town of Wilmington, in 1850 under the Town of St. Armand, and at last, from 1855 on, under the Town of North Elba.

An explanation of such seeming chaos is in order. We know that the Moodys were living in Keene in 1810. We know also that they moved to the present Town of North Elba (most of which was still part of the Town of Keene until 1850) in 1819. Why were they listed in Wilmington and St. Armand? In 1830 and 1840, the area in which the Moodys lived at Saranac Lake was legally situated in the Town of Wilmington. The Town of St. Armand was formed from Wilmington in 1844. About 1852, the area in which the Moodys lived was taken off St. Armand and added to North Elba. Even though the Moodys were listed in three different townships during the period from 1820 to 1855, they were, during all those years, actually living in the same geographical location: "the pines" in Great Lot 12, Township 11, Old Military Tract, in present North Elba.

The 1830 census of Wilmington is the only census that can give us a picture of the entire family. According to that census, the family consisted of the following:

- Jacob S. and wife Sally, heads of family.
- A female over age seventy and under eighty, probably the mother of either Jacob or Sally.

- Harvey, born 1808.
- A son, name unknown, born between 1811 and 1815.
- Jacob Smith, born 1813.
- Two daughters, names unknown, born between 1816 and 1819.
- Cortis, born 1822.
- Daniel, born 1826.
- Franklin, born 1828.

This adds up to eight children in 1830. Martin was born in 1833 and daughter Eliza in 1837, making a total of ten children born to Jacob S. Moody.

An additional female on the 1830 census, age about nineteen, was almost certainly Harvey's wife and not Jacob's daughter. Harvey was a married man in 1830, and his first child was born in 1831. His wife would have been with him in the 1830 household. It seems clear that Jacob S. Moody did indeed have a total of ten children rather than the seven reported by Donaldson. It stands to reason that he did. Large families were the norm in that era, and there were often a dozen or so children. Women ordinarily had a child every two or three years over a period of about twenty years. We can see that there was a large gap between Harvey and Jacob Smith, and more so between Jacob Smith and Cortis. This would have been most unusual. The three additional children with names unknown would fill those gaps.

Donaldson says that Jacob brought three children with him to Saranac Lake, two sons and a daughter, when there actually would have been three sons, and at least one and possibly two daughters. One of the unnamed daughters could have been born in Saranac Lake in 1819, shortly after the family arrived. Donaldson complicates the matter by saying that the daughter brought to Saranac Lake was named Eliza and died young with no issue. Jacob did indeed have a daughter named Eliza, but she was the last child born to him, in 1837, and did not die young. Donaldson did not mention this later Eliza. It is not impossible, of course, that an earlier daughter, who died young, might also have borne the name of Eliza.

Children of Jacob S. and Sally Brown Moody

This researcher has endeavored to make some sense out of the entire matter of the Moody children, and offers the following as a guide:

1. Harvey, born 1808 in Keene, New York, died 1890.

Children: Simeon, Phineas, Polly, William, Alonzo, Fayette, Richard, and Robert.

Donaldson shows the children correctly, but erroneously states that Richard's mother was Harvey's second wife. Only Robert was a son of the second wife. Richard was born in 1853, and Harvey's first wife Adelaide Hall (called Sally on some censuses), born in Vermont, did not die until shortly after 1860. Harvey took as his second wife Elizabeth Still Dudley, a widow, and had by her Robert, born in 1864. Elizabeth's children by her previous marriage lived with her and Harvey—Charles, Alonzo, Rosina, and Emogene Dudley, and another Dudley son, name unknown. (Harvey took on quite a burden in his old age!)

Phineas Moody guided with his father and is mentioned in old Adirondack books. Phineas enlisted in the Civil War as a substitute for his brother Alonzo in July 1863. He died on October 3, 1863, apparently from an illness contracted in the Army. He died in Central Park Hospital and is buried in New York City.

Harvey's son, William, also a guide, served in the Civil War, 96th Regiment, as a private for three years, from December 1861 to April 1865.

Harvey's son, Simeon, was also a well-known guide. He settled in Tupper Lake in 1857, where he guided and became prominent in village life. He opened the first store in Tupper Lake. (See *Mostly Spruce and Hemlock,* by Louis J. Simmons, 1976.) Simeon was born March l, 1831.

2. A son, name unknown, born between 1811 and 1816, according to 1830 Wilmington census.

This researcher toyed with the idea that this male may have been an error of the census taker, who showed two males older than fifteen and under twenty, when there may have been only one (Jacob Smith B. would be the second one).

This is somewhat unlikely, however. There are two other possibilities. This son may have died young. However, there is no grave for such a son in Saranac Lake. The most logical answer is that this son moved away from Saranac Lake upon reaching maturity, to make it on his own, and knowledge of him became lost over the years.

3. Jacob Smith B., always known as "Smith," born 1813 in Keene, New York, died March 22, 1890.

Smith married Jane Avery, daughter of Simeon Avery, the pioneer settler, in 1819, of the Averyville section of North Elba.

Children: Almeda Jane, Benjamin R., Hiram S. (called "Tidd"), Sarah (Sally), and James.

Donaldson incorrectly shows Almeda as "Armedie."

Benjamin R. was a prominent citizen of Saranac Lake, serving as Justice of the Peace, etc.

Hiram S. was a well-known guide. Donaldson says he was called "Ted," but a published list of Adirondack guides shows him as "Tidd."

Nothing more is known of Sarah.

James married Anna Blood. His descendant Richard Wyman is presently living in Lake Placid, on Averyville Road,[30] and is a good source of information on the "Smith" line.

4. A daughter, name unknown, born in Keene, New York, between 1816 and 1819.

5. Another daughter, name unknown, born in Keene, New York, or perhaps Saranac Lake, between 1816 and 1819.

One of these daughters could be Donaldson's "Eliza" who, he said, came to Saranac Lake with the family in 1819 and died young, without issue. One of them could have been born in 1819 after the family arrived in Saranac Lake.

There is no grave for any such daughters in Saranac Lake. If a daughter died young, what did Donaldson mean by "young"? According to the 1830 census, both of these girls were over the age of fourteen in 1830.

There is a strong possibility that neither of these daughters died young. They could well have married and moved away from Saranac Lake, and eventually the family may have lost touch with them or their descendants. Descendants may well make an appearance one of these days.

6. Cortis F., born 1822 in Saranac Lake, died October 30, 1902.

Children: Donaldson lists five children of Cortis: Cortez (properly Cortis), James, Frank, Abe, and Milo. He actually had three more. A son, Jacob S., died July 5, 1852, at the age of five years, five months and five days, and is buried beside his father in Pine Ridge Cemetery. Horton Duprey of Saranac Lake informed this researcher about the other two children: a

30 At this writing, Dick Wyman is living in Jay.

son, Henry William; and a daughter, Jennie, who married Edwin Stoner, a nephew of the famous Adirondack trapper, Nicholas Stoner.

Cortis's first wife, Martha J., died June 12, 1867 at age forty-four. His second wife, Elizabeth S. Snay, born 1851, died in 1923.

Cortis spent years guiding in Tupper Lake. He returned to Saranac Lake and died there in 1902. The house that he built at 588 Lake Flower Avenue was torn down a couple of years ago.

There has been much speculation about the correct name of this son. "Cortez" is the name given in all published accounts about him. Donaldson says his full name was Cortez Fernando and that it would seem his father "was a reader of history and an admirer of the conqueror of Mexico." Cortez is also the name on his death certificate.

There is, however, much other and compelling evidence that Cortis was his actual name. "Cortis F. Moody" is the name on his tombstone. Also, the tombstones of his first wife, Martha J., and his son, Jacob S., refer to them as the wife and son of Cortis, and he himself would certainly have been responsible for those inscriptions. The tombstone of his second wife, Elizabeth, refers to her as the wife of Cortis. As well, it has been reported to this researcher that old censuses show him as Cortis and public records concerning his namesake son show him as Cortis.

This researcher has chosen to accept Cortis as the true name. If this is correct, it is an enigma how the name Cortez came to be attached to this son. Its first appearance was in Street's *Woods and Waters,* published in 1860, and Street could be said to have introduced the name, misinterpreting the vocal sound of it. Cortis himself may have encouraged the continued use of so unusual a name. In any event, he was known simply as "Cort" in the North Country during his lifetime.

Whatever the truth of the matter, the name Cortez has become so ingrained in the public domain that all sources of publication continue to use it and probably always will.

7. Daniel, born 1825 in Saranac Lake (Alfred Moody says he was born "about 1830," but this is incorrect), died 1892.

Children: Donaldson said Daniel had four children: Alaric, Adelbert (Donaldson incorrectly listed him as Delbert), Vertner and Lizzie (Elizabeth, Mrs. W.H. Oldfield). However, he actually had another son, Cleveland Eugene (the father of Alfred Moody), making five children.

Daniel was a well-known guide and also a blacksmith. For a detailed account of Daniel and his children, consult Alfred Moody's excellent "Genealogy and Historical Sketches of Daniel Moody and his Father, Jacob Smith Moody" in the Adirondack Collection of Saranac Lake Free Library.

8. Franklin, born 1828 in Saranac Lake.

Franklin died, apparently at an early age, with no issue. He was still alive at the age of twenty-two, according to the 1850 census, on which he is listed as "William F." Apparently, his middle name was Franklin. He does not appear on census after 1850.

9. Martin, born 1833 in Saranac Lake, died 1910.

Martin married Minerva M. Reid, of Bloomingdale, on January 6, 1861. They had no children. Martin was sometimes listed as "Milo M." on early censuses. Apparently, his middle name was Martin.

Martin was the most famous of all of Jacob S. Moody's children. He moved to Tupper Lake in 1868, where he made important contributions to local history. There is a wealth of material on Martin in old books; *Mostly Spruce and Hemlock,* by Louis J. Simmons, is especially recommended for a detailed account of his career.

One story about Martin that appears in Donaldson is that he was a pallbearer at John Brown's burial in North Elba. This may be so. However, this information can be found nowhere else but in Donaldson's *History.* Ed Cotter, of John Brown Farm, has done enormous research on Brown and has a very large collection of material, and he says the names of the North Elba pallbearers are unknown and have never been listed anywhere.

10. Eliza, born 1837 in Saranac Lake (born when her mother was forty-eight!), died 1900 in Tupper Lake.

This daughter, strangely enough, is missing entirely from Donaldson's genealogical chart.

Eliza was the last born of Jacob's children. In 1855, at the age of eighteen, Eliza married William Johnson, from Saratoga County, who had just settled in Saranac Lake. When first married, Eliza and William lived with old Jacob. By 1860, they had their own residence in the North Elba part of Saranac Lake, but in 1865, they were living with Eliza's brother, Martin Moody. The Johnsons then moved to Tupper Lake and resided there the rest of their lives. It would appear likely they accompanied Martin Moody when he moved to Tupper Lake in 1868.

Eliza had two known sons: Ernest H., born 1856, and John F., born 1858. Ernest H. became a prominent figure in North Country life, as a guide and as superintendent of the great Whitney preserve at Sabattis.

According to Horton Duprey of Saranac Lake, Eliza was married for a second time to a man named Bushnell.

The foregoing is just a brief report of Jacob S. Moody's children. A great deal more information can be obtained from old North Country censuses, newspapers, public records, and gravestones.

* * *

[The following are notes from MacKenzie's file on the Moody family's ancestry.]

Alfred Moody claims in his article, "Genealogy and Historical Sketches of Daniel Moody and His Father, Jacob Smith Moody," that the following is Jacob S. Moody's line in America:

- William Moody, arrived 1633 in Newburyport, Massachusetts.
- His son Caleb Moody, born 1640 in Massachusetts.
- His son Daniel Moody, born 1683 in Massachusetts.
- His son Daniel Moody, born 1714 in New Hampshire.
- His son Richard Moody, born 1750 in New Hampshire.
- His son Jacob S. Moody—born 1787 in Unity, New Hampshire.

It has been said that William Moody was a son of George Moody, of Moulton County, Suffolk, England, and that George was famous for his good housekeeping and plain dealing.

It is also said that William's brother John came to America with him in 1633, arriving in Newburyport. John is said to be the ancestor of the famous evangelist Dwight Moody. Horton Duprey told this researcher an interesting story that would seem to corroborate this. He said that Dwight Moody once came to Saranac Lake and visited Cort Moody. This researcher found a confirmation in the *Essex County Republican* of September 14, 1899, reporting the recent visit of Dwight Moody to Saranac Lake to see his grandchild Irene (perhaps curing, for tuberculosis?). It would appear, then, that Dwight Moody and Cort Moody were distant cousins.

There are books published regarding the genealogy of the Moodys, and one is *Historical Notes Concerning Moody Family* by H.A. Moody (1947). This probably could be found in the genealogical section of a large library.

* * *

[Miscellaneous notes from MacKenzie's file on the Moody family.]

Miscellaneous Note #1

It is interesting to note that three of the Moodys married Dudley women.

1. Jacob S. Moody took Polly Kent Dudley, widow of Levi Dudley, as his second wife on July 25, 1855. (Levi Dudley died in 1854.) Jacob had stood up with her at her first wedding. She was the mother of Essex County District Attorney Arod K. Dudley.

2. Harvey Moody, son of Jacob S. and Sally Brown Moody, took as his second wife Elizabeth Still Dudley, a widow.

3. Fayette Moody (Harvey's son by Adelaide Hall Moody) married a Lucy A. Dudley on July 4, 1865, at Jay (*Essex County Republican*).

This has sometimes caused confusion for researchers.

Miscellaneous Note #2

Essex County Republican, Oct. 28, 1875: "Marriages: In Jay, N.Y., at the M.E. Parsonage by Rev. A. B. Bigelow, Oct. 19, 1875, Benjamin R. Moody of Saranac Lake and Elnora C. Jones of North Jay."

Harvey's son Simeon is said to have been one of the early settlers of Tupper Lake and to have had the first store there. He is supposed to have been the third settler in Tupper Lake, and then purchased the first and second settlers' holdings.

EIGHTEEN

The Thompson Clan: Sharing John Brown's Dream

This story, first published in the Lake Placid News *on June 26, 1980, won the 1982 McMasters Prize of the Clinton County Historical Society for Mary MacKenzie.*

One day in the year 1824, there rode down the Old Mountain Road to North Elba township a man who would become the patriarch of a legendary family. Already he was the father of four young boys: John,

Archibald, Henry, and Franklin, the latter an infant in his mother's arms. Five more sons and a daughter—Samuel, Leander, William and Willard (twins), Dauphin, and Isabelle—were born in North Elba.

He was Roswell Thompson, and he hailed from the neighboring hamlet of Lewis. Most historians have credited him with twenty-two children, but the evidence is clear: There were only ten. Even so, ten is a good round sum.

Roswell, fourth child of David and Mary Bliss Thompson, was born at Gilsum, New Hampshire, on February 13, 1795. An early settler of Lewis, there he met his wife, Jane Jenkins, born in New Hampshire in 1798. Jane, at least, was no stranger to North Elba. With her father, Jonathan Jenkins, she had lived on what is now the Wescott farm before 1810, moving to Lewis about 1815. Her mother was a Graeme, that Scottish clan of Sir Walter Scott fame, who pursued their eloping daughter, fair Ellen, and her brave Lochinvar, over "bank, bush and scaur" on Cannobie Lee.

In that year of 1824, but twelve families lived in all of North Elba. It was a wild and lonely place. Only ten years before, three hundred inhabitants and a substantial iron works had made of it a thriving and promising settlement. Two tragedies had caused a general exodus. In 1816—that infamous "year without a summer"—a prolonged arctic cold wave destroyed all crops, and near starvation followed. In 1817, the iron works shut down, leaving many without work. Now, in the clearings, the panther screamed again, and deer grazed unmolested in the abandoned fields. Still, a school remained, Eleazer Darrow had stayed on to run the gristmill and sawmills, and church services were held weekly at Squire Osgood's house.

The Thompsons settled on a state patent, Great Lot 299 of Township 11, Old Military Tract, just outside the present village of Lake Placid. A sweeping expanse of 168 acres, it spread from Mirror Lake to Wilmington Road and took in today's Northwood School, Cobble Hill settlement, Lake Placid Club's "Theonoguen," and some of its golf course. Later, the family owned altogether about a thousand acres of land in the township.

It was good land, eminently suited to the raising of cattle and the growing of hay, potatoes, rutabagas, and the like. Roswell lost no time in hacking a prosperous farm out of the forest primeval, and not a moment too soon. New offspring checked in punctually. The tenth and last, Dauphin, was born in 1838.

In 1839, the Thompson compound was "a string of log houses, sheds and cooper shop and blacksmith shop, all connected together," according to Timothy Nash.[31] In time, Roswell built a large frame farmhouse on the site. (Its last owner was the Lake Placid Club. Remodeled and enlarged, it served for years as "Mohawk" clubhouse, and was finally dismantled.)

It was here that Jane Jenkins Thompson died on May 5, 1868, and was laid out in a black merino dress in a Keeseville casket. ("We put white cuffs around her wrists," wrote her daughter Belle, "a black cap on her head, that embroidered handkerchief of mine around her neck pinned with a black breast pin. She looked so neat and swept, it seemed almost a sin to bury her away out of our sight.") And it was here, also, after fifty years in North Elba, that the old pioneer, Roswell Thompson, died on January 24, 1874.

By then, tragedy had mounted on tragedy. The Thompson family had come apart.

They were a hearty, industrious, close-knit tribe, those Thompsons, bound by loyalty and love. In 1849, the first crack appeared in the masonry. That was when a second patriarch and his bountiful brood rode into North Elba: John Brown came to town on a great new tide of settlement. The scenario was set. Violent death, tragedy, and separation were in store for the Thompsons, all growing out of their close alliance with that fervent abolitionist whose name would soon ring around the world.

Young Henry, blue-eyed, tall, and handsome, was the first of the Thompsons to haunt the Brown home. John's oldest daughter, Ruth, a cheerful, healthy girl of twenty, was there. The fond couple wed on September 26, 1850 (Ruth had "done well," her father said), and set up housekeeping with a good feather bed, washstand, large looking glass, a set of cane chairs, and some fine furniture from the local cabinet shop.

Henry Thompson hated slavery. He became a firm disciple, and a great favorite, of his father-in-law. In 1855, Kansas Territory was up for admission to the Union. Whether it would be voted free or slave hung in the balance. Some of John Brown's sons had moved to Kansas to fight for the "Free State" cause, and father John joined them. So did Henry

31 This quote is from a letter that MacKenzie had in her collection dated March 26, 1891, written by Timothy Nash to his niece Fannie Nash, in which he recounts a trip he took in 1839 over the old McIntyre road that ran from North Elba to Wilmington.

Thompson. Agonizing over the pain of separation, yet always mindful of his duty as he saw it, the young husband wrote to his Ruth:

> After reading your letter, I could hardly go to sleep, and when I did my mind wandered back to my mountain home. I saw my dear Ruth and pressed her to my heart. I awoke to find myself in Kansas, far, far from the dearest object of my affection. Should I be spared to fulfill my mission (for I feel I have a sacrifice to do to Baal) I should go home and be content to spend the remainder of my days in providing for my loved ones.

And again:

> It is a great trial for me to stay away from you, but I am here, and feel I have a sacrifice to make, a duty to perform. Can I leave that undone and feel easy, and have a conscience void of offense?

In the bloody and brutal skirmishes, Henry fought bravely and with a sense of right in John Brown's holy guerilla war against the "Slave Power" in Kansas. He was never to forget his role in the appalling "Pottowatomie Massacre." Wounded at the battle of Black Jack, he carried a bullet in his back the rest of his life. Suffering from "bilious fever," reduced to a skeleton, he came back home to comfort his wife, till his fields, raise his oats, and guide tourists up the surrounding mountain slopes. That John Brown could not enlist Henry in his Harper's Ferry raid was a sore disappointment to Brown. But Ruth put her foot down—"I cannot bear the thought of Henry leaving me again"—and, as a result, Henry lived to a ripe old age.

Henry and Ruth had five children and were deeply devoted to one and other all their lives. In 1863, with John Brown moldering in his North Elba grave, they set off for Ohio and Wisconsin. In 1884, they moved on to Pasadena, California, making the journey on the "immigrant train." Among their first friends were the Charles Frederick Holders, who originated the Pasadena Tournament of Roses. Henry worked as a carpenter until he was age sixty-five, when he retired to his picturesque little home above the Arroyo Seco, later part of the famous old Busch

Gardens. There he tended his cow, his orange trees, his roses. And on the long porch, under the shade of tall pepper trees, visiting celebrities from the east conversed with John Brown's daughter and son-in-law.

When Ruth died at age seventy-five, Henry was desolate. He lingered on until he was almost ninety-nine years old, a quiet, prophet-bearded man who would not speak of the past. But just before his death, he told his daughter Mame that he was afraid to die. He had done things in Kansas, he said, and "there is a God in heaven who will not forgive me."

Henry Thompson left a legacy to North Elba: the John Brown homestead. Henry built the plain, gaunt little house, with its back to the west wind, that is now one of the world's great shrines.

Henry's younger brothers, William and Dauphin, needed no prodding to go to Harper's Ferry, that first objective in Brown's wild, ill-conceived plan for slave insurrection. They, too, hated slavery. And so, both of them raw, inexperienced farm boys, they went off to the South with John Brown and his motley band. William was twenty-seven, a kind, amiable fellow, generous to a fault, who liked to tell funny stories. Dauphin was only twenty-one, a handsome lad, nearly six feet tall and well-proportioned, with blonde, curly hair and innocent blue eyes—the "pippin-cheeked country boy" in Stephen Vincent Benet's great epic poem, "John Brown's Body." He was quiet and read a great deal.

Harper's Ferry has been called "a unique American tragedy." The chaos and the violence there had the whole nation as an audience. It started on October 16, 1859. That night Brown and his men captured with ease the United States armory and arsenal, taking some hostages and finally holing up in the fire-engine house.

By daylight, the town was in hysterical ferment. Armed farmers, militia, and the Jefferson Guards poured in to rout out the raiders. In the wild crossfire, the town's mayor was killed, and some of Brown's men, stranded outside, were cruelly slaughtered and their dead bodies desecrated.

Brown, with what was left of his "army," was now trapped. He sent William Thompson and a hostage out with a flag of truce. Seized at gunpoint by the frenzied, half-drunken crowd (the Galt saloon was doing a booming business), William was made a captive in the Wager House hotel. There the mob thirsted to take his life. "Kill them! Kill them!" was the hoarse outcry in the streets.

A brief respite came when a young girl begged that his life be spared for a fair trial. But the mob soon dragged him, kicking and screaming, from the Wager. "Though you may take my life," William shouted, "eighty million will rise up to avenge me and carry out my purpose of giving liberty to the slaves!"

They hauled William to the bridge and shot him; before he hit the ground, a dozen balls were buried in him. They threw him off the trestlework into the Potomac. As he lay in the shallow water below, sharpshooters riddled his body with bullets. William, said a local historian, "could be seen for a day or two after, lying at the bottom of the river, with his ghostly face still exhibiting his fearful death agony."

Despite all the other horrors of that day, the shocking murder of William Thompson was singled out as a disgrace to the State of Virginia. The passing of 122 years has not blunted its barbarity.

Night came. John Brown, eleven hostages, and six raiders (one of them dead and two mortally wounded) huddled in the cold and dark of the engine house behind barred doors. At dawn, United States Marines, using a ladder as a battering ram, broke open the doors. Rushing in, they bayoneted Dauphin Thompson as he crawled beneath a fire engine. Mercifully, the young North Elba boy died instantly.

John Brown was captured alive, tried for treason and hanged; he came home to North Elba in a coffin. William and Dauphin Thompson, with other slain raiders, were buried like cattle in an unmarked grave beside the river Shenandoah. Paid $5 for his services, James Mansfield planted them in two large boxes, wrapping them first in the blanket-shawls they had worn at their deaths. There they lay while the Civil War raged over them.

In 1899, their bones were located and disinterred, brought to North Elba under military escort, and given a hero's burial beside John Brown's body. Forty years had wrought a profound change in the climate of public opinion. United States Marines killed Dauphin Thompson in 1859. In 1899, infantrymen of the 26th Regiment, stationed at Plattsburgh, fired a salute over his final resting place.

Perhaps a sadder tale is that of Belle Thompson, the one girl in that ill-starred family. Romance had rooted again in the Brown and Thompson households and, at age nineteen, Belle married John's son, Watson Brown.

A son, Frederick, was born in August 1859. Two months later, Freddy's father died in agony at Harper's Ferry. Just before the raid, a tender series of letters passed from Watson to Belle, which no one can read unmoved:

> I think of you all day, and dream of you at night. I would gladly come home and stay with you always but for the cause which brought me here—a desire to do something for others, and not live wholly for my own happiness. You may kiss the baby a great many times a day for me; I am thinking of you and him all the time.

The most famous is quoted by Benet in "John Brown's Body":

> Oh Belle, I do want to see you and the little fellow so much, but must wait. I sometimes think perhaps we shall not meet again.

And they never did.

For a time the young widow found solace in little Freddy. A remarkable pen portrait of the two appears in "Louisa May Alcott, Her Life, Letters and Journals." The famed author of Little Women and a Brown sympathizer, Alcott invited Mrs. John Brown, Belle, and Freddy to a tea party at her Concord home in 1860. In a letter to her newly married sister, Louisa May Alcott reveals:

> The two pale women sat silent and serene through the clatter; and the bright-eyed, handsome baby received the homage of the multitude like a little king, bearing the kisses and praises with the utmost dignity. He is named Frederick Watson Brown, after his murdered uncle[32] and father, and is a fair, heroic-looking baby, with a fine head, and serious eyes that look about him as if saying, "I am a Brown! Are these friends or enemies?" I wanted to cry once at the little scene the unconscious baby made.
>
> When he was safe back in the study, playing alone at his mother's feet, C. and I went and worshipped in our own way at the shrine of

32 The "murdered uncle" referred to here is Frederick, a son of John Brown murdered in 1855 during the Kansas guerilla skirmishes. MacKenzie does not mention him anywhere else in her historical writing.

> John Brown's grandson, kissing him as if he were a little saint, and feeling highly honored when he sucked our fingers, or walked on us with his honest little red shoes, much the worse for wear.
>
> The younger woman [Belle] had such a patient, heart-broken face, it was a whole Harper's Ferry tragedy in a look. When we got your letter, Mother and I ran into the study to read it. Mother read aloud. As she read the words that were a poem in their simplicity and happiness, the poor young widow sat with tears rolling down her face; for I suppose it brought back her own wedding-day, not two years ago, and all the while she cried the baby laughed and crowed at her feet as if there was no trouble in the world.

But Freddy, too, was taken from Belle, for the child died from diphtheria when four years old. His little headstone is in the North Elba cemetery: "Gone Home–Aug. 19, 1863."

Belle moved to Ohio and there married John Brown's nephew, Salmon Brown, in 1869. Two daughters, Jennie and Lydia, were born of the union.

For many years, the family farmed at Kilbourn, Wisconsin, where Salmon was also the village mayor. But old wounds were reopened, the old tragedy revived. A shameful thing had occurred at Harper's Ferry with the body of Belle's husband, Watson Brown. The Virginians had stolen it and taken it to Winchester Medical College, where it was mummified and used as an anatomical specimen. During the Civil War, a Union Army surgeon rescued the body and took it home to Indiana. In 1882, in a fit of conscience, he offered it to the Brown family. Belle was summoned to identify it, and then attended the burial at John Brown's grave in North Elba.

Belle died in 1907. By rare coincidence, her grave in Wisconsin Dells, Wisconsin, is only a stone's throw from that of Belle Boyd, the notorious Confederate spy.

Belle Thompson Brown's name lives on at North Elba. It is engraved on the plaque at the Brown farm honoring the women who aided John's cause.

William's twin Willard, a cabinetmaker, moved to Goffstown, New Hampshire, before 1860. Twice married, he had several children. Willard fought in the Civil War as a sharpshooter, specializing in shooting Southern sharpshooters. A true Thompson, he wrote from Washington, D.C., in 1862:

> God grant that this may be a land of liberty and that we strike at the very vitals of slavery. I will serve my lifetime in the cause of the government if they need my help to establish liberty. I should not feel right not to share the hardship.

Taken a prisoner of war at Gettysburg, Willard suffered the infamy of the South's cruel Libby and Andersonville prisons. Libby's warden, knowing of his link to John Brown, refused to exchange him. By mistake, he was exchanged anyhow, and re-enlisted. He was with Grant's army when it marched into Richmond and had the pleasure of seeing Libby Prison freed. Undoubtedly, as a sharpshooter, he avenged the slaughter of his twin William many times over. Willard spent his old age in Wisconsin, hunting and fishing, and wintering at the Milwaukee Soldiers Home, where he died at age eighty-nine.

The oldest Thompson brother, John, was elected North Elba's first supervisor when the town was cut off from Keene and organized in 1850. Leaving North Elba during the Civil War, he settled in Omro, Wisconsin, with his wife and three children, where he died.

Brother Samuel also moved to Wisconsin and sold patent looms. He died at Ironwood, Michigan, in 1892, leaving several children.

Leander served in the Civil War. A life-long resident of North Elba, he for years owned and operated the old sawmill on the Au Sable River, near the present site of the Olympic ski jumps. Also a carpenter, he had a hand in building many of Lake Placid's early structures, such as the first village hotel, Brewster's. He married Alma Demmon of North Elba, but had no children. He spent his old age in the Charles Davis home on Mill Hill, where he died in 1896 at the age of eighty-eight.

Franklin and Archibald were also life-long residents of North Elba. Franklin married Julia Demmon of North Elba and had six children. He died in 1897 at age seventy-three. Farmer and carpenter, as well as town assessor and justice of the peace, he owned the farm on Riverside Drive that later became Midrivers Farm of the Lake Placid Club. His century-old farmhouse, across the old iron bridge still spanning the Au Sable, was torn down about twenty years ago.

Archibald, lumberjack and renowned axe man, in middle age married Mary Brewster of North Elba and had three children. He died in 1901 at age eighty-one. A blithe and carefree spirit, he went to California in the Gold Rush of 1849, departing North Elba on the spur of the moment. His mother had sent him down to the spring for water. Filling the bucket, he suddenly set it down and, without a word of farewell, took off for the gold fields. Several years later, he came home. Going directly to the spring, he filled a bucket with water, strode to the house, opened the door and called out, "Hello, ma—here's your water!"

The descendants of Roswell and Jane Jenkins Thompson are scattered over the face of America. Some still reside at Lake Placid. The Thompson tenure spans 172 years[33] of North Elba history and encompasses a family legend unique in the annals of North Country pioneers.

NINETEEN
Henry Lyon and his Family
January 29, 1981

On these long, cold winter evenings, Henry Lyon hugs the stove in his cozy living room on Old Military Road and often thinks about the past. He has a lot to think about, for last August 4 Henry observed his ninety-second birthday.

He spent almost all those ninety-two years in his native Lake Placid. Henry remembers the first skating rink on Mill Pond's Hurley Bay, where George Alford cleared the ice on his own time for the children of the town. He remembers hurtling down the chute near Mirror Lake Inn on his homemade toboggan, and Sunday school at the old White Church under the tutelage of Miss Annie Newman, the quaint lady farmer of Bear Cub Road.[34]

He recalls when George White built the Opera House in 1895, and Ebenezer White hammered out caskets in the little shop next door; Halsey Snow's blacksmith forge, where the IGA now stands; Sid Mooney's harness shop; Weston, Bull & Mihill's general store on Mill Hill; and the sawmill on Mill Pond.

Much more: The old steel-coated Town Hall that burned down in 1915, the Victorian hotels, the Town Clock Livery, board sidewalks on

---

33 As of 1982, when this paper was delivered to the Clinton County Historical Society.

34 Now called Bear Cub Lane, County Route 26.

Main Street, the charcoal pit at Fawn Ridge—all the trappings of life in a small Adirondack village, when the horse held sway and kerosene street lamps flickered on Main Street.

Not forgetting, of course, the Stagecoach Inn on Old Military Road that Henry's ancestors owned and ran and brought to fame.

The roots of the Lyon family reach far back in North Elba's past. It was in 1847 that Henry's grandfather, Martin Chittenden Lyon, came over the Essex County hills from Willsboro to North Elba by ox team, hauling a stone boat piled high with household goods and furniture. (Henry still owns an Empire bureau and a graceful living room table transported on that stone boat.)

Martin was a week on the road. With him were his wife Amanda M. Blinn, wed at Willsboro on April 15, 1838, and three small children—Mary, Emma, and Oscar. Two more sons, Orville and Ira, were born at North Elba. Of the five, only Ira and Mary would survive childhood.

Martin, the son of Vermont natives Amon and Polly Boynton Lyon, was born at Chittenden, Vermont, on November 20, 1815. In 1838, his family located in Willsboro, and father and son became successful farmers.

But Martin wanted to move on and fend for himself. North Elba was building up and seemed a likely place to settle.

The Martin Lyons first lived on the farm now owned by Dr. George Hart in Averyville. Home was a log cabin located west of the present Hart farmhouse. Martin once shot a deer in the fields as he rested his gun across the logs of the cabin.

Farming was all very well but, after seventeen years in town, Martin Lyon began to think on other things. The outer world had found North Elba, and tourists would likely come in droves once the Civil War was won. Accommodations were scant. He thought of the Avery and Osgood holdings. Earl Avery was moving out of town, and so was the Iddo Osgood family. Both had choice, adjoining lands for sale on Old Military Road, the ideal situation for a wayside inn. In 1864, the Lyon family bought the large tract, embracing more than four hundred acres. Martin tagged a large addition on the west end of a house already on the land.

The resulting Lyon's Inn, widely known as "North Elba House," was a picturesque and charming hostelry, simply but comfortably equipped—a fireplace in almost every room, a tavern and dining hall, ample barns to lodge horses, and a general store as well. It quickly became a routine stop on the Elizabethtown-Saranac Lake mail and passenger stagecoach run, and a popular retreat for vacationers eager to explore the countryside.

The inn also housed the U.S. post office. Contrary to popular belief, though, Martin Lyon was not North Elba's first postmaster, but rather its seventh. On May 15, 1866, his son-in-law, Hiram A. Lusk, was appointed sixth postmaster, and the next year, July 8, 1867, Martin himself came to the office, holding it until May 4, 1886. Neither one did much to justify his title, for it was Martin's daughter, Mary Lusk, who took command, sorting and dispensing mail, selling penny stamps, and reading her patrons' postcards.

In short, Lyon's Inn was the polestar of North Elba—tavern, general store, and post office—and a fertile breeding ground for town gossip. John Stevens, recalling his arrival in North Elba in 1878, said of it, "Here elections were held, people gathered for sport and horse trading, drank hard cider and sometimes other liquids of a more stimulating character."

A further vignette appears in the diary of the famed Adirondack photographer, Seneca Ray Stoddard, who stayed there in September 1873:

> We decided to stop at the North Elba Hotel, a very pretty little 2-story house with wings extending out from the main part, accommodating about 25 guests. It is on the post road between Elizabethtown and Saranac Lake.
>
> Mr. Lyon, the proprietor, is one of those sturdy, farmer-looking men who, besides being Postmaster, Justice of the Peace and nobody knows what else, is considered to have a sort of fatherly interest in everything going on in the neighborhood. The literature displayed was of the most solid character: history, gazetteer, Congressional proceedings 'with the compliments of' the lawmakers, but we felt more like devouring the supper which was, like the literary food, substantial.

A strange lady once came to the inn. The incident was so curious that Mary Lusk's small, impressionable daughter Emma remembered it all her life. The lady, alien in dress and mysterious in manner, alighted from the stagecoach and quickly asked for lodgings. There, she sequestered herself for two weeks, taking meals in her room and peering furtively through the curtains at each stagecoach arrival. Then one morning she abruptly took the early stage and went on her lonely way. If no one else knew who she was, Emma did. She was, as Emma always told it, from Salt Lake City and one of Brigham Young's wives, fleeing her polygamous household and the long arm of the law.

In the 1880s, Martin's eyesight began to fail—he was totally blind the last years of his life—and the inn was up for sale. It went to the Russell E. Fisher family, who continued its operation until the turn of the century. By then the little wayside hostelry was going down the hill. The stagecoach era was winding down, great new hotels had risen on the shores of Mirror and Placid, and the tide of travel had turned northward to the new village on the lakes. The Fishers sold out to Melvil Dewey, who briefly used the land as part of the Lake Placid Club farm complex.

Maybe the golden days were gone, but it was not the end for Martin Lyon's inn. In 1904, Chancellor James R. Day bought the place for a summer retreat.

Chancellor Day was a prominent national figure in religion and education, president of Syracuse University from 1893 until his death on March 13, 1923, and a bewildering character as well. Despite his rank and fame, his life at Lake Placid was quiet. He relished the role of farmer, and kept a cow and grew vegetables. Aside from preaching now and then at local churches and lending morale to the Women's Christian Temperance Union, he seldom mingled with the town folk. Yet, so vivid and lasting is the impression he left on the community that even today, fifty-eight years of title change later, the old inn is still called "the Chancellor Day place."

Day was a man of massive physical frame, over six feet tall, and he could "roar 'til the windows rattled." Morris Bishop has said:

> What a man he was! Really, what an appalling fellow! Totally unscrupulous in advancing the interests of God, which he identified with his own, intellectually limited, vituperative in speech, unprincipled in dealing with facts, he was feared and hated as few college presidents have been. And yet, this is the paradox of Chancellor Day, he was totally devoted to Syracuse, building it anew, turning it from a poverty-stricken sectarian institution into the great

> University it is today. He was a man of mighty power, a great builder and maker, a great man. But still, he was an appalling fellow.

The redoubtable Day inhabited the old Lyon inn for nineteen years, and made of it an impressive and stately summer home. How much he changed its outward look, or whether he changed it at all, is not known, for no early photos of the inn have ever come to light. The interior rooms—including the handsome, lofty-ceiling common room and gallery—are likely much as Martin Lyon made them, save for Georgia pine paneling and twentieth century bathrooms.

Following the chancellor's death, the old landmark passed through several hands—Ancelin, d'Avignon, Hazelton, and others—and the ravages of time took root. Mr. and Mrs. Peter Moreau, who bought the place in 1977, have lovingly restored it to the glory of the Day tenure. Somewhere that great man must be roaring his approval " 'til the windows rattle." Most of North Elba's early landmarks have been destroyed by less-aware generations, if not by fire. The community is deeply indebted to the Moreaus for rescuing, polishing, and preserving this historic curiosity of our past.[35]

How old is the inn's east wing? Is it North Elba's oldest standing structure? No one really knows. Its stone foundation and sills of mighty, hand-hewn timbers attest to a venerable age. Actually, Justus Dart, who had a log cabin there, was farming the lot on which it rests as early as 1803. The wing may be a house built by Earl Avery when he bought his land from Osgood in 1851. A map of 1858 definitely shows a house on the site.

But what of the Martin Lyons? Before the inn was sold, wife Amanda had already invested in a new farm to the west, bordering Old Military Road. An outsized tract of about 231 acres, it stretched all the way from the Pratt farm past the entrance to Averyville Road,[36] up Chubb Hill to Carolyn Road. (In after years, much of it was occupied by the old Ruisseaumont golf links.) Martin built a farmhouse under the shelter of Peck Hill on Averyville Road. The house still stands and is now owned by Fredy Fluhmann. There Amanda Lyons went to her reward

---

35 After all the work Moreau put into restoring the Stagecoach Inn, the building stands empty as this chapter is being edited in 2005, gutted by fire three or four years ago.

36 Now Averyville Lane, County Route 23.

on September 23, 1895, and Martin followed four months later, on January 30, 1896.

Martin's son Ira bought the farm from his parents following his marriage to Addie Lewis of Wilmington. A founder of the old White Church and at one time town commissioner of highways, Ira farmed and lumbered his land for many years, and also manufactured cement bricks where the Raeoil storage building stands on Old Military Road. He built his first farmhouse on the lot across the road from Henry's home. When the village bought the lot, it burned the house down. His second home was the present Vernon Lincoln house next to Henry, but additions have been made.

By 1910, Ira had sold off the bulk of the farm, some of it going to the old Chateaugay narrow-gauge railroad for a track right-of-way. The railroad crossing on Old Military Road is still called "Lyon's Crossing."

Henry resides on the last unsold remnant of his father Ira's great farm.

Henry was married to Mabel Alford of North Elba on December 10, 1908, seventy-two years ago. At ninety years of age, she is still by his side. Daughter Marion Lyon Bullis resides in Plattsburgh.

In 1910, Henry built his present comfortable home, garnished with the memorabilia of a long life. It has been a good life. Born on August 4, 1898, Henry attended both the Little Red Schoolhouse and Lake Placid High School. As a boy, he skated Mill Pond and Mirror Lake on clampons, and became so proficient that in later years he gave skating lessons on Mirror Lake to guests from the hotels.

He once worked at the Lake Placid Club steam sawmill, just up from his house, and then become a carpenter, mostly helping to build great camps on the lake, including the Wise and Waterman camps on Buck Island. In 1917, during World War I, he went to Buffalo and worked in the Curtiss airplane factory. After two years, he returned home. He retired in his eighties, and not because he wanted to—it was just that he was too old for Workmen's Compensation coverage, and people were reluctant to hire him.

Henry shares the family tradition with other descendants of Martin Lyon, into the sixth generation, who have remained in town—Mrs. Calla Lyon Shumway (her son Charles lives in Saranac Lake) and Donald Lyon and his children Michelle and Michael. And with Martin Lyon's inn that still stands on Old Military Road, North Elba's last relic of the stagecoach days.

TWENTY

The Tender Family

Date Unknown

The Tender family came to North Elba in the 1830s. Alexis Tender is on the 1840 census, with wife, a son between five and ten, a daughter under five, and a daughter between ten and fifteen.

The Tenders do not appear on any further North Elba censuses, and therefore must have moved out of town before 1850. They obviously moved to Wilmington, New York, because Civil War rosters show Alexis Tender and his son William Wallace Tender as being residents of Wilmington. Wilmington censuses will reveal more about the extent of this family.

Alexis Tender was born July 4, 1801, at Portsmouth, Rhode Island. His parents were Robert and Rebecca Tender. Alexis gives his occupation as "lumberman" on the Civil War roster, but while living at North Elba, he was a farmer.

Alexis Tender's wife is given as Annes (Anne?) P. Ford on the Civil War roster.

Alexis Tender's son, William Wallace Tender, is shown on the Civil War roster as born in North Elba, August 10, 1842.

According to a manuscript found in the Gerrit Smith Miller collection at Syracuse University (undated, but appears to be 1840s), being a description of various lots in North Elba, Alexis Tender had his farm on Lot 103, Township 12, Old Military Tract, which became the Torrance farm in the 1860s: "[Lot] 103 lies on old road—is a good lot. The corner of the road has once been improved, some part of which is now occupied by A. Tender."

Apparently Tender also occupied twenty-five acres of Lot 102, across the road from the Torrance farm, for the manuscript states: "Lot 102 contains but 160 a. How is this? And Alexis Tender owns 25 a. of the lot."

Tender apparently never got a deed to either Lot 103 or the twenty-five acres of Lot 102. He may have been buying Lot 103 from the state on contract, and he never fulfilled the contract. In any event, Gerrit Smith, land speculator from Peterboro, New York, got Lot 103 by patent from the state in 1849.

Truman Jacobs got a patent from the state of twenty-five acres of Lot 102 (lower part). On September 2, 1838, Truman Jacobs signed an instrument in which he gave to Alexis Tender "the privilege of tilling and using all the lands that Truman Jacobs formerly tilled in the Town of Keene [North Elba was then part of Keene]."

Tender was apparently farming quite a large tract of land during his residence in North Elba.

TWENTY-ONE
The Peacock Family
April 19, 1979

One hundred thirty-three years ago, there were Peacocks in North Elba, and there are Peacocks here today. One, of course, is Lake Placid's mayor, Robert Peacock, who dispenses milk and cream to the community, as well as law and order. And there are Beanes and Bickfords and Trussells and Pattersons and Barneys and Benedicts, and a Williams, who have a Peacock in their pedigree.

Our story opens in 1845. The setting is England. Two brothers, Joseph and William Peacock, are poring over a map of lands located in a remote outpost of America—the Town of North Elba in the Adirondack Mountains. Gerrit Smith of Peterboro, New York, owns the lands, and they are for sale.

Joseph and William had long harbored a dream of emigrating to America and taking up a brave new life as farmers. Sight unseen, they chose two lots from the map and, from across the Atlantic, closed a deal with Gerrit Smith.

A year passed. Joseph, now twenty, sailed for America alone, finding his way to North Elba early in 1846. He soon married Tryphena Osgood, a young girl native to the town.

William, twenty-eight, followed his brother in 1847, with other family members. His little flock contained himself, his wife, Louisa Herring, a three-year-old son, and ten-month-old daughter, his brother, Thomas James, eighteen, his young sister Eliza, ten, and his father and mother, James and Sarah Mott Peacock. After a miserable seven weeks at sea, they disembarked at Quebec in July and took a boat again down the St. Lawrence. Landing at Three Rivers, Quebec, they performed a grievous errand. The baby daughter had died aboard ship on the long ocean voyage. With heavy hearts, they buried her in Canadian soil.

The Peacocks traveled from Canada to Malone by various means. At Malone they found no further means of transportation, and so they set out afoot through the wilderness, carrying in their arms the small son and a few belongings, walking over fifty miles through almost unbroken forest. The tale of that long-ago trek, with all its hardships and privations, is still told in the Peacock family. Reaching the western edge of North Elba, the little English party put up overnight at the Dan Ames farm in Ray Brook, now the site of the Saranac Lake golf course. The next day found them at Joseph's log house.

The brothers had chosen lots on the east side of the present Adirondack Lodge Road, with a stunning view of the Great South Range—Marcy, Colden, McIntyre, and Indian Pass. There was only one drawback: The lower lot was mostly swamp. The matter was resolved by slicing the two lots down the middle, each brother taking one-half farmland and one-half bog. They are still there, the wide, wind-swept fields of Joseph and William Peacock, now owned by Langdon Laws and the Martin Alger family.

William set about building a second log cabin. His family soon increased by two members, for in July 1848 his wife gave birth to twins.

Brother Thomas James settled in neighboring Keene. Brother Joseph eventually moved his family to California, taking along the father and mother, James and Sarah. Sister Eliza, at sixteen, married William Walsh, a North Elba farmer from Ireland.

It was hard going at the William Peacock farm on Adirondack Lodge Road. Land had to be cleared, crops planted. The log cabin offered no luxuries. Lacking boards for a door, William hung a blanket over the entrance, and there it remained for several years. A trap door in the floor led to a cellar hole where "vittles" were stored. Outside, they banked the cabin with earth against the chill winds. And then, on a raw winter day in January 1852, the cabin burned to the ground. Dishes, bedding, provisions, clothing—all were lost. William hefted his axe and started building anew.

At the outset, William had few close neighbors. But North Elba was growing, and new families were moving in. Some were black people who had been given lands by the humanitarian Gerrit Smith. In the spring of 1849 arrived a man whose name, in a few short years, was to ring around the world. He was John Brown, and he settled with his family just across the woods from William. The Peacocks and the Browns soon became fast friends.

In 1859, William found some greener grass on the other side of his fence. Over the Au Sable River and through the woods, at the end of Bear Cub Road,[37] lay a bountiful tract of land. It, too, looked out on the romantic Great South Range. There was good potato soil and a maple wood for harvesting sap. William bought the land and moved his brood down the road, building yet another log cabin; this one would house the family for the next twenty years. Now there were eight children to feed, including a second set of twins. The John Browns were again near neighbors, for they also had moved to a tract near the Bear Cub Road. William worked some of the Brown land on shares.

Life at North Elba moved in measured pace. But in the outside world, stirring events were unfolding. William's good friend and neighbor, John Brown, stormed the federal arsenal at Harper's Ferry on October 16, 1859, died on the gallows at Charlestown, Virginia, on December 2, and came home to North Elba in a coffin. In 1861, North and South met for the first time in the battle that opened the Civil War. William was age forty-four, an Englishman by birth, the patriarch of a large family. Yet only four months after hostilities began, he answered President Lincoln's call for volunteers. Enlisting in Company C, 118th Regiment on August 11, 1861, he fought in the Civil War for three years. Many other North Elba husbands and fathers laid down their plowshares and followed him.

Back on the farm, in the late 1860s, William drummed up a profitable trade with the lumber camps near Tupper Lake. He contracted to supply food at Big and Little Wolf Ponds for some years. In the winter, hay was piled on lumber sleds at evening. Rising hours before daybreak, William and his sons would load twenty-five to thirty bushels of potatoes and two or three quarters of beef on the hay. As early as 3 a.m. they would be gliding through the village of Saranac Lake, and out onto Lower Saranac Lake by daybreak. The sleds would usually arrive in camp by 9 p.m., to the wild cheers of lumberjacks. The Peacocks delivered not only food for man and beast, but mail as well.

37 Now called Bear Cub Lane, County Route 26.

By 1879, the family had so prospered that William and his sons built a proper house. It still stands on Bear Cub Road,[38] escaping destruction by a hair in February 1939 when a violent tornado whirled through the Peacock farm. A large machinery barn literally exploded, its sides bulging before they collapsed, and a brooder building was torn from its moorings and lifted into a tree. The house, however, suffered only minor damage.

William died on May 5, 1889. He had served his town well as hard-working farmer, overseer of the poor, justice of the peace, assessor, town auditor, and inspector of elections. There were still Peacocks to spare on Bear Cub Road. More houses rose on their lands, then including Henry Uihlein's Tableland Farm and another lot adjoining Heaven Hill.

William's son, Joseph Richard, took over the original house and farm. His son, Morton, grew up there, and Morton's son, Mayor Bob, grew up there, too. Potatoes were the main product until Morton inherited the farm and started a dairy herd. After attending Cornell, Bob returned and added poultry to the certified milk and seed potato enterprise. He left the farm in 1946 and went into the commercial dairy business with Carl Thornton on Parkside Drive, buying the latter out in 1955.

Bob has been mayor of Lake Placid since 1959, an unprecedented term of twenty years.[39] He treasures his family keepsakes. Among them is a table once owned by John Brown, given to William Peacock by Mrs. Brown when she left North Elba for California in 1863.

There are still Peacocks in Lake Placid. William's sister, Eliza Peacock Walsh, bore six children. Some of her descendants stem through her granddaughter, Nellie Walsh Beane. They are Sidney Beane, Esther Beane Bickford, Louise Beane Trussell, and their children. Others descend through her daughter, Mary Walsh Patterson—Mrs. Alfred Barney Sr. and her family, and the William Patterson family. Eliza was also an ancestor of Eunice Benedict McCasland.

The descendants of William Peacock now of Lake Placid are Ernest Williams, Morton Peacock, and Mayor Robert Peacock and children. Thomas Steinbeck, president of Paul Smith's College, is William's great-great-grandson.

38 Now called Bear Cub Lane, County Route 26.

39 Peacock served another fourteen years as mayor, until 1993, for a total of thirty-four years.

Six generations of Peacocks have lived in North Elba. Peacocks worked the farm on Bear Cub Road[40] for 101 years, until it was sold to Herbert Kieckhefer in 1960. The old Peacock homestead is now a century old. Standing square against the west wind, it presides tranquilly over ancient lilacs and apple trees. It has the look of a house that will stand another one hundred years.

TWENTY-TWO
The Flanders House: John Brown's First Home at North Elba
March 15, 1996

Many years ago, New York State erected one of its historical markers on the north side of Route 73 (Cascade Road) in North Elba, about three miles east of Lake Placid village. Long vacant, the site is now occupied by a house, just west of the Fairway Motel and the road leading into the Craig Wood Golf and Country Club. The marker reads, "John Brown occupied a house on this site in 1848–50 while clearing the land now known as John Brown's Farm."

Aside from its historical significance as the first dwelling place in North Elba of the famed abolitionist John Brown, the site has additional local historical value. A number of North Elba pioneers occupied it, including Elijah Bennet, Jonathan Dart, and Allen McArthur, dating back to the days of our first colony. The land is a part of Great Lot 110 of the Old Military Tract, Township 12, which extends back to what is today the Craig Wood Golf Course.

After the demise of the Elba Iron Works and the disastrous "year without a summer" in 1816, most of the early settlers moved out. A few new settlers occasionally drifted in, but there were never more than ten or twelve families in residence at any one time until a new wave of settlement began in the 1840s.

One of those who drifted in during the late 1820s was Chapin Flanders, who appears in our 1830 census with a wife as well as a son and daughter, both children under the age of five. Chapin bought and settled on Lot 110 and built an abode directly on the highway, very close to the present house and the historical marker. Remnants of an old stone foundation, almost

40 Now called Bear Cub Lane, County Route 26.

certainly that of the original Flanders dwelling place, exist today very close to the present residence. Antique square nails have been dug up in that location. Flanders also had a barn on the premises.

Chapin Flanders' stay in North Elba was brief. He moved down to Au Sable Forks in the Town of Jay before 1840 and never returned to North Elba. He did, however, retain ownership of the house and farm for some years, renting it out from time to time.

The first to rent the Flanders place seems to have been Robert Scott, who moved up from Keene to North Elba in the latter part of 1840. He lived in the house for perhaps a year, while he was building his own house and farm buildings just down the road. In time, Scott had a very large farm operation and became prominent in North Elba history. Scott's Cobble was named for him. His farmhouse, situated on the east side of the golf course road, eventually became a small hotel known as the Mountain View House. This burned down in June 1903 and a new house, built on the site, still exists, owned by the Lichtenbergs.

Although there undoubtedly were other tenants following Scott, John Brown was the next person of record to rent the Flanders farm, in 1849. The Browns had been living in Springfield, Massachusetts, and John was engaged in the wool business there with Simon Perkins. He had already become quite active in the anti-slavery movement. In 1848, while involved in that crusade, he heard of Gerrit Smith, a wealthy abolitionist of Peterboro, New York. Smith had purchased most of the Town of North Elba—aside from the High Peaks area—from the state and had been giving away numerous forty-acre lots to free blacks of New York, with the idea that they would establish farms there and become useful and productive citizens. By 1848, a few black families had already settled in North Elba, but they were having difficulties. The winters were long and cold, they had no experience in farming and no money to sustain them until the farms could yield a living—and besides, their lots had not been surveyed, and many did not know whether they had settled in the right location.

John Brown called on Gerrit Smith at Peterboro in April 1848 and presented a plan. Brown said that he would himself take up a farm in North Elba, teach his black neighbors how to farm productively, and be "a kind of father to them." Gerrit Smith took an immediate liking to John Brown and fell in with his plan enthusiastically. (He would loom large in

Brown's later militant anti-slavery activities.) John then travelled to North Elba and inspected the scattered Negro farms. He fell in love with the Adirondacks on the spot, a love that would endure and grow stronger over the next ten years. He felt at home here, more than he had in any other place, and he would, at the last, choose North Elba as his burial place.

John's wool business was then in dire straits, and a mountain of debt was piling up. Nevertheless, he would not abandon his plan to move to North Elba with his family. In 1849, he rented the Chapin Flanders place for $50 a year, intending to live there until he could build a house on a farm of his own.

John Brown arrived in North Elba in May 1849. With him were his wife Mary and seven of his children—sons Owen, Watson, Salmon, and Oliver, adult daughter Ruth, and two small daughters, Annie and Sarah.

There are but two known accounts concerning the Flanders house and farm on Cascade Road and the family's mode of life and experiences in that period. The first summarizes the memories of John's oldest daughter Ruth and appears in F. B. Sanborn's *Life and Letters of John Brown* (Boston: Roberts Brothers, 1885) as follows:

> Mrs. Ruth Thompson has given some anecdotes of the pioneer life at North Elba, whither she went at the age of 20. She says:
>
> "Before moving to North Elba, father rented a farm, having a good barn on it, and a one-story house which seemed very small for a family of nine. Father said, 'It is small, but the main thing is, all keep good-natured.' He had bought some fine Devon cattle in Connecticut, near his birthplace; these my brothers Owen, Watson and Salmon drove to North Elba. At Westport he bought a span of good horses and hired Thomas Jefferson (a colored man, who with his family were moving to North Elba from Troy) to drive them. He proved to be a careful and trusty man, and so father hired him as long as he stayed there, to be his teamster. Mr. Jefferson, by his kind ways, soon won the confidence of us all. He drove so carefully over the mountain roads that father thought he had been very fortunate in meeting him. The day we crossed the mountain from Keene was rainy and dreary; but father kept our spirits up by pointing out something new and interesting all the way. We

stopped occasionally to get a cup of water from the sparkling streams, that were so clear we could see the bottom covered with clean sand and beautiful white pebbles. We never tired of looking at the mountain scenery, which seemed awfully grand. Father wanted us to notice how fragrant the air was, filled with the perfume of spruce, hemlock, and balsam.

"The little house of Mr. Flanders, which was to be our home, was the second house we came to after crossing the mountain from Keene. It had one good-sized room below, which answered pretty well for kitchen, dining-room, and parlor; also a pantry and two bedrooms; and the chamber furnished room for four beds,—so that whenever 'a stranger or wayfaring man' entered our gates, he was not turned away. We all slept soundly; and the next morning the sun rose bright, and made our little home quite cheerful. Before noon, a bright, pleasant colored boy came to our gate (or rather, our bars) and inquired if John Brown lived here. 'Here is where he stays,' was father's reply. The boy had been a slave in Virginia, and was sold and sent to St. Augustine, Fla. From there he ran away, and came to Springfield, where by his industry and good habits he had acquired some property. Father hired him to help carry on the farm, so there were 10 of us in the little house; but Cyrus did not take more than his share of the room, and was always good-natured.

"As soon as father could go around among the colored families, he employed Mrs. Reed, a widow, to be our housekeeper and cook; for mother was very much out of health...."

"Father had been planning ever since a boy how he could help to liberate the slaves at the South, and never lost an opportunity to aid in every possible way those who were escaping their bondage. He saw in Mr. Smith's proposal an opening through which he thought he might carry out his cherished scheme. He knew that the colored people who might settle on those Adirondack lands were inexperienced. Most of them had lived in cities, and were unused to the hardships and privations they must necessarily undergo in making homes in that wild mountain region. Therefore, as soon as we had got fairly settled, father began to think what he could do to help the new colored settlers to begin work on their lands. The greater number of them were intelligent, industrious people, and glad to do the best they could, but many of them had been cheated badly by a land-surveyor, who took advantage of their ignorance, and got them to settle on lands that did not correspond with the deeds Gerrit Smith had given them. Some of them began working on low land that was hard to cultivate; and when they found they had been cheated they were discouraged, and many went back to their city homes. Father felt deeply over the way so many of them had been treated, and tried to encourage and help them in every way he could. He spent much of his time in surveying their land, running out their lines, and helping them to locate on land actually belonging to them; and he also employed several of the colored men to cut the timber off a part of the farm where he now lies buried. He bought a quantity of provisions for them, and some cloth to be made up into garments...."

"Westport is the town on Lake Champlain, south of the mouth of the Au Sable, from which travelers commonly start in going into the Adirondack wilderness by Keene; and it was through this town that father usually went to and from North Elba. On one of his trips home from Springfield, in the winter, he hired a man to take him from Westport to Keene, but could not get any one to carry him over the mountain to North Elba that afternoon. Being very anxious to get home, he started from Keene on foot, carrying a heavy satchel. Before he came within several miles of home, he got so tired and lame that he had to sit down in the road. The snow was very deep, and the road but little trodden. He got up again after a while, went on as far as he could, and sat down once more. He walked a long distance in that way, and at last lay down with fatigue in the deep snow beside the path, and thought he should get chilled there and die. While lying so a man passed him on foot, but did not notice him. Father guessed the man thought he was drunk, or else did not see him. He lay there and rested a while, and then started on again, though in great pain, and made out to reach the first house, Robert Scott's. (This was afterwards a noted tavern for sportsmen and travelers and became known far and wide

> as 'Scott's.' It is now kept by Mr. Scott's kinsman Mr. Ames, and is the nearest hotel to the 'John Brown Farm,' where father lies buried.) Father rested at this house for some time, and then Mr. Scott hitched his oxen to the sled and brought him home to us. Father could scarcely get into the house, he was so tired."

The only other in-depth account of the Flanders house and the John Brown family's stay there comes from the pen of Richard Henry Dana Jr., who visited North Elba in June 1849. Dana's account of his visit, entitled "How We Met John Brown," appeared in the *Atlantic Monthly* of July 1871. A much more detailed and precise account of his visit appeared in Dana's journal, published by the Massachusetts Historical Society [*The Journal of Richard Henry Dana Jr.,* edited by Robert F. Lucid (Cambridge, Mass.: The Belknap Press of Harvard University Press, 1968)]. We have chosen the journal account as our source.

Richard Henry Dana Jr., born in 1815, was a noted maritime lawyer of his day and worked for the Free Soil Party in its fight for freedom for fugitive slaves. He became best known, and indeed famous, as the author of *Two Years Before the Mast,* published in 1840. The book was a best-seller, was widely imitated, and is still read today.

In late June 1849, at the height of his fame, Dana took a trip into the Adirondacks. Theodore Metcalf, an experienced traveler, accompanied him. The pair journeyed from Connecticut to Vermont, and at Burlington took to a boat and crossed Lake Champlain to Westport. Here they secured a guide, Villeroy S. Aikens, an open wagon, two strong mules, and a driver by the name of Tommy. The party journeyed from Westport to Keene, where they spent the night. At 5:30 the next morning, June 23, they set out for what is now the Town of North Elba.

By 8 a.m. they had reached North Elba and stopped at a cabin for breakfast. In Dana's words:

> In this remote region, almost every man who has a decent place takes strangers to lodge & eat, receiving compensation, rather in the way of a present than of regular pay. The place belonged to a man named Brown, originally fr. Berkshire Mass—a thin, sinewy, hard-favored, clear-headed, honest-minded man who

> had spent all his days as a pioneer farmer. On conversing with him, we found him well-informed on most subjects, especially in the natural sciences, & he had books & had evidently made a diligent use of them. Having acquired some property, he was able to keep a good farm & had confessedly the best cattle & best farming utensils for miles round. His wife looked superior to the poor place they lived in, wh. was a cabin with only four rooms, & was out of health. He seemed to have an unlimited family of children, from a nice cheerful healthy young woman of 20 or so [Ruth], whom we all liked very much, & a full-sized red-headed son [Owen] that seemed to be foreman of the farm, down by every grade of boy & girl, to a couple that could hardly speak plain. He also had two Negro men, one called Mr. Jefferson, & a Negro woman. How on earth all these lived in that cabin was beyond our apprehension & almost beyond belief, & yet Aikens said he had often lodged here—in the garret, to be sure—where were three beds beside his own.

The Brown family, of course, at this date had been in North Elba barely a month. Apparently, previous occupants of the house had been accustomed to taking in travelers for the night. Dana continued:

> Miss Ruth was very kind, & with the aid of the Negro woman, whom all the family called Mrs. Wait, got us an excellent breakfast of corn cakes, poor tea, good butter & eggs & unlimited supply of the best of milk. After breakfast we made our arrangements to go to Adirondac, wh. must be done on foot, through the woods. A young farmer named Nash undertook to guide us, & we sent Tommy and his mules to Osgood's, a regular tavern about 3 miles below, to stay until our return.

Osgood's was North Elba's first inn—and, in 1849, its only inn. It was located just west of and adjacent to the present Uihlein Mercy Center. "Nash" was undoubtedly Timothy Nash, who had come to North Elba with his father in 1840.

Dana, Metcalf, Aikens, and Nash then set out through the woods for the McIntyre iron mines, on the other side of Indian Pass, a trek of about seventeen miles, according to Dana. Nash apparently accompanied them only part way. Dana gives a long and detailed description of the journey through Indian Pass to the little mining village of Adirondac, their stay and experiences there, and their climbing of Mount Marcy.

At 11 a.m. on June 26, Dana, Metcalf, and Aikens set out on the return journey through the pass to North Elba. After clearing the pass, they completely lost their way, much to their anxiety, as they had no food, blankets, or warm clothing. After a fatiguing tramp "up hills and down dales, thru swamps and thickets, over fallen trees," they came at nightfall to a clearing in which, most fortuitously, stood a dilapidated and deserted shanty, where they spent the night.

Leaving the clearing on the morning of June 27, the men discovered a path and followed it, and after a couple of hours, to their great relief, came out upon a highway. No dwelling was in sight. The men opted to turn to the left, and their instinct proved correct because, after a two-mile walk, they reached a house. To their astonishment and relief, it was the John Brown house, where they had breakfasted only four days earlier. Wrote Dana in his *Journal:*

> Three more ragged, dirty & hungry men seldom called at a house for a breakfast. The Browns were very attentive, & Ruth immediately got us a large pitcher of the best of milk, with sweet bread & butter, until we were both afraid & ashamed to eat more. Mr. Brown was just sending off a wagon in the direction of Osgood's, & kindly ordered the man to call & tell Tommy to come up with the mules. In the meantime we took to the garret and lay down on the beds & fell asleep, & were called when Tommy & the mules appeared. The sight of the wagon & mules made our hearts revive, & taking a kind leave of the Browns, we got into the wagon & rode to Osgood's. It was a comfort to be carried by something else than our own legs.

After an overnight stay at Osgood's Inn, Dana climbed Whiteface Mountain on the 28th. He again stayed at Osgood's that night. The next morning, June 29, the three men started out for home. Wrote Dana:

> After breakfast started for home. Tommy seemed glad at the prospect of seeing Westport again, from wh. he now had been absent just a week, & we were not un-willing to become travelers again in our pleasant carriages in civilised clothing, on easy seats, with two good animals to draw us along. We stopped at the Brown's cabin, on our way, & took affectionate leave of this family, wh. had shown us no little kindness. We found them at breakfast, in the patriarchal mode. Mr. & Mrs. Brown & their large family of children, with the hired men & women, including three Negroes, all at the table together. Their meal was meat, substantial and wholesome, large quantities of the best of milk, good bread & butter, Indian meal cakes & maple molasses.

Thus, most fortunately, through the auspices of Richard Henry Dana Jr. and his three visits with the family, we have been afforded a glimpse of the Browns and their way of life at the little Flanders house on the Cascade Road. The life of the Brown family at the Flanders place was certainly spare and frugal, but there seems to have been an abundance of good food on the table at all times. Their life, of course, was no different from that of their neighbors at North Elba, where the usual hardships of pioneer life were endured. It has not been recorded how many acres of the Flanders land had been cleared and were under cultivation.

Years afterward, of course, Dana became aware that the Brown he visited in 1849 at North Elba was none other than the famous John Brown of Osawatomie and Harper's Ferry.

One could assume from Dana's use of the term "cabin" that the Flanders abode was a log cabin, but it is evident he used the word in its literal definition—"a small one-story dwelling of simple construction." According to the record, this was a frame house and not a log cabin. Aside from the fact that Ruth always referred to it as a "house," the 1860 and 1865 censuses clearly indicate the Flanders abode was of frame construction, a rarity in the North Elba of that era.

Although the Brown family occupied the Flanders house for two years, John Brown himself spent little time there. He devoted much of the early summer of 1849 to putting the farm in order, visiting his black neighbors, and surveying some of their lots. In August 1849, he returned to Springfield, hoping to salvage his wool business, now in chaos. He had previously decided to ship all his best wool to England, gambling on a better price there. In August, he boarded a steamer for England, arriving in London on the 17th. After visiting Paris, Brussels, and Hamburg, he was back in London by September 17 and offered the wool at auction. The results were disastrous, and he returned to Springfield the last week of October 1849 thoroughly disheartened. During the next year of 1850 he was mostly absent from North Elba, attempting to wind up the wool business, now in staggering debt. His son Owen was running the Flanders farm during his absences.

On one of his return trips to North Elba, in September 1850, John exhibited his prize Devonshire cattle at the Essex County Fair and was present at the wedding of his daughter Ruth to Henry Thompson of North Elba on the 25th. In October, he again left for Springfield. That winter he decided to move his family back to their former home in Ohio, where his older sons could keep an eye on them while he was battling his creditors in the courts. It was in March 1851 that the Browns left the Flanders farm for Akron, Ohio. They would return to North Elba in June 1855, but not to the Flanders house. This time they moved into their newly built house on the present John Brown Farm.

The state historical marker on Lot 110 is, of course, erroneous as to dates. The Browns were in residence there 1849–1851, not 1848–50 as the marker reports. John was indeed clearing some of his own land (purchased from Gerrit Smith in November 1849) during his sojourn at the Flanders farm. Note Ruth's statement, "He also employed several of the colored men to cut the timber off a part of the farm where he lies buried."

Chapin Flanders continued to own the house and farm on Lot 110. The 1855 census indicates the premises were then uninhabited. The 1858 French's map of North Elba shows a dwelling place on Lot 110 close to the highway, but it names no occupant, suggesting that the house was then vacant. It would not remain so for long.

Shortly before 1860, and very probably in the year 1859, Cyrus Taylor moved up to North Elba from the Town of Jay, where he was born on April 6, 1817, to Jay pioneers Israel Sr. and Rhoda Harmon Taylor. With him was a son Samuel, born in Jay on April 13, 1850, by his first wife Mary Lee, who had died. With him also was a new wife, Mary E. Beede, born in Keene Valley in 1839, whom he married in 1859. Ten more children were born to Cyrus and Mary E. at North Elba, six daughters and four sons.

It is probable that Cyrus Taylor moved directly onto the Flanders farm upon his arrival in North Elba. He would have been renting it at first, as it is of record that Flanders continued to own it for some years. In 1864, Chapin Flanders deeded Lot 110 to two of his sons, one of whom was Conant Flanders (always known as "Cone").

The full story of the Taylor farm at North Elba has not yet been investigated, but a few details are presently known or can be conjectured and are offered here.

The 1860 and 1865 North Elba censuses, as well as the 1876 Gray township map of North Elba, clearly show Cyrus Taylor living in the Flanders house. As has been said, the censuses label the dwelling as a frame house and not a log structure. It seems likely that an addition was eventually tacked on. Cyrus had a very large family, and it is doubtful that all could have been crowded into the original Flanders dwelling.

From the evidence at hand, it would appear that Cyrus Taylor in time bought Lot 110, or at least a part of it, from Flanders. The 1866 assessment roll reveals that he also owned contiguous Lot 116 of 160 acres (it was assessed to his wife Mary E.), which is fully occupied today by the Craig Wood Golf Course. This confirms local legend that the old Taylor farm was "on the golf course." Cyrus probably built a second house on Lot 116—the old farmhouse that stood on the edge of the golf course for many years and was finally torn down in recent times. The old Taylor farm would have been located, then, on both Lots 110 and 116.

Cyrus was a blacksmith as well as a farmer, and his blacksmith shop was located somewhere on his land, perhaps on Lot 110. Cyrus was also a justice of the peace of the Town of North Elba for some years. H.P. Smith's *History of Essex County* (1885) states that he had been a justice for "about 12 years" as of that date.

Cyrus Taylor died on August 2, 1893, and his wife died the next year, on February 18, 1894. Both are buried in the North Elba Cemetery. Of his five sons, only one, Phineas, lived out his life in North Elba, evidently carrying on the farm. The other four sons moved to neighboring towns of Essex County. Son Samuel did return to Lake Placid in his old age and died here on March 3, 1929. He, too, is buried in North Elba Cemetery. Of Cyrus's six daughters, three remained in North Elba.

It seems clear that Cyrus Taylor had continued to own and preserve the Flanders house, because his son, Phineas, was living in it upon its demise. The following news report appeared in the *Elizabethtown Post and Gazette* of November 22, 1900:

'AN OLD NORTH ELBA LAND MARK GONE

> The house in which Phineas Taylor lived (the old Flanders place, one of the oldest in the neighborhood) located near the Mountain View House in the Town of North Elba, burned to the ground Saturday forenoon. Mr. Taylor was not insured, the insurance on his furniture having expired a few days ago. The furniture on the first floor was saved. That in the upper part of the house perished, also the vegetables in the cellar. The total loss is about $2,000. This is a particularly severe blow to Mr. Taylor, as he is a one-legged man and depends on his daily labor for support.
>
> The great North Elba pioneer, the late Robert Scott, lived in the house above-mentioned before he built what is now the old part of the Mountain View House.

The fact that the famous John Brown had also resided in the old landmark was not mentioned in the article, and was obviously unknown to the editor.

If this news report can be relied upon for accuracy, it is apparent that the Taylor house that burned down in November 1900 was the original Chapin Flanders house. It had endured for some seventy years.

In Alfred L. Donaldson's *A History of the Adirondacks* (Century Publishing Co., 1921, reprinted Purple Mountain Press, 1996), Volume 2, page seventeen, appears a photo of a house, labeled "Cone Flanders House, about one-half mile from Scott's, where John Brown once lived." Experts and old-timers have repudiated this photo, claiming that it is labeled erroneously, that the dwelling pictured is not the old Flanders house, but instead one located on the other side of the road. We concur. In his text, Donaldson erroneously stated that the Flanders house "was still standing in 1920," when it had, of course, burned down in 1900. It is obvious the photo was taken many years after 1900, probably in 1920.

A number of Cyrus Taylor's descendants still reside in North Elba and Lake Placid. Among them are attorney John Taylor Wilkins; Michael and Raymond Damp and Mary Damp Bagg; Kenneth Torrance, Rollie C. Torrance, Loren W. Torrance, Pamela Torrance Green, Gertrude Torrance Hare and Carol Torrance Hoffman; and Shirley Seney, former mayor of Lake Placid and now supervisor of North Elba.

After the Flanders house burned down, the site remained vacant for half a century and passed through a number of ownerships. Grace Wolf and Margaret Ronconi of New Jersey bought the site in the late 1950s and built the present house situated on it. In 1985, Raymond Edgley purchased a large tract in Lot 110, including the Flanders site.

The site of the old Flanders house, where John Brown once lived, is now occupied by Todd and Lisa Rissberger. The Rissbergers bought the Wolf and Ronconi house, along with six acres of land, from Raymond Edgley and moved in on May 13, 1995.

TWENTY-THREE
The North Elba Black Colony

The body of this chapter has been compiled from a number of individual monographs on the North Elba black colonists, a very few of which were undated but mostly marked as having been compiled in 1994, though one significant piece came from a letter dated August 4, 1987. The introductory section combines two items: one undated, the other from July 8, 1998.

In the 1840s, Gerrit Smith of Peterboro, New York, a well-known and wealthy abolitionist, philanthropist, businessman, and politician, owned large tracts of land in New York State. Much of this land was situated in the Adirondack Mountains, including the Town of North Elba in Essex County. The village of Lake Placid is now located in this township.

Gerrit Smith decided to give away forty-acre plots to free blacks of New York State who measured up to his standards of good moral character, industriousness, and temperance. Owning such property would enable them to become full citizens and vote, and to leave city life and become self-sufficient on little farms of their own. Accordingly, he appointed a committee to choose three thousand recipients and, beginning in 1846, proceeded to draw up deeds to those chosen.

Hundreds of the Smith deeds were for land in the Town of North Elba. North Elba was first settled in 1800; in the late 1840s, a number of white people were living and farming successfully in the town, where the soil was very fertile and suitable for agriculture.

Of the hundreds of blacks given land in this settlement, only a handful actually came and started farms. The first of these families arrived in 1848.

These black people had never been farmers. They had been cooks, coachmen, barbers, and the like. Clearing the land and starting a farm was a very difficult undertaking for these city people, who also had to learn how to farm. The noted abolitionist John Brown moved to North Elba at that time for the very purpose of teaching these black people the rudiments of farming. Most, however, found such a life too difficult or not to their liking, became discouraged, and moved out. The Gerrit Smith colony, therefore, could not be termed a success.

The North Elba censuses[41] from 1850 to 1870 list only thirteen black families. By 1870, only two blacks were left: Lyman Epps and Josiah Hasbrook Jr. Hasbrook left in 1871. Most stayed less than five years. There were very likely others who came to North Elba and remained only a year or two, not long enough for a census to record them.

The Lyman Epps family was the only one that remained in North Elba permanently. The last member of this family died near Lake Placid in 1942. The most accomplished man in the black colony was William Appo. He was not strictly a member, since Gerrit Smith had not given him land. With his own money, he bought 132 acres of land in 1848. Appo died at North Elba in 1880.

The North Elba censuses show the following black families. There were very likely others who came to North Elba and did not remain long enough to be recorded on censuses.

Thomas Brown, born in Ulster County. Came in 1850, last on the 1855 census.

William Carasaw, born in Watervliet, came from Troy in 1849. Fought in the Civil War from North Elba. Left shortly after the Civil War.

---

41 Census records from the nineteenth century in New York State record data taken every five years. The federal census was taken at the end of every decade, and a supplementary state census was taken in between.

Isaac Craig, born in New Jersey, came from Jefferson County, New York. Apparently died in North Elba shortly before 1860. The Craigs arrived in 1853. Mrs. Craig appears alone on the 1860 and 1865 censuses as a housekeeper for a white family.

Lyman Epps, born in Connecticut, came from Troy in 1849. This family was the only one that remained permanently.

Silas Frazier, born in Ulster County. Came in 1854. Left shortly after 1860.

Josiah Hasbrook Sr., born in Ulster County, came from Newburgh in 1849. All of the family except Josiah Jr. left North Elba shortly after 1855.

Josiah Hasbrook Jr., born in Ulster County. Stayed in North Elba after his family left. Fought in the Civil War from North Elba. Came back after the war and stayed until 1871.

James H. Henderson, born in Virginia, came from Troy in 1848. This was the first black family in North Elba. He died in North Elba in 1852, and his family then moved out.

Samuel Jefferson, born in Albany, came from Troy in 1848, was last on the 1855 census.

Thomas Jefferson, born in Albany, came from Troy in 1849, was last on the 1855 census.

Lewis Pierce, born in Virginia. Came in 1850, was last on the 1855 census.

John Vinson, born in Rensselaer County, came from Troy and appears only on the 1855 census.

Leonard Worts, born in Ulster County, came in 1855 and was last listed on 1865 census.

The Epps Family of North Elba

Lyman Erastus Epps Sr. was born free in Colchester, Connecticut, on December 29, 1815. No members of the Epps family were ever slaves. Lyman's father was a full-blooded Indian. His mother, Candace, according to the 1855 North Elba census, was black.

Lyman Sr.'s first wife was Patience Noble of Connecticut. She apparently died young, and there is no evidence of any children born of this marriage. As a young man, Lyman moved from Connecticut to New York City, where he met and married his second wife, a mulatto, Amelia Ann Miller (her tombstone gives her name as Anna), born free in Kings County, New York, in November 1817. Their first child, Evelene, was born in Westchester County,

New York, May 26, 1845. The couple then moved to Troy, New York, where their second child, Lyman Epps Jr., was born on June 19, 1847.

When Gerrit Smith held his lottery, Lyman Epps Sr. received the southwest quarter of Great Lot 84, Township 12, Old Military Tract (forty acres), at North Elba. He moved here, supposedly in June 1849, with his wife and two children.

In old age his son, Lyman Jr., often stated that the Eppses crossed Lake Champlain by ferry on their journey to North Elba and first met John Brown at Westport on the New York side of the lake. Brown was also bound for North Elba with his family and, according to Lyman Jr., the two groups joined forces there and made the forty-mile trip to North Elba together. This account has not been authenticated. In any event, a close friendship arose between the two families that lasted for the entire period of the Browns' residence in North Elba.

According to the censuses and the cemetery tombstones, Lyman Epps Sr. and his wife Amelia Ann had the following children:

Evelene, born May 26, 1845, in Westchester County, New York. Died September 19, 1908. Never married.

Lyman Jr., born in Rensselaer County, New York, June 19, 1847. Died November 19, 1942. Never married.

Albertine Thompson, born September 6, 1849, according to 1900 census, at North Elba. Died July 6, 1927, at Mount Kisco, New York. Married William Appo. One daughter, Maud, also known as Albertine Enid.

Twin to Albertine, unnamed. Lived but a short time. Burial place unknown.

Albert M., born December 1852, according to 1900 census. Died November 1937. His tombstone says he was born September 23, 1849, but all early censuses indicate he was born in 1852.

Amelia Ann (shown on some censuses as Ann Amelia), born December 4, 1853, died October 2, 1875. Never married.

Clara, born March 31, 1856. Died as an infant June 19, 1857.

Kate Isabel, born December 14, 1857. Died May 6, 1929. Married a Robinson. Children unknown.

All the children, with the exception of Albertine Appo and Albertine's twin, are buried in the North Elba Cemetery.

Lyman Epps Sr., his wife and his children were all labeled "mulatto" on early censuses. Lyman Sr.'s mother Candace is shown living with the family on the 1855 census, age eighty-two, and is labeled "black." Lyman Jr.'s obituary states that she had been a slave and all her life bore the scars of the lashes she received when a slave, but there is no authentic confirmation of this.

The Eppses lived on Lot 84 in a log cabin until 1863. This was a wilderness lot just south of the later Peacock farm on Bear Cub Road.[42] While it was isolated and well off the beaten track, Lyman Epps Sr. by all accounts carved out a productive farm. He may have acquired knowledge of farming before coming to North Elba. He wisely balanced his crops. In 1854, he harvested fifteen bushels of rye, thirty-five bushels of corn, twelve bushels of peas, and three hundred bushels of turnips. His four milking cows produced three hundred pounds of butter, and he combed thirty pounds of wool from his twelve sheep. He also owned seven other head of cattle (perhaps for beef) and two oxen. There is no evidence that anyone else in North Elba in that early period was able to raise corn.

In the early 1850s, the Town of North Elba built a road into the Epps property, linking it with Bear Cub Road. That road is still in existence today.

On September 8, 1863, Lyman Sr. purchased the south half of Lot 88, Township 12, Old Military Tract (eighty acres) from Henry and Ruth Brown Thompson and moved there, farming the acreage until 1894, when he sold out to Hattie J. Green. This land, on Bear Cub Road in North Elba, is now part of the Cornell-Uihlein Experimental Potato Farm. The well hole of the old Epps farm was in evidence there some years ago and perhaps can still be found, just opposite the entrance road to Heaven Hill Farm. Lyman Jr.'s obituary indicates that after he sold the farm, Lyman Sr. built a house at 5967 Sentinel Road, Lake Placid, in which the family lived until the death of Mrs. Epps Sr. This has not been investigated.

Lyman Sr. was also a well-known Adirondack guide in his early years at North Elba, guiding tourists into the High Peaks region. His name appears in several old Adirondack travel books, and he is credited with having cleared an early trail, known as "the Epps Trail," into Indian Pass, apparently starting from his house on Lot 88.

The Eppses were prominent in North Elba and Lake Placid life and were highly regarded. Father and children had excellent voices. They sang at John Brown's funeral with a rendition of "Blow Ye The Trumpets,

42 Now called Bear Cub Lane, County Route 26.

Blow," and also sang in local church choirs. Lyman Sr. gave singing and melodeon lessons to local white families.

Lyman Sr. formed the first Sabbath school for children in North Elba and was one of the teachers. He was also a charter member in 1875 of North Elba's first formal church, the Union Church—better known as the "White Church" for the frame building's color—serving both Baptists and Methodists. When the Baptist Church was built in the village in 1882, he was a charter member, and he was one of the founders of the Lake Placid Public Library. He is reported to have driven Mary Brown and children by horse and wagon to Malone in 1863 on the first leg of their journey to California.

Lyman Epps Sr. died at Lake Placid on March 23, 1897, at the age of eighty-one. His wife Amelia Ann died at Lake Placid on November 19, 1902, at the age of eighty-five. Both are buried in the North Elba Cemetery.

The esteem in which the senior Mr. Epps was held is evidenced by the fact that four area ministers officiated at his funeral in the White Church: Reverend Thomas Watson of the White Church; Reverend C. J. Sevelle of Saranac Lake, former pastor of the Lake Placid Baptist Church; Reverend George H. Holcomb, pastor of the Lake Placid Baptist Church, and Reverend George T. Lemmon, pastor of the local Methodist Church. Four of his neighbors shared the honor of carrying him to his last resting place. His obituary says that he was "a highly respected citizen" and that "it was a pleasure to listen to him because he used such choice language and was so well informed, and more than this because of his gentle dignity and benevolence."

The Epps family was the only black family of the original Gerrit Smith colony to remain permanently at Lake Placid and North Elba. Of the children, daughters Evelene, Albertine, and Kate eventually moved away. While still in North Elba, in the early 1870s, Albertine married a black musician and composer from Philadelphia, Pennsylvania, William Appo, who had bought a lot there from Gerrit Smith in 1848 and spent his summers there. He was forty years older than Albertine. Their daughter Maud was born about May 1872. Appo died at North Elba on January 19, 1880, leaving his property to Albertine. Albertine later deeded the lot out to various people, including her brother Lyman Jr. After leaving North Elba after 1900, Albertine and her daughter lived in various places, including New York City, Los Angeles, and Mount Kisco. Albertine died at Mount Kisco on July 6, 1927, and her body was cremated.

Albertine's daughter Maud married Irvin LaFollette, apparently a white man. They lived in San Francisco, where Maud died on May 6, 1946. Her name is given as Albertine Enid LaFollette on the death certificate, and she is listed as "white."

Late in life, the Epps son Albert had mental problems, and he was a patient for some time in the Harlem Valley State Hospital at Wingdale, New York, where he died in November 1937. Through the efforts of prominent North Elba people, his body was brought back to North Elba for burial.

Son Lyman Jr. remained in Lake Placid all his life. He seems to have worked as a farmhand early in life, and in his later years was an employee of the Town of North Elba. He was a popular and much-loved citizen, and he was given much publicity over the years by area newspapers because he had been personally acquainted with John Brown. Some of his stories were probably a bit exaggerated. He lived for many years at 5967 Sentinel Road, Lake Placid, and then boarded at a house on Cascade Road.

Lyman Jr.'s obituary states that in his youth he aspired to wrestling and boxing, which was not approved by his family. However, whenever a traveling show visited the town, he immediately signed up as an attraction. Until his last year, he walked four or five miles daily, and was a familiar figure on the streets of Lake Placid.

Lyman Jr. was considered a local treasure and was honored at a number of functions. In the summer of 1942, just before his death, he was the guest of honor at the unveiling of his portrait at a tea given at the Adirondack Community Church in Lake Placid. For years he sang "Blow Ye The Trumpets, Blow" at the annual pilgrimage of members of the John Brown Memorial Association to the Brown farm and grave.

For the last year of his life, Lyman Jr. lived at the County Home, where he died on November 19, 1942, the last local survivor of the Gerrit Smith black colony at North Elba. Funeral services were held at the Adirondack Community Church, and pallbearers were Harry W. Hicks, Godfrey Dewey, Wales Wilson, and George LaLonde Jr.

Lyman Epps Jr.'s obituary and tombstone say that he died at 102 years of age, but this is incorrect. As he advanced into old age, he kept adding years to his life. The old censuses are very clear that he was born in 1847, making him ninety-five years old when he died.

The family name is spelled "Eppes" on early censuses, in some newspaper reports, and elsewhere. However, the name appears as "Epps" on deeds and the family tombstones, and it appears that Lyman Sr.'s children finally adopted the spelling of "Epps."

William Appo

William Appo was born free in Philadelphia, Pennsylvania, around 1808 to John Appo, a free black man who ran a confectionary store. William Appo received a good education, and he became a leading black musician and composer of his day. His instrument was the horn, and he was also a vocal performer. He played in orchestras in Philadelphia and New York, and he was a member of a black orchestra that toured Europe in 1837. In 1837, he established a studio in New York, where he taught instrumental music until about 1870.

The evidence seems clear that, at first, he stayed at North Elba only in the summer months, and it was his summer retreat. His wife died in 1863. About 1870 he retired from teaching and moved to North Elba, living there full-time. He married Albertine Epps, a daughter of Lyman, who was forty years younger than he, and they had a daughter.

[The following is excerpted from a letter MacKenzie wrote, dated August 4, 1987, responding to an inquiry into William Appo.]

I have some information on Appo in my files that I believe will be of interest to you. Am I correct in assuming you are a descendant of William Appo? Here is the story:

William Appo was the only black man I know of who came to North Elba on his own. He may have had friends here. He did not receive a grant from Gerrit Smith but bought property with his own money. On July 11, 1848, he bought from Gerrit Smith 148.6 acres of Lot 87, Old Military Tract, Township 12, here in North Elba. I have an address for him at this time of 4 Orange Street, next to 8th Street, Philadelphia, Pennsylvania. The purchase price was $148.60.

He apparently planned to establish a small settlement on this acreage because on January 20, 1852, he and his wife Elizabeth A. of Chester,

Delaware County, Pennsylvania, sold to Samuel Brown of Baltimore from Lot 87 "Lots 7-8-9-10 according to plan of village in Lot 87, Township 12, Thorn's Survey, each lot being twenty feet front and rear and two hundred feet each side."

This Lot 87 was finally disposed of as follows: William Appo's wife Albertine Epps sold a part to Lyman E. Epps and part to Anna Newman in 1900 and part to Edward Brewster in 1903. In 1906, Albertine and her daughter Maud E. of Los Angeles, California, deeded the last of the lot to Anna Newman. The latter acreage had a house and barn on it, which the deed says were "occupied in or about 1888 by said Albertine Epps Appo as a place of residence."

I have a copy of William Appo's will dated April 21, 1877, in which he left all of his property in North Elba to Albertine.

William Appo first appears in North Elba on the census of 1860. He is not on the census of 1855, so he apparently moved here between 1855 and 1860. The census has him as fifty-two years old, living alone without wife or children, as being born in Pennsylvania and as being a farmer and music teacher. I was quite surprised that you said his wife Elizabeth Brady died in Burlington, New Jersey, in 1863. Apparently, she did not come to North Elba with William.

I note that William's will gives the names of his children as Helen A. Cook, St. John Appo, Maud Epps Appo, and Catherine Johnson. But he must have had another son, William Appo Jr. "William Appo (colored), born 1843," is on our roster of North Elba men who fought in the Civil War. He was a private, enlisted 1861, and died at Bull Run [on] August 30, 1862. He is buried on the Bull Run battlefield. The number of his regiment is not given. I do not believe he was with Negro Regiment 26; if I recall correctly, that had not yet been formed in 1861. William Jr. must have joined his father in North Elba after 1860, because he enlisted in the Army at North Elba.

As you state, William Sr. married Albertine Thompson Epps. (This name is spelled both Eppes and Epps in numerous records. I do not know which is the original correct spelling but I always use Epps because that is the way the Epps children spelled it and the way it appears on the tombstones here.) You say they were married in the early 1870s. Albertine was born in 1850 and therefore was some forty years younger than William. I note you say their daughter Maud was born about May 1872.

As you guessed, the wrong information is on file at the Brewster Library in Elizabethtown about William Appo's tombstone inscription, and I will take it upon myself to have them correct their records. I went down to our North Elba Cemetery and found the following: William Appo died January 19, 1880, and is buried in the Epps family plot. The Elizabethtown file is of course completely incorrect in showing Anna as William's wife—she was the wife of Lyman Epps.

I do not find it so strange that Albertine waited several years to probate William's will. There was probably no particular need for immediate action.

Several years ago I found William Appo's obituary in the *Essex County Republican* of Keeseville, New York (one of our county newspapers), of January 29, 1880. It is very brief and merely says, "Mr. Appo died January 19, 1880, after a long illness, paralyzed three years. He left a wife and one child."

The Appos and Eppses were our two leading black families and they were close to the John Brown family. Both the Eppses and William Appo were very musical and gave lessons to the local residents. Among William's pupils was John Brown's daughter Ruth. Apparently, William's instrument was the melodeon. He is supposed to have sold his melodeon to Ruth, who married Henry Thompson. This melodeon is now in the John Brown log cabin museum in Kansas, donated by some of Ruth's descendants.

The daughter Maud was apparently always (or later in life) known as Enid. Enid Appo LaFollette, Albertine's daughter, was in possession of a lot of Epps family material and in the 1920s sold it to a bookstore in San Francisco, California. Dr. Boyd Stutler, who had one of the largest John Brown collections in the world, purchased it from the bookstore. I was acquainted with Dr. Stutler. Enid was said to be living in Mount Kisco, New York, in the 1920s.

Incidentally, in 1887 Albert Epps, Kate Epps, Albertine, and Maud were all living in New York City.

I have quite a lot of information on the Epps family and their background should you want it. It is quite interesting. They were an outstanding family at Lake Placid. The last of them here, Lyman Epps Jr., died in 1942.

Freeman's Home: Thomas Brown and Benjamin Landrine

The name Freeman's Home or Freedman's Home was applied for some years to the so-called "Cascade" settlement of North Elba, in the vicinity of the Bobrun Road,[43] supposedly because a number of Gerrit Smith's black colonists were granted lands there. Evidence suggests that several black people did settle and build log cabins there. At the time of the Smith grants, the area was unsettled.

In a talk to the Lake Placid-North Elba Historical Society in 1965, C. Walter Goff of Cascade shed some light on the settlement at Freeman's Home, as follows:

> Gerrit Smith conceived the bright idea of obtaining a large grant of land and bringing colored families here in the North. Negro settlements comprised the whole area of Cascade and the surrounding territory. In rambling around I have run across several of their little plots of land and old log cabins—decayed logs with stones in the corner. One of those cabins was back of Bushy's filling station [Michaud–Whispering Pines campground]. There was one on the Bobrun Road near the bridge, one on the grounds of North Country School, and one in the woods back of Goff's house.

The only documentary evidence of these black settlers is in reference to Thomas Brown and Benjamin Landrine.

The 1850 census lists Thomas Brown in the household of Robert G. Scott, age forty-eight, a person over twenty who could not read or write. The 1855 census listed him separately as a farmer, fifty-five years old, born in Ulster County, with a log house worth $25. He stated then that he had resided there for five years. He left North Elba before 1860.

The written "recollections" of Fern Thew Davis, who was born in 1880 in North Elba, daughter of Eugene and Eliza Thew, also mention Thomas Brown. According to these "recollections," Eugene Thew arrived at Cascade in 1877 with his wife and children to run a mill with "Perkins Chase." [There is a question about this name—his last name may have been Perkins.] When the Thews reached Freeman's Home, they found that the mill had burned that morning. Perkins Chase and his family of three children had lived in the upper floor of the mill. The few neighbors had a "bee" and in one day built a new log house for the family. There was no lumber for the gable and roof, so they went to Tommy Brown's cabin, long abandoned, and removed

43 The entry road to the bobsled track, off State Route 73.

his roof and gable and put them on the new log house. Tommy Brown had been gone so long the neighbors did not expect he would ever return.

The above would indicate the Brown cabin was in the vicinity and was one of those mentioned by Walter Goff. The late Elisabeth Thew McDonald of Glens Falls, formerly of Lake Placid, who grew up in the Cascade settlement, remembered playing on land locally known as the "Tommy Brown lot."

Tommy Brown does not seem to have worked his own farm. Fern Thew Davis said that he worked for James Davis, who lived for a time in the Cascade settlement, and also for Robert Scott, a farmer on the Cascade Road who also ran an inn for tourists. James Davis is said to have sold mittens, socks, shirting, cheese, butter, candles, etc., to Tommy Brown, indicating Brown raised neither produce nor cattle on his holdings.

There is no record of a Gerrit Smith grant to a Thomas Brown in the Freeman's Home area. Smith did grant a Thomas W. Brown of New York City forty acres in Lot 63, the southeastern half, Township 12, and it can be assumed this was the same man as the Tommy Brown of Freeman's Home. In any event, Lot 63 was and is wilderness land southeast of the later Wescott Farm in Averyville, and unfit for cultivation. Like so many of the North Elba black colonists, Tommy Brown must have finally settled on land for which he never received a formal deed.

Gerrit Smith granted Benjamin Landrine, apparently of New York City, the southeast quarter of Lot 140, Township 12, forty acres, on the east side of present Route 73, out in Freeman's Home. Round Lake occupies the greater part of this southeast quarter, and Landrine certainly found little acreage to till. Instead of simply squatting on a better lot elsewhere, as so many of the Smith grantees did, Landrine then bought from Gerrit Smith the whole of Lot 133, Township 12, 160 acres on the west side of Route 73, directly across the road from Lot 140.

Landrine was in North Elba in 1849 and may have arrived earlier. In September 1849, J. McCune Smith, a black doctor from New York City and one of Gerrit Smith's selection committee for land grantees, visited North Elba to see how the colonists were faring. In a letter to Gerrit Smith dated February 6, 1850, Dr. Smith reported:

> Mr. Landrine had cleared about two acres, and was vainly trying to reach water by well digging. He has since given up in

> despair and is now in this city [New York] wishing to sell his lot (which he bought from you) at $4 per acre.

It was the ultimate irony. The lot he was given had too much water and the lot he bought had none.

Landrine does not appear on the 1850 census. It is obvious he never returned to North Elba.

Thomas Thompson

The origin of the names "Thompson Hill" and "Thompson Brook" in the vicinity of the Cascade settlement has always been a mystery. There is no evidence whatever that North Elba's pioneer Roswell Thompson family ever owned property or lived in this area, and North Elba never had another Thompson family until modern times. The places known as "Thompson Hill" and "Thompson Brook" have always been the hill that goes up toward Lake Placid from the entrance to the Old Mountain Road, and the small brook that runs under the road on this hill.

Gerrit Smith did grant lots in North Elba to a number of black families named Thompson, but none of these lots was located in the Freeman's Home perimeter, and no black Thompsons ever appeared on censuses. Still, one or more Thompsons could have lived in the area for a short time, following the practice of squatting on land not deeded to them. There seems to be no other explanation for the origin of the ancient names "Thompson Hill" and "Thompson Brook."

In his *History of Essex County* (1885), under the Town of Jay, H. P. Smith reports the following:

> Thompson, Thomas (colored) is a hammerman for the J. & J. Rogers Iron Co.; is a native of North Carolina, was born a slave July 16, 1846. He left his master's plantation in 1862 to seek his liberty, and made good his escape into the Union Army at Suffolk, Virginia. For two years he was employed by the officers of Company K, New York State Volunteer Infantry, as their cook, and then enlisted in the same company and served until discharged in 1865. He then came to North Elba, and later to Jay, where he learned iron making and hammering, which he has successfully followed for the last ten

> years. Since he came north he has by industry and frugal habits acquired some property and a good education. He is a member and class leader of the first M.E. Church of Jay.

Thomas Thompson has not been found on a North Elba census, but it is possible he did live here for a time after the Civil War. He would not, of course, have been a member of the original Gerrit Smith colony. He could have been the elusive Thompson of Freeman's Home.

James H. Henderson

James H. Henderson was one of the first settlers of the black colony at North Elba. At the age of thirty, he came from Troy, New York, in the summer of 1848, with wife Susan M., thirty-two, five children under the age of ten, and his mother Sally, sixty-eight. He and his mother were born in Virginia, and his wife in New York State.

Gerrit Smith had given him forty acres, the southwest quarter of Great Lot 83, Township 12, a wilderness lot just south of the later Peacock farm on Bear Cub Road.[44] Henderson apparently chose not to live in this wild and isolated spot, although Henry Dickson did successfully develop a farm on his adjoining forty acres of Lot 83.

In 1848, we find the Hendersons living on Lot 93 in Township 12. This lot is located along Old Military Road, mostly on the north side. The western boundary is Bear Cub Road and Church Street and it extends easterly through the Jewish and North Elba cemeteries. A triangle of the lot lies on the south side of Old Military Road and includes part of Pine Brook Farm as well as the pond and converted barn house at the corner of Bear Cub and Old Military Road. Lot 93 is a small lot compared with other Great Lots, containing only 87.4 acres. Pine Brook runs through it, which would have been a good source of water and the land was easily accessible and suitable for farming.

The story of Lot 93 and its settlement is convoluted and difficult to construct from Henderson's confused account and other sources. It is clear that Pliny Nash, a white man (brother to Remembrance Nash and uncle to Joseph V. Nash, of North Elba) acquired the lot from Gerrit Smith in the late 1840s under a contract calling for ten equal payments. The

44 Now called Bear Cub Lane, County Route 26.

purchase price was $174. Nash was a shoemaker by trade and he may not have farmed to any extent.

In any event, in 1848 Nash allowed James H. Henderson to live on five acres of Lot 93. Henderson cut down trees, plowed the land, and built a frame house (unusual for that time)—on the face of it, a risky course of action, since he did not own the land. The families of Samuel and Thomas Jefferson then came along and were allowed to settle on another part of the land.

At this point John Brown stepped into the picture. Apparently, Nash wanted to divest himself of the lot, the three blacks wanted to acquire ownership, and John Brown wanted to help his black friends secure title. On June 30, 1849—to all appearances, with the cooperation of Pliny Nash—Brown forwarded to Gerrit Smith a draft for $225 as full payment for principal and interest on the Nash contract, and asked that a deed be given for Lot 93 to Samuel and Thomas Jefferson, James H. Henderson, John Brown, and Jason Brown. For whatever reason, within a short time John Brown changed his mind. He withdrew his offer on Lot 93 and on November 8, 1849, formally requested Smith to apply the $225 instead on his own individual purchase of Lot 95, where he eventually lived and on which the Brown grave and farmhouse are located.

What happened subsequently to Lot 93 is not entirely clear. Henderson continued to occupy his five-acre plot without title to it. The two Jeffersons left North Elba in 1850 for unknown periods of time. At this point, Henderson, believing the Jeffersons had bought Nash's contract and were about to sell the lot to an outside party, became very apprehensive about his future and petitioned Gerrit Smith for a deed to his five acres. Smith turned him down but, as will be seen, the matter would shortly be of no concern to the Hendersons.

Nash must have continued to live on and claim the property, because he made four payments to Smith on his contract, the last one in 1853. The Jeffersons eventually returned to North Elba and appeared on the 1855 census, presumably again living on Lot 93.

Henderson comes through as an industrious and intelligent man, able to read and write, although his spelling was quite dreadful. He seems to have farmed successfully at North Elba from the outset. His letter of January 29, 1849, appearing in a black publication called *North Star* and extolling the virtues of North Elba, said, "There is no better land for grain.

We get from twenty-five to fifty bushels of oats to the acre.... The farmers here get 45¢ per bushel, cash on hand, for their oats." He added that potatoes and turnips were plentiful, as much as four hundred bushels per acre. (Potatoes became a major cash crop in North Elba in that era as they could be sold in quantity to the local starch mill for 20¢ a bushel.)

Henderson must have been respected and liked by the white residents, for at the North Elba town meeting of March 4, 1851, he was elected an inspector of elections. His children almost certainly would have attended the local school.

He was a shoemaker as well as a farmer and evidently carried on a brisk trade. James McCune Smith, the black doctor from New York City, reported to Gerrit Smith on February 6, 1850, "Mr. Henderson, a shoe-maker from Troy, had his sign hanging out (the first and only in the township) and appeared to drive a good business."

To all appearances, Henderson was determined to make a go of the Gerrit Smith experiment and to raise his family and live permanently at North Elba. But in 1852, his dream of a good life in the Adirondacks came to a sudden and tragic end. Ruth Brown Thompson told F.B. Sanborn (as reported in his *Life and Letters of John Brown,* 1885):

> He [John Brown] did not lose his interest in the colored people of North Elba and grieved over the sad fate of one of them, Mr. Henderson, who was lost in the woods in the winter of 1852 and perished with the cold. Mr. Henderson was an intelligent and good man and was very industrious, and father [John Brown] thought much of him.

John G. Fay, in a letter to the *Lake Placid News,* published in the December 11, 1942 issue, gave a more detailed account of Henderson's death by hypothermia. John Fay's father, Gilman Fay, had a farm adjoining the later Wescott farm in Averyville during the 1850s, and it was to the Fay domicile that Henderson wandered that snowy day in 1852. Said John Fay:

> One wintry, snowy day a colored man, whose name I cannot recall, came through a trail from a cabin near John Brown's farm. Mother advised him to stay all night since it was snowing so hard

> and his tracks would be covered, but he insisted on going home. He said he had a compass. The third day his people came to inquire about him. He was found within a half mile of his home. He had walked around a tree nearly all night, so they thought by the hard beaten path. He had torn his compass to pieces, became tired, sleepy and foggy, and he was sitting in what the searchers described as a peaceful sleep.

Henderson's family left North Elba after the tragedy, probably returning to Troy, and no longer appeared on censuses. There is no grave marker for Henderson in the North Elba Cemetery.

Samuel and Thomas Jefferson

Samuel and Thomas Jefferson are assumed to have been brothers. The 1855 census lists Thomas as black and Samuel as mulatto. They came from Troy, New York.

Samuel, born in Albany, seems to have been the first of the brothers to arrive here, in 1848. He was then forty years old, with a wife Jane, listed in the census as black, also forty, born in Rensselaer County, and two sons listed as black—William, sixteen, and Samuel, nine—born in Rensselaer County.

According to Ruth Brown Thompson in Sanborn, Thomas arrived a year later, in May 1849, simultaneously with the John Brown family, whom he met up with at Westport, New York, on his way to North Elba.

Said Ruth:

> At Westport he [John Brown] bought a span of good horses and hired Thomas Jefferson (a colored man, who with his family were moving to North Elba from Troy) to drive them. He proved to be a careful and trusty man, and so father hired him as long as he stayed there, to be his teamster. Mr. Jefferson by his kind ways soon won the confidence of us all. He drove so carefully over the mountain roads that father thought he had been very fortunate in meeting him.

Thomas, then thirty-two, born in Albany, came with wife Jane, listed in the census as mulatto, then thirty-three, born in Greene County, and two sons listed as mulatto—Gerrit, five, and Harrison, two, both born in Rensselaer County.

When the author Richard Henry Dana Jr. came to North Elba in June 1849 and visited at the Brown house, he found Thomas Jefferson in the household and eating meals with the Browns.

Samuel Jefferson must have liked what he saw at North Elba because he would seem to be the Jefferson who addressed a meeting of Gerrit Smith grantees in Troy on November 1, 1848, describing North Elba favorably and urging that no grantee part with the land Gerrit Smith had given him. (*North Star,* November 10, 1848)

Samuel and Thomas had been given adjoining forty-acre parcels, the northwest and northeast quarters of Subdivision 1, Lot 23, Township 12, Richard's Survey. Lot 23 was deep wilderness land, far to the west of present Adirondack Lodge Road and far to the south of present Bear Cub Road.[45] It is still wilderness today, and part of the state Forest Preserve. Access would have been most difficult, and it is evident the Jeffersons did not attempt to settle on their grants. William Carasaw had also been granted forty acres in this lot, and he, too, settled elsewhere.

We find both Jeffersons living on Lot 93, Township 12—the same lot whereon James H. Henderson was squatting.

Samuel and Thomas Jefferson left North Elba, probably in early 1850, possibly because they had not obtained title to their shares of Lot 93. One returned to Troy, and the other moved to Westport, New York. They do not appear on the 1850 census.

At what point the Jeffersons returned to North Elba cannot be accurately determined.

Samuel Jefferson may have moved back after James Henderson's death in 1852. In 1854, he raised five hundred bushels of potatoes and owned six head of cattle, two horses, and two pigs.

The 1855 census suggests that the Thomas Jefferson family did not return until 1854.

Presumably, the families of Samuel and Thomas Jefferson again occupied Lot 93 when they returned to North Elba, but their second sojourn was short. Both families were gone by 1860, never to return.

---

45 Now called Bear Cub Lane, County Route 26.

It is the firm belief of this compiler that it was the conclave of Henderson and the Jeffersons on Lot 93 that inspired Alfred L. Donaldson's preposterous tale in his *History of the Adirondacks* (Century Publishing Co., 1921, reprinted Purple Mountain Press, 1996) of a squalid black shantytown near the White Church, composed of a defeated ragtag collection of runaway slaves.

In the first place, Donaldson falsely depicted the North Elba colony as one for fugitive slaves, when it was entirely composed of free Northern blacks, most of them born in New York State. Secondly, his notion that the colony was a miserable failure from the start is misguided.

Said Donaldson:

> The farms allotted to the Negroes consisted of forty acres, but the natural gregariousness of the race tended to defeat the purpose of these individual holdings. The darkies began to build their shanties in one place, instead of on their separate grants. Before long about ten families had huddled their houses together down by the brook, not far from where the White Church now stands. The shanties were square, crudely built of logs, with flat roofs, out of which little stovepipes protruded at varying angles. The last touch of pure Negroism was a large but dilapidated red flag that floated above the settlement, bearing the half-humorous, half-pathetic legend "Timbuctoo," a name that was applied to the vicinity for several years.
>
> Here occasionally, always overnight, new faces appeared and disappeared—poor, hunted fugitives seeking the greater safety of the Canadian line. Those who stayed permanently were roused to spasmodic activity by Brown, who induced them to work for him or some of his scattered neighbors. But, unless directed by him, they did nothing for themselves or for their own land.

This lurid tale, of course, is entirely refuted by the individual stories of the black colonists and the fact that there never was Underground Railroad activity in North Elba. We know the colonists settled on their own lots, built their own cabins, and tilled their own soil diligently, some with considerable success. There is not a scrap of evidence that they huddled together in slum fashion.

Also, they were not fugitive slaves, and when they chose to abandon their North Elba grants they had relatives, friends, and a former home awaiting them elsewhere in New York State.

How could Donaldson have concocted such a tale, so at odds with reality?

Donaldson's history owes a lot to information supplied by old-timers. One of his main consultants in North Elba was Byron R. Brewster, born in North Elba in 1845. He worked for the Brown family in boyhood and would have remembered many of the black colonists and where they lived. He undoubtedly told Donaldson of the concentration of blacks on Lot 93. There was, after all, a total of sixteen black people living on the land—eight Hendersons and eight Jeffersons. All three houses were possibly close to Pine Brook, a handy source of water.

Lot 93 is located along Old Military Road, mostly on the north side. The western boundary is Bear Cub Road[46] and Church Street, immediately adjacent—in Donaldson's day—to the old site of the White Church. (The church building was relocated in later years.) The boundary line of Lot 93 extends easterly through the Jewish and North Elba cemeteries. A triangle of the lot lies on the south side of Old Military Road and includes part of Pine Brook Farm as well as the pond and converted barn house at the corner of Bear Cub and Old Military Road. Pine Brook runs through it at the western boundary. The locale fits exactly the site of the black shantytown described by Donaldson.

Donaldson's approach to history was sometimes appalling. He had an unfortunate penchant for accepting simple, basic accounts and then embellishing and exaggerating them beyond all resemblance to the truth. It is very clear he did so in this instance. His healthy imagination transformed three small independent farms into a crowded ghetto, and the entire black experience in North Elba was thus distorted and trivialized.

There are many errors and misconceptions in Donaldson's entire chapter on John Brown and the black colony. It is a poor source for authentic information and should be avoided.

The Hasbrooks

The correct spelling of this name is in question. Various documents show both "Hasbrook" and "Hasbrouck." "Hasbrook" predominates in the

46 Now called Bear Cub Lane, County Route 26.

North Elba records. Probably the name was originally Hasbrouck but in later years only the spelling Hasbrook was used.

Gerrit Smith made three grants of land in North Elba to Hasbrooks: John Hasbrook, Lot 257, west half, Township 11, eighty acres; Josiah Hasbrouck, Lot 9, southeast quarter, Subdivision 4, Township 12, thirty-five acres; and Simeon G. Hasbrouck, Lot 98, northwest quarter, Township 12, forty acres.

It seems clear that only Josiah Hasbrook settled here. Although the 1850 census labels Hasbrook as "John," this most certainly was an error as later censuses show this family as headed by "Josiah."

Josiah Hasbrook Sr., born in Ulster County, New York, arrived at North Elba in 1849 at age thirty-four, from Newburgh, New York. With him was wife Susan, thirty-three, born in Dutchess County, and five children—four sons and a daughter. Another daughter was born in North Elba. Josiah's mother was a slave and was said to have received her freedom from "General Hasbrouck" (perhaps Jonathan Hasbrouck of Newburgh?).

Gerrit Smith had granted Hasbrook the southeast quarter of Lot 9, Subdivision 4, Township 12, thirty-five acres. This is rather isolated land east of the Adirondack Lodge Road near the foot of Mount Van Hoevenberg.

It certainly was not the choicest of the Gerrit Smith lots, but that is where the family must have settled and built a log cabin. Oddly, the 1866 assessment roll shows Josiah Hasbrook assessed for Lot 87, Township 12, 148 acres, located on Bear Cub Road[47] near Heaven Hill Farm, but Hasbrook decidedly was never the owner of that land. William Appo was the true owner of Lot 87 for many years. Did Appo perhaps allow the Hasbrooks to live on Lot 87 for a time?

It seems from the 1855 census that, early in that year, Leonard Worts, with his wife and son, moved in with the Hasbrooks. The two families may have been related, as both Josiah Sr. and Worts were born in Ulster County. In any event, by 1860, most of the Hasbrook family had departed from North Elba. Three of the children did remain here. In 1860, Josiah Jr. and Harriet were listed as living in the Leonard Worts household, and son Simeon was listed as living in the Henry Thompson household. It could be speculated that Leonard Worts had taken over the Hasbrook property.

47 Now called Bear Cub Lane, County Route 26.

By 1865, all the Hasbrooks were gone from North Elba except Josiah Jr., who the census listed as "In Army."

On August 23, 1862, Samuel B. and Clara M. Thompson had deeded to Josiah Hasbrook "forty acres to be laid out in a square form off the NE corner of Lot 108, Township 12." The consideration was $124.50 "previously paid in work to them." This was property on River Road,[48] and the grantee was quite probably Josiah Jr., as Josiah Sr. had left North Elba before 1860. There is no evidence Josiah Jr. ever lived on this lot. Obviously, the deed was in payment for work he had done for the Thompsons. He sold the property to Palmer E. Havens on August 27, 1863, for $75.

Josiah Hasbrook Jr. was born in Fishkill, New York, in 1843. He served in the Civil War from North Elba as a private in Company B, 26th Regiment, Negro Troops. He enlisted at North Elba on August 17, 1864, for one year, was mustered in on September l, 1864, and was honorably discharged on August 28, 1865. He served in South Carolina for a year and for a short time after discharge stayed in the South, visiting black people, telling them they were free and giving them what help he could.

At the time of Josiah Hasbrook Jr.'s enlistment, he purchased the west half of Lot 74, Township 12, eighty acres, in North Elba, from Palmer Havens and wife, for $400. The deed for this purchase was dated August 22, 1864. This land had been part of the original Horatio Hinckley farm (later and now Heaven Hill Farm) and was situated on the west side of Heaven Hill off Averyville Road.[49] Havens had bought the land from Horatio Hinckley on September 2, 1863. When Josiah returned to North Elba after the war, he settled on his new eighty-acre farm for a brief time. On November 12, 1866, he sold it to Judson C. Ware of North Elba for $400.

When Josiah returned from the war, his mother and sister came to live with him for a time. The mother had been gone from North Elba for years, and sister Harriet had left after 1860 and apparently had married. In a letter of November 14, 1865, Jane Thompson of North Elba wrote to her daughter Belle Brown in Ohio:

> Josiah Hasbrook has come from the war and his mother has come and is keeping house for him. She bro[ugh]t two children,

48 Now called Riverside Drive.

49 Now Averyville Lane, County Route 23.

> one five and the other two years old. The youngest is Hariet's, and she is coming in the spring. So you can see J. is in or will be in hot water. We are sorry for Josy. [One wonders what the last two sentences imply.]

On November 4, 1868, Josiah married Jane Ann Hazzard of nearby Bloomingdale. Jane's father Avery Hazzard had settled there in 1851. In the late 1840s, Gerrit Smith had also established a black colony in the Bloomingdale-Loon Lake area similar to the North Elba black colony, and it could be assumed Avery Hazzard originally settled in Bloomingdale as part of that colony. In any event, Hazzards lived and farmed there for many years, well into the twentieth century. There are many Hazzard graves in the Bloomingdale cemetery. The last one of that family in Bloomingdale, George W. Hazzard, died on September 28, 1948.

Josiah and Jane Ann continued living in North Elba for several years. In 1870, Jane Ann bought twenty acres from Amanda M. Lyon in Lot 78, Township 12, on Old Military Road. This was the old Wiles property, and the original Wiles frame house was probably still there. Jane Ann sold the property to Myron T. Brewster of North Elba on February 14, 1872. It appears from the census that the Hasbrooks were living on this land in 1870.

The 1870 census presents some questions. For the first time it labels Josiah Jr. "mulatto" instead of "black," as in the past. It also labeled Jane Ann "mulatto," as are the children listed.

A child, Stephen, eleven months old, is obviously Josiah and Jane Ann's son. But whose children are Lucy, eleven, and Hester J., six? Could they be Jane Ann's by a previous marriage? Also in the household is a black man, Jeremiah Miles, twenty-two, working on the farm, born in Virginia. Might Josiah have brought him North on his return from the war?

In 1871, Josiah and Jane Ann Hasbrook moved to a farm in Westport, New York, later to Worcester, Vermont, where Josiah was elected president of a local chapter of the Grand Army of the Republic, and finally to Amherst, Massachusetts, where Josiah died in August 1915 at seventy-five.

Josiah Jr.'s obituary mentions the many acts of kindness and help of the John Brown family toward the struggling inhabitants of the black colony, and that Josiah Jr. received his first schooling under Sarah and Annie Brown; also, that Josiah Sr. had once been lost for three days in the winter woods of North Elba and had been rescued by a search party organized by John Brown.

The obituary also states that Josiah Jr. attended John Brown's funeral and, after that, he worked "for seventeen years" with the widowed Mary Brown, but of course that length of time is in error as Mary Brown left North Elba for California in 1863, four years after her husband was buried. It also states that Josiah Jr. accompanied Mary Brown as far as Malone on her journey to California.

Cyrus Thomas

None of the Gerrit Smith black colonies were intended as havens for escaped slaves, and there is not a shred of evidence that North Elba was ever a station on the Underground Railroad. Still, it would not have been unlikely for a fugitive slave to appear now and then at a colony such as Timbucto. Cyrus Thomas, however, was the only black at North Elba for whom a runaway slave status is clearly defined.

The passage of the Fugitive Slave Act in 1850 had enraged John Brown and he had preached that all fugitives should resist the law at all costs, arm themselves, and refuse to be taken alive.

Wrote his daughter Ruth Brown Thompson:

> Our faithful boy, Cyrus, was one of that class, and it aroused our feelings so that we would all have defended him, if the women folks had had to resort to hot water. (Villard, *John Brown: A Biography Fifty Years After,* 1910.)

Cyrus Thomas had appeared on the Brown doorstep the very next morning after the family's arrival in North Elba in May 1849. In F.B. Sanborn's *Life And Letters of John Brown* (1885), Ruth Brown Thompson describes the occasion:

> We all slept soundly; and the next morning the sun rose bright, and made our little home quite cheerful. Before noon a bright, pleasant colored boy came to our gate (or rather, our bars) and inquired if John Brown lived there. 'Here is where he stays,' was father's reply. The boy had been a slave in Virginia, and was sold and sent to St. Augustine,

> Florida. From there he ran away, and came to Springfield, where by his industry and good habits he had acquired some property. Father hired him to help carry on the farm, so there were ten of us in the little house; but Cyrus did not take more than his share of the room, and was always good-natured.

Cyrus Thomas appears only on the 1850 North Elba census, as black, living in the John Brown household, age twenty-three, laborer, born in Florida. He was not granted land by Gerrit Smith and his stay in North Elba was probably of short duration.

Lewis Pierce

At the age of thirty-five, Lewis Pierce, born in Virginia, came to North Elba in 1850 from an unknown place of residence in New York State. He came alone, as either a bachelor or widower.

Gerrit Smith had deeded to Pierce the northwest quarter of Lot 115, Township 12, consisting of forty acres, and there is every reason to believe he settled on it. Lot 115, adjoining the present Craig Wood Golf Course directly on the north, was fairly accessible and also capable of cultivation.

In 1855, Pierce was living in a log cabin valued at only $10.

It must have been small, but then he had no wife or children to house. The farm was valued at $300, and he appears to have been industrious and successful. In 1854, he harvested between eighteen and twenty bushels each of wheat, oats, and rye, and also eight hundred bushels of potatoes, more than any other of the black residents. He also kept sheep, owning eleven head in 1854 that produced thirty-three pounds of wool. In addition, he had two horses and two pigs.

Oddly, in spite of this rather enviable record, Lewis Pierce left North Elba after 1855. Leonard Worts, another black resident, took over his farm at some time between 1855 and 1860. Whether Worts had an arrangement with Pierce or simply squatted on the farm after Pierce departed is unknown.

Lot 115 is much closer to River Road (Riverside Drive) than to Route 73 (Cascade Road), and access to it was most probably gained from River Road. Old maps—one as late as 1963—do show a dirt road going into Lot 115 all the way from Intervales Farm on River Road, and this was no doubt the original road into the Pierce farm. One old-timer today, Emmabelle

Williams, remembers the road and believes it led to a camp in the interior. It is believed this road is not in existence today, but traces probably remain.

Today, Lot 115 is in the hands of private owners, except for the northeast quarter, owned by the state of New York and part of the Forest Preserve. It is uninhabited woodland.

Henry and Hannah Dickson

The Dickson name has been variously reported as Dickson, Dixon, and Dickinson, but it would appear the correct name is Dickson.

Henry Dixon (sic), black, age forty, born in Maryland, and his wife Hannah, mulatto, age forty, born in Schoharie County, New York, appear on the 1855 North Elba census, living in a log home valued at $50. They stated they had lived in North Elba for six years. They are not on the 1850 census. The census taker must have missed them, because in a letter from Ruth Brown to her mother Mary Brown, dated October 31, 1849, Ruth mentions "Dickinson," proving that the Dicksons were indeed here as early as 1849. They came from Troy, New York, and apparently had no children.

Gerrit Smith granted Henry Dickson forty acres in Lot 83, Township 12. This was a lot in the wilderness just south of the later Peacock farm on Bear Cub Road.[50] While it was isolated and well off the beaten track, it is evident that was where the Dicksons actually settled. Their placement on the 1855 census indicates they were living in the Bear Cub Road sector. Further, Ruth Brown's letter states, "Mr. Epps & Dickinson have moved into the woods & living in their new houses." This implies that Epps and Dickson may have been living near each other, and Lyman Epps' grant was also in this same Bear Cub Road sector.

The Dicksons must have been an industrious and hard-working pair. They had immediately built a log cabin in 1849. There is evidence that in the space of a few years they had carved a productive farm out of the wilderness. When John Brown Jr. visited his father at North Elba in 1858, he wrote to his brother:

> I am fully convinced that North Elba is the country for us to come to....I can get Mr. Dickson's place (forty acres, with five or

50 Now called Bear Cub Lane, County Route 26.

> six improved, or at least cleared), with a good log house, a frame barn, twenty by thirty feet, for $150.

An anecdote from Salmon Brown's recollections of North Elba in the 1850s, published in the *Adirondack Daily Enterprise* in May 1913, provides a rare glimpse of Mrs. Dickson. Salmon recalled the community meetings held at the schoolhouse. Everyone brought food for themselves and their animals. Picnic-style, they ate dinner out-of-doors and in rigs. Said Salmon:

> I recollect an old colored lady by the name of Dickson brought a big rutabaga as large as a baby's head in a sack for her dinner. She took it out and laid it on the desk with the air of a queen. She was well known for her economical habits.

There is one cryptic reference to Mrs. Dickson in a letter from John Brown, then living in Akron, Ohio, to Henry and Ruth Thompson at North Elba, dated August 10, 1852:

> We are quite obliged to our friend Mrs. Dickson for remembering us, are glad she is with you, and hope you will do a little towards making her home with you happy on our account, as we very much respect her, and feel quite an interest in her welfare. (F.B. Sanborn, *Life And Letters Of John Brown,* 1885)

It appears that, for some reason, Mrs. Dickson was living with the Thompsons for a period of time. Her husband was still alive, but perhaps was away for a while.

In spite of obvious success, the Dicksons left North Elba. The year of their departure is not known. They do not appear on censuses after 1855.

Lot 83 was eventually acquired by the State of New York through tax sale and is now part of the state Forest Preserve. There is no local anecdotal tradition of any settlement on this isolated lot, and there is no remaining visual evidence.

Isaac and Jane Craig

Isaac and Jane Craig came to North Elba in 1853. The 1855 census gives his age as fifty-four and hers as forty-nine, and lists no children. They are labeled "black," and Craig's profession is given as "shoemaker," but he must surely have been a farmer also. He was born in New Jersey, and Mrs. Craig in Saratoga, New York. They came to North Elba from Jefferson County, New York.

Gerrit Smith granted to Isaac Craig forty acres in the northwest quarter of Lot 43, Township 12. This is wilderness land well off the Averyville Road,[51] east of Alford Pond, and today part of the state Forest Preserve. There is no evidence it was settled at any time, and it is unlikely Craig ever lived there.

Instead, there is sufficient evidence that the Craigs actually settled on Lot 44, Township 12, off Averyville Road, although no deed is recorded in their name. This lot is today predominately occupied by the Placid Meadows development of Phil Thayer. It is just to the west of Lot 51, once occupied by black colonist Silas Frazier and presently the site of the Dr. George Hart farm and the remainder of the Placid Meadows development. The 1860 census shows the Craigs living along Averyville Road next to the Fraziers. Further, Edwin Cotter of John Brown Farm has an old Burr map of Essex County containing notes on the margin (supposedly in the handwriting of William Appo), one of which places Craig in Lot 44. Also, the outlet of Alford Pond, a main tributary of Ray Brook, which runs across Lot 44, was called Craig Brook a hundred years ago, and is still known as Craig Brook.

An article in the *Elizabethtown Post* of October 31, 1907, entitled "Averyville, So-Called," describing the old farms in Averyville, had some interesting comments on Craig:

> The farms of Messrs. Wood and Ola Alford include a portion or all of Round or White Lily Pond [Alford Pond], which has an area of twenty acres and empties into Ray Brook through Craig Brook. Craig Brook takes its name from one of the Negro families of that name, located near it, by Gerrit Smith's colonization scheme. The last time the present writer passed the place he picked and ate apples from trees planted by the Craigs and found the mold and sideboards of a plow. The apples were not Baldwins or Spys—just apples.

---

51 Now Averyville Lane, County Route 23.

Phil Thayer reports that in the clearing and development of Placid Meadows, many large piles of stones were found, indicating that the land had once been farmed. Whether these date from the Craig years or possible later farming operations is unknown.

In 1855, the Craigs had a log cabin valued at $25.

It seems that Isaac Craig died between 1855 and 1860, because he is missing from censuses after 1855. Mrs. Craig is still listed in 1860 and 1865, but as housekeeper in the household of Charles Willard, a white man in his sixties. Willard was probably the same man as the Charles Willard who appeared on the 1850 North Elba census with a wife Charlotte. He is not on the 1855 census. Apparently, his wife died before 1860 and he was then a widower. Two totally unconnected children were also in the Willard household in 1860: David Goodrich, seven, and Laura A. Goodrich, nine. They are not listed in 1865.

Evidently, Mrs. Craig had wished to remain in North Elba and had found employment. It appears that Willard took over Mrs. Craig's farm, as censuses position him next to the Fraziers, and in 1865 he was living in a log cabin valued at $25.

Nothing further is known of Mrs. Craig.

Silas and Jane Frazier

Silas Frazier, born in Ulster County, New York, and his wife Jane, born in Orange County, New York, joined the black colony at North Elba late, in 1854. Both were born about 1820. The 1855 census lists them as mulatto. There were no children in the household.

Frazier was not a Gerrit Smith grantee. He bought the northwest quarter of Great Lot 196, Township 11, thirty acres (this was a 120-acre lot), from a Peter Smith of Newburgh, New York, who was probably the original Gerrit Smith grantee. Lot 196 was an inaccessible lot deep in the wilderness just west of the present Whiteface Inn road. There is no evidence that the Fraziers ever attempted to develop the lot or live on it.

Instead, there is ample evidence that the Fraziers settled on Great Lot 51, Township 12, on Averyville Road,[52] although it is believed no deed to the property was recorded in their name. The Dr. George Hart farm and the Placid Meadows development of Phil Thayer occupy Lot 51 today.

52 Now Averyville Lane, County Route 23.

Old censuses show the Fraziers living in Averyville. Further, the Burr map of Essex County that Edwin Cotter of John Brown Farm has, with the supposed notations on the margin in the handwriting of William Appo, places Frazier in Lot 51.

Further, part of Alford Pond lies in Lot 51, and on the 1876 O.W. Gray map of North Elba it is called "Frazier Pond." (Gray erroneously places the pond in adjoining Lot 43.) The name Frazier Pond probably endured until the Alfords established farms in this area in the 1880s.

Frazier could not have farmed the whole of Lot 51. It is known that Martin Lyon occupied part of it for a number of years, from the time of his arrival in North Elba in 1847. It has been said that Lyons' log cabin was west of the present Hart farmhouse.

The 1855 census reported that, in 1854, Silas Frazier had raised seventy bushels of oats, two tons of hay, and six bushels of wheat, no small accomplishment for only one year of residence. By 1855, he had also built a log cabin, valued at $50. He may have erected a frame house thereafter, as the real estate was valued at $400 in 1860, and the 1865 census shows a frame house on the property, then occupied by Robert Ross, valued at $400. The personal estate of the Fraziers was also valued at $400 in 1860.

In his recollections of North Elba published in the *Adirondack Daily Enterprise* in March 1914, Salmon Brown had some interesting things to say about Silas Frazier.

According to Salmon Brown, Frazier was a mixture of white, black, and Spanish, and he had quite a reputation as a fighting man. At that time, in the Town of Keene, there lived a rival fighting man by the name of Riley Blood, a staunch Democrat and a hotelkeeper. Blood had no use for colored persons. When Silas Frazier appeared at one of his turkey shoots down in Keene, Blood made insulting remarks to him and then attacked him. Frazier, however, emerged as winner of the fisticuffs.

It is not known when or why the Fraziers left North Elba after 1860. They do not appear on the 1865 census or thereafter.

A Jane Frazier of Westport, New York, appears on a list of pensions granted for Civil War service as of September 1879, she being the widow of a Civil War veteran. This may be the same person as Jane Frazier of North Elba, and Silas Frazier may have served in the Civil War.

William Carasaw

According to the deed record, Gerrit Smith granted William "Carason" the southwest quarter, Subdivision 1, of Lot 23, Township 12, forty acres. All other documents—letters, censuses, and the Civil War roster—clearly show the name as "Carasaw" or "Carrasaw." The recording clerk could easily have mistaken "aw" as "on." The weight of evidence favors the name of Carasaw.

William Carasaw came to North Elba from Troy, New York. He was born in Watervliet, New York, in 1820. With him was his wife Eliza, age twenty-one, born in Montgomery County, New York. Three sons were born in North Elba: John in 1853, James in 1855, and Frederick in 1857.

The 1855 census indicates the Carasaws arrived here in 1850, but a letter from Ruth Brown to her mother (who was away from home) indicates they were here in 1849. The letter, from North Elba and dated October 31, 1849, states, "I with Mrs. Carasow have got the girls' dresses made good."

Lot 23 was deep wilderness land, far to the west of present Adirondack Lodge Road and far to the south of present Bear Cub Road.[53] It is still wilderness today and part of the state Forest Preserve. Access would have been most difficult, and it is highly unlikely that Carasaw made any attempt to clear his lot and settle on it.

It is useless to conjecture where Carasaw actually did live. In three separate censuses, he is positioned in three entirely different locales in North Elba and among three entirely different sets of neighbors. Perhaps he moved around. In 1855, he had a log house valued at $40. The 1860 census credited him with no real estate, perhaps an error on the part of the census taker since his household is shown as an independent one. In 1865, he had a log house valued at $50. This last census suggests he was living in the Bear Cub Road area.

The 1855 census valued his farm at $100. It was not particularly productive. He grew one hundred bushels of potatoes and produced one hundred pounds of butter. However, he was the only black farmer to make maple sugar, producing a hefty four hundred pounds in the spring of 1855. He owned six head of cattle, two horses, and two pigs.

In August 1864, Carasaw enlisted for service in the Civil War. He was mustered in on September 1, 1864, and served for one year as a private in

53 Now called Bear Cub Lane, County Route 26.

Company A of the 26th Regiment of Negro Troops. He was honorably discharged on August 28, 1865.

The Carasaws left North Elba after the Civil War, having lived here for at least sixteen years.

Leonard Worts

This name has been spelled in various ways on a number of documents—Wort, Worts, Wurts, and Wortz. It appears as Worts on the original Smith grant and on the 1866 assessment roll, and that is assumed to be the correct spelling.

Leonard Worts, born in Ulster County, was living in the Town of Keene in 1850. Early in 1855, he moved into North Elba with his wife Deanna, also born in Ulster County, and an adopted son Charles, sixteen, born in Dutchess County. Leonard and Deanna's ages vary sharply on three censuses and are thus difficult to determine, but it appears they were over fifty when they arrived here. Deanna's true name is also in question. It appears as Deanna, Dianah, and what appears to be Dreamer.

It seems evident the Wortses moved in with the Josiah Hasbrook family when they arrived. The two families may have been related. By 1860, most of the Hasbrook family had departed from North Elba, but we find that three of the children had remained. Harriet Hasbrook, sixteen, and Josiah Hasbrook Jr., eighteen, were living with Leonard Worts that year. This also points to a relationship.

The 1860 census labels Leonard Worts and his wife as illiterate. They had a personal estate of $200 and real estate valued at $50. The adopted son was then gone from the household.

Gerrit Smith had granted Leonard Worts the northwest quarter of Great Lot 253, Township 11, forty acres. Like a number of the black colonists, Worts never lived on the land he was given. He could not possibly have settled on Lot 253 in any event. It is far up on the west shore of Placid Lake and was then completely inaccessible.

Worts may have continued to live on the Hasbrook property for a short time after the senior members of the family departed, but he was clearly living elsewhere by 1860.

Former North Elba Historian Ida Lockwood told this compiler that Leonard Worts "lived out at the Country Club" (Craig Wood Golf

Course). This approaches the truth. The 1866 assessment roll shows Worts in possession of the northwest quarter of Lot 115, Township 12. While it does not embrace the Craig Wood Golf Course, Lot 115 does adjoin it directly on the north.

As readers may remember from the story of Lewis Pierce, Lot 115 is much closer to River Road (Riverside Drive) than to Route 73 (Cascade Road), and access to it was most probably gained from River Road. Moreover, Worts' placement on both the 1860 and 1865 censuses shows him surrounded by River Road inhabitants, indicating the census taker's path of travel.

Gerrit Smith had granted to Lewis Pierce the forty-acre lot on the northwest quarter of Lot 115, and Pierce had lived on and successfully farmed it for a number of years. It can be fairly assumed, then, that after Pierce's departure from North Elba some time between 1855 and 1860, Worts took over his farm. Whether this was by arrangement with Pierce or an opportunistic move on Worts' own initiative is unknown. A search of records at Elizabethtown might provide an answer.

Lot 115 is today in the hands of private owners, except for the northeast quarter, which is owned by the State of New York and part of the Forest Preserve. It is uninhabited woodland.

It is interesting to note that the 1866 assessment roll also shows Worts in possession of the south half of Lot 253—eighty acres—up on Lake Placid. This must have been totally in error because Worts had originally been given only forty acres of Lot 253, and that was the northwest quarter. It is highly unlikely that he ever paid taxes on this lot. The 1866 assessment roll is, in any event, an enigma. In many cases, it does not reflect true ownership of land and should not be relied on for accurate information.

In spite of the fact that the Wortses remained in North Elba longer than most of the black families, very little has been learned about them. It is not known when they left town. The 1865 census lists them still living in a log house valued at $50. It gives his age as sixty and hers as sixty-two.

Samuel Drummond

Gerrit Smith gave Samuel Drummond the northeast quarter of Lot 135, Township 11, forty acres, in Ray Brook.

On his trip to North Elba in September 1849, J. McCune Smith found Drummond on the lot and reported to Gerrit Smith in his letter of

February 6, 1850, "Mr. Drummond also, whose wife and children are in Township 11 on a clearing of four or five acres, is miserably idling his time here, if not criminally."

Drummond does not appear on the 1850 census. He apparently threw in the towel and left shortly after J. McCune Smith's visit. His stay in North Elba was most probably less than a year.

Samuel F. Hall

[Compiled by Edmund Cotter[54]]

Smith gave Samuel Hall the southwest quarter of Lot 114, Township 11, forty acres. Hall was from New York City.

On August 28, 1849, Owen Brown wrote to his brother John Jr., "Have raised a fine log house for Pappa Hall" (it was hard to read but it looked liked "Pappa").

In a letter John Brown addressed to "Dear Children" (Ruth and Henry), dated October 6, 1851, found in F.B. Sanborn, page 108, he wrote:

> Wish you to say to Mr. Epps that if Mr. Hall does not soon take care of the boards that are falling down about the house he built, I wish he and Mr. Dickson would go and take them away, as I paid for them, and am the rightful owner of them. I wish to have them confine themselves to those of the roof and gable-ends. I mean to let Hall have them if he will occupy the building, or have anyone do it on his account; but I do not mean to have him let them lie there year after year and rot, and do no one any good. I wish this to be attended to before the snow covers them up again.

John Brown's remark, "let them lie there year after year," indicates that the boards (and Hall) were there the winter before the letter—that is, the winter of 1850—and maybe also in 1849.

Owen Brown's letter referred to Hall's "fine log house." Perhaps Hall built a frame house later.

---

54 Cotter was curator for many years at the John Brown Farm State Historic Site, just outside Lake Placid. He was considered the foremost expert of his day on the life of John Brown. Cotter and MacKenzie were the best of friends.

[Note by Mary MacKenzie:] Lot 114, Township 11, is in the Ray Brook area, a long way off the Old Military Road, and certainly in a deep wilderness area. It seems doubtful Hall would have built there. Perhaps he was squatting on another lot, as so many of the grantees did.

Curiously, Hall never appears on a North Elba census. Did the census taker miss him?

Thomas Elliott

The name of Thomas Elliott surfaces in an intriguing tale of John Brown and a Bible.

In July 1940, Allen H. Davis, a Lake Placid native, approached D.C. Ball and offered to sell him a Bible with an interesting history. D.C. Ball was president of Oakite Products and had a summer home, "Far Horizons," on Cascade Road for some years.

The story that Davis told Mr. Ball seemed straightforward enough. The Bible, said Davis, had once belonged to John Brown himself. Brown had given it to Thomas Elliott, an escaped slave from Virginia who had found his way to North Elba and its black colony in the early 1850s and was then working on the John Brown farm. Elliott soon went to work for "Ben Demmon" on the Intervales Farm on River Road,[55] and stayed there until Mr. Demmon's death in the 1870s, when he departed for New Jersey. When Elliott left North Elba, he gave the Bible to Allen Davis's mother, Flora Brown Davis. It came into Allen's possession when his mother died in 1932.

His mother, Davis added, thought a lot of Thomas Elliott, for he had been very good to her when she was a child living on the Demmon farm. Davis further mentioned that he was sixteen when Thomas Elliott, then a white-haired man of perhaps eighty-five, paid a visit to his old home in North Elba in 1902.

Mr. Ball evidently bought Allen Davis's story because, on July 17, 1940, he bought the "John Brown" Bible as well, for the sum of $20.

There are a few problems with this story.

Aside from the problems, the Davis-Demmon-Elliott connection should be explained, as Davis did not fully allude to it in his written statement to D.C. Ball. Alpheus Demmon, who came to North Elba

55 Now called Riverside Drive.

in 1855, was the actual owner of Intervales, although his son Ben did help him run the farm. Alpheus first had a farm near the present Lake Placid Club skeet field. He did not acquire Intervales until 1867. Alpheus Demmon was the great-grandfather of Allen Davis and the grandfather of Allen's mother, Flora Brown Davis, to whom Elliott gave the Bible.

Neither Alpheus nor his son Ben died in the late 1870s, as Allen Davis related. Ben moved to Lewis, New York, in 1881, took up a farm, and died there in 1888 at the age of fifty-two. Ben probably left North Elba because his father Alpheus sold Intervales in 1880. It could be surmised that 1880 was also the correct year that Elliott departed. Alpheus Demmon died at Lake Placid in 1890.

The most serious discrepancy is that Thomas Elliott does not appear on any North Elba censuses of the 1850s and 1860s. Was he concealed when the census taker came around because of his escaped-slave status? He does appear on the 1870 North Elba census as living with the Alpheus Demmon family—a farm laborer, mulatto, born in North Carolina. (Note the designation of "mulatto.")

Elliott's age is not clearly shown on the 1870 census. It appears to be twenty-four, but could possibly be twenty-eight. If twenty-four, he would have been just a child in the early 1850s, and it is unlikely he would then have been in North Elba as an escaped slave and have known John Brown. Even in 1859, the year of John Brown's death, he would have been only thirteen. If twenty-eight is correct, the chances improve that he knew and worked for John Brown, but it is still questionable.

Moreover, Davis says that when Elliott visited his old home of North Elba in 1902, he was a white-haired man of "perhaps eighty-five." He would, of course have been no more than sixty, and perhaps only fifty-six, but to a boy of Davis's age then, sixteen, he might have seemed very old.

Many details of this story must be viewed with suspicion. It is significant that Elliott does not appear on the censuses of the John Brown years and is never mentioned in Brown family correspondence as other family helpers were.

Was Thomas Elliott a member of the early black colony of North Elba? Or did he actually arrive here after the Civil War? Did the Bible sold to D.C. Ball once belong to John Brown? Or did D.C. Ball buy a pig in a poke? And if the Bible story was a hoax, who was responsible for it—Elliott or Davis?

Mrs. Wait

Richard Henry Dana Jr. in his *Journal* [*The Journal of Richard Henry Dana Jr.,* edited by Robert F. Lucid (Cambridge, Mass.: The Belknap Press of Harvard University Press, 1968)] reports his trip to North Elba in 1849 and his visits at the John Brown house. He mentions a "Mrs. Wait" working in the Brown household:

> Miss Ruth was very kind, & with the aid of the negro woman, whom all the family called Mrs. Wait, got us an excellent breakfast.

No Wait appears on the 1850s censuses. Her stay must have been short.

Mrs. Reed

Ruth Brown Thompson, in F.B. Sanborn, said:

> As soon as father could go around among the colored families, he employed Mrs. Reed, a widow, to be our housekeeper and cook, for mother was very much out of health.

In her letter to Mary Brown of October 31, 1849, Ruth Brown said:

> Mrs. Read has been quite active about getting a barrell of soap made this some time. She has had hard work too get ashes enough but I think she will finally succeed.

No Reed or Read appears on the 1850s censuses. Her stay must have been of very short duration.

Jeremiah Miles

Jeremiah Miles was not a Smith grantee. He came to North Elba after the Civil War and was living with Josiah Hasbrook Jr. in 1870. Perhaps Hasbrook, who fought in the Civil War, brought him up from the South when he returned to North Elba at war's end.

John and Margaret Vinson

Little has been learned about John and Margaret Vinson, two other black people listed on the 1855 census. He was twenty-three, born in Rensselaer County, and she twenty-two, born in Connecticut. The Vinsons were not Smith grantees. They had arrived in North Elba from Troy, New York, only one month before the census was taken, and had no house. It can be assumed they moved in with the Dicksons, as they are listed directly following the Dicksons on the census. They do not appear on censuses again, and may have left North Elba with the Dicksons. Perhaps there was some relationship.

William Thomas

Gerrit Smith gave William Thomas forty acres in the southeast quarter of Lot 141, Township 12. This lot is far to the east of River Road.[56] Apparently, Thomas came to North Elba to view his property and, not being able to find it, had a survey made by surveyor Wait J. Lewis. Lewis reported to him, "This is a mountain lot and it is not fit for cultivation. The lot is worthless except for its timber, which may in time be valuable. I think the lot is hardly worth paying taxes on it."

Wait's survey and assessment of the lot were correct. In Stephen Thorn's notes for his survey of 1804 appears the following: "Lot 141, Township 12. Mountainous—timber, mostly evergreen." This lot is in the area of the Sentinel Range.

While Thomas apparently visited North Elba, he never settled here. The survey was made in May 1849.

Walter Hawkins

In a letter to Edwin Cotter of John Brown Farm, dated February l, 1966, Boyd Stutler, a John Brown authority, said:

> Walter Hawkins, a young lad, spent considerable time under John Brown's roof. He went on to Canada, became a minister and later a Bishop of the British African Methodist Church. I believe he stayed with the Browns while they were living in the Cone Flanders house.

---

56 Now called Riverside Drive.

No other mention of Walter Hawkins has been found. He does not appear on a North Elba census. The above Hawkins information is probably in the Boyd Stutler collection in the archives of the Ohio Historical Society. It appears that Hawkins was another one of the transient blacks who briefly worked for John Brown.

TWENTY-FOUR
They Called it Timbucto?

In November 1997, Mary MacKenzie was asked to review an article on John Brown and the North Elba black colony that was scheduled for publication in the Winter 1998 issue of Orion *magazine, a bimonthly publication of the Orion Society, Great Barrington, Massachusetts. The article, "They Called It Timbuctoo," was written by Katherine Butler Jones. The following is an excerpt from the critique Mary sent back to* Orion.

Now is the time to comment on the name Timbucto. There is not a shred of evidence that the blacks gave that name to their colony. The evidence is strong that it was a name conjured up by John Brown. The first appearance of the name Timbucto is in John's 1848 letters to Willis A. Hodges, the head man of Gerrit Smith's other black colony in the Adirondacks, at Loon Lake, about thirty miles from here. These letters were reprinted in Villard's history and in the *New York Evening Post* of December 21, 1859—and, as far as I know, can be found nowhere else.[57] The year 1848 was also the last time the name appeared for close to a century. In that intervening time period, Timbucto does not show up anywhere—not in any of the rest of the Brown family correspondence, not in the reminiscences and letters of either black or white people, not in any newspaper stories, not in any accounts of any kind about the black colony at North Elba.

As far as the historical record is concerned, a place called Timbucto did not exist.

The name does not surface again until Alfred Donaldson's *History of the Adirondacks* (Century Publishing Co., 1921, reprinted Purple Mountain Press, 1996), and Donaldson's only possible sources were the Brown-Hodges letters in Villard. It is from the Donaldson account, and the Donaldson account

57 MacKenzie's handwritten footnote: "A few original letters are in private hands."

alone, that people have plucked the name of Timbucto and accepted it as a legitimate and widely used name for the black colony. It is very obvious, and my firm belief from all the research I have done, that the black people—and also the white people—of North Elba never knew of this name, never used it, and that it was only a term used by John Brown in his correspondence with Hodges, simply to distinguish it from the Loon Lake colony, known as Blacksville. (This latter colony was in existence but a short time because the soil there was infertile and unfit for farming.) There is absolutely no evidence anywhere that anybody but John Brown, and perhaps his family, used the name Timbucto. Of course, it never appeared on maps or in public records.

In spite of all the above, I have come to the conclusion that the name Timbucto is much too charming a myth to annihilate, and to perpetuate the myth is no great sin. After all, we can always say that one person did use the name. Besides, the myth has become so embedded in the public domain that it would be almost impossible to dislodge it. I have promised myself that I will keep this secret and never tell anyone the truth of the matter, and I am sure Jones would not want to divulge it.

I only ask that John Brown be given credit for the name Timbucto, and not the blacks themselves.

And I insist that the sentence, "The red flag hoisted over their lands with the name Timbucto," be eliminated posthaste. Jones borrowed this "red flag" from an outrageous and mean yarn in Donaldson about the blacks living in a sordid shantytown with that stupid flag waving over it. This tale is incredibly erroneous and comes directly from Donaldson's well-known fertile imagination. With this preposterous tale, Donaldson did a terrible disservice to those good and intelligent blacks and their valiant efforts to carve out a life in North Elba on their own individual plots. Of course, he trivialized the entire story of the black experience at North Elba.

PART TWO

The Golden Age of Hotels

TWENTY-FIVE

Joseph Nash: Jovial Father of the Village of Lake Placid

August 16, 1979

It was a fresh June morning in 1839, but the two barefoot boys trudging the Old Military Road were tired and hungry. Three days out of Willsboro, on Lake Champlain, they had already walked close to fifty miles—and, besides, they were driving a herd of young cows.

They were bound for the Plains of Abraham, on the remote west line of Essex County. Passing Elizabethtown and Keene, they had now crossed the shadow of Pitchoff Mountain beyond Keene's Alstead Hill.

Joseph, thirteen, and Timothy, fifteen, were the sons of Remembrance Nash, a farmer and shoemaker and a direct descendant of Thomas Nash, who had come to America in 1637. Their mother, Nancy Kellogg Nash, had died in 1833. Born in Duxbury, Vermont, they had moved to Willsboro with their father and three sisters a few years back. But now Remembrance had purchased some land from Roswell Thompson on the Plains of Abraham, and the family would shortly settle there. Meanwhile, the brothers were bringing over some of the cattle.

Abruptly they emerged from the great woods into brilliant sunlight. They had reached the first cabin clearing on the Plains, that of Oliver Bartlett. No men were about, but Mrs. Bartlett gave them a hearty midday meal and directions to the Thompson farm.

Less than twelve families were then living on the Plains. Roswell Thompson had a string of log houses, sheds, cooper, and blacksmith shops.

The boys stayed overnight at the Thompson farm and then began the journey back to Willsboro. Taking a shorter route, an abandoned road winding over the Sentinel Range, they reached Willsboro at nine o'clock that night. They had walked forty-two mountain miles in thirteen hours.

That was how Joseph Vernon Nash, who was to mold Lake Placid's history as few others would, first saw what would become the Town of North Elba.

Seven months later, on a brisk day in January 1840, the Nash family moved to the Plains, lock, stock, and barrel.

Joe Nash was an enterprising lad. Legally bound to his father's service until he was twenty-one, he still found time for outside jobs. At twenty, he bought from his father the balance of his minority. Over the next three years, he worked for his brother Tim at $11 a month, saving $100 the first year alone.

Joseph Nash, Landowner

Soon, Joe Nash became a cattle drover, moving herds as far as Albany. As he plied the mountain roads in the dust of the drives, he dreamed of the farm he would have on the land he wanted to buy, back in North Elba. It was Gerrit Smith land, 160 acres, second to none in the township, and it was going for $240. Miles from settled land, shelving up from the west shore of Bennet's Pond (Mirror Lake), fronting Whiteface and the Sentinels, it was clothed in virgin forest and deep, dark soil. It covered all of Main Street, as it now exists, to the high school, all of Grand View Hill and much of Signal Hill. Except for pasturelands that Nash cleared, this entire tract was then true wilderness, with thick growths of tamarack, balsam, pine, and maple.

Joe bought it in 1850, built a three-room, flat-roofed cabin on the lakeshore, and began felling timber. After he cleared the land, he planted crops and brought in sheep and cattle. Nash maintained a maple sugar grove where the Hillcrest Avenue village park is now located. His farmhouse and barns stood on what is now the northwest corner of Main Street/Mirror Lake Drive and Saranac Avenue. Of course, Saranac Avenue did not exist then. A narrow wagon track ran along the thickly wooded shores of Mirror Lake southward through a great forest to the old coach road (Old Military Road), which was the only link with the outside world.

On October 15, 1851, he married Harriet Brewster, a schoolma'am. She was the daughter of Thomas Brewster, who had come to North Elba from Jay in 1841 on the great new tide of settlement.

Harriet Brewster was an admirable woman, dowered with true grit. Good-humored, sturdy, and spirited, she was bred to the rough Adirondack frontier life and hunted and fished like a man. She was to prove the ideal helpmate and companion to Joe Nash.

Joe had but one conveyance, a heavy wagon hauled by an ox team, and his cabin was not much to offer a bride. He had only a bed, a stove, a chest, chairs carved from barrels, and a rough plank table. Harriet did not mind. Still, it was a wild and lonely place, with the nearest neighbor miles away. The moon rose over Cobble Hill to the sound of loons laughing.

Deer, Canada geese, and great blue herons visited the lake. In the winter, wolves howled up on Placid.

Panthers still roamed the woods. One night the couple was jolted awake by cries from the sheep yard. Joe jumped up, grabbed his loaded rifle and, rushing out, saw a panther jump the fence with one of his sheep. The next day he gathered a posse. The men tracked the big, tawny cat to the spot where the Holiday Inn[1] now stands. Finding the remains of the sheep, cunningly concealed with leaves, they set a trap.

They caught the panther, measuring eight feet, nine inches from its nose to the tip of its tail—but the $10 the catskin brought looked even bigger.

Joe now built a small frame house above his cabin on the land where the Lakeside Motor Inn (Hilton annex) now stands. Painted barn-red, it was ever after known as "Nash's Red House." An unusual feature was a double-decker backhouse, accessible from ground level and from the second floor as well via a boardwalk extending from the bedroom.

It was not lonely now. Joe's father Remembrance had moved in with them. The first of five children arrived in 1854, and Harriet's brother, Benjamin Brewster, bought the Great Lot just to the north and built a log cabin. Three daughters grew to maturity and married: Harriet Green, Carrie Lamb Ware—both now deceased—and Fannie Williams, now in her ninety-third year.[2] The Williams and Lamb families now represent the local descendants.

About 1859, Joe purchased from Luther Lyman another 160 acres adjoining his property on the south for $240. An outlay of $480 had netted him 320 acres, a tract worth millions today.

Meanwhile, North Elba was astir with strange activity. Outlanders began to appear on the farm roads. A man and woman came all the way from Boston on horseback. Painters, writers, mountain climbers, sportsmen—all were trekking in for a look at the unspoiled wonders of the wild. Travelers seeking a bed began to pound on the Red House door.

Joseph Nash, Innkeeper

If no one else knew which way the wind was blowing, Joe Nash did. He put an addition on his house, and by 1855 had turned innkeeper for

---

1 As this chapter is being edited, the Lake Placid Resort Holiday Inn has just switched its franchise, becoming the Crowne Plaza.

2 Written in 1979.

the summer tourist trade. Business was up and doing. Harriet set a good table, and even Adirondackers drove from fifteen to twenty miles away of a Sunday to down one of her broiled trout and venison dinners.

Overnight, Nash's became the place to stay. It was difficult to reach and not much to look at, with its motley assortment of barns and outhouses. For all that, the house breathed hospitality, and the view was unsurpassed. Hordes of the talented, well-known, and well-heeled passed through its doors. One was Charles Loring Brace, author, social worker, and philanthropist. Brace seems to have been the first to conceive the idea of an Adirondack Park. He wrote one of the earliest editorials about the Adirondacks, appearing in the *New York Times* of August 9, 1864.

Other patrons of note were the distinguished painter of the Adirondacks, Sanford Gifford, and Matilda Fielding, whose name was immortalized in the "Hitch-Up Matilda" floating log walkways at Avalanche Pass.

The heady success of the Nash hostelry was not hard to fathom. The key was the personality of the owners. No account of the Red House was valid without a close look at those two warm and lovable characters, universally known as "Uncle Joe" and "Aunt Harriet." Alfred Donaldson has told it well:

> Everybody knew and liked Uncle Joe. He was a short, stout, well-rounded little man of kindly heart and jovial disposition. He wore a Horace Greeley beard on the outskirts of a broad mouth, and his hair was slanted upward, giving him a look of constant surprise. Two clear and deep-set eyes met yours squarely, and usually twinkled with humor, for Uncle Joe liked to hear or tell a funny story.
>
> Like her husband, Aunt Harriet was chatty, jovial, kind-hearted and open-handed.

In its long career, Nash's received only one unkind notice. According to an 1872 guest, A.D. Mayo, the house was "beastly," his dinner was "something fearful to partake of," and his breakfast "execrable." Mayo did, however, leave to posterity a brief glimpse of the Red House attesting to its enormous popularity.

> We found Nash crowded to suffocation, trying in a blind way to cipher out the problem of accommodating the hundreds of visitors

> in a house where not 25 can be comfortably stowed. I was promoted to the only vacancy—a sort of anteroom to a chamber beyond, where a whole family of children were piled away in four beds.

Impressed with the success of his brother-in-law, Benjamin Brewster built a small hotel on his own land in 1871, later known as Lake Placid Inn. Joe followed suit in 1876, raising another hotel, the Excelsior House, on the ridge above the Red House. Rented out the next year, he sold it to John Stevens in 1878. The Excelsior House burned to the ground on Christmas Eve 1885 and was replaced by the famous old Stevens House.

Joe, the story goes, once offered to sell his whole tract to a Mr. Jerome, a Connecticut clockmaker, for $2,500. Jerome protested. It was too cheap for all those beautiful views. "I'll heave in all the views, too," Joe said.

Jerome did not buy, but plenty of others wanted a piece of the pie. Always quick to interpret the signs of the times, Joe saw clearly what his holdings were meant to hold. He sold plots upon which were later erected the Grand View Hotel, the Allen House, and the great Mirror Lake House. To J.Q. McLenathan, Nash sold a house that became the Homestead Inn. Nash sold a lot to Frank Stickney, who built the first store on Main Street. To his daughter Carrie, Nash gave a lot upon which she built and ran the Lakeside Inn.[3] He also gave lots to others to induce them to build.

He was farmer Nash no more. He was, over the years, town supervisor, commissioner of highways, and justice of the peace. He had choice land to sell, a thriving lumber business, and often functioned as the village bank.

On May 20, 1884, Joe rose early, went to his piazza, and took his usual morning walk. He knew his time was short; his heart had troubled him for some months. At 8:30, Frank Stickney went to Joe's room and found him tipped out of his chair.

Joe Nash, founder of Lake Placid village, was gone. He had lived fifty-eight years, long enough to witness the birth of the great resort he had foreseen, on land that he had once tilled.

---

3 The original Lakeside Inn, built in 1883, was destroyed in a fire on Friday, March 13, 1959. It was replaced by the Lakeside Motor Inn, built in 1961, which became the Hilton Hotel's lakeside complex.

There never was such a funeral. Seventy teams came, thirty-nine stretching from the Red House to the little red Baptist church. Mourners spilled out of the doors.

Harriet lived another seventeen years, selling off the balance of the farm for homes and stores. She saw the farm incorporated as a village—not, as might have been, under the name of Nashville, but as Lake Placid, New York.

The Red House lived much longer. Although a section was torn down in 1895, it was not entirely demolished until 1961, to make way for the Lakeside Motor Inn.

One hundred forty years have passed [as of 1979] since Remembrance Nash came to North Elba. Many of his descendants still live here. The Nash line of Lake Placid is now into the seventh generation. For all we know, their ancestor, jovial Joe Nash, could be looking down right now at the site of his old farm, where a panther once jumped his sheep. He could be whistling in wonder, "How about all that? And what are those strange flags, snapping in the breeze off Nash's pond—those flags with the five interlocking rings?"[4]

TWENTY-SIX

School Days: Public Schools in North Elba and Lake Placid

November 2001

Schools and schooling have always had high priority in Lake Placid and its township of North Elba.

Our first settlers arrived in 1800, and by 1810, about forty families were in residence on the fringes of the present village. Even back in that pioneer setting, education was of prime importance. There was a log schoolhouse, and Fanny Dart was the first teacher.

That first colony was a success until 1817, when most of the inhabitants moved out, primarily due to the hardships and privations caused by the "year without a summer," 1816. For the next quarter of a century, no more than twelve families inhabited North Elba at any

4 Written as Lake Placid was preparing to host its second Winter Olympiad, in February 1980.

one time. Regardless, although there is no record of a formal school building, there is ample evidence that the few children somehow received an excellent education.

Little Red Schoolhouse

In the 1840s, a new tide of immigration came to North Elba, and by 1850, about forty families again resided here. A schoolhouse, ever afterwards to be known as "the little red schoolhouse," was built in 1848, as near as can be determined. One of the first teachers was Henry Markham, from nearby Wilmington, who went on to become governor of California (1891–95). "Little Red" originally stood on the northwest corner of present Sentinel Road[5] and Summer Street, just outside village limits. It was not abandoned as a school until 1915. In 1925, it was sold, and the building was moved one block over to Johnson Avenue. It is still in existence.[6] With a few modifications, it has served as a dwelling house from 1925 to the present, and is now the home of the James McCasland family.[7]

"Little Red" is surely one of our most historic buildings and should be preserved. It was much more than a seat of learning. For many years in the nineteenth century it was the only public building in town—not even a formal church existed—and, of necessity, it was used for almost all public gatherings, religious, social, and civic. When North Elba was set off from the Town of Keene as a separate township, in 1850, our first town election was held there. It served as the North Elba Town Hall for many years. Several denominations held church services here, and John Brown once gave a talk to the townspeople.

Averyville School

An early school that may have predated "Little Red" existed in the Averyville section. It stood on the site of the present (abandoned) old school building. In 1888, it was moved to Frank Alford's farm to be used as a shop, and the present school building was erected in its place. There is no evidence that the original school still stands anywhere in Averyville.

The 1888 Averyville School closed at the end of the term in June 1932. The last teacher was Winifred Ryan. The building sold at auction in 1936

5 Now called Newman Street.

6 Street address: 43 Johnson Avenue.

7 As of the fall of 2005, Little Red was the home of the James Wilson family.

to the Otis family, who used it for some years as a vacation cottage. For a long time it has been a part of the Malone family summer residence property. Sadly, it has long been neglected and now presents a very shabby and forlorn appearance. An effort should be made at some level to restore this historic little building. There have been no additions made to it, and the bell tower readily identifies it as an old rural schoolhouse.

North Elba School

In 1850, Gerrit Smith deeded to School District #4 a small triangle of land on which the present building rests, opposite the entrance to the Adirondack Lodge Road, on Route 73. The first schoolhouse there, built in the 1850s, was of logs and was in use for some years. In 1886, it was torn down, and the present frame building was constructed on the same site. An addition was made to the west end in 1920. The school closed in 1936. The last teacher was Katherine O'Rourke. In 1941, the district trustees voted to sell the building, and Walter and Gertrude (Torrance) Hare purchased it and turned it into a private home.[8] The building no longer resembles an old rural schoolhouse.

Cascade School

In 1879, the population in the Cascadeville section of North Elba had reached such proportions that a school was needed. On March 30, 1879, Sabrina Goff deeded half an acre of land to School District #6, and a schoolhouse was built that year near the entrance to the bob run road [Mount Van Hoevenberg]. Jacob Wood, grandfather of our local golf champion Craig Wood, was awarded a contract to build the school at a cost of $240. This school served the Cascadeville community until 1940, when it closed. Albert Goff then purchased the property and turned the school into a vacation home, and then a retirement home. The Goff family still owns it.[9] This little school is lovingly preserved and is unmistakably an old country schoolhouse, bell tower and all.[10]

---

8 As of the winter of 2004, the couple still lived there.

9 Albert Goff deeded it to his nephew, Harold Goff; Harold's widow, Marie Goff Senecal, still lived in it as of the winter of 2004. The homes of Harold and Marie's children surround the old schoolhouse.

10 Old photos of the Cascade School, however, do not show a belfry.

Ray Brook School

A one-room schoolhouse existed in the hamlet of Ray Brook in the very early days, and appears on the 1876 Gray township map of Essex County. This was not located on the site of the present school building, but on the road leading to the present federal prison off Route 86. It either burned down or was torn down. The present building on the Old Ray Brook Road, off Route 86, was built between 1903 and 1905 to accommodate the children of employees at the newly built Ray Brook State Hospital for tuberculosis patients, and it was in use for many years. After it closed as a school, Ray Brook residents used the building as a community center. Charles Damp now owns it and occupies it as a home. He has made many additions and improvements, but he has retained the bell tower so that the central core of the building still has the look of an old schoolhouse.

The Modern Schools

It can be seen that five of North Elba's original rural schools are still with us, covering a period of a century and a half of our history. Not many communities can make such a claim.

By 1870, 349 people were living in North Elba, but there still was no village of Lake Placid. Only two families, those of Joseph Nash and Benjamin Brewster, were living in what is now the incorporated village. Both families had large farms bordering on Mirror Lake. Their children attended the Little Red Schoolhouse, far out in the township.

In the 1870s, Nash began to sell off his land. Two hotels had been built, and a village was taking shape along a Main Street that had once been Nash's cow path. Growth was rapid. By 1890, the township population had tripled to 1,117. Most of the newcomers were living in what had become known [though not yet incorporated] as the village of Lake Placid, and stores, homes, churches, hotels, and even a library had made an appearance.

The growing number of children begrudged the long walk out to the Little Red Schoolhouse. In 1885, Mrs. May Stickney, the local librarian, started a private or "select" school in the second story of a large boathouse below Main Street on Mirror Lake, built and owned by Martin Brewster, and located on the site of the present "Bear Haus" building at 2427 Main Street. Students reached the second story of the boathouse from the street by a long suspended walkway that led directly to the schoolroom door.

Tuition was rather modest, but the pupils had to furnish their own desks and chairs. Mrs. Stickney excelled in penmanship and expected the same of her students.

By 1887, after Mrs. Stickney's school had been in operation for just two years, it had become very clear that only a public school could adequately serve the expanding population. Many community members advocated a two-room school, but only a one-room school was erected in 1888, directly across from the present town hall and below the modern high school on Main Street. The first teacher was William Barker, and children from age six to sixteen attended.

As had been predicted, the school soon ran out of space and had to be enlarged. The size of the addition is unknown but it seems to have been a modest one. The date is also in doubt, but it most probably was in 1895 when the school was admitted as a Union Free School. Also in 1895, the first board of education was organized, consisting of Lemuel S. Parkhurst, George T. Chellis, Charles N. Davis, Reuben W. Clifford, and Edwin Kennedy. The board appointed William Almon Andrews principal of the Union Free School in 1895, and he served until 1899. C.M. Strock is said to have served as principal in 1899 and 1900.

Predictably again, the first addition proved anything but adequate. Population continued to rise by leaps and bounds, and the village was incorporated in 1900. Finally, at the beginning of the new century, the residents seriously addressed the problem of the education of its children. Accounts vary, but the most reliable one reports that it was 1900 when a large, two-story wing was added on the north of the schoolhouse. It seems definite that it was 1902 when another large two-story wing was added on the south, and then a second story and a third-story balcony room was added above the one-story original central building.

The village now had a rather imposing wooden structure known as the Lake Placid High School. Total enrollment was 335. The New York State Department of Education chartered the school as a High School in 1901 through the Board of Regents. Reportedly, one or two students—including Ida Billings Lockwood—received high school diplomas in 1901, but there were no graduation exercises. Formal commencement exercises began in 1902, when there were three graduates: A. Burton Davis, Roseanna

Merrill, and Abe Feinberg. Graduation exercises were held for many years in the town hall, across Main Street, there being no auditorium in the school. William Almon Andrews apparently served as principal again from 1901 to 1903.

The years passed, the population of Lake Placid continued to rise, and the school again began to run out of space. As early as 1916, the school board began to tackle the matter of an entirely new school to replace the wooden building that had become, in so few years, inadequate and antiquated. On March 27, 1916, the people of Lake Placid approved a bond issue of $125,000 to build what the *Lake Placid News* called "the most elaborate, best equipped and highly priced public school in the Adirondack section."

There remained the matter of where the new school would be located. Seven different sites were proposed. For the next two years, community factions bickered and quarreled. It was finally agreed that the new school would he built on the rise of land a few hundred feet back of the old wooden school.

Nothing happened for several years, while other matters were ironed out and World War I intervened. During this period, for lack of space, the school conducted kindergarten in the Prunier block, just up the street, which once stood next to the Edge in Sports building.[11]

At last, in September 1922, Lake Placid's children moved into a splendid, three-story yellow brick building, complete with auditorium and gymnasium and all modern equipment and devices. There were 129 teachers and 653 students. H.G. Coons became principal of the new school when it opened in 1922 and remained through June 1931.

The Lake Placid Club purchased the old wooden school. They cut it into three sections, which were moved to the Club's Westgate area, down Parkside Drive, opposite the former village tennis courts. They converted these sections into living quarters for Club employees. In the form of these three sections, Lake Placid's old wooden high school stood, amazingly, for another seventy-six years. The three buildings were torn down in 1998, when they were close to a century old.

On July 2, 1930, the board of education adopted centralization, and the school became Lake Placid Central School.

---

11 2640 Main Street.

In too short a time, it happened again: The grand new school ran out of space. By the early 1930s, several rooms were rented in the North Elba Town Hall for second-grade classes, and the first grade was conducted in the basement of St. Eustace Episcopal Church.

It was generally agreed that an addition should be put on the present building, one sizeable enough to suffice far into the future. Architect H.O. Fullerton of Albany was hired. The addition went under construction in 1934 as a project of President Franklin D. Roosevelt's noted Works Progress Administration, utilizing local labor. The addition was completed and opened in 1936. David G. Allen was principal.

Probably few in the community had envisioned the result. Here was a building of which a community the size of Lake Placid could be very proud, indeed. The new central section was of Palladian neo-classical composition, and the new north wing exactly matched the old school—now the south wing—in all its fine details. The new school was declared a most successful example of additive transformation. It remains Lake Placid's most beautiful and distinguished public building.

The years passed and minor additions were put on the rear and north end. By the 1970s, the school had again become seriously overcrowded. It was clear that only a separate elementary school could begin to solve all the problems. Land was purchased on Old Military Road near its junction with Averyville Road,[12] and a fine elementary school was built in 1974. An addition was made in 1997.

In 1999, the community approved a major program of additions and renovations at both schools, valued at $11.5 million. This great project was completed in the fall of 2001. It includes not only the physical changes but all manner of innovations in technology, courses of study, and existing facilities to prepare Lake Placid's children for success in the twenty-first century.

Kindergarten and the first through fifth grades are housed in the elementary school on Old Military Road. The high school and the middle school of sixth, seventh, and eighth grades are in the large Central School building.

---

12 Now Averyville Lane, County Route 23.

TWENTY-SEVEN
Mountain View House and Robert G. Scott
1993

We have seen that, between 1870 and 1880, three pioneer hotels were built on the Nash and Brewster farms on the west shore of Mirror Lake, and a village to be called Lake Placid was in the making.

Out on the plains of North Elba—the storied Plains of Abraham—the resident farmers viewed all this upstart activity with mixed emotions, maybe a smidgen of envy, but definitely a goodly measure of disdain. After all, North Elba, beyond the outskirts of today's incorporated village, had by then been a settled community for some seventy-five years, and had been catering to travelers and tourists for close to half a century. Osgood's Inn on Old Military Road existed from at least 1833 to Civil War times, and Hanmer's hotel on the River Road[13] from 1869 until destroyed by fire in 1873. The North Elba House, or Lyon's stagecoach inn, on Old Military Road, had opened its door in 1864 and was still in business.

And then, of course, there was Robert Scott's old wayside inn on the road to Keene, newly enlarged and renamed the Mountain View House. Robert G. Scott was one of North Elba's great pioneers. Born in Stoddard, New Hampshire, on March 17, 1805, he had come as a small child to Keene, New York, shortly after 1810 with his father and mother William and Martha Scott. He helped to carry on the family farm when his father died in 1825, married Laura Farrington of Keene, and then struck out for himself. In 1840, he and Laura moved up to the future Town of North Elba, having purchased from Gerrit Smith a fine and fertile tract of 240 acres bordering the Keene highway—Lot 117 and the north half of 118, Township 12, Old Military Tract. Only nine other families were then living in what is now North Elba.

With true grit, the couple proceeded to hack a farm out of the wilderness. For a few years, they made do with a log cabin. By 1850 they had erected a substantial frame farmhouse directly on the highway, at the base of a little mountain that came to be known as Scott's Cobble, about a half-mile east of today's golf club road. In time, Scott's became probably the finest of North Elba's grand old pioneer farms. Crops were grown

13 Now called Riverside Drive.

there in abundance, and the land supported oxen, horses, cattle, sheep, hogs, chickens, and even a flock of turkeys.

By all accounts, Rob Scott presented a rather unusual appearance, especially in old age. Although wiry and strong as an ox, he was small in stature. He has been variously described as shaggy as a wild bear, dark of skin, and with a face "like a baked apple wrought into human mold." Under that unprepossessing exterior was a heart of gold. Everybody loved Rob Scott. A more giving and caring man never lived, and Laura was cut out of the same cloth. The Scotts had no children of their own, but the house never lacked the prattle and laughter of young people. It was reportedly the scene of more wholesome merriment during pioneer days than any other place in North Elba. In 1848, the Scotts adopted Laura's nephew, three-year-old Jacob Wood, upon his father's death, and brought him up as the son of the house, although he retained the name of Wood. They also adopted Martha Scott, daughter of Rob's brother Samuel. Martha came from Michigan to live with them at the age of ten, after her father's death. A third adopted child was Lucy, whose heritage is unknown.

Then, too, Rob Scott could never turn away a jobless, drifting farmhand looking for a roof over his head. There was always plenty of help on the farm. One of the hands was Tommy Brown, a member of North Elba's famous black colony, who could not seem to make a go of farming for himself.

Neither, in those early years, could the Scotts turn away the occasional tourist seeking a bed or meal on that lonesome plateau at the verge of the wilderness. It goes without saying that offers of payment were embarrassing and politely refused.

The historian, Reverend J.T. Headley, who wrote one of the first travel books about the Adirondacks, gave a vivid portrayal of Scott's in his *The Adirondack; or Life in the Woods.* In a rough wagon, along with five other passengers (two of them women), Headley made his first trip to North Elba in the early 1850s. Night had fallen when the party reached Scott's clearing after a harrowing ride over the Old Mountain Road from Keene. They found the solitary Scott house dark and silent as the grave. A few loud halloos fetched Rob to the door in his nightshirt. The family regularly went to bed with the birds, but all now cheerfully turned out and, by the time the horses were cared for, a brisk fire was crackling in the stove and a pan of shortcake baking for supper. This, with tea and wild strawberries the children had picked that day, made an excellent meal. Somehow, they found room to stash the party away for the night, and within two hours from arrival time, that lonely dwelling was again dark and silent.

At dawn little Jacob went down to the Au Sable with his fish pole and came back with a mess of bright, fresh brook trout for breakfast. It was, according to Headley, a breakfast fit for a king.

But he was even more overwhelmed by the scene that awaited him outside the farmhouse. This great plateau was ringed by the highest peaks of New York State: to the north, Whiteface, swimming in a sea of mist; to the south, Marcy, Colden, McIntyre, Wallface, massive summits pushing and shouldering each other in savage grandeur. Wrote Headley, "The little clearing is destined, in my opinion, to be as well known in a few years as Catskill Mountains or the White Mountains of New Hampshire. I had never heard of it before, and am surprised that its peculiar location has not attracted more attention."

Headley had a long talk with Rob and found him "a great wag and bubbling over with humor." From what source did he draw his strength and sense of fun in this isolated place, Headley wondered. When winter came, was it not grim and desolate beyond endurance? "Do you never get lonely?" he asked. "No." Rob said, "I never was lonely but twice in my life, and then I was in New York City. Both times I was there I got very homesick."

Other men of distinction visited Scott's in those early years, but none more distinguished than Horatio Seymour, then governor of New York State. Governor Seymour had discovered and was devoted to the Adirondacks, often traveling throughout the region. On his trips through North Elba, he never failed to stay at Scott's and admitted that Rob's wit was the best entertainment he found in all the Adirondacks. Another frequent visitor was John Brown, who from 1849 to 1851 was a next-door neighbor, living in the little Flanders house just down the road.

By the late 1860s, the trickle of tourists had swelled to a stream. Rob had enlarged his farmhouse, and it had become a proper wayside inn with regular rates for room and board, called simply "Scott's." It was known far and wide for its excellent meals, its homelike comfort and hospitality. There was now plenty of space. The children were gone from the nest, grown up, and married. Lucy married Augustus Holt of Keene, and Martha married

Moses Ames of the pioneer Ames family in Ray Brook. At twenty-one, Jacob married Amelia Mooney of Keene and moved into a house of his own across the road from Scott's. Another marriage in the family was that of Rob's niece, Mary Ellen Scott, who came from Michigan to visit and met and married Andrew Baker of Saranac Lake in 1866. Andrew built a rambling cottage for his bride, and it was in this cottage that Robert Louis Stevenson spent the winter of 1887–88 in Saranac Lake with the Bakers.

Alfred B. Street, author, poet, and New York State law librarian for more than thirty years, stayed at Scott's about 1865, taking off from there on his famous trek into Indian Pass and up Mount Marcy, fully reported in his book, *The Indian Pass.* He, too, was deeply affected by the serenity and beauty of the setting, the good food, the richness of the farm and the magnificent mass of mountains encircling it, "truly a most glorious frame for this little picture of peace and plenty, this garden-spot of swaying and glittering grain. The place smiles an oasis of meadow and grainfield, in the midst of mountain forests."

Scott's was now the perfect place to stay on the way to Indian Pass and Marcy, and stalwart young guides were always available in the area.

Rob himself was an expert woodsman and hunter and knew the North Elba wilderness like the back of his hand. A close friend was the famous old local guide, Bill Nye, and the two became deeply involved in North Elba's most intriguing mystery, which, oddly enough, started out as a Scott family legend.

A few years before his death in 1825, Rob's father William Scott had gone hunting alone for moose in the region out toward Indian Pass. It was on this excursion that he discovered the mysterious Scott's Ponds on top of Wallface Mountain, which were afterward named for him. William became lost in the intricate mazes of the forest and wandered a day or two, bewildered and uncertain of his bearings. Then from a large ledge adjoining his evening camp, the glitter of a rich metal, brought to life by the leaping fire, danced on his rapt eye. Breaking off some of the mass, he carried specimens home in his pockets. It was reported by no less an authority than Winslow C. Watson[14] that spoons of purest silver were fabricated from William Scott's ore. At any rate, it was not long before he

14 Author of, among other works, *The Military and Civil History of the County of Essex, New York* (Albany, N.Y.: J. Munsell, 1869).

set out for a return visit to his El Dorado. Never again, of course, was he able to find it.

This family tale haunted Rob Scott all his life. He finally enlisted the aid of his friend, Bill Nye, and the two men combed the mountain fastnesses for several years for that elusive ledge of silver ore—without success. William Scott's lost silver mine lives on in legend. If it ever has been rediscovered in the hills of North Elba, no one has owned up to it.

One A.D. Mayo stayed at Scott's in August 1869, and he also was deeply moved by the magnificence of the scenery. He arrived by way of Keene to find a bountiful roast of mutton "smoking on the board" outside the house (barbecues were ritual at Scott's). The Charles Loring Brace family was just leaving, but there were a number of other guests—"a very quiet High Church rector with his chatty little wife," three young New Yorkers in full rig for an adventure among the lakes, and a genial elderly lady and her lively niece. Mayo secured a comfortable room "whose three windows framed as many matchless views."

Rob took him for a pleasure drive in a spruce, two-horse wagon down through Wilmington Notch. Interestingly, Mayo noted that "the rough road was enlivened by crowded wagons full of tourists, for this is one of the great avenues of approach and egress." Evidently, even at this early date, North Elba was awash with summer people.

Rob had cut a trail to the top of Scott's Cobble for his guests' enjoyment. From that little observatory, Mayo spent a morning feasting on the incredible panorama: the full circle of giant mountains with their gorges and slides, Indian Pass so clear-cut in the bright sunlight that it seemed he could leap from his little mountaintop straight into its rocky depths. Afterward he wrote, "This plateau of Scott's is destined to become one of our most attractive summer resorts."

And so it would be in the space of a few years. By the early 1870s, Rob and Laura were getting on in years and ready to retire. They turned the place over to Rob's adopted niece Martha Scott and her husband Moses Sampson Ames. Mose Ames was an upstanding young man with large ambitions. He had plans for the old Scott farmhouse-inn, and soon it entered upon its halcyon days. Just when Mose and Martha added the huge wing that came out flush with the highway is not clear, but it was reportedly there in 1877. Scott's was now the Mountain View House, an attractive small hotel with a capacity for forty guests. Initially, terms were $7 to $8 a week, $2.50 a day, and 50¢ a meal. It was generally open from June 1 to November 1.

The Mountain View House prospered. Still popular with hunters and fishermen, it also continued as a springboard for the trek into Indian Pass and the climbing of Marcy and other high peaks of the south range. It advertised "the healing air of these high plains," and now guests came for the entire summer season. The table fare was plain but delectable, for it was fresh from the farm, which continued in operation. It had telegraph service installed as early as 1880.

What it lacked in size, the Mountain View House made up in prestige. Only the "best" families stayed there. It was a wonderful place for children. The farm animals provided constant entertainment, and the wild, open meadows invited unbridled play. Whole families came for the summer, bringing along their own servants and nannies. It was a place, too, for those who valued serenity and quiet pleasures above the sophisticated social life of the luxurious hotels now up on the lakes.

The hotel register from 1879 through the season of 1902 contains some well-known names: Dr. E.L. Trudeau, State Surveyor Verplanck Colvin, Seneca Ray Stoddard, and even some of the Cabots from Boston. Henry Van Hoevenberg often rode over on his horse from his Adirondack Lodge to use the telegraph facilities, staying for dinner and the night. A delightful entry in the register of 1880 is the neat little pen and ink sketch Mr. Van drew of his newly erected log hotel on Heart Lake.

Guests came from many states, often returning year after year. Surprisingly, there were guests from India, Mexico, France, Germany, England, and Canada. One party from Philadelphia noted in 1886 that they had just completed an eighty-five-mile tramp from Westport on Lake Champlain through the High Peaks.

The Ames children and their friends had great fun scribbling in the register fictitious and outrageous names. "John Brown's Body" came for dinner. And then there were George Henry III, Duke of Limerick, Ireland, His Royal Knobbs Prince George of Hartford, and Lady Grace Gardner and maid of Blarney Castle, Ireland. But two members of the British peerage actually did stay at Mountain View House in October 1889. Lord Stanway of Warwick and a baron from Chester, name indecipherable, accompanied by several attendants, arrived in a private coach drawn by four horses.

Rob and Laura did not live to witness the transformation of their little inn. That old pioneer Robert G. Scott went to his reward on December 9, 1875, at the age of seventy, and his great-hearted Laura, sixty-eight, followed him a few months later, on June 29, 1876.

Nor did Moses Ames live to witness the full success of his Mountain View House. He died suddenly of typhoid fever in 1887 at the age of forty-four. He had served two terms as North Elba supervisor. His wife Martha Scott Ames carried on the hotel, assisted by her son Robert Scott Ames. Robert Scott Ames was North Elba supervisor in 1891–93 and served as Lake Placid postmaster from 1913 to 1922. He, as well as his two daughters, Bertha Ames Bolum and Martha Ames May, are well remembered by Lake Placid old timers.

At the turn of the twentieth century, the Mountain View House still drew its fair share of summer guests. It was now easier of access. The railroad had come to Lake Placid in 1893, and a Mountain View conveyance met the train each morning.

On a chilly day in early June 1903, before the hotel opened for the season, Robert's wife started a fire in a stove upstairs to warm a bedroom for her baby's bath. It was early morning, and Robert had gone to the barn to attend to chores. Suddenly he was summoned to the house to put out a fire that had started in a chimney. It was too late for action. In no time, flames were darting everywhere, and within a few hours Mountain View House burned to the ground. At least one member of that family had a sense of history. Despite all the terror and turmoil of the day, someone thought to rescue the guest register from the burning building. It was lovingly preserved over the years and exists today, one of the few records we have of our summer visitors a century ago.

The Ameses immediately built a new house on the site of the Mountain View House and lived in it for many years as a private home. That house, now known as Olympic Heights and owned by Horst Lichtenberg, is still there in the lee of the little mountain called Scott's Cobble. And the old Scott farm is again the haunt of summer people. Efficiency units in the house are rented out from July through October.

Another house with a close bond to the old Scott clan is also still with us. In 1880, Jacob Wood, Rob and Laura's adopted nephew, built the handsome farmhouse on Adirondack Lodge road that stands on the hill just above the first bridge. After his death in 1896, it was for years a notable summer boarding house, operated by his widow and daughter Hattie.

In contrast to Rob Scott, Jacob Wood was a giant of a man and bore himself like a Viking. He was a mighty hunter and woodsman like Rob, and was often quoted in *Forest and Stream* magazine. His six children became prominent in local affairs, and his son, Charles, was the father of Lake Placid's famous golf champion, Craig Wood. It is a happy circumstance that the Craig Wood Golf and Country Club, named in honor of Jacob Wood's grandson, is only a stone's throw from the old Scott farm.

Afterword: The Mystery of Lot 79

Mystery surrounds the early years of Great Lot 79, Township 12, Town of North Elba. Justus Dart of New Hampshire, who came to North Elba in 1803, first owned it. Thorn's Survey of 1804 shows Dart then living on Great Lots 85 and 86, but he could not have stayed there very long because Iddo Osgood soon obtained a patent to them from the state. After the Thorn survey, Dart received a state patent to Lot 79 and probably lived on it and farmed it.

On October 1, 1811, Justus Dart deeded Lot 79 (deed book "B," page 213, in the Essex County Clerk's Office) to William Scott of Stoddard, New Hampshire,[15] for $192, deed recorded September 19, 1812. This deed uses both the names of Justin and Justus in the wording—Justin in the beginning, and Justus twice afterward. James Wilson and Malcolm McMartin of North Elba's pioneer colony were witnesses to Dart's signature.

Up until recently, Lot 79 was always known by old-timers in North Elba as "the Scott lot," and it is very probable that William Scott lived on and farmed it for a few years before he moved down to Keene, where he first appears on the 1820 census. (Hattie Wood, in an interview, said that the William Scott home in Keene was on Alstead Hill and was a log cabin.) He then deeded the lot to his son, David Scott.

Twenty-eight years later, David Scott sold Lot 79 to his brother, Robert G. Scott, as recorded in Essex County Deed Book "EE," page 187: "David Scott to Robert G. Scott—$64.00. Deeds Lot 79, Township

---

15 MacKenzie's note: Stoddard was very near Keene, New Hampshire—also near Alstead, New Hampshire.

12, containing over 160 acres. Recorded August 7, 1848." Robert Scott apparently farmed this lot along with his own farm.

According to Donaldson's notes in the Saranac Lake Library, Moses Ames bought the Robert Scott house in 1877 and put on the big addition.

In an interview, Hattie Wood said that the "Scott lot" in North Elba may have been the first place that William Scott lived. Moses Ames apparently owned it in later years, and when he died, Martha Scott Ames inherited it, according to Hattie. This has not been confirmed at Elizabethtown.

TWENTY-EIGHT
The Peru Iron Company on Lake Placid
Date unknown

The great Peru Iron Company of Clintonville, on the Au Sable River in Clinton County, built the outlet dam on Lake Placid about 1850, owning and maintaining it for over forty years, until August 1893.

The Peru Iron Company was organized in 1824. For more than half a century, it was a vital force in the economy of northern New York. The business was centered in Clintonville, and not only extensively mined the iron ore at Arnold Hill but also operated huge blast furnaces, foundries, rolling mills, and factories for the manufacture of nails, ship anchors, and other iron goods—with saw mills and grist mills besides.

Waterpower was, of course, of prime importance in its operations. During the spring freshets, the Au Sable was in full flow, but in summer droughts was often at a dangerously low level. In order to have some control over water level, in about 1850, the company secured patents from the State of New York to Great Lots 237 and 256 in Township 11, Old Military Tract, on Lake Placid, which contained the head of Lake Placid's outlet, and built a wooden dam at the site of the present outlet dam. It is interesting to note that a letter written by Jason Brown, John Brown's son, made mention of the dam going out in 1857 in high waters. It can be assumed a new dam was immediately put into service.

D.H. Hurd's *History of Clinton and Franklin Counties, New York* (J.W. Lewis & Co., 1880) states on page 229, "The Company owns the dam at Lake Placid, by far the largest reservoir on the river, with the exclusive privilege of using it at will, in this possession having a decided advantage over all rival corporations on the river."

It is clear, then, that Peru Iron Company built the dam on Lake Placid for the sole purpose of controlling the flow of outlet waters into the Au Sable River. It had no mills or lumbering or charcoal-making operations on the lake. For many years, the level of the lake fluctuated with the alternate storing and drawing off of water.

Beginning in 1870 with the building of the Hall camp, summer camps and hotels began to rise on the shores of Lake Placid, and by 1893, there were more than a dozen camps and several substantial hotels. All suffered great annoyance and hardship from the constant fluctuation of the lake level caused by Peru. In July 1893, roused to action by Col. Abraham G. Mills, the camp and hotel owners organized the Shore Owners' Association of Lake Placid with the main purpose of securing title to the outlet dam from Peru.

The company, now known as Peru Steel Ore Company Limited, was, in fact, quite willing to relinquish title. Financial reverses had visited and almost paralyzed its enterprises. As a matter of record, it would soon cease to exist. On August 18, 1893, Peru deeded four acres of Great Lot 256, on which the dam was located, to Abraham G. Mills and Preble Tucker, acting as agents for the Shore Owners' Association, as follows:

> Deed dated August 18, 1893, consideration $1,500 and the further consideration that the parties of the second part shall keep and perform the covenant hereinafter set forth as to establishment and maintenance of level of the waters of Lake Placid.
>
> Peru Steel Ore Company Limited to Abraham G. Mills and Preble Tucker, both of the City of New York.
>
> 2/3 interest in 4 acres, more or less, in square form, and in storage dam and appurtenances thereon, out of southwest corner of Lot No. 256 in Township 11, Old Military Tract, situate in Town of North Elba, and described as follows [shows metes and bounds].
>
> Parties of second part covenant and agree to establish and maintain a surface level of the waters of Lake Placid at a point not

> lower than three feet and four inches below the top boards of the coping of the south abutment of the present Lake Placid storage dam but, the lowering of the lake by the parties of the second part in the month of November of each year, for the purpose of enabling shore owners, during the winter, to clear and improve the shores, shall not be considered a breach of this covenant.

By a deed dated August 22, 1893, for a consideration of $1, the same property, with the same restrictions, was deeded by Preble Tucker and Katharine L. Tucker, his wife, of the City of New York, to the Shore Owners' Association of Lake Placid. It is not known why Abraham G. Mills was not included as a grantor.

The Shore Owners' Association at once rebuilt the wooden dam, replacing it with a masonry dam in 1901–02, and also cleared the shores of dead trees and debris. The association has always maintained the agreed water level. In earlier years, the level was occasionally lowered in the autumn to permit camp owners to repair docks and piers, but for a long time the policy of the association has been to maintain the lake at a uniform level year round.

TWENTY-NINE
William B. Nye: Discoverer of the Hudson's Source

From the New York State Conservationist, *February–March 1969.*

There is a breed in the Adirondacks today that calls itself guide. Let the outlander beware. The last genuine article passed over the hills some seventy years ago.

These mountains have often been host to vanishing species. But of all the noble fauna that are gone, none was nobler than the Adirondack guide. Around 1900, he disappeared from the landscape with the earlier wolf and the panther, and the woods never saw his like again.

It is a paradox that no other region of America ever produced the species. He was indigenous to the Adirondacks. To the wealthy sportsman, who began to visit the area after 1850, the guides were nature's royalty, and he described them in superlatives—loyal, honest, cheerful, patient, superb spinners of tales, expert in the lore of woodcraft, handy with the rod, gun, paddle, and skillet, eager to please, tireless, and brave. There must have been a few rascals, lazy louts, and low-bred fellows among them, but most of the old-time guides probably were an extraordinary new breed of American.

The six most famous guides of 1850 to 1900 were John Cheney (the "Mighty Hunter"), Orson ("Old Mountain") Phelps, Alvah Dunning ("The Hermit"), Mitchell Sabattis (the Abenaki Indian), John Plumley (Adirondack Murray's "Honest John"), and William B. Nye. The first five were lucky enough to number among their clients well-known writers who popularized and immortalized them in the literature of the period. Only Bill Nye lacked a high-powered press agent and, consequently, much of his story is lost for all time. His fame has rested on a slight, amusing tale of Avalanche Lake, once widely circulated and even today found in an anthology or two, and a powerful portrait taken by that photographer extraordinaire of the Adirondacks, Seneca Ray Stoddard.

Prior to 1850, guiding in the Adirondacks was only a sideline. With the frantic scramble of hunters, fishermen, mountain climbers, and bird watchers to the great North Woods, many enterprising men, wise in the ways of the forest, adopted it as a profession. Wrote one guide buff in 1879, "The Adirondack guide is born, not made. He falls, so to speak, out of his log cradle into a pair of top boots, discards the bottle for a pipe, possesses himself of a boat and a jackknife and becomes forthwith a full-fledged, experienced guide."

An Old Testament Character

Not so Bill Nye. Bill emerged full-blown from the pages of the Old Testament. Long, silky hair rippled over massive shoulders. An uncombed beard flowed to his lapels. Bristling eyebrows met over a commanding nose and under a noble expanse of forehead. His was the hot eye of a prophet, the iron-molded jaw of a biblical patriarch leading his flock to the Promised Land. He was nearly six feet tall and powerfully made. Certainly, his appearance was arresting, and may very well have been slyly calculated, for some of the noted guides cunningly invented a character for themselves to snare the city trade. In fact, "Old Mountain" Phelps was something of a humbug as a guide—lazy and inefficient, more entertainer than woodsman—whose flamboyant personality cancelled out his sins of omission.

William B. Nye was born in Berlin, Vermont, in 1816. What brought him to the primitive and out-of-the-way North Elba is a mystery. Oddly, he began his career as a seafaring man, far removed from the mountains on which he left his signature. Disappointed in love, at nineteen Bill went off on a whaling voyage, then shipped as first mate on a brig for a three-year cruise. He moved to Charleston, South Carolina, and with his own boats engaged in transporting slaves and tobacco along the palmetto-lined Ashley River. During all of his later life, he carried about with him a peculiar dried fish he had gaffed off the island of Madagascar, identified by Professor Albert Bickware of New York as a trunk or box fish, a strange denizen of tropical seas with head and body completely encased in fused, bony plates and the reputation of being poisonous.

Bill was a stubborn Yankee of the breed that originally settled the High Peaks area of the Adirondacks. Often silent and morose, he was withal a very nice, "big, queer fellow with a keen sense of humour"[16] and a little dog always at heel. Typical of all guides, who had learned their own insignificance among the grand mountains, he refused to tolerate any display of superiority on the part of a client, whatever his station in life. Those who expected fawning servility were in for a jolt their first night out in the woods.

In spite of (more probably because of) many eccentricities, Bill was extremely popular and rated the very best of the North Elba guides. He appeared in the township of North Elba, which later encompassed the famous resort village of Lake Placid, in 1851. A bachelor all his life, he boarded out with various families: the Jackson Brewsters, the Joseph Nashes, and the Widow Weeks. Finally, he established himself in a small cabin on the Au Sable River on a site just south of the Olympic ski jump, very near his favorite trout pool, still locally known as Nye's Hole. From here, he built a sawmill and a starch factory and, in the spring, he ran a sugar works on the John Brown farm across the river. Soon he seems to have tired of his sawmill and factory; he sold the property to Timothy S. Nash in 1854, and turned to guiding full time.

---

16 Russell M. L. Carson, from his chapter on Nye Mountain in *Peaks and People of the Adirondacks* (Garden City, NY; Doubleday, Doran & Company, Inc.1928), p 167.

"Hotel" vs. "Independent" Guides

Bill was that rarefied creature, the "independent" guide, as opposed to the "hotel" guide, who was several notches down in the pecking order. The independent guide was often hired a year in advance. A note in the North Elba census for 1875, "Men generally command good wages in this town, as this is the place where people take guides for the woods in the Adirondacks," indicates he was well paid. He received from $2.50 to $3 a day, furnishing boat and all other equipment required for camping except food, which cost the employer $2 for each per week.

Bill pioneered many of the mountain trails in the Lake Placid area. He cut the first path up Whiteface from the Lake Placid side at his own expense, the first trail from Adirondack Lodge to the summit of Marcy, and did much to make a suitable track through Indian Pass. He originally built most of the trails for Henry Van Hoevenberg when Van Hoevenberg started Adirondack Lodge at Heart Lake, as well as most of the old trails on the north side of the main Adirondack range.

Bill broke into print by virtue of a pleasant little episode that occurred in 1868 at Avalanche Lake. The tale was told and retold in the backwoods belt, and even Bill himself could be induced to recount it (to men only) in his quiet, quaint style around an evening campfire.

Bill was guiding the Fielding family from lower New York State. Mr. Fielding was a small, excitable, rabbity man. His wife—by name Matilda—was tall, plump as a partridge, and possessed of an iron resolve. The fourth member of the cast of characters was niece Dolly, about seventeen, and an exceedingly comely and vivacious girl, if we are to believe Bill's rueful comment: "I tell you, boys, when I look at such a girl, I sometimes feel as though maybe I have made a mistake in living alone so long."

Their trip had been a grueling one, although the overweight Matilda had taken it in stride. It led from Nash's inn at North Elba [the Red House] through Indian Pass to the iron works,[17] then on to Mount Marcy and back by way of Avalanche Pass. The first day's journey ended in a tramp of four miles by torchlight through a night "darker than a stack of black cats." The intrepid Matilda, insistent on gaining camp, carried her shoes in her hand for the last mile.

---

17 That is, the defunct McIntyre iron works, at what was known as "the deserted village" of Adirondac, in Newcomb township. Adirondac is still the main southern trailhead to Marcy.

Now at Avalanche on the fourth day, the party faced a dilemma. The narrow lake, wedged between precipitous granite walls too sheer to climb, had to be forded. The trail, in fact, led through the water. Ladies could not be expected to wade the deepest part, which came to the armpits. Moreover, any female wearing the cumbersome costume then de rigeur for an Adirondack outing was doomed to sink like an anorthosite boulder.

Hitching Up Matilda

A pow-wow ensued and Matilda, with a great show of Victorian modesty, at last consented to be carried over on Bill's powerful shoulders. The nervous Mr. Fielding then allowed it was only polite to see the ladies safe first and appointed Matilda to man the first run. What seemed a further impasse—Matilda insisting on riding sidesaddle, Bill demanding she sit astride his shoulders—was averted when Mr. Fielding persuaded his wife to throw away her delicacy and do as Bill asked. With Dolly calling, "Hold your horse, aunt!" the fording proceeded. Matilda, however, kept slipping further and further down on Bill's back, and when he arrived at the deepest part her well-padded derriere dangled just above the water.

"Hitch up, Matilda! Hitch up, Matilda! Why don't you hitch up?" screamed Mr. Fielding from shore, dancing around among the rocks, while Dolly laughed merrily. The more Mr. Fielding cried "Hitch up!" the more Mrs. Fielding hitched down, but by leaning far forward, Bill landed her safe and dry.

The risqué adventure somehow leaked out, although the ladies never told of it in Bill's presence, and "for thus showing so much regard for the feelings of a bashful man and a bachelor, I shall be grateful to them to my dying day," said Bill.

Floating rafts of logs chained to the rocks at each end have since spanned the crossing at Avalanche Lake and to this day are called "Hitch-up-Matildas."

The Colvin Survey

Never were the North Country guides more truly tested (and Bill Nye was among them) than in aiding the great Verplanck Colvin topographical survey of the Adirondacks conducted by the state. Begun in 1872 and continuing for a quarter century, the survey was roundly criticized by some, mainly because Colvin did not complete a map of the whole region. Until the survey, however, the interior was largely a terra incognita, geographically unknown. Lakes, ponds, rivers, and mountains never before mapped were located and measured and land boundaries were defined and, equally important, Colvin impressed upon the citizens of New York the priceless heritage they possessed in the vast wilderness of northern New York.

The guides not only guided for Colvin. They were his pack mules, and he could never have conducted his survey without them. Their skill was infinite, their loyalty fathomless, their trials horrendous.

The guides built bough houses and log huts for shelter, carried supplies forward from camp to camp, chopped trees into huge lengths for campfires, cleared trails, and cut brush from the line of sight of the leveling instruments. They transported baggage and heavy instrument boxes, sometimes weighing over a hundred pounds, across streams, up mountains, and through passes. They hauled timber for signal trees along tortuous trails, up through dense dwarf forests, over ledges and the open rock of mountaintops, the transportation of a single timber often taking a day's work from three powerful men. Boots often froze to their feet. A guide ascending Marcy on November 1 to bring a theodolite down had both ears frozen in a wind sweeping the summit at seventy mph.

The terrain was so difficult that even the guides, themselves, occasionally became lost. Provisions were often reduced to "cracker crumbs dealt out by the spoonful," mainly due to Colvin's slap-dash organization, and guides were then sent out hunting with the hounds that invariably accompanied the party. One, returning with the only meat he could procure, carried seventy-five pounds of bear flesh on his back, and received nothing but wry looks for his efforts.

The Highest Springs of the Hudson

In the early days of Colvin's survey, it was gospel that Avalanche and Colden were the highest lake springs of the Hudson River. On September 16, 1872, Verplanck Colvin and Bill Nye rewrote geography. On that day the two men made not only the first recorded ascent of Gray Peak, fifth highest of Adirondack summits, but also the then-sensational find of another loftier pond source of the Hudson, little Lake Tear-of-the-Clouds, nestled in the bosom of Marcy.

Colvin's crew had been engaged in survey work on the crest of Marcy. A halt was called when a bank of clouds settled on the mountaintop. Most of the party then returned to Lake Colden camp with instruments and luggage, while Colvin, Bill, and his hound set out to find and climb virginal Gray Peak. Their adventure, as recounted in detail by Colvin in the best lavender prose of the period, captures the excitement and glamour of the then-untrodden forest ways.

The two men plunged down Marcy through dense thickets of scrub balsam that tore their rubber coats to ribbons. Groping in a pea-soup fog, they aided their descent by grasping at dwarf trees and even the tail of Bill's whimpering hound. Finally, the side of Marcy lost its downward slope.

> The hound here commenced to sniff the ground fiercely, gave tongue and was off in pursuit of some wild creature, in high excitement. Hark! What sound was that! Are we called? Or is it the echo of the hound's deep tongue? We shout, and quickly after, three mountains answer from the fog in echo! Hark! The deep, near answer of old Marcy; the southward voice is Skylight; the faintest westward echo Colden! Shout louder! Shout again! The answers of the mountains shall tell us where to go. Point towards Marcy's echo. The Gray Peak lies the other way toward the dull, no-echo way.

And so it does. At length, forgetting cold and wet and fog, scaling slippery rocks and fighting thickets with new ardor, the two explorers stand on the pinnacle of Gray, rejoined by the effervescent hound. The echo to their halloos now comes only from distant peaks.

It grows bitter cold. Even the staunch Bill shows pleasure, and the hound slavers in joy, at the proposal to descend. Now the men determine to find the mysterious lake called Perkins, seen so many times from the top of Marcy but never visited, and believed by the guides to drain to the river Au Sable. But which way does it lay? They have no compass bearings, and the fog swirls down. They call to the mountains again, and the dull, fog-voiced echo replies, "Southward."

Down they go, hanging by roots, slipping, sliding, leaping. Now the hound finds signs of game once more and rushes off in hot pursuit. At length they emerge on the edge of a little cliff, at the foot of which runs a stream amid black mossy rocks.

Discovery of Tear-of-the-Clouds

> Descending, we hasten to drink of the gurgling water. But scarcely have we sipped when we start back and gaze at each other with astonishment! Can it be? Is it possible? This stream tells a strange story, and surely it flows westward to the Hudson! The water is warm or tepid, and has not the usual icy temperature of the mountain brooks. It must come from a pond or lake, and this lake cannot flow to the Au Sable and the St. Lawrence, but to the Hudson! Oh! Unfortunate lakes Avalanche and Colden, so long famed as the most elevated in New York! Your glory has departed! Shame! To be deprived of it by this little mountain pool! For while you fail to reach an altitude of 3,000 feet, the barometer here tells that we are over 4,000 feet above the sea.
>
> And interested, and excited, by the hope of discovery, we commenced to ascend the stream, hurrying along on the slippery boulders, leaping from rock to rock. Suddenly, before us, through the trees gleamed a sheet of water, and we shouted our 'hurrah,' for there were Marcy's slopes beyond, while the water of the lake was studded with those rocks which we had looked at with our telescopes from Marcy. It was the lake, and flowed, not to the Au Sable and St. Lawrence, but to the Hudson, the loftiest lake spring of our haughty river!
>
> First seen as we then saw it, dark and dripping with the moisture of the heavens, it seemed, in its minuteness and its prettiness, a veritable Tear-of-the-Clouds, the summit water as I named it.

The first fine romance is, of course, long gone from the Adirondacks, but it was in full bloom on the day Colvin and Nye stood on the shore of the little mountain tarn. Their discovery became a nine-day wonder, lasting until the final mysteries were swept from the uncharted corners of the wilderness.

In the remote southwest segment of North Elba township, facing the giants Marcy, Colden, and McIntyre, stands a memorial to Bill, the 4,160-foot-high Nye Mountain. Dr. W.W. Ely of Rochester, an admirer and patron, named it in about 1873. Nye is one of the so-called trailless peaks of the Adirondacks, although a path near the top comes across the col from neighboring Street Mountain. Few have known its lonesome summit aside from those select cardholders of the Forty-Sixers' Club, who have scaled all forty-six Adirondack peaks four thousand or more feet high. It is doubtful whether Bill himself ever stood at the top, although he is known to have hunted along its flanks. The first recorded ascent was on June 27, 1921, by Robert and George Marshall and Herbert Clark.

Bill Nye and the mountain named for him were pulled into the famous story of William Scott's lost silver mine when Scott's son, Robert, a good friend of Bill's, enlisted him to aid in the search for the mine. By process of elimination, they arrived ultimately at the base of Nye Mountain—and there the story, for all practical purposes, ends. In time, a legend grew that Bill actually did find the silver on Nye and was able to retire comfortably in his old age. Once a year, he was seen to set off furtively for the old family homestead in Vermont, carrying a heavy-laden pack basket on his shoulders.

About 1880, then in his sixties, Bill retired permanently to the family farm on Berlin pond, not far from Montpelier, Vermont, which he shared with his sister, Mrs. Sarah Pratt, and her son, George. Soon he became a familiar, patriarchal figure on the streets of Montpelier, his long, white hair floating like thistledown over rugged shoulders. Bill was a teller of wildwood tales in his declining years. He claimed to have officiated as a marshal at the funeral of John Brown at North Elba, and exhibited with pride a collar that he said the fiery abolitionist wore at his hanging.

Never a violent man, Bill died of violence in his seventy-seventh year. In the early morning hours of Lincoln's birthday, February 12, 1893, a fire, apparently originating from a candle in Bill's bedroom (he refused to use a kerosene lamp), consumed the Pratt home, barns, and outbuildings. The aged Mrs. Pratt made desperate efforts to save her brother, trapped in his inferno, but was driven back by flames. "Roasted to Death!" blared the headlines of the *Vermont Watchman.* Bill's charred remains were taken from the ruins in the cellar and buried in the village cemetery, but not before large crowds from Montpelier, Northfield, Barre, and the surrounding countryside had viewed them in fascinated horror. Bill's dried trunkfish and John Brown's collar were also consumed in the flames.

THIRTY
Ski T Farmhouse
February 1999

The so-called Ski T farmhouse, located on Riverside Drive opposite the Olympic ski jump complex, is an important historic landmark of the Town of North Elba. It is one of the very few buildings dating from the mid-nineteenth century still in existence here, and has a long and colorful history. The house is situated on Great Lot 101, Township 12, of the Old Military Tract, which contains altogether eighty-four acres of land.

In the early 1840s, Gerrit Smith of Peterboro, New York, a wealthy landowner and a leading abolitionist of his day, purchased much of the land in North Elba from the State of New York, including Lot 101.

On August 4, 1853, Gerrit Smith sold Lot 101 for $200 to John P. Alger of Saratoga Springs. It would seem that Alger had plans to erect a starch mill on the Au Sable River, which flows through 101. He did not, however, immediately establish such a starch mill, but very shortly—on May 23, 1854—gave a deed to Lot 101 to William B. Nye.

It would seem Bill Nye was occupying Lot 101 before he received a deed to it, and probably was buying it on time. It may have been in 1853 that he built a dam and substantial sawmill on the Au Sable several hundred feet upriver from the present Olympic ski jumps. Upon receiving his deed from John P. Alger, he entered into an agreement with Alger allowing him to build a starch factory on the river just below the sawmill, and to take water from the sawmill dam. These two mills would operate side-by-side for years. The starch mill proved an economic boon to the farmers of North Elba. It manufactured starch from potatoes, and potato growing became a big business here, with large quantities sold to the starch mill. Another business soon came to Lot 101. William Weeks built a blacksmith forge just across the main road from the mills, and was deeded fourteen acres of land. For many years, Weeks carried on his trade of blacksmith and also had a log home on the premises.

Bill Nye must have soon tired of his sawmill, for on November 4, 1854, he sold it—along with all of Lot 101, except for the Weeks purchase—to Timothy S. Nash of North Elba for the handsome sum of $1,400, reserving the right to Alger to continue the starch mill.

The evidence strongly suggests that it was William B. Nye, and not Alger, who built a house, as well as the sawmill, on Lot 101. Nye's sale to Timothy Nash included "a dwelling house on the same lot." It is the opinion of this researcher that this original dwelling house is the present Ski T farmhouse—which, of course, has had additions and improvements over a period of almost 150 years. There is no record or indication that the original house on the property was ever burned or torn down. It can therefore be conjectured with some assurance that the present house was built in 1853 or 1854. The house that Nye built must have been rather substantial. In that period, it was one of just a few frame houses in town, most of the residences being log cabins. On the 1855 and 1860 censuses, it was one of the highest-valued dwellings in town, listed at $500.

New owner Timothy S. Nash was a solid North Elba citizen. Born in Duxbury, Vermont, he had come from Willsboro, New York, to what is now North Elba in 1840 at the age of sixteen with his father, a brother Joseph, and three sisters. Brother Joseph would become renowned as one of the two co-founders of Lake Placid village. At the first town meeting in 1850, Timothy was elected superintendent of common schools. He served as North Elba supervisor from 1851 through 1853, and again from 1864 through 1866.

Nash moved into the farmhouse with his wife and three children. He carried on a family farm as well as the sawmill. The sawmill seems to have been successful, with six employees and a monthly payroll of $120. Nonetheless, Nash failed to pay off the mortgage he had given Bill Nye for the purchase price. As a result, he lost title to Lot 101, along with the house and mill. It was sold at public auction on July 13, 1858, and was bid on by Asahel M. Nye and wife, apparently relatives of Bill.

Now Timothy Nash's family stepped in to save for him the land, the house, and the mill. Remembrance Nash, Timothy's father, bought the property from Asahel Nye on September 13, 1859. Willsboro couple Ira A. Boynton and his wife Adeline Zanetta, who was Timothy's sister, then acquired the property. Timothy continued to occupy the house and run the mill. On May 2, 1859, Timothy was appointed North Elba postmaster, and a room of Ski T became the North Elba post office until March 21, 1861, when the Nash term ended.

Ira Boynton gave Lot 101 back to Remembrance Nash on January 11, 1860. Timothy continued in possession of the house and mill. During this period, Ira Boynton was also living somewhere on the land. The 1876 Gray map of North Elba indicates that a house had been built somewhere between the Weeks blacksmith forge and Ski T, and it can well be assumed that Boynton built it and lived in it. Here he opened a general store, said to have been the first store in North Elba. He also moved the North Elba post office to his house after his appointment as postmaster on March 21, 1861. He served until April 21, 1863. The Boyntons then moved to Brasher Falls, in St. Lawrence County, New York. This researcher has never found anyone who recalls the old Boynton house. It must have been torn down a very long time ago.

Timothy Nash was not running the sawmill in 1865, although the family was still living in the house and farming the land. It has been rumored that shortly after this, Timothy's wife left him, taking the children with her. In any event, Timothy soon left North Elba and moved to Minnesota, where he lived out his years.

Palmer E. Havens of Essex, New York was next to acquire Lot 101. Havens never lived in North Elba, but was speculating in Elba real estate.

Lot 101 then came into the possession of Joseph Hanmer (two-thirds ownership) and Edwin Miller (one-third ownership), who contracted on February 12, 1867, to buy the property from Havens. The price was $1,500. The two moved into Ski T farmhouse. Miller was working in the Weeks forge. Havens already had sold the sawmill outright to Leander Thompson of North Elba's famous Thompson family, along with a small parcel of land on the river. Thompson began running the sawmill in 1866 with his partner, D.E. Farrand, and continued to operate it through the 1870s. Thus, the sawmill property was at last severed from the rest of Lot 101, now reduced to about seventy-nine acres.

Hanmer and Miller received a deed on December 2, 1873, when they had paid the purchase price in full. Meanwhile, Joseph Hanmer had given Lot 101 an entirely new look. He had come to North Elba from Black Brook, near Au Sable Forks. About 1869 he built a hotel somewhere on Lot 101 and named it

"Hanmer's Hotel." It seems to have been a substantial, two-story building. Old historical accounts of Lake Placid and North Elba have completely overlooked and never mentioned his hotel, but this researcher found the story of a visit to it in the *Essex County Republican* of July 28, 1870, as follows:

> From the steps of our hotel in North Elba it [Whiteface Mountain] looms up proudly magnificent, its cold summit now lost in the clouds and now bathed in sunlight.
>
> Mr. Hanmer has a house that answers every necessary purpose for this locality and has a great deal of transient custom from persons visiting John Brown's grave, and parties passing from one point to another during the season of summer pleasure travel. The accommodations are excellent, and the meals got up in a style to suit the most fastidious.
>
> N.B. Trout for breakfast.

Sadly, Hanmer's Hotel had a short life. The *Essex County Republican* reported its demise according to a dispatch from North Elba dated April 11, 1873:

> Hanmer's Hotel burned today about 4 o'clock. Building total loss. Most of the effects on first floor were saved—none in the chambers or cellar. Insurance of $2,500 on building and furniture, partly in Glens Falls Company. Real loss $2,800. Origin of fire unknown.

Exactly where did this hotel stand on Lot 101? It would seem likely that it was near Ski T farmhouse, and possibly on land that is now part of the house property. A search of the land might produce evidence, but that evidence would have to be in the form of charred material. Any remnants of foundations could be those of barns once on the property.

On July 20, 1882, Joseph Hanmer deeded his two-thirds ownership of Lot 101 to Joanna Lamb, sometimes called Joanna Hanmer, who was living in his household. Hanmer died at Lake Placid in 1887 and is buried here. On December 1, 1882, Joanna Lamb and Edwin Miller deeded their interests in Lot 101 to Aletha Taylor, wife of Charles Taylor, of North Elba.

Charles Taylor had already purchased the old sawmill and its small lot, and now his family moved into the farmhouse and began farming the land.

Taylor, born in 1835, came from a pioneer family of neighboring Jay. He moved up to North Elba in 1865. This researcher does not know how long Taylor ran the sawmill on the Au Sable, but it was in full operation in the 1880s, and he was the last one to run it. The Taylors sold Lot 101, with its house and farm buildings, on July 17, 1890, and it was probably then that the sawmill ceased operation. Taylor also had a sawmill on Mill Pond in Lake Placid. He died here on May 20, 1898. He had nine children, and some of his descendants still live in Lake Placid.

The new owner of Ski T was Judson C. Ware of North Elba. Ware was born in neighboring Keene in 1842 to an old pioneer family. When his mother died, he came to North Elba to live with his maternal aunt, Mrs. Horatio Hinckley. The Hinckleys came here in 1839 and were the first owners and developers of what is now Heaven Hill Farm. It was there that Judson Ware grew to manhood. He enlisted for service in the Civil War and spent three years in Company K, 96th Regiment, New York Infantry. He was a sergeant major, and then was promoted in the field to second lieutenant. He was twice wounded in action.

Judson became prominent in the life of North Elba. He was town supervisor in 1875 and 1876, after which he was elected Essex County sheriff, serving in that post for some years. Upon his retirement as sheriff in 1889, Judson looked about North Elba for a good property. He was still fairly young and wanted to spend the rest of his life working with animals and the soil. Lot 101 greatly appealed to him, and he bought it.

Judson Ware was probably the first to bring this farm to its full potential. It became known as one of the better farms in North Elba. A photo given to this researcher by a Ware descendant is the only known photo of the farm. In the photo, the fence posts shown are along the main highway, now Route 73. An odd structure at the extreme right on the main highway may be the remains of the old Boynton house. The old sawmill can be seen further up the road. A structure in the middle background may be an old Weeks building.

Judson Ware died in 1908, bringing to a close this particular chapter in the story of Lot 101 and Ski T farmhouse.

Early in the twentieth century, the famous Lake Placid Club began buying up many of the grand old pioneer farms of North Elba. This enabled the club to supply its table economically with poultry, eggs, milk, cream, butter, beef, pork, potatoes, and vegetables raised on its own lands.

Eventually the club owned some two dozen of the old North Elba farms, one of them the Judson Ware farm on Riverside Drive. It is not clear as to what purpose this farm served. It was not one of the Club's milk-producing farms, like the Intervales and Midrivers farms farther down Riverside Drive. It may have been acquired as a desirable adjunct to what the club called its "river" farms, and hay and vegetables were probably the predominant crops there. The club gave the Ware farm the name of "Au Sable Valley Farm," sometimes referred to simply as "Valley Farm."

Aside from the photo given by the Ware descendent, this researcher has never been able to find a photo showing the farm buildings of Ski T at close range at any stage of its history. A photo of 1927 gives a view of Valley Farm from the top of Intervale ski jump, now the Olympic complex. There are a number of barns and outbuildings shown in that photo. At what period of the farm's history these were erected is unknown. It is possible some of them were very old. In any event, none of these buildings, with the exception of the house, exists today.

In the fall of 1923, the Au Sable Valley farmhouse underwent a great improvement. The club converted the first floor into a charming, old-fashioned tearoom, with a beautiful stone fireplace. A hot-air furnace was installed, as well as hot and cold running water, modern plumbing, and a telephone. The club named the house "Ski T," and that name has stuck for seventy-six years. No matter who comes and goes on these premises, Lake Placid and North Elba natives have called the place "Ski T" and still do. It may be a long time before the name dies out.

The Lake Placid Club intended Ski T as a clubhouse and little restaurant for its winter colony. Those using the ski jumps and toboggan runs nearby now had a warm and cozy place for relaxation and enjoyment of hot coffee and doughnuts. It would also be a great stopping-off place for trampers, snowshoers, horseback riders, and sleighing parties. Most importantly, the Club built a new, two-mile cross-country ski trail from the upper golf links down to the bridge across the river on Riverside Drive, and thence past the big red barn to Ski T. Ski T, therefore, was undoubtedly the first so-called ski lodge on the continent. It became enormously popular with Lake Placid Club members and famous for its chicken and steak dinners.

The Club hired David Milne and his wife to manage the new Ski T clubhouse and restaurant, and thus added another outstanding personality to the list of those who inhabited the farmhouse over its long history. David and May ("Patsy") Milne managed and lived at Ski T farmhouse during the winters from 1924 until 1928, summering at Big Moose Lake. Ski T restaurant was also open in the summer under management other than the Milnes.

David Milne was a painter. His artistic talents had already been recognized. A Canadian, born in 1882 near Paisley, Ontario, he had studied at the Art Students League in New York City and then began painting in earnest in the United States. For some years, he supplemented his income as an artist with odd jobs. When he came to Lake Placid, his paintings had already been exhibited in the United States, Canada, and England.

Milne found beautiful Lake Placid and North Elba ideal for landscape painting. During his winters here, he roamed the countryside as often as he could and executed many paintings in the village and out in the township. One of his paintings, titled *Marcy, Colden and McIntyre*, was included with several other Lake Placid scenes of his in exhibitions in Canada during that country's centennial year of 1967. It seems to have been painted from the top of the hill facing Ski T farmhouse, and it shows the ski jump hill and the road—now called Route 73—coming down the hill from the North Elba plains, with the three tall mountains in the background. Unfortunately, Ski T farmhouse is just out of the picture's frame.

Milne left the United States for good in 1929 and spent the rest of his life in Canada. He died at Bancroft, Ontario, on December 26, 1953. Since then, major exhibitions of his works have been held in Canada, and he is today considered one of Canada's most important artists.

David Milne's son, David Milne Jr., visited this researcher in March 1995. He brought with him copies of just about all the paintings his father had done in Lake Placid and North Elba for identification of locale, and there were a good number of them. These paintings are now mostly in private hands.

How long Ski T served as a clubhouse and restaurant is unknown, but it would not have been much beyond the 1930s. The Lake Placid Club began to divest itself of its farms in the 1940s, and thereupon Ski T farm was sold and broken down into parcels.

Thus ends the ancient history of Ski T farmhouse. It has had a number of owners over the intervening years. The house today includes about four acres and is owned by Ann Stowe.

This house has had a long, rich, and interesting history and worthy inhabitants, has been lovingly preserved and, of course, has been enhanced by attractive additions for almost a century and a half. We may well ask of it, what lies ahead?

THIRTY-ONE
The Mill Pond Story
August 1, 1974

Chubb River rises in the Adirondack High Peaks region, close to Nye Mountain, and winds northerly through North Elba township for some ten miles, emptying into the West Branch of Au Sable River. As it enters Lake Placid village, the outlets of Lake Placid and Mirror Lake join it. A rather mysterious stream of many moods, seldom visited in its forest terrain, it disappears underground at one point in its journey. It is partly navigable by canoe and rowboat, highly prized by trout fishermen, and has a major attraction in beautiful Wanika Falls.

The Chubb's first appearance on a map was in 1804, following Stephen Thorne's state survey of North Elba. It then bore the name of Pond Creek, but several years later, it was rechristened Chubb for Joseph Chubb, a pioneer farmer on the Old Military Road.

As early as 1809, this stream was first harnessed for waterpower. In that year, state Comptroller Archibald McIntyre founded the Elba Iron and Steel Company, with a capital stock of $100,000. Damming the river to form what is now the Lower Mill Pond at Lake Placid, the company proceeded to build a rather elaborate industrial complex for the manufacture of bar and hoop iron, steel, anchors, and nail rods from local ore. Soon, many buildings fringed the shores of Lower Mill Pond: two forges, an agent's dwelling house, boarding house, bloomers' house, storehouse, two large barns for workers' barracks, a blacksmith shop, sawmill, grist mill, and three charcoal houses.

Plagued by misfortune, the forge was abandoned by the Elba Company in 1817, but it was partially continued in operation by Eleazer Darrow for his own personal use another ten years. The buildings then gradually fall into decay or were dismantled, and by 1850, little evidence of Lake

Placid's first industry remained but a crude dam. The latter was replaced by a concrete dam when Lake Placid village began operating a municipal electric power plant in 1905 just below the former iron-works site.

It was not until the early 1850s that industry again returned to the Lake Placid area of the Chubb. By 1855, Messrs. Smalley and Flagg, a partnership formed for the operation of a sawmill, had built a wooden dam on the Chubb several hundred feet above Lower Mill Pond, and a second, much larger, body of water, which came to be known simply as Mill Pond, was created from the Chubb flow. The sawmill erected on the north side of the dam passed through many owners before it ceased production and was razed around 1920. Later in the nineteenth century, a second mill for the manufacture of shingles and lath was erected directly across the river from the sawmill.

The sawmill and Mill Pond came into existence at a time when the site of the present village was practically uninhabited. Suddenly, a settlement began to rise about them, and it can be said that Lake Placid rose and grew and flourished on the lumber milled there.

Among the many owners and operators of the mills were Loyal C. Rich, Arvilla E. Blood, Carlos and Harvey White, Charles Taylor, and Benjamin F. Brewster. During the latter's tenure, the pond became known as Brewster's Pond. George Stevens, of Stevens House fame, was also an owner. The last to own and operate the sawmill was the partnership of Wallace Murray and Phelps and Apollos (better known as Paul) Smith, with Abe Ling as manager. Title to the dam and pond then passed to Paul Smith's Electric Light & Power & Railroad Co., which maintained the dam and ran a substation there, connecting their plant into the Lake Placid village generator for the production of electricity. Paul Smith's deed passed to Niagara Mohawk Power Corporation. In 1967 the latter conveyed title to M. Frances and Louise E. Brewster, granddaughters of the same Benjamin Brewster who had once owned and operated the sawmill. The deed specified that never again would the site be used for the production of electricity.

It is a long time since the Chubb meandered lazily through a primeval forest, and lumbermen floated logs and pulpwood down to the pond from Averyville. In winter, logs were drawn and dumped on the ice to await the spring freshets that sent them down to join the great drives on the Au Sable River. Nobody knows how many hundreds of thousands of board feet passed through the pond in the old days of Adirondack lumbering.

It is quite a while, too, since the railroad came to town in 1893, and the present station was built on the shores of Mill Pond in 1905, and Frank Williams cut and drew ice from the pond for its water cooler. (Sometimes Frank waited too long and had to haul the ice out with a wagon from shore, but how he did that is another story.) Orange Weaver discovered an oil deposit in the pond—or thought he did. Some people were mean-spirited enough to say it was run-off from the new garage that appeared down on Hurley Bay, now that someone had invented the automobile.

It might be said that Lake Placid's great winter sports program was born on Mill Pond. One of the early toboggan slides was there, and the first skating rink in town. George Alford, among others, voluntarily scraped it for the children. Charlie Jewtraw, a local boy, learned to skate there, starting his world-famous career as a speed skater. He was to win the first gold medal awarded to any contestant at the first Winter Olympic Games, held at Chamonix, France, in 1924. Many other Lake Placid boys who went on to national fame as speed skaters tested their first blades on Mill Pond.

Both the upper and lower ponds and their shores are steeped in the early history of Lake Placid. For a long time this lower section of the village was known as Newman, in honor of Miss Anne Newman, an eccentric but benevolent Philadelphian who fell in love with the mountains, made North Elba her home, and farmed a large tract of land on the Bear Cub Road,[18] now known as Heaven Hill Farm. In 1891, Miss Newman succeeded in having a second local post office, named Newman, established at the bottom of Mill Hill. This went out of existence when the present modern post office serving the entire village was erected near the [Olympic] Arena, and the name Newman is seldom used now except by old-timers.

There have been many changes on the shores of Mill Pond. The old iron bridge, the slaughterhouse, and the blacksmith shop are long gone, as are the American House hotel and the old plank road up Mill Hill. The railroad is gone,[19] the station now used as a museum by the local historical society. But the old George White Opera House still stands.[20] Here, wandering companies of actors, musicians, and

18 Now called Bear Cub Lane, County Route 26.

19 The railroad returned in 1980 for a short run. More recently, in 2000, a tourist train started running between Lake Placid and Saranac Lake, which is still in operation as this is being edited.

20 Now housing a restaurant, Lisa G's.

vaudevillians once entertained the community, dances were held, and the first phonograph ever seen or heard by most Placidians was exhibited. It became, in time, a hardware store, an A&P, and now in shabby gentility houses an antique shop. And the old post office building still stands, occupied by the Raeoil Company.[21] Once it played a prominent role as the bank in an early "wild west" bank-robbery film shot in Lake Placid. Those were the days (the 1920s) when Placid was a favorite locale for silent movies filmed by the old Long Island studios, pre-dating Hollywood.

The dam and Mill Pond itself, and the plump trout it nourished, are gone. When the dam at last gave out in 1970, the beautiful little body of water that had seen the history of a century and a quarter went also, and the Chubb reverted to its ancient channel. Many houses and buildings, and the small park on Station Street planted in shrubs and trees by the Garden Club in 1961, have been left high and dry. The landscape on River and Station Streets looks sad and incomplete today.[22]

THIRTY-TWO
Intervales Farm

In a letter dated May 30, 1994 to the owners of property on River Road, Mary MacKenzie tells the history of the Intervales Farm.

I believe I can give you a fairly comprehensive account of your big red barn on River Road[23] and the farm called Intervales, formerly owned by the Lake Placid Club.

The Lake Placid Club purchased the large farm that included Intervales from Byron R. Brewster. I have two different purchase dates in my files: 1905 and 1907. The correct year can easily be determined from deed records in the Essex County Clerk's Office in Elizabethtown.

It appears that the club completed the construction of the big red barn in 1909. The following appears in *Lake Placid Club Notes* of July 1909:

---

21 Now housing a restaurant, the Downhill Grill.

22 Since MacKenzie wrote this chapter, the Mill Pond dam has been restored—twice. The most recent rebuilding came in 2001.

23 Now called Riverside Drive.

> At Intervales the new Holstein stable on the edge of Riverside Drive is being lengthened to 200 ft., and like the Club stables at Highland, Tablelands, Bolderwood and the certified milk house, has cement floors, running water and all modern appliances, making them all a great advance on anything heretofore seen in this section.
>
> (Note: In its 1914 Handbook the Club states the barn was "160 ft" long. You [the letter writer] probably know the actual correct length.)

This is the only printed reference I have ever found as to the date of construction. I would interpret it to mean that during construction, begun in 1909, the Club decided to make the barn longer than originally planned. This is confirmed in a beautiful photo of the barn under construction contained in the Moses glass photo plate collection at the local Center for the Arts. In this photo, the barn being built appears to be the very same size as the finished version.

There are also two interesting photos of the barn and Intervales farmland in *Lake Placid Club Notes* of December 1913 and November 1924. The 1913 photo shows a rather substantial barn addition across the rear (construction date unknown). In the 1924 photo, the barn is gone and silos have been added. There is, of course, today an addition on the north side, but I do not know when it was built.

I am going to give you a rather complete history of Intervales Farm, feeling you would be interested. To avoid confusion, I am simplifying the account to some degree.

The State of New York originally owned all of the Town of North Elba. Gerrit Smith purchased great Lots 106, 107, and 108, Township 12, of 180 acres each, which later contained both the Intervales and Midrivers farms of Lake Placid Club, from the state in the mid-1840s. Smith was the man who founded the famous black colony at North Elba, which brought John Brown to town.

In the early 1860s, brothers Archibald, Samuel, and John Thompson were deeded the three lots. The Thompsons, though, had already started farming the lots several years before 1860. They had actually bought the land on time in the 1850s through a contract of purchase and sale. A Thompson farmhouse was definitely in existence there by 1858. It appears on the French map of 1858 and was located on precisely the same spot as the [William] Harries house today. It is my firm belief that the back part of the Harries house is the original Thompson farmhouse built circa 1855.

These Thompsons who first farmed Intervales and built the Harries house were from our most interesting pioneer family. They were sons of Roswell Thompson, who settled in North Elba in 1824. Roswell had ten children altogether—nine sons and one daughter—and the family became closely allied to John Brown. One son, Henry, married John Brown's daughter, Ruth. The one daughter, Belle, married John Brown's son, Watson, who was killed at Harper's Ferry. Two Thompson sons, William and Dauphin, went to Harper's Ferry with John Brown and were killed in the action there. Some Thompson descendants still reside in Lake Placid and are our oldest pioneer family.

In the mid-1860s, Palmer E. Havens of Essex, New York, bought all this land from the Thompsons as an investment. He never lived here, and soon—on September 24, 1867—sold all three lots to Alpheus C. Demmon and his wife Almira Farrand Demmon, who had come to North Elba in 1855 from Waterbury, Vermont. The purchase price was $3,600, a lot of money for that day and age.

For quite some years, the Demmons lived and farmed successfully on what finally became Intervales. They had five children. Two sons fought in the Civil War from North Elba, and one was killed in action at Fair Oaks. One of their daughters married another Thompson son, Franklin, who in 1872 acquired a chunk of land out of the Demmon farm—Lot 106, and thirty-five acres of Lot 107, on the north side of the Chubb River. Franklin built a farmhouse and barns on Lot 107, bordering on the Au Sable River, just across the present bridge. This land became the later Midrivers farm of Lake Placid Club, and the new housing development across the bridge occupies a part of it.

Alpheus Demmon retired from farming in the early 1880s, and at that time sold his farm, consisting of Lot 108 and most of Lot 107, to Byron R. Brewster. Brewster also purchased from others contiguous Lots 113 and Lot 114 of 160 acres each, as well as the Franklin Thompson farm occupying Lot 106 and part of Lot 107.

Byron R. Brewster was the grandson of Thomas Brewster and the son of Jackson Brewster, who settled in North Elba in 1841. They were descendants of Elder Brewster of the Mayflower, and became important in the pioneer history of Lake Placid. Byron served as mayor of Lake Placid village soon after its incorporation. This large farm of Byron Brewster on River Road,[24] along the Au Sable River, said to contain some nine hundred acres, became one of the best-known and most-prosperous farms in northern Essex County. Brewster ran it for some twenty-five years and then, about 1905, sold the entire acreage to the Lake Placid Club.

The old Franklin Thompson farmhouse and barns across the bridge were then still in existence. This portion of the farm the Club named "Midrivers." The old Thompson-Demmon farmhouse (now Harries) and outbuildings were also still in existence, and this land on the road side of the river the Club named "Intervales," and it was where they soon erected your big red barn.

It is impossible to ascertain how much acreage the Club might have assigned to Midrivers and how much acreage it might have assigned to Intervales. It also had purchased the old Ware farm opposite the ski jumps on River Road [Riverside Drive] near the entrance (the original farmhouse built in the 1850s still stands there). Most of the time Melvil Dewey lumped these three farms together and called them the Club's "River Farms." At various times he gave conflicting figures for individual and total acreage. Melvil was often quite careless about facts, and I hesitate to quote his figures.

At any rate, the land on which your red barn rests has been farmed for the better part of 140 years. The Club used Intervales exclusively for a Holstein milking herd, and the acreage was then probably devoted entirely to meadows and hay. All the ancient outbuildings are long gone, but the red barn remains and, as I said, the original farmhouse still stands.

The Midrivers barns and farmhouse built by Franklin Thompson in the early 1870s were torn down about 1963.

I believe the Club divested itself of all the land occupied by its "River Farms" except for the piece where the skeet field is now located.

THIRTY-THREE
Lake Placid House (Brewster's)
Date unknown

It was springtime of 1871, and farmer Benjamin Brewster was making history at his farm on the west shore of Bennet's Pond. He was building

24 Now called Riverside Drive.

a hotel on a knoll above his farmhouse. As things turned out, it would be the first hotel within the limits of what is now the village of Lake Placid.

To be sure, down the road a few hundred feet, the farmhouse of his brother-in-law, Joseph Nash, called by many "the Red House," doubled as an inn for summer people, but it could hold no more than twenty-five guests, and then only when they were packed in like sardines. Ben Brewster aimed to have a real hotel, with ample room for fifty to sixty people.

The matter of building a hotel had been urged upon him by Charles Loring Brace, of New York, a noted author, philanthropist, and social reformer. Brace was enamored of this romantic, out-of-the-way spot. He had been patronizing the Red House since 1860, and he often strolled over for a chat with Ben Brewster. His family was finding Nash's too cramped for comfort, he confided. Why didn't Ben erect a real hotel? He would, Brace promised, keep it filled with family, relatives, and friends. Ben bought the idea, borrowed some money, and with North Elba's master carpenter Franklin Thompson bossing the job, the hotel was rapidly completed and opened for business on July 4, 1871.

"It will be conducted strictly on temperance principles," reported the *Essex County Republican*, "and in conformity with rules which the most fastidious could approve."

The official name was Lake Placid House, but it was known locally simply as Brewster's.

Historian Alfred Donaldson, who had a penchant for hyperbole, gave a false picture of the early Lake Placid House. In his *History of the Adirondacks* (Century Publishing Co., 1921, reprinted Purple Mountain Press, 1996), he described it as ugly, jerrybuilt, and primitive in the extreme—unpainted, two-storied, with only ten rooms, nails for coat hooks, barrels for tables, doors leading nowhere, and a leaky roof.

Unpainted it may have been for a time, but otherwise a different story is told by Seneca Ray Stoddard's 1873 photo of the Lake Placid House. It was, in fact, a commodious, three-story, sturdy and honest structure, and quite attractive in a backcountry fashion. And Stoddard's Adirondack guidebook of 1876 reports "rooms large, comfortably furnished, and the table good." Capacity was sixty, and terms were $8 to $10 a week.

The name of Benjamin Thomas Brewster was now one to be reckoned with. Born in neighboring Jay on October 20, 1829, the youngest of eleven children, he had come to North Elba from Jay in 1841 at the age of twelve with his parents, Thomas and Polly Lewis Brewster, his sister Harriet, and brother Jackson. Thomas was a direct descendant of Elder William Brewster, who had arrived in America aboard the Mayflower. First settling out on the plains of North Elba, Thomas Brewster's final home with his son, Jackson, was a log cabin on what became the Lake Placid Club upper golf course.

Before 1850, pioneers had shunned Placid Lake and Bennet's Pond.[25] Early settlement was confined to the outlying plains of North Elba. In 1850, Joseph Nash, who married Ben's sister Harriet, bought a large tract of land on the west shore of Bennet's Pond. The next year, 1851, Ben Brewster became the area's second citizen, acquiring a tract north of Nash.[26] Nash's farm extended from the present Hilton down to the Central School and over Grand View Hill to the outlet of Lake Placid. The Brewster farm extended from the Hilton over to Lake Placid, taking in most of Signal Hill. It then continued around the north and east shores of Bennet's Pond, encompassing the land later occupied by the main Lake Placid Club buildings. Altogether, Ben's lots had a total of 517 acres. Never mind that 225 of them were under water (Placid Lake, Bennet's Pond, and Mud or Echo Pond). The remaining land was mostly fertile and fully capable of sustaining a large family such as Ben's. He married Julia Ann Washburn, of Keene, in 1854, and fathered eight children.

Nash and Brewster started off in log cabins, but by the late 1850s both had erected substantial frame farmhouses. Ben's domicile was located at the rear of the present Colonial Cottage[27] of Mirror Lake Inn and was always called "the long house" because of its configuration. In 1871, the Nash and Brewster families were still the sole occupants of what is now the incorporated village of Lake Placid.

---

25 Later called Mirror Lake.

26 In his Adirondack diary entry for Thursday, June 28, 1849, Richard Henry Dana, Jr. says that, following a climb to the summit of Whiteface Mountain, his party made "a short visit to Brewster's cabin" before returning to Osgood's inn for the night. Like many other North Elba settlers, Ben Brewster may have been buying his land on the isthmus between Placid and Mirror Lakes on time. Though he acquired the deed to his land in 1851, he appears to have been settled upon it as early as June 1849. If this is so, then Brewster would have been the first settler in the territory of the Lake Placid's Upper Village, not Joe Nash, preceeding his brother-in-law's settlement there by a full year.

27 Demolished in September 2006.

Ben's hotel flourished. Charles Loring Brace lived up to his promise, bringing family, relatives, and friends. By word of mouth, other distinguished city-dwellers were attracted to the new hotel and its scenic delights. Lake Placid House was a woodsy sort of place, with no frills, and its clients were the sort of people who liked woodsy places—hikers, mountain climbers, boaters, birdwatchers, and fishing folk. A climb up Whiteface was a routine diversion. A boathouse was well stocked with canoes and Adirondack guideboats. Guides and horses were supplied to answer every need or whim of the outdoorsman. Two of the early guides were young half-brothers from Vermont, George and Albert Billings. Each soon married a Brewster daughter.

The Brace family came for fifteen years. The children of Calvert Vaux, one of the architects of Central Park, and the children of the well-known actor and singer, DeWolf Hopper, spent summers of their youth at the Brewster hotel. The register of the 1880s, still in existence at the local historical society's railroad station museum, reveals the names of prominent people who went on to build camps on Lake Placid. Pranksters (probably Brewster children) scribbled in the register the names of Chester A. Arthur, Grover Cleveland, P.T. Barnum, and Lydia E. Pinkham of vegetable compound fame, but Chester A. Arthur Jr., of Washington, D.C., son of the president, actually did stay at the Lake Placid House in July 1884.

Soon after the hotel opened, a significant event occurred. Among the guests in the early 1870s were a Mrs. Monel and her daughter, Mary, a young woman of considerable literary talent. Mary Monel fell deeply in love with the pristine little body of water at the foot of Lake Placid House. It had been known as Bennet's Pond for some seventy years in honor of North Elba's first settler Elijah Bennet. Mary now christened it Mirror Lake and, to commemorate the occasion, meticulously wrote down in the hotel register a poem of her own creation, entitled "Mirror Lake, Formerly Bennet Pond." The name Mirror Lake immediately caught on with both summer and local people, and almost overnight, it was made official. Mary Monel later married Judge Frederick Scott Wait, and the couple acquired Nytis Lodge on Lake Placid. Here, the woman who named Mirror Lake spent her summers until her death on February 13, 1927, at Greenwich, Connecticut.

Ben ran the hotel until 1876, then leased it for three years to a brash young man by the name of Henry Allen. Henry livened things up a bit.

Fond of parties and balls, he staged several at what he called "Allen's Hall" as entertainment for the locals during the long, dreary winters. An elaborately printed invitation to Henry's Christmas ball of 1877 came to light some years ago. "Yourself and ladies are invited," it began. Tickets sold for $2, a princely sum in those days. Henry Allen went on to fame with his Allen House and Grand View Hotel.

In 1880, Ben returned to Lake Placid House, ran it for several years, and then turned the management over to his son, Martin. In 1883, the Brewster long house was turned into a laundry and help's quarters for the hotel, and Ben built himself another home, a stately Victorian residence befitting his new station in life. Forty years later, it became the Mirror Lake Inn. Though Ben had now retired from farming, his lands were still intact.

Not so the Nash lay-out next door. Things were booming there. Nash had sold off a good many lots, and a village was taking shape on the west shore of Mirror Lake. By the late 1880s, hotels, homes, churches, and stores mottled the landscape. The old life was gone. Was it time to move on?

John and George Stevens, who had just built their great new Stevens House on the hill above the Nash farmhouse, were casting covetous eyes on the Brewster farm. In 1887, they made Ben an offer he could not refuse. For $25,000 he sold to John and George Stevens his entire original farm, including the Lake Placid House. The only exceptions were the new residence and a few small parcels previously deeded out. The purchase price was impressive at the time but, even so, had Ben waited a few years, he might have doubled it. As things were, the Stevenses turned a handsome profit over the years, selling the hotel and lots for summer cottages and camps. Besides, a large segment of the land was converted into the Stevens House golf course. Ben and his wife lived on in their new house for a time and then moved to Vermont.

The Stevens brothers, with their own grand hotel to maintain, had no interest in running Lake Placid House. They leased it out, waiting for a buyer to come along. And come along he did, in the person of George W. Baldwin of Keeseville. Baldwin was an Adirondack photographer of no small ability and had just established a studio in Saranac Lake. He bought Lake Placid House, with quite some adjoining land, on March 8, 1893, for $13,000. It may be wondered why he was willing to invest in a small hotel that had seen its best days. Its prestige of being Lake Placid's first hotel had faded, and a number of new and luxurious resorts had eclipsed it. It had, in truth, become something of an anachronism in a village that was now a nationally recognized summer resort.

There may have been plans for expansion. Very shortly, on November 17, 1893, Baldwin deeded a half interest to Hilton L. French, general passenger agent for the Chateaugay Railroad at Plattsburgh. In any event, Baldwin and French made few changes and retained ownership for only four years. Baldwin remained in Saranac Lake for a few more years and then moved to Rutland, Vermont, where he died in December 1930 after being struck by a car. Baldwin's photos of the Saranac-Placid area around the turn of the twentieth century are of historical importance and are rare collector's items today. A number can be found in the Adirondack Research Room of the Saranac Lake Free Library.

The next owner was George W. Cushman, of Malone, who acquired the property on June 8, 1897, for $17,000 plus a mortgage of $8,000. It was Cushman who totally transformed Ben Brewster's little pioneer hotel and gave it a new and dramatic image.

At staggering cost, a huge addition now swallowed up the original Lake Placid House. The result was a spacious and imposing four-story structure. An unnamed architect finished off the facade in a style that might be called Adirondack Gothic. In these last years of the twentieth century, the building comes across as grandiose and even a bit absurd, but it was greatly admired in its day. Dominating the rise of land between the two lakes, the new Lake Placid House was quite a sight. Given its size and location, it shows up in the majority of the early Lake Placid picture postcards and photos.

On April 17, 1899, George W. Cushman deeded the hotel with all furnishings to Lake Placid House Company. Consideration was $50,000, but there were also frightful encumbrances totaling over $33,000. It is not known whether the company was a Cushman corporation and merely an extension of his ownership, or whether it was an entirely new player. Whatever the answer, the hotel, still engulfed in expansion debt, went into mortgage foreclosure. It was sold at a referee's sale on November 21, 1902, to Michael J. Callanan of Keeseville. Following his departure from Lake Placid, Cushman became manager of the Meacham Hotel over on Lake Meacham.

Title soon passed to Branch and Callanan, and that firm sold the hotel to Steven B. Ayres, of Spuyten Duyvil, the Bronx, on August 1, 1911. By now, and somewhere along the line, it had taken on the new name of Lake Placid Inn, probably directly after its enlargement. Ayres was an absentee owner. Even before his purchase, and as early as 1909, the name of Frank W. Swift had become synonymous with the hotel, and would continue so. Swift was definitely the manager in 1909, and also under Ayres ownership. Swift was obviously first leasing the place, and may have been buying from Ayres under contract. A formal deed from Ayres to Swift (Mrs. Helene Swift was actually the grantee) was not given until August 8, 1916.

Old-timers today well remember the names and persons of Frank Swift, his wife Helene, and his children Bill and Betty. Frank became one of Lake Placid's best-known and most astute hoteliers, and the family was active in village life. Frank Swift was born in East Orange, New Jersey, in 1879, the son of Frank Cole Swift and Mary Wing Swift. Before coming to Lake Placid, he had managed the Tahawus House Hotel in Keene Valley and the Maplewood Inn at Elizabethtown.

During the Swift years, the hotel did well. While it could not offer all the diversions of Lake Placid's more elegant hostelries, it was a pleasant and comfortable vacation locale. In that era, guests utilized all the accommodations at Lake Placid Inn, and employees were housed in tents on platforms erected on the hillside lot now occupied by Judge Harold Soden's residence. A short roll from tent to lake was a good way to start the day.

In 1920, Frank Swift bought the Northwoods Inn on Main Street and sold Lake Placid Inn to B.E. DeMurg, who formed the Lake Placid Inn Corporation. Frank and Helene Swift went on to create Lake Placid's first fireproof hotel, the Marcy. Frank's last stand was a second Lake Placid Inn (the renamed Alford Inn) on Main Street, next to the Marcy.

From the beginning, ill luck hounded DeMurg. In the spring of 1920, while workmen were readying the hotel for the season, the top story was severely damaged by fire. Hasty repairs were made, and the hotel opened. Late in the summer, another fire broke out and the entire Lake Placid Inn burned to the ground. The core of it had endured for half a century.

Ben Brewster did not live to see the demise of his Lake Placid House. Upon the death of his wife in 1911, he left Vermont and came back to Lake Placid, moving into a house on Saranac Avenue with his son Emery. The house still stands and has been absorbed into the Town House Motel operation.[28]

---

28 2267 Saranac Avenue.

The old Brewster farm was now scarcely recognizable. Showy summer homes, a church, and a golf course occupied Brewster Hill. Winter sports had arrived at Lake Placid, and the village had installed a toboggan chute on the hill next to Ben's former Victorian house. The Stevens boys had built a road around Mirror Lake in 1889, following Ben's old cow path (the same road we traverse today); where Benjamin Brewster had once pastured his cows, the buildings of the exclusive Lake Placid Club stood.

Even the name of the farm hill, always called Brewster Hill, had been changed. It was now Signal Hill. In the late nineteenth century, during his great Adirondack survey, state surveyor Verplanck Colvin had erected one of his signal towers on the brow of the hill, directly opposite the present James LaFountain residence.[29] The tower was utilized in Colvin's reconnaissance triangulations of the area and remained in place for years. Inevitably, the name "signal" became attached to the hill.

By 1913, Lake Placid had become a Mecca for the silent movie industry, and it filmed scores of outdoor melodramas here for the next fifteen years. Local people were hired as extras. In July 1914, one script called for an elderly gentleman to play Father Time, and Ben Brewster was chosen. He was eminently suited for the role. Ben was now eighty-four years old and had a long, white beard. When told his face would soon be seen all over the country, Ben was not impressed.

"Well, I'm known all over the country anyhow," said he.

He may have been right. At any rate, he was known and respected all over northern New York. With the building of his hotel, he had dispatched the little settlement at Bennet's Pond on its long journey as a resort, and he and his family had become prominent in local affairs.

Just five months after his stint as Father Time—on December 19, 1914—Benjamin Thomas Brewster died at the age of eighty-five. Members of the Lansing family are his only descendants now living in Lake Placid. Two others, Kathleen Lansing Ruiz and Norma Jean Lamb, maintain second homes here. The site of the old Lake Placid House is occupied by the Clune House of Mirror Lake Inn and the James Owens residence (the house with the famous wall), just off Interlaken Avenue and looking out over Mirror Lake Drive.

---

29 Formerly the old MacDonald house, built 1895 (per MacKenzie). Now 49 Norton Road.

But visible evidence of the old Ben Brewster landmarks is not entirely lacking. About 1900, the long house was cut in half. One half was moved a short distance to the very edge of the lake and became a separate residence, which Dr. Buchbond owned for many years. In 1911, the other half of the long house was demolished. Constantly altered, refurbished, vamped up, and beautified for close to a century, the house on the lake is now the outstanding summer home of Dieter Heckmann.[30] Though it in no way outwardly resembles the pioneer Adirondack farmhouse it once was, in its heart are the timbers and framework of the old Brewster place. Ben's long house is still there on Bennet's Pond.

THIRTY-FOUR
Albert H. Billings
July 30, 1988

Albert H. Billings was born in Windsor, Vermont, in 1853, son of Alonzo Billings and Alma Silver Billings. In the early 1870s, Albert and his older half-brother George Billings left Vermont and came to what is now the village of Lake Placid. Both Albert and George found jobs at the Brewster hotel, Albert acting as a hunting, fishing, camping, and mountain climbing guide for the guests.

In 1875, George married Benjamin Brewster's daughter Elsie, and shortly afterward Albert married Elsie's sister Ella. As a wedding present, Brewster gave Albert and Ella a piece of land he owned on the east shore of Mirror Lake, now part of the Lake Placid Club complex.[31] The couple occupied the property for some years, building a rather large house near the lakeshore and farming on a small scale. Albert continued guiding and also worked as a carpenter.

In time, Albert decided he would like to "modernize" the old Adirondack guideboat. He was not the first or the last, of course, to make such a decision. The Adirondack guideboat evolved over decades, and in the late nineteenth century, many boat builders were adding their own refinements to the unusual craft. This researcher is not familiar with

30 112 Mirror Lake Drive.

31 The last piece of the Lake Placid Club complex was demolished in January 2002.

the Billings innovations. At any rate, during the winter months, Albert began building his own version of the Adirondack guideboat. These boats are now rare collectors' items. The work was done in the upper part of Albert's boathouse on Mirror Lake. The exact year he started this venture is unknown. It was probably in the late 1880s.

Albert and Ella sold their place to John Fraser and moved over to the west shore of Mirror Lake, where the village of Lake Placid was evolving. In the 1890s, they built a house on Mirror Lake Drive. It is still standing, enlarged and modernized, and is now known as the Colonial Cottage[32] of Mirror Lake Inn.

John Fraser and his wife turned the old Billings farmhouse into a boarding house and christened it Bonnieblink. In 1895, Bonnieblink became the first clubhouse of what was to become Melvil Dewey's famed Lake Placid Club. Renamed Lakeside and greatly enlarged, the building was torn down in 1946, as was the original Billings boathouse some years later.

In 1897, on the site of the present Holiday Harbor,[33] Albert established a boathouse-marina on Lake Placid and named it Billings Landing. Here he ran a boat livery and provided docking facilities for rowboats, canoes, and the early motorboats of camp owners on the lake. Here he also continued building his Billings guideboat and other non-standard rowboats, besides repairing and refinishing boats of the camp owners. His boathouse was enlarged in 1899 and 1902.

Albert Billings died in 1903. Two of his employees, Thomas H. George and C. Herman Bliss—the latter of whom was chief boat builder for Albert—ran the business for Mrs. Billings for a year. In 1904, they purchased the entire establishment, and the business became known as George & Bliss. The building of rowboats at the old Billings Landing continued only a few more years. In February 1919, fire destroyed the entire marina, which had been greatly expanded by George & Bliss, but it was quickly replaced.

The firm of George & Bliss was in business until 1963, and was followed by various owners. All the old marina buildings at Holiday Harbor have been torn down in recent years, but docking facilities are still provided.

Albert's wife Ella died in 1931. Both are buried in the North Elba Cemetery at Lake Placid.

---

32 Demolished in September 2006.

33 In 2006, site of the Lake Placid Marina.

Albert and Ella had three daughters: Ida (Mrs. Homer) Lockwood, Marian (Mrs. Arthur) Brettle, and Beth (Mrs. James) Owen. Mrs. Lockwood and Mrs. Brettle are deceased, but it is believed that Mrs. Owen still survives and is living with her daughter Ann in Ohio.

THIRTY-FIVE
The White Church Story
August 6, 1987 and September 1, 1998

From 1800 until 1875, the citizens of North Elba lacked a formal church building. In those three-quarters of a century of fluctuating fortunes and population, a religious sensibility nonetheless flourished.

In the early days of our first colony (1800–1820), when close to three hundred people inhabited the Plains of Abraham, the predominant affiliation was Congregationalist. The noted Cyrus Comstock, a Congregationalist circuit rider with headquarters at Essex, New York, furnished sustenance for the soul, conducting church services, marriages, and funerals at North Elba, probably in the log schoolhouse.

With the almost total failure of the colony in 1817 due to the infamous "year without a summer" and the closing of the Elba Iron Works, North Elba became something of a ghost town. For some twenty-five years, no more than twelve families resided here at any one time, but a religious sentiment persisted. Church services were held regularly at the home and inn of Iddo Osgood on Old Military Road. ("On the Sunday we went to Squire Osgood's meeting," a letter of October 14, 1826, reports.) Iddo himself, a lay minister, conducted the services, and later they were presided over by his son Dillon, who became an ordained Congregationalist minister.

The Little Red Schoolhouse made an appearance on Sentinel Road[34] in the late 1840s and soon became the place of Sunday worship. By now, Methodism had come into fashion; with the death of Dillon Osgood in 1860, that old mainstay of the pioneers, Congregationalism, went into decline. A new influx of population was inaugurated in the 1840s,

34 The portion of Sentinel Road where the Little Red Schoolhouse stood is now called Newman Road. In 1925, the Little Red Schoolhouse was moved one block over to 43 Johnson Avenue.

and by the 1860s, the inhabitants of North Elba began to hunger for a formal place of worship—although, simple farmers all, they felt there was insufficient money in the community to undertake such a project. Still, in 1868, a substantial group banded together and entered into a formal covenant to build a church, open to all religious denominations, and to cost no more than $1,500. The signers of the covenant pledged tentative amounts totaling about $1,100. Seven years were to pass before the church became a reality. A charming legend of its purported origins, recounted in Alfred Donaldson's *History of the Adirondacks* and long accepted as gospel, is reprinted here as part of the White Church story:

> In the early [1860s] and Seventies there wandered over the Plains of Abraham an itinerant tinker, known to every one in North Elba as "Old Beard." Whether this was his name, or merely a reference to his hirsute face, is an unsolved mystery. Probably the latter, for his head was an unkempt tangle of overgrown hair and beard, and his expression was reduced to a pair of eyes in perpetual ambush. His clothes were the logical sequel to such a head-piece—a costume of shreds and patches. He is reported to have worn them as faithfully as a tree does its bark. He removed them only when it became necessary to add a patch or to patch an addition. This he did so often that the clothes of his later life were but a crazy-quilt reminiscence of an ancestral suit.
>
> Beneath this unpromising exterior there lurked a tinker of more than usual skill. He was more than a mender of pots and kettles, and dabbled in original creation. Mr. George A. Stevens had a ring which the old man made for him from a silver quarter, and he told me that no one ever equaled Old Beard in the making of a trout-hook. His hooks were the delight of all the sportsmen of his day.
>
> Old Beard wandered about from house to house, doing a job where one was needed, and often taking his pay in a meal or a night's lodging. He had no home and no relatives and, unless he slept with a customer, he spent the night in the open, or uninvited in some barn. His only deep attachment was for two dogs which always followed at his heels, and their names—Jennie Lind and Betsey Baker—were as familiar through the countryside as his own.

> In the course of time he grew so old and feeble that he could no longer pursue his vagrant calling. Claiming to have neither relatives nor money, he was taken to the poorhouse. Here a fresh suit of clothes was offered him, but he stubbornly refused to relinquish his old one. Soon after, he died in it, suddenly, one day. Then the reason for his refusal was fully explained. As his coat of many rags was peeled off, some of the half-rotten patches split open and were found to contain bills of various denominations. This most surprising discovery led to a thorough investigation, of course. It showed every patch to be double, and each to be lined with paper money. The total yield was $350—the surreptitious savings of a lifetime.
>
> This money had to be advertised, according to law, but no claimants for it appeared. The finding of it was, of course, known to every one, and finally the suggestion was made that it be used to build a church. The growing community had long desired to build a regular place of worship, but had felt too poor for the undertaking till Providence brought to them this possible windfall. The poormaster consented to give the money on condition that seven men would pledge themselves to pay fifty dollars each in case any relative of Old Beard should ever turn up. But none ever did.
>
> The church was completed in 1875. It still stands and is a monument to a vagabonding tinker, who unconsciously spent his life in hoarding and secreting funds for its erection.

Regretfully, little if any of the tale tallies with the truth. Ordinarily, it would be sacrilege to destroy a legend that has long been cherished locally, but in this case, it would be a greater sacrilege to ignore the vital role of North Elba citizens, who gave so much of their time, labor, money, and love to the building of the White Church.

The "Old Beard" story seems to be typical Donaldson nonsense. Over the years, much of what he reported has proved to be erroneous, and competent historians no longer want to use him as a source. If there was anything Donaldson loved, it was a good, colorful yarn, and there were plenty of old guides and old-timers around to assuage his appetite, often at the expense of the truth. Donaldson accepted anything that was told to him and, even more irresponsibly, proceeded to embellish tales by adding tidbits from his own fertile imagination. He never attempted to verify these tales by studious research.

To begin with, it is clear that Donaldson was unaware of "Old Beard's" actual name. He could easily have determined it, because the man was buried in North Elba Cemetery and his name, Stuart Baird, is on his tombstone.[35] The locals called him "Old Baird." Donaldson obviously mistook it as "Old Beard," and therein lies the core of his tale. The "beard" sparked his imagination. He delighted in giving the man a great, shaggy beard and a head of uncut hair—"an unkempt tangle of overgrown hair and beard, and his expression was reduced to a pair of eyes in perpetual ambush." This is pure Donaldson prose. There is no authentic material to be found anywhere to sustain this extravagant description. Then he dressed Baird in rags held together by patches—and again, there is not a shred of reliable evidence to warrant such a description. Donaldson gathered information from George Stevens about Baird, which is on file in his correspondence in the Adirondack Research Room of the Saranac Lake Free Library, but Stevens said absolutely nothing about such a ludicrous appearance.

Certainly, an itinerant tinker like Baird would not have been voted the best-dressed man of the year. But it is difficult to believe that a man who served the public would have been as repulsive and disgusting as Donaldson's "Old Beard" and have been invited to stay overnight in a customer's home.

Donaldson intimates that Baird operated only in North Elba, but, of course, such a tinker would have covered the whole North Country. He certainly was working in the Au Sable Forks area when he made the silver ring for George Stevens, because Stevens was living there at the time and did not move to North Elba until years later.

Donaldson also claims that Baird went to the poorhouse in his old age. He seems to place the poorhouse in North Elba, but that would not have been correct. None of the Essex County towns had their own poorhouse; a central county poorhouse at Whallonsburg served them all. Donaldson also says that Baird died in the poorhouse, and when he was divested of his

35 The tombstone actually reads "Beard." The "Baird" spelling was used in a newspaper article on the man's passing.

rags—which he had always refused to relinquish—the patches were found to conceal a cache of $350, sufficient to build the Old White Church at North Elba.

Fortunately for us, an article appeared in the *Essex County Republican*, published at Keeseville, of October 30, 1873, which throws considerable light on Stuart Baird. It is as follows:

> North Elba, Oct. 19, 1873.
>
> Stewart Baird, commonly known as "old Baird," the tinker, came to the house of widow Rich on the night of the 17th last, got up in the night and he did not feel well, took some medicine and went back to bed. Got up again at daylight, went out of the door, came back, sat down by the stove and died instantly. They found on his person $199.15 in money, which was taken charge of by the poormaster, R.G. Scott, who will make arrangements for his burial and will also try and find his friends.

This article is very revealing. Stuart Baird had not gone to the poorhouse in his old age. Donaldson must have assumed this because the town poormaster took charge of the matter. Baird was still plying his trade as a tinker and had come to North Elba, where he stayed overnight at the house of the widow Rich (which was located on the Adirondack Lodge road). Certainly, if he had been as disreputable as Donaldson made him, the widow Rich would hardly have allowed him in her house. After Baird's death, $199.15 was found on his person, a sum considerably less than the $350 Donaldson reported. The newspaper article says nothing about it being found under patches in ragged clothing.

The poormaster at North Elba, Robert G. Scott, took charge of the matter. Under the circumstances, this would have been a usual procedure. Baird apparently had no permanent residence, and no one knew of any relatives or close friends. The poormaster had no connection with the county poorhouse. The poormaster had Baird buried in the North Elba Cemetery, buying a plot for his grave. Stuart Baird's tombstone—which bears the legend that he was born in Scotland, and died October 18, 1873, at seventy-seven years—is quite large and very respectable. The cost of the plot and the tombstone would have taken a large part of the $199.15 found.

It is certainly possible, and indeed probable, that if any money was left over, it could have been applied toward the building of the Union Church then being planned, but it would, of course, have been just a drop in the bucket.

In any event, the death of Baird occurred five years after the church was first proposed and initial pledges made, and was hardly the instrument of its construction.

In the fall of 1873, Moses Ames of North Elba donated the site for what was to become the Union Church on Old Military Road, and the foundation was partly laid. Quite some progress was made in 1874.

Donations for completion were earnestly solicited, and most North Elba people gave willingly and generously. The guests at Brewster's new hotel in Lake Placid contributed, and during the winter of 1874–75, various "sociables" were held as fund raisers, including one at Joseph Nash's inn and another at the house of William Hall, where net proceeds of the evening were $36.95.

At long last, in the summer of 1875, North Elba's first church, dedicated as Union Church but ever after known fondly as the White Church, opened its doors. The final cost of construction is unknown.

It was a plain, homely little building, but a church it was, shared by both Methodists and Baptists. Transient ministers served the local Methodists, who were already organized as a sect. The local Baptists did not formally organize until August 1879. The Reverend D.R. Pope was their first pastor, from 1880 until 1884.

But neither sect remained long at the White Church. It was the ultimate irony. After years of blood, sweat, and tears devoted to creating the White Church, both the Baptists and Methodists took flight and erected separate buildings of their own. The village of Lake Placid had come into being following completion of the White Church, and the burgeoning population and summer guests found it inconvenient to travel several miles for Sunday worship. The Baptists opened their new church on Main Street in 1885. On August 23, 1888, a small wooden Methodist church on the site of the present stone building was dedicated.

Was the White Church doomed? Providentially, no. There had appeared in North Elba in 1872 an eccentric but well-heeled lady by the name of Miss Anna Newman. Forsaking the high society of her native Philadelphia, Annie had purchased what is now Heaven Hill Farm and had turned gentlewoman farmer with a vengeance. Many are the delightful legends surrounding this quaint Betsey Trotwood,[36] but that is another story. Equal to, if not greater than, her interest in her farm was her love of the little white church at the crossroads. Annie was determined to keep it open and did so until her death, providing the funds for its survival. Here, regularly, each Sunday afternoon she conducted a Sunday school, giving credit cards to the pupils for learning verses from the bible. These cards could be traded at local stores for merchandise. She treated the entire Sunday school to picnic outings at various farms, and at nearly all times had as servant in her house some member of her Sunday class.

Annie Newman died in 1915. It was the beginning of the end for the White Church. From that time until 1929, the building was mostly idle. In 1929, the local Grange rented it, and in September 1930, the Grange bought the old edifice, removed the steeple, and made interior changes. The organization utilized the former church for many years as a place for meetings and social gatherings. When the Grange disbanded, the Placid Memorial Hospital acquired it and has since used it as a storehouse.

Something of the White Church remains with us. Following the Grange purchase, Willis Wells, then chairman of the North Elba Cemetery Association, had the pulpit and other church furniture placed in the chapel of the North Elba cemetery. Our Lake Placid-North Elba Historical Society has possession of the original church bible. The name Union Church stamped on the front cover is a wistful reminder of an act of love a hundred years ago in North Elba.[37]

---

36 Reference to a character in the Charles Dickens novel, "David Copperfield." Trotwood was Copperfield's aunt and surrogate mother.

37 In the late 1980s, Placid Memorial Hospital sold the land where the White Church stood to the Olympic Regional Development Authority for the construction of a new Olympic Training Center on the site. ORDA planned to demolish the White Church, but the North Elba Zoning Board of Appeals approved a last-minute request from a small, nondenominational Christian congregation to move the building to a donated lot behind the Lake Placid Jewish Cemetery. The building was trucked to its new home on June 16, 1988. Three months later, the Trinity Chapel congregation held its first worship service in the building on its new site. That congregation has occupied the White Church building ever since.

THIRTY-SIX

Stevens House

Date unknown

It is no use looking for a village called Lake Placid on a map of 1876.[38] No such entity existed then. The present upper village, from the Town Hall north to Placid Lake, was occupied solely by the great farms of Joseph Nash and Benjamin Brewster. The present lower village contained nothing but a sawmill.

Regardless, the west shore of Mirror Lake buzzed with activity in the summer months. Joe Nash had been taking in summer boarders at his red farmhouse since 1855, and in 1871 Ben Brewster had built a proper hotel, called the Lake Placid House (or just plain "Brewster's"), on his farm. In the summer of 1875, both places were overflowing with guests, and hordes of would-be patrons were being turned away. What the area needed, reckoned Joe Nash, was another hotel. He had become pleasantly well-to-do from the tourist trade and could afford to build one.

Accordingly, in the spring of 1876, Joe erected a second hotel overlooking Mirror and Placid Lakes and named it the Excelsior House. The site, chosen for its breathtaking views, was on the crest of the hill above his Red House, and directly opposite the present site of St. Agnes Catholic Church.

Joe had no intention of running Excelsior House himself. It was purely an investment, and he fully expected to sell it at a handsome profit. Moses C. Ferguson leased and ran it the first two summers and then built his own hotel, the Grand View. In 1878 a buyer for Excelsior House came along—John A. Stevens.

John Stevens was then thirty years old and living in Plattsburgh. He and his younger brother George had often talked about owning an Adirondack hotel. It was only a pipe dream, for neither one had any capital to speak of. Still, when John learned that Excelsior House was for sale, he managed to scrape up enough cash from friends and family for a down payment and signed a contract to buy the hotel plus forty acres of land. The purchase price was $9,000, payable in installments.

38 The best-known old Essex County map is the Gray's map, published in 1876.

On March 8, 1878, John Stevens, with a load of provisions and a pocketful of optimism, came over the wretched wagon roads from Plattsburgh to open his hotel. Only three families were then in residence at that small settlement on the west shore of Mirror Lake: Nash, Brewster, and Benjamin Wood, a recent arrival.

John immediately renamed the hotel the Stevens House. It was a pretty little structure, three-and-a-half stories high, with a broad veranda and an observation lookout. Capacity was ninety, and terms were $2.50 a day and 75¢ per meal.

That first summer, 120 guests registered. For the next three years, the hotel was filled to capacity, and John was able to pay off the contract, receiving a deed from Nash on August 9, 1881. It had been agreed that he would take in as partner his brother George, eight years his junior, but first he sent George to business school in Burlington, Vermont. George began assisting at the hotel in 1881 and became a full-fledged partner in 1883.

In December 1881, the brothers secured the first telegraph line to Lake Placid, from Saranac Lake, furnishing and drawing with their own teams all the poles needed for the entire line. This proved a clever move, inducing city businessmen to spend long vacations at the Stevens House.

All went famously until Christmas Eve 1885. At 8 o'clock on the morning of December 24, the upper rooms caught fire from an overheated stovepipe, and the entire building burned down.

Though the loss was enormous, both financially and psychologically, the brothers were made of the right stuff, and their credit was good. In March 1886, they commenced building a new hotel on the site. Forty workmen were employed.

By May 14 the framework, including a tower, was almost complete when a weird thing occurred. That night the structure was caught in the teeth of a freak whirlwind; the nearly completed hotel was torn from its moorings and went crashing down the hill. Every man jack in the township volunteered to help clear the debris. The tale of that community bee has been handed down for generations.

The mettle of the brothers had again been tested, and had again prevailed. Rebuilding commenced at once and continued at a rapid and remarkable pace. A great new Stevens House opened on July 4, 1886.

"Imposing," "stately," "palatial," and "commodious," pronounced E.R. Wallace's guidebook. It was indeed a splendid structure, built on lines of classic simplicity. It was four stories high, with a wide, encircling piazza on the ground floor and a central observation tower. The appointments were lavish—spacious parlors and dining rooms, hardwood floors throughout, carved wood furniture, bedding and carpets from Arnold Constable, with the best forty-pound hair mattresses and wire springs on every bed. Lighted by gas and warmed by steam, it had a hydraulic elevator, and a steam pump forced water to all parts of the house. There were hose attachments to fight fire, probably the main reason why this second Stevens House escaped the usual fate of the old wooden Adirondack hotels.

The water supply was more than ample. The Stevenses had built a dam on the outlet of Lake Placid, creating a small pond, and a hydraulic pump forced a steady supply of clear mountain water through a mile or so of piping up to the hotel's reservoir on the east side of the building. When the municipal water system was established just after the turn of the twentieth century, the dam was abandoned and the reservoir filled in. Today, more than a hundred years later, the foundation of the old pump house and remnants of the dam can still be found on the outlet.

The new hotel could hold two hundred guests, and rates were $3 a day. A week after the opening, on July 10, a Raymond excursion[39] of 110 came, leaving on the 15th, and constant new arrivals filled the hotel. Then, during the first week in September, the sterling reputation of the Stevens House was sealed for all time. President Grover Cleveland and his bride arrived, attended by several aides and even Cleveland's mother-in-law. The Clevelands were spending their honeymoon (with plenty of company) over at the old Prospect House—later called Saranac Inn—on Upper Saranac Lake, and made a side trip to Lake Placid to view the scenery. Two days and two nights were spent at the Stevens House, and a grand ball was held in Mrs. Cleveland's honor in the beautiful new ballroom.

Aside from the sumptuous service and accommodations, a big drawing card was the scenery. All the trees on Signal Hill had long since been cut down, and the site commanded a magnificent panorama, looking out on Mirror and Placid Lakes, primeval forests, and a full circle of the great peaks of the higher Adirondacks. Said Wallace's guidebook, "The view obtained from the piazza

---

39 A commercial tour operator, famous in the 1880s.

and observatory is one of the grandest any region affords. Tourists who have traveled in Europe are filled with surprise and admiration when surveying this spectacle, admitting that it surpasses anything they have ever beheld."

What is more, the hotel advertised its freedom from "those pests," blackflies and mosquitoes, due to its high altitude and fresh breezes, a claim that might be hotly contested by citizens on the hill today.

The brothers now flung all caution to the winds and took their boldest step yet. In 1887, only a year after the construction of the new hotel, they purchased for $25,000 the adjoining Brewster farm of several hundred acres. This included the little Brewster hotel, Lake Placid House, most of Signal Hill, and choice acreage on Placid Lake. What to do with all that land—and another hotel—had not yet been resolved but, as usual, the brothers' instincts were right on target. The deal turned out to be a real moneymaker. They soon sold the Lake Placid House. They mapped the land on Signal Hill and Placid Lake for cottage lots. Sites for summer homes and camps were soon in great demand, and the Stevenses could supply the best—for a price. Most of the luxurious dwellings built on the Stevens cottage lots around the turn of the twentieth century are still in existence.

In July 1889, the Stevenses installed a newfangled electric plant at the hotel. Said a Lake Placid correspondent for the *Essex County Republican*, "The electric light by which the Stevens House is now illuminated is not only a great attraction to the house, but shows the ever increasing energy and enterprise of the Stevens Bros. and adds not a little to the beauty of our pleasant little village."

With the future assured, each brother took a wife. John married Hannah Morey and would have one son, Kenneth. George married Frances Flanders of Au Sable Forks and would have four sons.

One more setback occurred in 1893, but it was quickly remedied with the usual Stevens aplomb. An annex, which they had built soon after the new hotel, burned down in February. The Stevenses were occupying it that winter and barely had time to escape in their nightclothes. A new annex was soon in evidence. By now, several attractive cottages had also been added to the hotel complex.

In the years before the railroad arrived at Lake Placid, stages connected guests with trains in Saranac Lake and Westport. There was also a daily stage via Wilmington Notch to Au Sable Chasm.

On August 11, 1897, four years after the railroad had reached Lake Placid, a second United States president was a guest at the Stevens House. President William McKinley, staying at the Hotel Champlain near Plattsburgh, made an excursion to Lake Placid via the Chateaugay Railroad, accompanied by Vice President Garrett A. Hobart and Secretary of War Russell A. Alger and their families. At the Lake Placid station, thousands had gathered to see the distinguished visitors, who proceeded to the Stevens House for a gala luncheon. The front of the hotel was decorated with Adirondack greenery, and the luncheon tables with native flowers. Afterward, members of the presidential party promenaded on the hotel piazza, admiring the view. They also visited John Brown's farm and grave. As the president was leaving the grave enclosure, someone began singing "John Brown's Body" in low tones, and all present joined in the refrain.

In the next three years, the brothers took two more bold steps. First, they built a large five-story addition on the west end, complete with soaring battlements. This increased capacity to four hundred. The Stevens House was now truly a "grand" hotel and a fine example of Second Empire architecture.

Golf was becoming a leading pastime at Adirondack resorts, and in 1900 the brothers converted their unsold lands on Signal Hill into a challenging little nine-hole golf course. Guests had only to walk a short distance from the front door to the first tee. The course, probably the most scenic in the Adirondacks, lured still another breed of client to the hotel and became one of its main attractions. George himself became an accomplished golfer. Around this time, they installed tennis courts on the site of the old reservoir.

In those early years, the brothers built up a steady and exclusive clientele. Gentleman sportsmen crowded the place. George and John knew the woods and were avid and accomplished hunters. Both led many an expedition of guests into the wilds of the Adirondacks, and Canada as well. In fact, a pack of hounds was kenneled on hotel grounds for years for use in hunting safaris.

Boating was another popular pastime, and the boys had a large and well-stocked boathouse on Placid Lake's Paradox Bay. Of distinct advantage to them was the busy little fleet of pleasure boats owned and operated by a third brother, Henry Stevens, whose *Ida*, *Nereid*, and grand old *Doris* plied the lake waters to the delight of tourists. Stevens House guests could board the pleasure craft at the hotel landing dock on Paradox Bay. Locals well remember Henry's son, Arthur, who piloted the *Doris* and *Doris II* on the lake for fifty-eight years.

All this time, a resort village had rapidly been taking over the old Nash and Brewster farms, energized by the building of pioneer hotels like the Stevens House. In 1900, the village was incorporated as Lake Placid. It is time now to take a closer look at those two movers and shakers who helped, in no small measure, to shape our environment.

John and George Stevens were Adirondack originals of staunch and stubborn Yankee heritage. They were born on the family farm in Black Brook township, Clinton County, to Curtis and Lucy Sherman Stevens, John in 1848 and George in 1856. Their grandfather, Asher Stevens, had settled the farm soon after the Revolution. Adirondack woods and waters were in the boys' blood, and they hunted and fished, it seemed, almost from the time they could walk.

Early on, the boys lost their father, who died at forty-six from the effects of being gored by a bull. Along with their brother Henry, they assisted their mother on the farm until her remarriage, and then struck out on their own at a tender age, mostly as farm hands. At fourteen, George was working on a farm in Vermont. The family had codfish for dinner every night, and George could not abide codfish. He soon left. The boys went on to other occupations, and both were salesmen for the Isham Wagon Co. in Plattsburgh when John bought the Excelsior House.

John and George loved people; they were born hoteliers, natural hosts, and great raconteurs. But more than that, they possessed what Hemingway called "grace under pressure," and they would not and could not tolerate defeat. Both were large, well-built men, and strong, although John had been somewhat frail in boyhood. John was the gentler one. Both were warm and genial with guests, but George's employees knew his darker side—he had at times an explosive temper and could be a hard taskmaster.

The two could probably have run the town and village completely on their own, with huge success. In his lifetime, George was North Elba supervisor, member of the state Assembly, president of the Bank of Lake Placid, and an officer of the Shore Owners Association, the State Hotelmen's Association, and the Adirondack Resorts Association. John was village mayor from 1908 to 1910, and good roads and streets were his hobby. During his term, he macadamized Main Street and built concrete sidewalks. He was also a great promoter of winter sports and was one of those who brought ice harness racing to Mirror Lake in the 1880s. His stable of trotters became famous.

In short, John and George Stevens were uncommon men, and one can even think of them in terms of those biblical "giants in the earth." Blessed with vision, courage, strength of character, vitality, and charm—and a good deal of horse sense—they became legends in their own time and loom larger than life today.

In 1905, John retired from the hotel to pursue other interests and sold his half interest to George. He died in 1913 at his home on Main Street, now the St. Eustace Episcopal rectory. Descendants now living are Mrs. Mary Rounds Tagliarino of Plattsburgh, Chris Rounds of Boyne City, Michigan, and their children.

During George's sole stewardship, the hotel became the most famous in the Adirondacks. In this era, musical entertainments came to the fore at the hotel. Talented musicians were brought in, capable of performing concerts as well as the lilting dance music of the day.

George A. Stevens died suddenly of a heart attack on September 17, 1920. His funeral was the largest ever held in the Adirondacks. There are no living descendants. His one grandchild died at the age of seventeen.

Now the mantle of hotel management descended upon the shoulders of George's sons: Paul, Hubert, Raymond, and Curtis. They acquired a large complex: the main hotel with 136 rooms and fifty-one baths, the annex with thirty-nine rooms and ten baths, a laundry, power house, employees' dining room and kitchen, garages, ice house, blacksmith shop, barns, four cottages, and the golf course.

The four boys had been raised as a rich man's sons, indulged, educated at prestigious schools. All were personable and, as well, outstanding sportsmen—hunters, golfers, speedboat racers, and, finally, gold-medal bobsled champions at the 1932 Winter Olympics. Of the four, only Raymond seems to have had a true talent for and interest in the hotel business. Mainly under his guidance, the hotel continued to thrive. Even without a firm hand at the wheel, it probably would have survived, riding as it did the crest of the Roaring Twenties. It received its greatest publicity in those frenetic times.

Now it was the favorite haunt of high-placed politicians. Governor Al Smith of New York stayed there, as well as state Comptroller Morris E. Tremaine and scores of New York City political VIPs. Governor Franklin D. Roosevelt, the third U.S. president to enter the Stevens House door, breakfasted there with local political bigwigs on September 11, 1929. The guest register listed an assortment of ambassadors, senators, congressmen, and eminent judges, including U.S. Supreme Court Justice Charles Evans Hughes. Other notables were famed aviatrix Ruth Nichols, Joseph P. Tumulty (who was formerly secretary to President Woodrow Wilson), and the great Metropolitan Opera star Amelita Galli-Curci.

In 1925, the sons borrowed huge sums to completely overhaul the aging hostelry. It was a foolish, extravagant, and futile move. But no one suspected then that the Great Depression would overtake the land—and, after that, vacation patterns would undergo a vast upheaval, spelling the end of the great Victorian hotels. The automobile had not yet wholly supplanted the horse, and the word motel had not been coined. Every room in the hotel was lavishly redecorated and refurnished. The kitchen went all-electric, and a basement level was converted into the finest grill in northern New York, with a sunken dance floor (Ben Bernie's famous band played there that summer).

Came those black days in October 1929, when Wall Street crashed and the bubble of prosperity burst. The Great Depression settled in and, locally, the Stevens House was one of its first victims. The sons were broke and, saddled with debt and unpaid taxes, the hotel was put up for auction in 1933. It was in disputed title and a maze of claims for years. A new company attempted to hold things together in the 1930s. The hotel was rented to outside interests each summer until 1941. Guests came, but in minuscule numbers compared to the past. One spark of the old life did remain—the grill, which became enormously popular with the young people of Lake Placid. Many an old-timer is still around to recall, with nostalgia, dancing at the Stevens House grill of a Saturday night.

The Stevens House went into bankruptcy in 1940 and was not opened for guests the summer of 1941, but the grill was leased out—and to none other than Raymond Stevens. (Ray had continued in the hotel business as manager of various resorts, including Sun Valley.) He hired Lazlo Bartell's broadcasting orchestra, and locals happily patronized the grill. The Lake Placid Ski Club's annual ball and an Alumni Association benefit dance were held there in August. Neither the hotel nor the grill was ever opened again. It was fitting that a Stevens presided over that last hurrah of the grand old resort.

Throughout World War II, the hotel remained idle and empty. Because of huge unpaid tax liens, Essex County finally received base title in 1943 and attempted a sale, but no one wanted the tired and forlorn old dowager. In 1947, a buyer at last appeared: Margaret Nohowel and her Signal Hill Colony Inc. Title passed on September 21, 1947. The demolition of the Stevens house was immediately under way. All at once, there was a hole in the sky up there on Signal Hill where that great house had dominated the landscape for sixty-one years.

The boathouse on Paradox Bay, the annex, and the laundry building were preserved. The annex was sold to Mr. and Mrs. Isadore Urfirer in 1948. Completely renovated, it served as an inn under several owners until 1967, when it was torn down. The boathouse saw various uses until 1972 when it, too, was razed. Only one building is left to remind us of what once was: the old laundry, still in existence in an altered state. First serving as the Signal Hill Art Center for concerts and plays, it later became the up-scale Frederick's restaurant, and is now a condominium.

The golf course is long gone, and no hint of it remains. The hotel property and golf course were parceled into building plots, and the whole of Signal Hill is now a choice residential district. Ironically, few residents can boast of that great scenic outlook once so widely advertised; tree growth and numerous buildings have seen to that. Artist Averil Conwell's delightful murals of Stevens House scenes can be found at the North Elba Town Hall. Originally commissioned for and displayed at Frederick's restaurant, Nancy and Fred Richards recently gifted them to the community.

Of all Lake Placid's golden age hotels, the Stevens House was the most famous and surely the most beloved. The community deeply mourned its demise. But Harry Coonrod, a former employee, left with us an eloquent and meaningful epitaph when he said, "The passing of the Stevens House is not a passing into oblivion. It is, rather, a graceful retreat into memory."

THIRTY-SEVEN

Grand View Hotel

Updated February 10, 1995

As Joseph Nash began to understand North Elba's vast potential for tourism, he got into the real estate business and began to sell off lots from his vast holdings. One of the first to acquire a slice of Joe's pie was Reuben Clifford, who invested in several lots. In 1878, Clifford sold a lot to Moses Ferguson, who had been renting and operating Joe Nash's Excelsior House. The lot was located at the top of the Nash farm hill, overlooking lakes Mirror and Placid, and commanded what probably were and are the most spectacular mountain views in all the Adirondacks. Only twenty years before, Joe Nash had trapped a panther on the very spot where Ferguson in 1878 erected a little hotel aptly named the Grand View. A small, plain but tidy building, it boasted three stories capped with an observation lookout and an encircling veranda amply stocked with rocking chairs.

Two more hotels soon rose on the slope of hill below the Grand View and opposite the present post office: in 1880, the Allen House (dubbed "mammoth" by a contemporary county newspaper); and, in 1883, the Mirror Lake House, eventually the largest and most luxurious of its time. The infant village emerging from a wilderness now had five well-frequented houses of accommodation (including the Lake Placid House), and an embryonic Main Street was taking shape along Joe Nash's cow path.

Henry Allen, proprietor of the Allen House, was, like many another pioneer Adirondack hotelkeeper, originally a farmer. Born in Ripton, Vermont, on April 23, 1848, he was one of five brothers who fought in the Civil War. For a time he farmed in Lewis, near Elizabethtown, New York. In April 1874, the young man moved to North Elba, hired out to a farmer, Deacon Alpheus Demmon, and soon married the farmer's daughter, Sarah.

Simple farmer or no, Henry Allen was a born entrepreneur, sensing at once which way the wind was blowing up on the hill off Mirror Lake. In 1876 he rented Ben Brewster's small hotel, ran it until March 1880, and later that spring built his own Allen House, which opened that summer. At the same time, Henry Allen operated a stage line between Lake Placid and Au Sable Forks.

Moses Ferguson's Grand View was having its ups and downs. "Mose," as he was called (little is known of him beyond his name), seems to have been unsuited to the tourist-catering business. For a couple of years he ran the Grand View himself. In 1880, he leased it for three years to Andrew J. Daniels and clergyman Henry C. Lyon. In 1881, Ferguson and his wife Louise, then living in the Town of Au Sable in Clinton County, New York, sold the Grand View to Henry Allen for $4,275, subject to two mortgages—one held by Reuben Clifford for $1,800, the other by Byron R. Brewster for $446—and also subject to the Daniels-Lyon lease, which expired May 1, 1883. From 1883 until 1886, Allen operated the Grand View in conjunction with his Allen House. His purchase of the Grand View was propitious, for his Allen House burned to the ground in 1886 and was never rebuilt.

In his little book, *Lake Placid: The Adirondack Village that Became World Famous* (Glencraft Printing, 1968), George Carroll devotes a chapter to a purported honeymoon stay at the Grand View by President Grover Cleveland and his bride in the summer of 1886. Unfortunately for the Grand View, this account is erroneous. County newspapers (especially the *Elizabethtown Post* of September 9, 1886) tell the true story. In September 1886, the Clevelands instead actually stayed for two nights at Lake Placid's Stevens House, where a grand ball was held in their honor.

In 1885, Allen had built a telephone line from the Allen House through the wilderness to Saranac Lake, and probably switched the line to the Grand View after the Allen House burned down.

In 1894, the opulent Mirror Lake House also burned to the ground, leaving the Grand View the sole public house on the hill, which, in the natural order of things, had come to bear its name.

The village of Lake Placid was rapidly expanding, and Henry Allen, a man of broad vision, proceeded over a span of years to acquire additional land and enlarge his Grand View by degrees. By 1900, the hotel had attained its final proportions. The result was, next to the Stevens House, the largest, most gracious and imposing public place of accommodation in the now nationally recognized summer resort of Lake Placid. It would, along with the Stevens House, dominate the skyline of Lake Placid village for generations. No substantial outer alterations were made in after years.

From the start, the ingenious Allen's new creation was eminently successful. His dining room's bill of fare rivaled that of the finest New York restaurants. The story goes that one night in 1897, the renowned hotelier Paul Smith of St. Regis Lake, a rough-hewn Adirondack original who inspired many a legendary tale, came to the Grand View to sample one of its famous dinners. For dessert, he took only custard pie. Allen was in the kitchen when out came Smith's waitress laughing uncontrollably. She was finally able to gasp, "That old gentleman took the custard pie up in his hands to eat it."

The appointments of the Grand View were lavish. It also had an elevator of the hydraulic type, operated by an enormous steam pump. Curiously, the steam pump was not replaced by an electric motor until the 1920s. Just when electric lights first came to the Grand View has not been recorded. It certainly must have been years before the village electric plant went on line in November 1906. It is known that in the summer of 1889, the Stevens House installed its own electric plant, and it is reasonable to assume that, not to be outdone, the Grand View soon followed suit.

Henry Allen inaugurated the hotel's permanent policy of engaging an orchestra for dancing and musicales in the great ballroom. The hotel's boathouse on Mirror Lake was amply stocked with rowboats and canoes. Tennis courts were provided and all manner of entertainments devised to divert a prosperous, worldly, and eminent clientele. Strolling paths were cut through the beautiful woods down to the outlet of Lake Placid, punctuated by rustic gazebos for rest and relaxation.

In the wintertime, when the hotel was closed, Henry found another outlet for his energy and enthusiasm. A good judge of horseflesh, he acquired a few fine horses, and in the 1880s and 1890s, he became involved in ice harness racing on Mirror Lake, Lake Placid's first and pioneer winter sport.

One problem that plagued all the early hotel owners was water. There was water, water everywhere, as far as the eye could see, but no conventional waterworks to service their large-scale requirements. If anyone was equal to the challenge, it was Henry Allen. As early as 1881, he built a dam on the outlet of Lake Placid, some distance down the hill in back of the Grand View. With the installation of a hydraulic ram, a wealth of sparkling Adirondack water was pumped up the hill through an elaborate pipeline to the Allen House. The Mirror Lake House hooked on to the system.

When the Mirror Lake House and Allen House burned down, the Grand View became the sole beneficiary of the water system. Henry built a thirty-by-forty-foot, 250,000-gallon reservoir surrounded by an ornamental iron fence, directly behind the hotel. Subsequently, so plentiful was the supply that Henry went into the waterworks business with Byron Brewster and began to provide the surplus commodity to parts of the growing village.

Had it not been for the cunning Stevens brothers, John and George, hosts of the rival Stevens House over on Signal Hill, this idyllic state of affairs might have continued indefinitely. But the Stevenses cannily built a second dam on the outlet upriver from Henry Allen's, installed a pump, piped a goodly supply of water to a reservoir at the Stevens House, and also began to sell surplus to villagers. The community now had a water system of sorts, served by two separate waterworks.

Lake Placid's famous "War of the Waterworks" began in earnest. Allen and Brewster soon found, to their chagrin, that the Stevenses, with a pump and dam farther upstream controlled by the temper of the owners, could take the lion's share of the water, causing severe shutdowns in the partners' system. The partners sought a solution by tapping a brook near Whiteface Inn and laying seven miles of four-inch pipe, the water to flow by force of gravity directly into village street pipes. Some of the pipe had been laid when a stretch of state land brought Allen and Brewster up short. Allen and Brewster petitioned the state for permission to cross the land. Reportedly, they were outraged when, through the machinations of George Stevens, who was then serving in the state Assembly, their project was effectively quashed.

Annoying shutdowns continued. Finally, at the turn of the twentieth century, Allen and Brewster persuaded the Lake Placid Club to buy them out. The Club soon sold the water system to the village, which then proceeded to build a three-million-gallon reservoir on Mount Whitney, never utilizing the Grand View reservoir. The village also bought the Stevens waterworks and, at a reputed total cost of $40,000, installed the municipal water system as it exists today.

The Grand View reservoir, an empty hole but with its ornamental fence intact, was still in existence decades later. Now, after a century has passed, traces of both the Allen and Stevens dam abutments are still in evidence on the outlet of Lake Placid.

In 1901, Henry Allen sold the Grand View Hotel to Thomas Parkes and built the National Hotel in the lower section of Lake Placid, which he conducted until failing health forced his retirement. The beloved and respected pioneer hotelman, also sheriff of Essex County for three years and North Elba supervisor for two years, died at Lake Placid in December 1916 at the age of sixty-eight. He left no children, unless one believes that the Grand View Hotel deserves that distinction.

Thomas Parkes was born in England. Arriving in America as a young man, he became involved in the hotel business in New York City, eventually owning and managing the Hargrave Hotel there. Parkes continued the lofty traditions of the Grand View, keeping the place open from June into October. It was Parkes who established the popular baseball diamond that existed for years on Grand View grounds. The scene of lively matches between guests and employees of the Grand View and those of rival hotels, the field was also used by the local high school and various other North Country baseball teams. It was even a practice area for the Lake Placid polo team in the 1920s.

Thomas Parkes died in 1910. About 1913, his widow, Grace Riley Parkes, sold a half-interest in the Grand View, as well as a full interest in the Hargrave Hotel, to Morton B. Marshall.

Marshall, a native of Ticonderoga, New York, was a seasoned hotelman who had been and still was the manager of the famous old Saranac Inn on Upper Saranac Lake. Marshall's long career in the hotel business included the Alexandria and St. Andrew in New York City. In 1915, he acquired Mrs. Parkes' remaining half-interest in the Grand View, becoming sole owner.

By 1916, the property consisted of more than seventy acres, down to Mirror Lake on the east and through beautiful woods down to the outlet of Lake Placid on the west. Besides the main hotel, there were two annexes—an overflow room annex and an annex used mainly for storage and employee housing—plus a cottage known as Robin's Nest and a boathouse on Mirror Lake.

It was in 1916 that Morton B. Marshall began to envision a great new role for the Grand View Hotel property. He succeeded in getting local businessmen and New York City capitalists interested in financing a new, year-round, fireproof, 150-room hotel with numerous cottages. No less a firm than that of the great Frederick Olmsted, designer of Central Park, was to be called in for overall planning and landscaping. E.C. Whiting of the Olmsted firm actually made a casual survey of the property in June 1916. His description of the hotel is interesting—"a big wooden ark of a typical summer hotel type." Negotiations in Lake Placid and New York City were intense into 1917, when the project was abruptly abandoned, probably due to the intervention of World War I. Henceforth the Grand View would remain unchanged.

Marshall sold the Grand View in 1922 to the Placid Hotel Corporation, of which Walter Arnold Ruykeyser seems to have been the principal stockholder. Placid Hotel Corporation was completely in Jewish ownership, and from this time forward until its demise, the Grand View's clientele was exclusively Jewish. Up until this time, no major hostelry in Lake Placid had admitted Jews, a practice prevalent in the Adirondacks as well as many other resort areas. The Grand View's policy marked the beginning of the end of religious discrimination in many local hotels.

During the Placid Hotel Corporation era, the hotel was always under the personal direction of Ruykeyser who, in the 1920s, was instrumental in designing for the Soviet government what was to be the largest asbestos mine in the world, and who lived in Russia for a year. Under Ruykeyser, the hotel received a long-delayed overhauling. Lobby, public rooms, and bedrooms were completely renovated. The day of grand balls had passed, and Henry Allen's splendid ballroom was converted into a cafe or casino, always with an orchestra for dancing.

Because of its size and amenities, the casino, known as the Alpine Grill, was a popular choice for fund-raising entertainments by area organizations in the 1920s. Occasionally, Broadway and radio personalities were brought in to enhance the festivities.

Northwoods Sanatorium of Saranac Lake held a dance and impromptu auction there in August 1925. Premier orchestra conductor Paul Whiteman stepped in to lead the Grand View orchestra for dancing, and Benny Rubin, Schubert musical comedy star, sang.

The huge sum of $10,000 was raised at the grill in July 1929 for the benefit of the Lake Placid and Saranac Lake synagogues. Two of Broadway's most famous names were present. Eddie Cantor, then starring in *Whoopee* on Broadway, acted as master of ceremonies, and the great Sophie Tucker—of stage and vaudeville fame—was hostess of the prestigious affair.

Just before the 1932 Winter Olympic Games, a parcel of the hotel land was sold to the Town of North Elba for the site of the indoor Olympic Arena. The old employee housing annex that occupied part of the land was then torn down.

From 1931 to 1956, the old hundred-room hostelry was under the management, and then the ownership, of the dynamic Edgar V.M. Gilbert of New York City, who also had an interest in Lake Placid's St. Moritz Hotel for a time. The hotel could then accommodate 250.

Gilbert loved Lake Placid and vigorously promoted it as a resort. He updated the hotel in many ways. Despite the Grand View's ripe old age and now unfashionable facade, despite the Great Depression and the gradual winding down of the grand-hotel era, his strong and engaging personality attracted people like a magnet. The Grand View was never livelier than during the Gilbert days. It provided constant entertainments and, as in the past, a dance orchestra was always in residence.

During World War II, the Grand View took on a Continental aura as a Mecca for European refugees, particularly those from Hitler's Germany. Gilbert made every effort to provide the customs of the lost homeland. "Afternoon coffee and Schnecken on the porch" was a featured ritual. From the broad veranda, guests looked out nostalgically on a mountain landscape reminiscent of the summer retreats they had once known.

During the war, Gilbert served a stint as food director for the American Red Cross in Africa. When Lake Placid boys came into his orbit, he saw to it they received special rations, and plenty of them. Following the war, he joined the firm of H. Hentz Co., New York stockbrokers, with whom he was associated until his death in 1962. He was the founder and donor of the E.V.M. Gilbert annual art awards at Brandeis University.

Edgar Gilbert closed the doors of the Grand View in 1956. They were never again opened. The times were a-changing. Vacationers no longer came for an entire summer season, and they were bypassing the faded old Victorian hotels for the new breed of cabins and motels. In 1960, the property was sold to Robert Hanke, of Rye, New York, who had no immediate plans for development. At last, vacant for several years, the once grand edifice on Grand View Hill, sole remaining relic of Lake Placid's "golden age" of summer hotels—the core of it dating back eighty-three years—was demolished in 1961. A Holiday Inn[40] soon rose on the site.

The twenty-four-room overflow annex, just to the northwest of the hotel, had previously been sold to Fred Wertheim and was not included in

40 Now a Crowne Plaza franchise.

the demolition. This last remnant of the famous old Grand View burned to the ground in January 1966.

THIRTY-EIGHT
Cascade House
March 27, 1980

On a visit to North Elba in 1858, John Brown Jr. wrote to his brother, "From Keene we came by a new road, laid south of the old route over the mountains. This new road is the most romantically grand and beautiful that I ever saw in my life."

He referred, of course, to Cascade Lakes Pass, and his sentiments have been echoed down the years by hordes of travelers. "Remarkable," "picturesque," "astonishing," "savage," "sublime"—these are a few of the adjectives lavished on that long, narrow fault valley and its two lakes, wedged between the precipitous Pitchoff and Cascade Mountains. It is, without question, a place of wild, bleak, sinister beauty. Its lakes are black as night and suggest bottomless depths. An avalanche seems poised at the top of every beetling cliff.

North Elba owns just a small part of the pass, but has laid claim to much of its history.

As early as 1810, the Elba Iron Works was mining ore on the south shores of the upper lake. Locally, the lakes were first called Square Pond and Long Pond, and Cascade was known as Long Pond Mountain. Pitchoff went by the name of Keene Mountain. Briefly, the lakes became Walton's Ponds, probably for pioneer Oliver Walton of Keene. Then, for many years, they were known and shown as Edmonds' Ponds, for William Edmonds, who lived not far to the east.

With the abandonment of the Elba mine about 1814, Cascade Pass returned to its wilderness ways, known only to neighboring hunters and fishermen and the ravens who traditionally nested there.

In those days, the road from Keene to North Elba was far removed from Cascade Lakes. Generally known as the Old Mountain Road, it climbed Alstead Hill in Keene and threaded a gorge on the north side of Pitchoff. Much of this ancient route is still visible. A primitive wagon track, it was steep, rough, rutty, boggy, stony, treacherous, and lamentable. Finally, in

1858, the state surveyed a bypass road from Keene to North Elba through Cascade Pass, and completed it in 1859.

Over this new route passed the mail and sightseers bound for North Elba. It undoubtedly won more friends than Old Mountain Road. Still, one early wayfarer described it as "ten miles of rocks and mud holes," and the stretch through the pass as "a narrow and dangerous causeway, a corduroy so narrow that the hubs of the wheels almost impended over the water." And since the reins of the stage were often in the hands of a one-armed driver, travelers must have feared for their lives.

The glory days of Cascade Pass had just begun. For years, its sole habitation had been a little log shanty occasionally occupied by fishermen. In 1878, Nicaner Miller and his wife Ellen Goff Miller built a small summer hotel on a handkerchief of land between the two lakes. They named it Cascade House in honor of the fairy-tale streamlet that hangs on the mountain like a bridal veil. In no time, the name Cascade was pinned also to Edmonds' Ponds and Long Pond Mountain.

The next year, the U.S. Government opened a post office at Cascade House under the name of Cascadeville (changed to Cascade in 1904, and discontinued on January 1, 1919). Miller was the first postmaster. In the winter months, the post office operated out of a farmhouse in the Cascade settlement. Today, an old envelope postmarked "Cascadeville" is a choice collector's item.

Cascade House was a hit from the start. The place became famous for boating and trout fishing, and Mrs. Miller starred as the cook. Fifty years after his visits there, Dr. Addison Baird reminisced, "I can still taste in imagination those freshly caught trout with appetizing toasted bread and hot tea for supper."

Directly and conveniently past the front porch ran the main highway. Here the Elizabethtown-North Elba stage made a routine stop, and passengers disembarked for revival and refreshment. In winter, the precarious main road was ignored, and horse and coach took to the icebound lakes.

Until 1893, when the railroad came to Lake Placid, the stagecoach was the mainstay of all the broad countryside. Bringing people, mail, packages, and gossip, its window-rattling arrival was the event of the day, and its weather-beaten drivers the heroes of the hour.

In 1861, the mail stage (usually a buckboard) was running once a week between Elizabethtown and Saranac Lake, the thirty-four-mile trip consuming eleven hours. By the 1880s, a coach was running daily. Tally-hos met every train and steamer at Westport and proceeded to Elizabethtown, where connections were made for North Elba. Four-and six-horse coaches were primed for the adventurous climb over the mountains. It was four hours to Cascade House, and the fare was $2—$2.50 to Mountain View House, farther up the road. Travelers could board a connecting stage to Adirondack Lodge at Torrance Corners.

Many are the names of the intrepid early drivers: Arnold Partridge, William Hanchett, H.R. Reynolds, and Person & Judd, to name a few. In 1882, Ashley Leach took over the route and purchased fine new coaches and horses. In later years, Agnew Bros. of Elizabethtown operated the line.

Despite the railroad and the automobile, the Essex County stage survived well up into the twentieth century. In 1919, a veteran driver boasted of not missing a trip or losing a horse for thirty years.

In 1883, the Millers sold the Cascade House, and for the next ten years it prospered under the partnership of J. Henry Otis and Warren F. and Sidney H. Weston, the latter pair also owners of a general store, inn, and forge in Keene. The Cascade House was handsomely enlarged, and a boathouse, bowling alley, and tavern room were added.

Between 1893 and 1906, the hotel reached its zenith of popularity under the magic wand of the widowed Mrs. Ednah M. Weston. Still a Mecca for trout fisherman, it also provided lavish amusements: boating, climbing, outdoor picnics, drives to scenic curiosities, progressive hearts parties, dances in the ample parlors, chafing-dish suppers, and tennis and ping pong tournaments. The gala climax of the season was "Float Night" on Upper Cascade Lake. Boats festooned with flags and Japanese lanterns floated up the lake in single file, returning abreast. There they formed into a pontoon bridge, and the boaters joined in song while music played in the background and echoed far up on Pitchoff Mountain.

The Goff family of Cascade sold milk, vegetables, and beef to the hotel and also provided hayrides, a baseball diamond in back of the one-room Cascade Schoolhouse, and a pocket-sized golf course on the Goff farm.

Mrs. Weston's pampered guests returned year after year. A cherished hostess, she was equally loved by her help; despite taking meals in a separate dining hall, employees ordered their meals from the same menu used by hotel guests.

The great forest fire of 1903 roared through Cascade Pass, devastating Cascade Mountain and the southern slopes of Pitchoff. Walter Goff, fifteen, with horse and wagon, outraced the fire to Cascade House and carried off Mrs. Weston and her daughters in the nick of time. Rabbits, porcupines, and deer fleeing the fire raced the road with them. A pair of fish hawks that had nested and reared their young for years near Cascade House were great favorites of the guests. As the fire raged, they circled the lakes with plaintive cries and then disappeared, never to return. Miraculously, the fire swept around the hotel clearing. The Cascade House came through the holocaust unscathed.

Following Mrs. Weston's retirement in 1905, the hotel went into a gradual decline under various owners: Horace Nye, J. Henry Otis, and W.D. Slattery. It had a brief renaissance in the early 1920s. None other than Miss Abigail Harding, President Warren G. Harding's sister, was a frequent visitor, costume balls were staged, and a "wireless telephone"—the only one in the Adirondacks—was installed, enabling guests to hear the latest stock exchange and baseball news.

In 1923, the property passed into the ownership of the Lake Placid Club—all the buildings, both lakes, and 1,440 acres of land, including Pitchoff and Cascade Mountains. The Club had ambitious plans for its new branch. They stocked the lakes with about fifty thousand fingerling trout. The hotel was spruced up with renovations, plate-glass picture windows, new baths, balconies, fireplaces, outdoor tearoom, fresh paint, and new furniture at a cost of $65,000.

Bathing, fishing, mountain climbing, boating, tennis, putting, croquet, bowling, and crossword puzzle contests were served up, and guests loafed on Cascade's cool porch, idly watching Bridal Veil Falls. But the place was not a great success. The sun shone briefly there, and the new breed of sun-worshippers found it gloomy and forbidding.

Cascade House did not open in the summer of 1927, for the state had closed the stretch of highway dipping down to the hotel and was blasting a replacement road out of the back ledges. One old-time Cascade resident has insisted that the state's blasting operations sounded the death knell of the old Cascade House. Its roofs, he said, were riddled with holes where stones plunged through clear to the basement.

Whatever the reason, the Lake Placid Club never opened Cascade House again. The buildings were torn down and the entire 1,440 acres were sold to New York State, becoming a part of the "forever wild" Forest Preserve.

Like all mysterious and romantic spots, Cascade Pass has its share of myths and legends.

The first is the oft-told tale that the two lakes were once a single body of water divided in the mid-1800s by a landslide. Numerous avalanches indeed thundered down the sides of Cascade and Pitchoff in both the nineteenth and twentieth centuries, but none divided one lake into two. The 1812 patent for the Elba ore bed very definitely described the two lakes exactly as they appear today. That they were one lake far back in the mists of geologic time is probable, but not within the memory of man.

Other yarns feature the lakes as the watery grave of numberless humans and beasts of burden. In the old days, they say, horses and wagons sometimes lost their footing on the narrow road and plunged into the lake, taking with them passengers who were seen no more. Only one of these tales appears to be authentic. A peddler and his wagon actually did go over the bank, but whether this gentleman drowned, no one now can say.

The only recorded accidental death at Cascade Pass is that of George Slawinski of Detroit, Michigan. In August 1926, Slawinski, seventeen, left the Cascade House and proceeded to scale a high cliff about seven hundred feet up Cascade Mountain while a party of his friends went swimming in the lake. Losing his footing, he hurled down the steep rock face to the hotel reservoir and died instantly.

Other embroideries still circulate about the origin of the popular Stagecoach Rock. Adirondack historian Maitland DeSormo has diligently ferreted out the true story.

In the mid-1930s, a maintenance crew was giving the Pass road a periodic checkup and came upon a large boulder recently dislodged from the side of Pitchoff. The problem was reported to Donald Rogers of the state highway department and Bill Petty of state conservation.

There was sufficient space for a small parking area, and the boulder was nudged there and tilted upright. The two directors then agreed that, suitably engraved, it would make an ideal monument to the old stagecoach route through the pass. A suggestion was quickly shot down that the rock be carved, buried nearby, and later "accidentally" unearthed and reported as an archeological find.

Lewis Brown of Chazy, a monument designer, drew a working sketch of a stagecoach and made a rubber stencil for the stonework. With the aid of Brown's stencil and the region's first portable sandblaster, Wilfred Carnes of Carnes Granite Company in Au Sable Forks set about engraving at the Pass. By nightfall, he had not finished. Aware that vandals abound, even in the Adirondacks, the Carnes party pitched a tent over their truck body and spent the night there.

Wilfred Carnes's carved coach and its riders, though English in concept, are an affectionate reminder of the burly Adirondack stages rumbling through Cascade Pass a century ago. A great tourist attraction, the rock adds much to the climate of the pass.

Stagecoach and Cascade House are gone, but the Pass still lures fishermen, campers, tourists, climbers of Pitchoff and Cascade—and rock hounds.

There are caves on Pitchoff, discovered in 1949. And Cascade Mountain is a rock hound's paradise. State geologist Ebenezer Emmons was the first to sift through its treasures in 1841. (Emmons was also probably the first to ascend Cascade, although that credit has been given to Lon Pierce.)

On Cascade are found the ancient Adirondacks' richest specimens of Grenville, among the oldest recognized rock formations on Earth. Landslides have laid bare the primary limestone. Here on the mountain and in the bed of the stream are rare and colorful minerals and semiprecious gems: green diopside, black augite and magnetite, blue calcite, rose quartz, brown sphene, hornblende, labradorite, jasper, scapolite, idocrase, and other Grenville contact minerals.

"High up the precipice a series of caves occur, which are the peculiar deposits of the gems and minerals, and almost rival in beauty and variety the caverns of eastern story," said historian Winslow Watson in 1869.

"No one can be found now who knows of their existence," said historian Russell Carson in 1927.

There are some who say, in 1980, that the caves are still there.

THIRTY-NINE

Castle Rustico

Date unknown

Everyone knows about Henry Van Hoevenberg and his great log hotel, the Adirondack Lodge. Few, however, know the story of William Fox Leggett and his great log hotel, Castle Rustico.

By one of those odd historical crotchets, writers over the past century have romanticized and immortalized Van Hoevenberg ad infinitum while virtually ignoring Leggett, probably the most dashing and romantic figure in all of Lake Placid lore. And, though Castle Rustico predated Adirondack Lodge and outlived it by half a century, it has been accorded a mere footnote in local history. David Ackerman's recent book, *Placid Lake 1893–1993* (The Shore Owner's Association of Lake Placid, 1993), gave them some long-needed attention, but the picturesque Castle Rustico and the provocative Leggett deserve to have even more of their stories told.

We have seen that the first village hostelry, Ben Brewster's little Lake Placid House, was built on Mirror Lake in 1871, ushering in our golden age of summer hotels. By then, eyes had already turned northward to the beautiful and secluded Placid Lake, with its unspoiled and uninhabited shores and islands. In 1870, the first summer camp—built by Monroe Hall, a prominent Plattsburgh lawyer—made an appearance far up on the east lake. Among the next outlanders of record to build on the big lake were William Fox Leggett and his wife Ida Frances.

In 1873–74, Ida Frances Leggett purchased parts of Great Lot 273, about midway up the western shore. The land had considerable lake frontage and included a chunk of the west side of Moose Island. On the mainland, near the mouth of a pretty little stream that tinkled its way through the premises, the Leggetts erected a rustic log cabin from trees felled on the property. Ida Frances, with childlike perception, christened the stream Fairy Brook. It was later and is now known as Minnow Brook.

Both William and Ida Frances were from the world of the New York theater. William was a Shakespearean actor of some renown. He bore so astonishing a resemblance to the great tragedian of the era, Edwin Booth, that he was facetiously referred to as Edwin Booth Leggett. Ida Frances, an actress who appeared in humorous sketches, would be labeled a comedienne today. How these two people from the esoteric world of the stage discovered Lake Placid at so early a date can only be surmised. Quite likely, they learned of the wild beauty and welcome serenity and isolation of the area from guests of the Brewster hotel.

And what prompted these two people to enlarge their little cabin into a huge, three-story house of public accommodation is also a matter for speculation. The Leggetts' great log hotel, with the bewitching name of Castle Rustico, opened for business the summer of 1879. William and Ida Frances catered exclusively to fellow actors and actresses and other artists of various persuasions. The guests must have staged their own entertainments, and the atmosphere of Castle Rustico could not have been less than magical. It would be interesting indeed to know the identities of those guests, but nothing about them has come to light.

Seneca Ray Stoddard's guidebooks of the 1880s gave a concise picture of the hotel's unconventional appearance: "Castle Rustico is on the west shore opposite Moose Island—an immense gabled structure of logs, rough outside and rustic in, surrounded by primeval forests, grotesque, weird, and attractive. It is commanded by W.F. Leggett, who with his efficient lieutenant, and supported by faithful retainers, receives the wayfarer right royally."

The *Essex County Republican* reported: "Mr. Leggett has really a fine log house. It will pay anyone to go and see it; it looks fine from the lake. Mrs. Leggett has a very fine piano and she knows how to handle the keys."

Castle Rustico was the first hotel directly on Lake Placid, and was claimed to be the largest log structure in the world and larger than Adirondack Lodge. The only access was by boat. In those pioneer times, Captain Theodore White's little steamer *Mattie* made trips around the lake twice daily and obligingly transported guests and their baggage to and from the hotel.

William Fox Leggett, the king of Castle Rustico, was born April 12, 1839, presumably in or near the village of West Farms, Westchester County, now in the borough of the Bronx. His ancestors had settled there upon arrival in America from England in the late 1600s, and the name Leggett was a prominent and important one in that area for generations. William's father and mother, William Fox and Sarah C. Hull Leggett, were Quakers, and he was a lifelong member of the Society of Friends in New York City.

William trained for the stage and was especially drawn to Shakespearean roles, to which he devoted his entire acting career. He did not, however, appear in full-scale productions. Unfortunately for him, the great Edwin Booth was performing during the same period. Booth had his own theater in New York, where for years he staged and starred in major Shakespearean plays. William's amazing physical resemblance to Booth was a great handicap. Unable to compete one-on-one with Booth, he confined himself to one-man shows in minor theaters, acting out memorable Shakespearean roles in full costume. Still, strikingly handsome, physically deft and vital, he achieved considerable notice and might be called the poor man's Edwin Booth. A June 1867 playbill of the old French Theater, on 14th Street, records his appearance there for six nights in roles from *Richard III*, *Romeo and Juliet*, and *The Merchant of Venice.* He was then twenty-eight years old. It is entirely possible he went on tour throughout the country with his one-man productions.

The wilderness setting up on Lake Placid had great appeal for the Leggetts. They had come home. There is every indication they renounced the New York stage once they found Lake Placid. During the 1880s, they remained at Rustico all year, rattling around alone in their great, drafty domicile in the winter months. They claimed they never felt lonely there, and they were not reclusive. Having made friends among the townspeople, they often waltzed down the frozen lake to visit. One local inhabitant reported that the Leggetts attended one of Henry Allen's balls at his Allen House in March 1881, "and tripped the light fantastic like a boy and girl of 20."

The Leggetts gave the North Country a dose of culture. During the summer, both William and Ida Frances presented their monodramas to guests at local hotels. In the winter months, they traveled about northern New York, performing in some of the larger villages to crowded houses and high praise from the press. They were in Keeseville at least twice, and their second appearance, sponsored by the Moonshine Racquet Club, was reported at some length in the *Essex County Republican* of December 15, 1887. William, in authentic costumes, acted out scenes from *Hamlet*, *Richard III*, and *The Merchant of Venice*, and Ida Frances presented "her inimitable humorous creations." A splendid portrait of William, the only likeness known to exist, accompanied the article.

Abruptly, and reportedly in 1888, the Leggetts ceased to operate Castle Rustico as a hotel. They had usually been booked to capacity, and running such an operation may have become a burden. On the other hand, they had made a pleasant discovery—their extensive acreage was highly desirable, and lots could be carved out and sold at elevated prices. Ida Frances had already deeded out two lots: one to Clarence M. Noble, the other to local artist Lydia Amanda Brewster.

The property was originally recorded in the name of Ida Frances, but in 1893 she deeded it over to William, probably because she was then in ill health. The exact year of her death is unknown, but it seems certain that William lost his beloved helpmeet and companion before 1900. In 1902, a few repairs were made to Castle Rustico. In 1903, William did the unforgivable. He removed the logs from the second and third stories of Castle Rustico and replaced them with modern shingles. Mourned the *Elizabethtown Post*, "This seems a pity to those who have always admired C.R., the largest rustic structure in the world."

The Leggetts had known some lean times, but in the years following Ida Frances's death, William found himself in comfortable circumstances. He had sold off more lots at inflated prices. Still, the lonely winters at Castle Rustico were now more than he could handle. He began spending the cold months at Buffalo, New York, conducting classes in elocution. It was there that he became acquainted with a young woman by the name of Margaret Burns Hendren, who was destined to bring a new dimension to the legend of Castle Rustico.

Margaret was one of his elocution students. Born in County Arnagh, Ireland, and reared in America, she was a healthy, bright, and cheerful young lady who claimed lineal descent from Robert Burns. She and William became friends. William was now growing old and failing in health, and the prospect of returning to Castle Rustico and living there alone and without assistance was distressing. William pleaded with Margaret to return with him to Rustico and serve as his housekeeper, nurse, and companion. According to Margaret, she resisted for almost a year, reluctant to leave a good job in Buffalo and fearing for her reputation in living alone in the same house with a man not her husband. Again, according to Margaret, she at length consented "to give up my social standing, a lucrative position and care for the poor, sick man to the best of my ability." The two left for Castle Rustico.

There is reason to believe that for the next six years Margaret, as general factotum, devoted herself unselfishly to William and Castle

Rustico. William sold more lots and could now afford to spend winters at southern resorts. He and Margaret were wintering at Southern Pines, North Carolina, when the old thespian died on March 30, 1910. Margaret brought his body to New York City, where it was cremated following funeral rites conducted under the Quaker formula.

Now followed the most extraordinary and famous will trial in Essex County history. The Society of Friends of New York City produced a Leggett will naming several beneficiaries. The Society and Margaret were left cash and the Lake Placid real estate in varying shares. Margaret thereupon produced a will of a later date, leaving William's entire estate to her alone. She hired Judge Francis Smith of Elizabethtown to represent her interests, and she and the Quakers waged a battle royal over the next few years in both Surrogates Court and the Court of Appeals. It was widely reported by North Country newspapers. On the testimony of two famous handwriting experts, Margaret's will was declared a forgery. It was not until 1914 that she and the Society came to an agreement on the division of the Lake Placid lands under the first and legitimate will. Margaret came into full possession of Castle Rustico.

For two summers after William's death, Margaret stayed at the Castle. In 1912, she built a cottage at 128 Hillcrest Avenue and lived there the rest of her life. Eventually owned and occupied by the Kenneth Torrances for many years, it is now the home of the Jason Winch family.

The intimate personal history of Margaret Burns Hendren is somewhat of an enigma and is of little relevance here. Suffice to say that she occasionally left Lake Placid for extended periods and returned bearing a new name. She was variously Mrs. Manley, Mrs. Baxter, and finally, in her last years, Mrs. Watson. Lake Placid remembers her only as Mrs. Baxter and her four sons as "the Baxter boys."

With Margaret's means extremely limited, Castle Rustico received little or nothing in the way of upkeep and repair. She and her children occasionally camped out there, but otherwise the Castle stood idle, empty, and neglected. In the 1920s, Margaret made a last-ditch effort to eke out an income from the old relic. Once again, the door of Castle Rustico was opened to summer guests. An ad appeared in the Delaware & Hudson Railroad's *A Summer Paradise* of 1927: "Castle Rustico, Mrs. M.H. Baxter, proprietress, Lake Placid, N.Y. Modern conveniences. Terms moderate. Also camping in the woods, fine location on beautiful Lake Placid. Write for rates and further particulars."

The venture could not have been much of a success or of long duration. Already the Castle was in the first stages of deterioration and poised for its journey downward to rack and ruin. By the 1930s, roofs and flooring had caved in, and Margaret had totally abandoned the place. If there was ever a haunted house at Lake Placid some half a century ago, it would have been Castle Rustico. Inevitably, the tumbledown wreck attracted exploring parties of young people from the village and the lake colony. Once entry had been accomplished, there was not much to see—in the old parlor a couple of mildewed and mouse-infested sofas, bits of sheet music littering the sagging floor and, yes, Ida Frances's grand piano, long silent and gone to ruin. The youthful adventurers whispered that William Fox Leggett's ashes were there, in an urn on the fireplace mantle and, of course, that his ghost lurked in the cobwebbed corners of his old domain.

Margaret Burns Hendren Manley Baxter Watson died at Lake Placid in September 1945, leaving four sons: Francis, William, Melvil D., and Alexander Baxter. Her grave is in North Elba Cemetery.

The wreck of Castle Rustico was long an affront to campers on the lake. In the late 1950s, Mrs. W. Alton Jones, who owned Camp Littlebrook next door, bought the property from the Baxter heirs for the express purpose of removing the old eyesore. What was left standing of the once noble landmark was torn down, and all the debris was burned or carted away. Thus ended one of the strangest episodes of Lake Placid history.

FORTY
Camp Woodsmoke (Formerly Echo Lodge)
July 1991

The Woodsmoke story begins with Echo Lodge, one of the early accommodations for summer people on Lake Placid. Tourists were not uncommon in the local area even in the 1850s, but it was not until the 1870s that Lake Placid began to lay down its roots as a village and prominent resort. Three small hotels then existed within present village corporate limits. Up on Lake Placid, a few summer camps had appeared, and William Fox Leggett's Castle Rustico, catering to artists of all kinds, was in evidence far up on the west shore.

Almon Thomas and his wife Rebecca, of Plattsburgh, New York, had observed the Adirondack invasion and invested in large parcels of Adirondack land, some of it through state tax sales, extending as far south as the old Totten & Crossfield Purchase.

One of their purchases was Lot 311, of 120 acres, in Township 11, Old Military Tract, Town of St. Armand, bordering Echo Bay at the head of Lake Placid. On October 13, 1879, the Thomases sold Lot 311 to Miss Adeline Mallory, also of Plattsburgh and possibly an acquaintance. The price was $400.

The Mallorys were an old Plattsburgh family, prominent in its pioneer history. As early as 1810 Adeline's father, John Mallory, who died in 1872 at the age of eighty-four, owned mills and possessed the sole right to furnish water to the inhabitants of Plattsburgh.

"Addie" Mallory was an ambitious lady. In the spring or summer of 1880, she built Echo Lodge as a hostelry for summer guests on the site of the present Camp Woodsmoke. The Lodge itself seems to have been a fairly small building, but was supplemented by tent accommodations. Although it was situated far up on the western shore of Lake Placid and was inaccessible by road, guests and their baggage were handily transported from the foot of the lake on Theodore White's little steamer *Mattie*, which made trips around the lake twice a day.

The next year, the summer of 1881, Miss Mallory permitted her sister and brother-in-law, Sarah C. and William P. Molloy, to build a little log studio on land contiguous to Echo Lodge. Sarah C. Mallory Molloy was a talented landscape artist, and for some years used the log building as a teaching studio as well as headquarters for the sale of her own Lake Placid paintings, which found favor with summer people. Nothing has been learned about Mrs. Molloy's credentials, and it is not known whether she was self-taught or had formal art training. Some of her work has occasionally surfaced in modern times. About twenty years ago Peggy O'Brien, Adirondack art authority, came across one of Molloy's Lake Placid landscapes, signed "S. Mallory Molloy." Also, two little primitive works titled *Lake Placid* and *Mirror Lake* appear in Possons' *Guide to Lake George and Lake Champlain and Adirondacks* (Glens Falls, N.Y.: Chas. H. Possons, 1888). Sarah signed them with her maiden name, "Mallory S.C."

Fortuitously, two informative articles describing both Echo Lodge and the Molloy studio appeared in the *Essex County Republican* in July and August 1881. It is interesting to note that the articles cited Adirondack air and climate as beneficial to consumptives.

That Echo Lodge was an instant success for Adeline Mallory is evident from these articles, but less than two years after its opening, on February 20, 1882, Adeline died suddenly at Plattsburgh of typhoid fever. Her brother and sisters, Richard P. Mallory of Cambridgeport, Massachusetts, and Caroline C. Mallory, Sarah C. Molloy, and Delia A. Marshall of Plattsburgh, inherited Echo Lodge. On October 31, 1887, Richard P. Mallory deeded his interest to his sisters. There is no evidence that the Lodge continued as a public accommodation for summer guests. Available clues suggest that the Molloys and their son Walter E. (known as "Wally"), as well as sisters Delia and Caroline, used Echo Lodge as a personal summer retreat, and that Sarah Molloy continued to occupy the little log building as an art studio.

Both Sarah Molloy and her husband William died some time before 1895 and son Walter inherited their interest in the Echo Lodge property. During the early 1890s, according to the local newspaper *Mountain Mirror*, Walter was living much of the time at Lake Placid, both summer and winter.

The Mallory family finally gave up Echo Lodge on October 19, 1895. Caroline C. Mallory, Delia W. Marshall, and Walter E. Molloy, all of Plattsburgh, sold the entire 120 acres of Lot 311 to John H. Prall, of New York City, for $4,500. Prall deeded the property to his wife, Sarah D. Prall, on July 27, 1903. The Pralls retained the name of Echo Lodge for the property, which served as the family summer home for the next quarter of a century. Mr. Prall died in 1918.

Records of the Shore Owners Association of Lake Placid state that the Pralls "built" their Echo Lodge in 1896, and describe it as "on the site of Molloy's." Important and very relevant questions must therefore be asked: Did the Pralls, as appears likely, tear down the original Echo Lodge and erect a new and larger camp? Or did the Pralls simply put an addition on the original Echo Lodge built by Adeline Mallory? This compiler has not been furnished evidence of any addition and thus must conclude that the Pralls demolished the original Echo Lodge and, in 1896, according to Shore

Owners records, erected on the same site what is today the main lodge of Woodsmoke. This would give the building an age of ninety-five years.

According to Kris Hansen, present Woodsmoke owner, Sarah Molloy's original log art studio still stands on the property, recently receiving major repairs. If so, it appears that it is now the oldest original structure still in existence on Lake Placid.

On March 18, 1918, Mrs. Prall deeded Lot 311 to Harvey Alford of Lake Placid, who subdivided the original 120 acres and sold parcels out to various individuals. In 1919, the parcel containing Echo Lodge and the log studio was sold to Mrs. W.H. Sharp, who occupied the place for some years.

Calvin Pardee III of Hazelton, Pennsylvania, then became the owner of the land containing Echo Lodge and the log studio. The Pardee family had been summering at Lake Placid for many years. Calvin Pardee III's grandfather, Calvin Pardee, a prominent Pennsylvania industrialist, first stayed at the old Ruisseaumont Hotel on Lake Placid beginning in the early 1890s. When his children grew up and married, he decided he would have a camp where he could bring his grandchildren. In 1908, he erected Camp Eagle's Eyrie on a large tract of land on Echo Bay just north of Echo Lodge and at the very head of the lake, under the shadow of Eagle's Eyrie hill, with Whiteface looming up behind. His son-in-law, Reverend Charles R. Erdman, a noted Presbyterian churchman of Princeton, New Jersey, had Camp Erdman next door. Pardee and Erdman were familiar names in Lake Placid for close to fifty years, and the two families made great contributions to the summer scene and community life.

Calvin Pardee died in 1923, and after his wife passed away in 1933 his grandson, Calvin Pardee III, affiliated with the Pardee family enterprises, acquired Camp Eagle's Eyrie, which he and his family enjoyed for many summers. The Pardee and Erdman camps were finally sold to the State of New York and were torn down. The tract is now part of the state Forest Preserve and has reverted to wilderness.

Calvin Pardee had also owned two thousand acres running up the Lake Placid side of Whiteface, including the top of the mountain. This tract was finally deeded to the State of New York and is today the nucleus of the Whiteface Memorial Highway complex on the peak of the mountain.

Calvin Pardee III probably bought the additional Echo Lodge property as a protection for the peace and quiet of Eagle's Eyrie. It is not known whether he himself ever occupied Echo Lodge.

Calvin Pardee III became an expert bobsledder, training at Lake Placid. He was also a skillful airplane pilot, serving in the Civilian Air Patrol during World War II. He died at the young age of forty-two in 1947.

Shirley (Kris) Hansen of Lake Placid, director of women's athletics at North Country Community College in Saranac Lake, bought Echo Lodge from the Pardee Estate in 1964. It had then lain idle for many years. She renamed the camp Woodsmoke.

Immediately opened as a summer camp for girls, Woodsmoke went co-ed in 1973 and offers day and live-in camp activities for both girls and boys between ages seven and fifteen. The agenda has constantly expanded and stresses the Adirondack experience. Today Camp Woodsmoke is one of the finest and most successful children's summer camps in the Adirondacks. Over the years the original buildings have been greatly improved, a number of new buildings have been added, and adjacent property has been acquired. The former Echo Lodge is still the main focus.

Kris Hansen is a member of the Camp Safety Advisory Council of New York State and is on the board of directors of New York State's Federation of Lake Associations.

FORTY-ONE
Allen House
Date unknown

Of all Lake Placid's great summer hotels built in the late nineteenth century, the Allen House had the shortest life span. It was in existence just six years, from 1880 to 1886. Yet, if only because of one of its uncommon features—an astonishing dining menu—it deserves a special niche in our history.

The Allen House was the creation of Henry Allen, whose biography has been given in some detail in the earlier chapter on the Grand View Hotel. In brief, Henry Allen was born in Ripton, Vermont, in 1848, served in the Civil War, and was originally a farmer. Arriving in North Elba in

1874, the young man hired out as a farm hand and soon married the boss's daughter, Sarah Demmon.

In 1871, Benjamin Brewster had erected a small, primitive hotel, the Lake Placid House, adjacent to his farmhouse on the shore of Mirror Lake. Henry Allen had no intention of spending his entire life on a farm. Seething with ambition and bitten by the hotel bug, he rented the little Brewster hostelry in 1876 and ran it successfully for several years. That same year, Joe Nash opened the Excelsior House atop Signal Hill. When a third small hotel, known as the Grand View, was erected on the Nash farm hill two years later, in 1878, it was time for Henry Allen to get into the act. Buying one of Nash's farm lots on the slope of hill below the Grand View and opposite the present post office, he began the construction of a hotel to put Brewster's, the Stevens House, and the Grand View to shame.

"Mr. Allen is getting his lumber on his building spot very rapidly," reported a correspondent for the *Essex County Republican* in March 1880. "I suppose he intends taking the shine off the other hotels when he gets his up."

During construction, on May 10, a minicyclone zipped through North Elba, doing considerable damage to the Allen framework. Despite this setback, the hotel was completed and opened in July 1880 under the name of Allen House. Architecturally, it was totally unlike the typical boxy Adirondack hotel of the period. And it was big, easily outclassing its three competitors. It could accommodate one hundred guests. Two enormous wings sprouted from a large rear section. A main attraction was a spacious encircling porch, from which guests could gaze out in rapture at the magnificent lake and mountain views.

Stoddard's Adirondack guidebook gave the whopping new hotel and its host high marks. "A great, roomy, rambling structure," said Stoddard. "Pleasant parlors facing the lake, a dining room 40 by 70 feet. The sleeping apartments are large, the principal ones having two windows." Native courtesy and wholesome friendliness were attributed to Henry Allen. "Mr. Allen is hearty and popular," Stoddard reported, "and is on the road to the presidency. He is sheriff now."

Rates at the Allen House were $8 to $10 a week and $2 per day. The hotel was open from June 1 to November 25.

The role of boniface suited Henry Allen to a T. But beyond his natural courtesy and warmth, he possessed a special vision and a penchant for solving knotty problems, such as the hotel's lack of water. He built a dam on the outlet of Lake Placid, and with the installation of a hydraulic ram, a wealth of pure mountain water was pumped up the steep hill to the Allen House through an elaborate piping system. In 1885, sixteen years before telephone service officially arrived at Lake Placid in 1901, Henry even built his own telephone line through the wilderness to Saranac Lake.

Henry loved parties and balls and had hosted many at the Brewster hotel. North Elba residents were delighted when he offered Saturday night dances at the Allen House, enlivening the long, dreary winters. Three were held in early 1881 alone, including a Masonic ball. Obviously, the place was equipped, at least partially, for winter occupancy. In fact, guests stayed through November for the hunting season.

By this time, the winter sport of ice harness racing had come to the North Country. Henry acquired some good horses and entered into the sport enthusiastically on Mirror Lake. A racing circuit was formed, including Lake Placid, Saranac Lake, Tupper Lake, and Plattsburgh. When contestants came to Placid, Henry erected a tent on his hotel grounds to accommodate their horses.

A visitor to the Allen House on August 6, 1882, reported a first-class establishment. The house was overflowing, with 125 steady guests in residence. One hundred sixty-five dinners were served that evening. The following menu for the day attests to a remarkable variety and Roman-banquet splendor of food:

> Consommé with French peas, English calf heads.
>
> Entrees: Broiled lake trout, anchovy sauce; baked California salmon, wine sauce; boiled corn beef and cabbage; Cincinnati ham; pickled pork, new string beans; leg of Essex County lamb, caper sauce; roast ribs of prime beef, China gravy; Adirondack suckling pig, applesauce; mountain spring lamb, brown gravy; loin of veal, herb dressing; saddle of mutton; sugar-cured ham; cutlets de agneau in crumbs au petit; banquette de veal, glade au champignon; macaroni d'Italien; ribs of spring lamb, saute de fin oignon; saute of kidney in wine; beef heart au tortuise with sauce rhubarb.
>
> Vegetables: New potatoes with cream, mashed potatoes, early green peas, summer squash, early cabbage, new beets, string beans, stewed tomatoes, new onions, lettuce.

Relishes: Cucumber pickles, Worcestershire sauce, celery salt, olives, French mustard, salad dressing, mushroom catsup, salad oil, pepper sauce, tomato ketchup, mixed pickles, chow-chow.

Pastry: Angel, fruit and striped cake, Queen pudding with brandy sauce, Charlotte de russe, Au Sable watermelon, nuts and raisins.

Tea, coffee, chocolate.

Here in the uncouth Adirondacks, in a small settlement barely one step removed from its log cabin culture, was offered the most sophisticated of cuisines. "The bill of fare," said the visitor, "is more inviting than that of city hotels." All of our early hotels served good food, but the likes of the Allen House menu have never been noted elsewhere.

Did Henry employ a French chef? Or, given his many-faceted talents, was the menu of his own device? It was reported only that the dining room was under the control of H. Oliver of Elizabethtown, assisted by Elsie Maders of Keeseville. Two clerks were employed that summer, James W. Steele and John Liberty of Elizabethtown.

For all its amenities and worldly ways, the Allen House was doomed. It was to go the way of so many of our old wooden hotels, with no means of fire protection and control. In 1886, Henry Allen's dream house burned to the ground and was never rebuilt.

Fortuitously, it was not the end for Henry Allen and his unique vision and restless energy. He went on to own and operate the Grand View and National hotels and play a major role in the development of Lake Placid as a famous summer resort.

FORTY-TWO
Mirror Lake House: From Modest to Magnificent
April 26, 1995

Lake Placid's third grand hotel to occupy Grand View Hill in the late nineteenth century was the Mirror Lake House. As was the norm for most of our early hotels, it started out in a modest way and soon received major additions.

Mirror Lake House stood side by side with Allen House and below the Grand View Hotel, on the slope of hill sheared off in modern times for our large village parking lot. Charles Green and his wife Hattie were the original owners and builders.

Joseph Nash was selling off his expansive farm on the west shore of Mirror Lake, and on August 31, 1880, deeded seventy-five acres to the Greens. The purchase price was a paltry $150—but, then, Hattie Green was Joe Nash's daughter. Charles, always known as Charlie, was born in the Town of Jay in 1859, the son of Jay pioneer Liberty Green, who had come from Scotland.

At Lake Placid, the hotel business was going great guns, and the young couple wanted a piece of the action. In the fall of 1881, they began erecting a resort of their own on a part of their large tract. They completed the building in the spring of 1882. Charlie and Hattie went down to the great Prime Brothers general store in Upper Jay and bought a passel of goods to furnish it: bedding, linens, lace curtains, dishes, cutlery, furniture, lamps, pots and pans, spittoons, chamber pots. An original purchase list still exists. All was trundled up from Upper Jay in installments by horse and wagon.

Opened that summer under the name of Mirror Lake House, Charlie and Hattie's hotel was a graceful little four-story structure with a three-story rear wing and could accommodate seventy-five guests. It had, of course, the obligatory wrap-around piazzas.

Why, in September 1882, the Greens deeded out their entire tract, including the hotel—and to the Prime brothers at that—after only two summers of operation is puzzling. Silas W. and Spencer G. Prime may have wanted to invest in the suddenly hot Lake Placid real estate market and made an offer the Greens could not refuse (the consideration in the deed was $6,500). On the other hand, the transfer may have been made to satisfy a debt. Certainly, the Primes were not in the hotel business. Their general store in Upper Jay (the historic old building was destroyed by fire only a few months ago) served all of Essex County, and they were moneylenders besides. Each amassed a tidy fortune in his lifetime.

In any event, there is no evidence the Primes ran the hotel themselves; they leased it out. Two of the known lessees were Duncan Cameron, owner of the Ray Brook House, and Charles J. Daniels, who had previously rented the Grand View. Mirror Lake House lost its next-door neighbor when the Allen House burned down in 1886, and then its only competitor in the immediate area was the Grand View.

Charlie Green continued in the hotel business locally with the Green House (later called the Adirondack) and the Homestead. He built the Hotel Albert that once stood on the site of our Olympic speed skating oval, naming it after his only child, Albert, who died at twenty-four. Charlie and Hattie also had a farm on Bear Cub Road,[41] now occupied by the Uihlein-Cornell potato farm.

A buyer for the Mirror Lake House soon came along. He was Ira D. Isham, a bachelor from Plattsburgh. His family had been manufacturing carriages in Plattsburgh for some years under the name of Isham Wagon Co. Although the *Elizabethtown Post* reported in 1888 that Ira Isham had purchased Mirror Lake House, a formal deed did not come from the Primes until September 1889. Only 7¼ acres were conveyed. The Primes had already sold several parcels from the original seventy-five-acre tract, including one for the erection of the old wooden Methodist Church.

Whoever installed it—Prime or Isham—an electric plant went into operation at the hotel in the summer of 1889. The night sky was suddenly ablaze with bright light streaming from every window. It was the talk of the town, a town that would still be dependent upon kerosene lamps for years to come.

In 1889, humongous additions were made to the Mirror Lake House. Whether or not the Primes were involved is unclear. Evidence suggests that it was Ira D. Isham who was responsible for most, if not all, of the transformation. By 1890, the Mirror Lake, incorporating the original building, was a magnificent, imposing palace of a place, the likes of which had never before been seen in the North Country.

The hotel went into the ownership of Ira's own company, Mirror Lake Hotel and Improvement Company. Taking on a new name, Mirror Lake Hotel, the partnership of Ira D. Isham, family member Harry S. Isham, and Andrew W. Peabody managed it. With accommodations for four hundred guests, it was one of the largest and most luxurious hotels of all time in Lake Placid. Its rates were commensurate with its opulence, a hefty $4 a day, subject to special terms by the week or season.

And it had everything: rich furnishings, polished hardwood floors, spacious halls and bedrooms with high ceilings, open fireplaces in all public rooms, a ballroom and orchestra, and a parlor on every floor—each

41 Now called Bear Cub Lane, County Route 26.

equipped with a piano. It also had electric lights and modern plumbing throughout, an excellent water system, an elevator, steam heat, a barbershop, daily papers, telegraph service, and brook trout for breakfast. Outside were tennis and croquet courts. A separate building on Mirror Lake housed bowling and billiard halls.

Then, too, the food was excellent and well-prepared, although existing menus list only a few real gourmet delicacies, such as pate de foie gras and soft-shell crabs with sauce tartar. The scenery was unsurpassed. Guides were on tap to take parties out into the wilderness, Lake Placid's famous Sam Barton being one of them. Stages arrived and departed twice a day for the railroad at Saranac Lake, and ran daily to Essex County destinations.

Unfortunately, the hotel had something else—heavy liens and mortgages against it that had financed the elaborate additions and furnishings. In spite of a brisk business, the hotel's future was precarious. Ira Isham had bitten off far more than he could chew, and by late 1890, he was in dire financial straits.

One of the mortgages soon foreclosed, and Mirror Lake Hotel was knocked down [sold] at a referee's sale in February 1891. George H. Holden of Burlington, Vermont, was the highest bidder, offering the pathetic sum of $6,650. The property, however, was still encumbered with liens and mortgages totaling over $20,000.

Ira Isham was gone from the great hotel he had created, but the name of Isham would continue in Lake Placid history. Ira's relative, Frederick A. Isham, came to Placid in 1899 and, along with his son Robert, conducted the prominent law firm of Isham & Isham for many years. Frederick A. Isham's sister, Ella Isham Chellis, had moved to Lake Placid in 1882. She was the grandmother of the Weaver children, one of whom, Lucille Weaver Ranney, still lives here,[42] having lived here all her life.

Although it was George H. Holden who received a deed to the hotel, he was actually only an agent for Paul Smith, that renowned, lovable, and colorful hotelier over at St. Regis Lake. Holden soon deeded the property to the Lake Placid Hotel Co., of which Paul Smith was president, his son Phelps vice president, Holden himself the secretary, and G.B. Blodgett the treasurer.

Under Paul Smith stewardship, the Mirror Lake House flourished and fast became the most talked-about resort in northern New York. Lake

42 At the time this chapter was written in 1995.

Placid itself was growing by leaps and bounds, headed for its incorporation as a village in 1900.

An interesting letter of this period has come to light. On April 13, 1892, hotel manager Charles E. Martin typed a message to Seneca Ray Stoddard, the Adirondack guidebook author. As manager of the Mirror Lake Hotel he had, Martin reported, along with several other gentlemen of New York, purchased Whiteface Mountain, and they would soon commence the building of a carriage road from the Mirror Lake Hotel to the top of the mountain.

Alas, a road up Whiteface would have to wait for another forty-three years. In the fall of 1894, Mirror Lake Hotel caught fire and burned to the ground. It was a terrifying spectacle. One more grand hotel vanished from the Lake Placid landscape, and the carriage road plan was soon forgotten.

FORTY-THREE
Whiteface Inn

In this letter written February 15, 1984, Mary MacKenzie answers an inquiry about Whiteface Inn.

The first hotel on the site of Whiteface Inn was called the Westside. Oliver Abel, a lawyer from Elizabethtown, New York built it early in 1882. At that time, the present road from the Saranac Lake road was not in existence,[43] and all the building materials had to be taken over the lake on a barge or boat. One boat loaded with sand for construction purposes sank, and presumably is still lying on the bottom of the lake off what is now known as "Sand Point."

The Westside opened on August 1, 1882. Its first guests were the Colburn family from Ansonia, Connecticut, who had been waiting with several of their friends at the Grand View Hotel, in Lake Placid, for the opening. The mountain behind the Westside was named Mount Colburn in their honor.

Mr. and Mrs. Abel managed the hotel until joined in the partnership by their son, William H. Abel, in 1887. The Adirondack Museum in Blue Mountain Lake has a diary of William Abel from the winter and spring

43 MacKenzie's note: There was a road into the Westside by 1887, according to William H. Abel's diary, which is lodged down at the Adirondack Museum.

of 1887, which is delightful to read. At that time, William was a young man very much in love with an Elizabethtown girl, and the diary is full of references to his adored "Puss" or "Christine." William spent the winter and spring of 1887 at the Westside, taking care of matters for his father, getting the place ready for the summer and bossing a crew of workers while they cut wood, painted, etc. He was quartered in the office until a faulty smokestack obliged him to move into one of the cottages. When spring came, he did a lot of work making maple syrup, and his father really gave him what-for when he burned a large part of the maple syrup crop. I am happy to report that William and "Puss" married that summer. They later went west, and William went into the railroad business.

In 1891, the Abels sold the hotel and adjoining land of four hundred acres to the Adirondack Company, which had been organized in November 1890. Its first officers were E.B. Bartlett, president; A.G. Mills, vice president; and Preble Tucker, secretary and treasurer. The company renamed the hotel Whiteface Inn in February 1891. In 1896, the annex to the north of the old hotel was erected, as well as the Wigwam, a recreational building and bowling alley. Mrs. Mabel Child leased and managed the inn from 1896 until 1901 and was very successful.

In 1901, the original old Westside was torn down, and on its site, a new building was erected. I have a portfolio of original photographs of the inn, cottages, and woodland walks of this period, which are very lovely. In 1902, the cottages Inwood and Overbrook were built, and they still stand. A few years later, the inn was considerably enlarged, and I have several postcards of it in the early 1900s.

On the night of May 20, 1909, the inn took fire and burned to the ground. It had survived only eight years. The Wigwam, although close to the inn, escaped harm and was used until 1932, when it was torn down. Balsams, Overlook, and Hillside cottages, and the laundry and stables also, were unharmed.

From 1910 to 1914, Mr. Halsey Wood, caretaker at the inn, and his wife took care of a number of summer boarders each year, using the cottages spared by the fire. In the fall of 1914, the Adirondack Company began the erection of a new building, and Whiteface Inn reopened in the summer of 1915. A wing was added in 1916, doubling the inn's capacity. This is the hotel building that still stands today.[44] Many improvements

---

44 The "new" Whiteface Inn was demolished in April 1985.

were made over the years, of course, and a convention hall and heated swimming pool were added, along with many cottages.

The new inn was managed from its opening in 1915 through 1929 by James J. Sweeney, and from 1930 to 1954 by Henry W. Haines. Whiteface Inn Inc. acquired the property in 1954 and hired a managing director, F. Burton Fisher, who served until his retirement at the end of the 1970 season. During Mr. Fisher's years, the hotel became a great center for conventions. He was an outstanding manager, and the hotel was a great success during his stewardship. After his departure, the place gradually declined. Perhaps it would have anyway, for these great old hotels have had to give way to the motel era. People no longer come to resorts to stay for the entire summer.

During the summer and fall of 1955, I worked at the Whiteface Inn as Mr. Fisher's secretary. I must say that I have never enjoyed any job as much as I did that one, and I loved the atmosphere, the food, and the people.

Following the 1980 Olympics, the owners of the inn—the MacKenzie Mountain Development Co.—went into bankruptcy. On September 20, 1981, a very sad event occurred: an auctioning off, piece by piece, of the contents of the inn–the lovely murals done by Averil Conwell, the carpets, the birch-tree ceiling lights, and all the furnishings. It is now, as you know, an empty shell.

I don't know what the corporate set-up is today, and you probably aren't concerned about that. An outfit called the Whiteface Resort still runs the cottages, the golf club (still very popular), and a cross country ski center on the property.

Incidentally, the original Whiteface Inn golf course was not the present one. I believe it was before 1900 that the Inn leased a piece of land now occupied by the W. Alton Jones Cell Science Center (across the Saranac Road from the Sterling animal place) and had a nine-hole course there for some years. Golfers were transported from the inn to the golf course by horse-drawn carriage. Upon completion of the new inn in 1915, the company built a new nine-hole course on the outlying section of the present course on land where the great fire of 1903 had destroyed the forest. In the early 1930s, this course was converted into an eighteen-hole course by enlarging it and extending it toward the inn. The present golf house was built in 1963.

It is difficult to come up with the names of the many famous people who stayed at the inn. In the first place, there were no early newspapers here. The first one began in 1893 and did not last long. The *Lake Placid News* began in 1905, but only a few scattered copies are in existence from 1905 to 1914. During the 1920s, the News did publish the names of guests at the many village hotels, but strangely enough, they never included Whiteface Inn—I suppose because it was outside the village.

There certainly had to be many prominent people who stayed at Whiteface Inn—it was that kind of place. I do know that New York Governor Nathan L. Miller vacationed there in the summer of 1921. And during the 1920s, Rosa Ponselle, a famous Metropolitan Opera star of the period, was a frequent visitor there. She had a camp on Lake Placid but spent much time at the inn playing golf. I think it was in 1929 that she was hit in the head with a golf ball while playing there, and the *New York Times* actually had the story on its front page, with a picture of her. Up to that time, the *Times* had never run a picture of an individual, not even the president of the United States, on its front page. This story was told me by the Associated Press correspondent who wrote the account.

The great Babe Ruth, of baseball fame, stopped off at Lake Placid in June 1939 and played golf on the Whiteface Inn course.

Along about 1961, I attended a big political gathering and luncheon at Whiteface Inn, when Nelson Rockefeller was the featured speaker. It may be that he and his party stayed there.

You ask for "special events," but I have never read or heard of any unusual affairs. In the old days, there were the usual balls and social events and parties. The inn was always a place where the "best" people went. The Lake Placid Club, of course, was the really "in" place, and a notch above all other Placid hotels, and most of the grand and newsworthy events took place there.

FORTY-FOUR
Bowling Alleys at Lake Placid
July 1999

Mirror Lake House

The village of Lake Placid had its first bowling alleys in 1889. In that year, one of its pioneer hotels, Mirror Lake House, built a huge addition, becoming one of the largest hotels in the entire Adirondacks. It was located opposite the present post office, on the west side of Main Street. In that year, the hotel erected several outbuildings across the street on Mirror Lake, including a boathouse, a laundry, and a structure housing a billiard room and bowling alleys. The hotel brochure of 1889 says, "Sources of pleasure and recreation are not wanting. Splendid tennis courts, croquet, boating, bowling, billiards, driving, rambles, etc. are a few of the features."

These bowling alleys were presumably not open to the public but only to hotel guests.

The Mirror Lake House burned to the ground in the fall of 1894. The outbuildings, including the bowling alleys, escaped the fire and shortly were purchased by the Lake Placid Club. There is no evidence, however, that the alleys were ever operated again and, in any case, the buildings were torn down shortly after the turn of the twentieth century.

Cascade House

At this point, the bowling alley at the Cascade House should be mentioned. While the Cascade House was not within village limits, being roughly six miles east of Lake Placid on a spit of land between upper and lower Cascade Lakes, it had a connection with and is a part of the history of the Lake Placid Club. This early hotel was located just a few hundred feet outside the boundary of Lake Placid's township of North Elba, but it has always been considered a part of North Elba history.

Built by Nicaner Miller, the Cascade House opened its doors in 1879. In 1883, it was sold to Messieurs Otis and Weston. It was then handsomely enlarged, and a boathouse, bowling alley, and tavern were added. From all accounts, the bowling alley continued in existence throughout the life of Cascade House. Following a number of owners, the Cascade House came into the possession of the Lake Placid Club and was, for a short time, one of its main clubhouses. Club literature of the 1920s mentions the bowling alley as a feature of the place.

Cascade House was closed for the summer of 1927, as the state was building a new highway past the hotel. For some reason, it never opened again. The buildings were torn down, probably in the 1930s, and the entire acreage was acquired by New York State for its Forest Preserve.

As with the Mirror Lake House, this bowling alley was undoubtedly not open to the public but confined to guest use.

Whiteface Inn

The only other hotel at Lake Placid known to have bowling alleys was Whiteface Inn on Lake Placid. These were of late origin. Three Whiteface Inns occupied this site. The third and last opened in 1915 and was torn down in 1985. In 1954, a separate Convention Hall was built on the grounds and four Brunswick-Balke alleys were installed on the lower level. These were in use until the 1970s, when the building was converted into cabanas. Again, only guests of the resort probably used these lanes.

The Parish House

Following the demise of the Mirror Lake House, Lake Placid was not without bowling alleys for long. St. Eustace-on-the-Lakes Episcopal Church was completed and opened in 1900. The first rector was Reverend William W. Moir, a man of considerable personal wealth. Reverend Moir was far ahead of his time, believing that the physical well-being of an individual was just as important as his spiritual well-being. He was especially interested in planning and providing wholesome physical activities for young people.

In 1901, Reverend Moir personally financed the building of a four-story church Parish House on Main Street on the west shore of Mirror Lake. The street floor contained a gymnasium, which was also utilized for church services, meetings, lectures, dances, and other activities. The floor below contained a game room with bowling alleys, pool and billiard tables. The ground, or lakeshore, level served as a boathouse. The church also maintained a skating rink on Mirror Lake. Although owned by the Episcopal Church, the Parish House was not intended for the use of church members only, but was open to all the people of the community. Noted the church Year Book of 1902:

> One of the chief attractions of the Parish House has been the game room, where the men, particularly, meet and spend pleasantly together the evening in social enjoyment. Bowling, pool and billiards are never-failing sources of recreation, and during the winter this room has proved valuable in furnishing in a wholesome manner what the social nature of so many men demands, removing in no small degree the dullness of the long winter season, when in

> former years there was no place in which they might gather and while away their time except in the four saloons in the town. The fees are moderate even to non-members.

The bowling alleys were a great success from the start. Tournaments were held for both adults and youngsters, and elaborate prizes were awarded to the winners. First run under church management, the game room was later leased out. Charles Osgood of Lake Placid managed the alleys for years.

In 1915, the Parish House was sold to George Stevens, but the game room was still in existence in 1916 under the management of William Carey. The last published mention of the bowling alleys was in November 1916, when the *Lake Placid News* reported: "The pool tables have recently been upholstered and the alley floors leveled at the Parish House."

Competition soon spelled the end for the Parish House bowling alleys, when the Lake Placid Masonic Lodge erected their large building next door, installing bowling alleys of the finest and latest make.

The former Parish House building survives today at 2515 Main Street.

Masonic Building

The Lake Placid Masonic Lodge building at 2511 Main Street was completed and opened in the latter part of 1916. The street floor was devoted to stores, and the second floor to the meeting rooms and offices of the Lodge. Early in 1917, the Lodge installed bowling alleys in the basement. "Four alleys of the best make, costing $600 apiece," opened on March 1, 1917. They were described as of regulation length, with a twenty-six-foot runway, and equipped with automatic pinsetters and Mineralite balls. Indirect lighting cast no shadows.

Jack Franke of the Rexall Pharmacy was the first to lease the bowling alleys. Others took over in the 1920s, including William Barry. Apparently, the alleys were refurbished in 1931 when Fred Cane, who had an adjoining barbershop, began leasing them. Fred Cane continued the operation for many years, and his name became synonymous with the place. The last lessee, in the 1950s, was Kenneth Cronk of Lake Placid.

Bowling during those years of the Masonic building was an enormously popular sport in Lake Placid. A good many leagues, for both men and women, were formed, and competition was keen.

By the late 1950s, the Masonic building bowling alleys had become antiquated and outworn and in need of replacement. The Masons at this juncture decided to close down the facility and rent the space out to business interests. They dismantled the alleys, renting the space to the Placid Printing Service, joined in December 1960 by the *Lake Placid News* office. It has been said that traces of the alleys were apparent for some years. This building still stands but is no longer in Masonic ownership.

The Saranac Lake Years

The absence of alleys at Lake Placid, after so many years, was a severe blow to the numerous and avid bowlers of the community. It was now necessary for them to travel to Saranac Lake, eight miles distant, where the nearest bowling alleys were located. For some forty years, these Saranac Lake alleys were the locale of Lake Placid's continuing lively league competitions. During those years, interest in, and love of, the sport of bowling never waned.

Bowl Winkles

Now, after so long a time, bowling alleys have returned to Lake Placid. In the summer of 1997, Bowl Winkles opened at 2750 Main Street.[45] The large building contains eight alleys, with all the latest improvements and components. The leagues are back competing in their hometown, and the great resort village of Lake Placid can offer one more sport to its many visitors.

FORTY-FIVE

The Lake Placid Club

The Lake Placid Club and its historic structures are no more, claimed by vandals, arsonists, wrecking balls, and time. The last building, The Agora Suites, was demolished in January 2002. The date of this essay is unknown.

When a man by the name of Melvil Dewey first came to the well-established summer resort of Lake Placid in 1890, he was already recognized in the academic world. He had, among other things, created and published the Dewey Decimal System for libraries, was state librarian and secretary of

45 Former home of the Grand Union supermarket.

the New York State Board of Regents, and had been the leading spirit in founding the American Library Association, the Spelling Reform Association, and the Metric Bureau.

Dr. Dewey was seeking a site for a small summer vacation retreat for intellectuals like himself and his wife Annie. He first bought a tract on the west side of Mirror Lake in Lake Placid. He soon had a change of heart. The largely undeveloped land on the east shore of Mirror Lake, populated by only a few old farmhouses and summer cottages, seemed to have greater potential. In 1894, he purchased five acres there, occupied by a modest farmhouse on the lake. The house was known as Bonnyblink.

Dr. Dewey opened Bonnyblink for business in 1895, calling it for the first few years Placid Club and Placid Park Club. Soon after 1900, it was renamed Lake Placid Club. Bonnyblink could accommodate only thirty guests and had but one bathroom, but it was an immediate success. Here, congenial people could vacation in a beautiful natural setting at moderate cost. The first members came mostly from educational circles—the place was sometimes referred to as "a university in the wilderness"—but quickly attracted well-to-do people of culture. By 1905, in just ten years, Bonnyblink had undergone a vast change. Swallowed up by major additions, it would henceforth be known as the Lakeside clubhouse of the Lake Placid Club. Lakeside continued to expand.

In the fall of 1904, an event occurred that would change the image of Lake Placid forever. Melvil came up with an incredible idea: He would keep open for the winter season of 1904–1905 a recently acquired cottage known as Forest, several hundred feet south of Lakeside and also on the lakefront. Forest had previously been a private home; the Club purchased it from Myron T. Brewster, a local resident. The year of its construction is presently unknown. Winter vacations amid ice and snow were then unheard of, but Melvil boldly ordered forty pairs of skis from Norway (not a pair could be purchased in America) and brought in a stock of skates, snowshoes, and toboggans. Ten Club members came for that first Adirondack winter outing, which was to firmly establish Lake Placid's claim to the title of pioneer winter sports resort of America.

The experiment was a rousing success. So many members signed up for the winter season of 1905–1906 that a winterized clubhouse had to be built immediately. Thus came into being Forest Towers in the summer and fall of 1905. It would become the middle house of the final winter clubhouse chain, containing fifteen guest rooms, seven baths, billiard and pool rooms, library, music room and stage, and large glass-enclosed piazzas. The taller tower had a powerful 9½-inch telescope for members who wished to study the starry skies under the guidance of the Club engineer, the famous Henry Van Hoevenberg. Forest Towers had a cellar, hot water heaters, and radiators, besides numerous fireplaces and open fires in private suites.

But immediately, facilities again proved inadequate for the demand by winter sports fans, and in 1906 a third winter house was built, called Forest Hall. This was the finest building of the three Forest clubhouses, with offices, recreation and game rooms, dining rooms, kitchen, library, 103 bedrooms, forty-seven baths, and forty-five open fires.

The original winter house, Forest, was gradually enlarged and became known as Lake Forest. Forest Hall was connected by a glass-enclosed solarium with Forest Towers, and Forest Towers was connected by glass-enclosed piazzas with Lake Forest. On the site was also an older cottage known as Wayside, located directly in front of Forest Towers.

Wayside was moved in the summer of 1915 to a site just south of Lakeside clubhouse. The village of Lake Placid was building a new road along the Club front and had to remove the entire knoll on which Wayside stood. This was an improvement, as the small hill had always obstructed the view toward Mirror Lake from Forest Hall and Forest Towers.

It can now be recognized that the present large wooden complex of the Lake Placid Club was at first three separate entities, connected by warmed corridors.

In the years 1915, 1916, and 1917, major changes occurred. Forest Hall was enlarged in 1915, and a sizable addition on the front of the building was made in 1917. Many improvements came to Lake Forest in 1916, and a large addition was built on the south end. Forest Towers also received a large addition and remodeling in 1917.

By 1918 Forest Hall, Forest Towers, and Lake Forest were practically unified and brought under one roof and would henceforth be referred to by the collective name of Forest. Doubled in size, the Forest complex was so improved and transformed that it had almost the look of a new building. These were the greatest improvements made in the Club's existence up to that point, and the changes and additions consumed a large fraction of the $630,000 spent on all projects in the previous three years. All kinds of innovative and attractive sleeping quarters, recreational and dining facilities, and offices were now assured.

Other exterior changes took place in later years. Interior changes were continuous over the life span of the Club. Dining rooms, offices, lounges, recreation rooms, library—in fact, all public rooms—were constantly shifted from one place to another.

In little over ten years, the Lake Placid Club had become fully established as the leading winter sports center of the United States. Aside from the buildings, all manner of sports facilities had been provided: a double-shuttle toboggan run, ski slopes and trails, ski jumps, skating, hockey and curling rinks, ice boats, and four-in-hand sleighs. In addition, unique festivities entertained the guests: hunting for the Yule log, Twelfth Night revels, the First Christmas Tree pageant, the mass singing of Christmas carols, Torch Night, Candlemas Night, ice gymkhanas, Hare and Hounds, and special New Year's celebrations.

In 1923, an enormous change was wrought at the Lake Placid Club, a climax to its remarkable expansion. Long a cherished dream of Melvil Dewey, the great brick Agora theater and auditorium unit, Agora east-wing suites, and the Annie Dewey Memorial Chapel were completed and opened. Agora west-wing suites were completed and opened in 1924. Melvil's wife Annie had worked on the plans for Agora and the chapel for ten years. She did not live to see her plans come to full fruition, for she died in October 1922. The total cost of the addition was $750,000, a huge outlay for that era. In the next several years, the priceless Tiffany windows, a local treasure, were installed in the chapel as gifts from Club members.

The last major addition to the Lake Placid Club was completed in 1930. This was Forest East Suites, a large five-story fireproof brick addition on the rear of the Forest aggregate. Housed in the new wing were ski and skate shops, a children's playroom, an extension to the Forest dining room, and twenty-five bedrooms with baths. At this time, fifteen new bedrooms with baths were also built atop the Agora suites.

The original Lakeside, in the early life of the Club the focal point for most summer social activities, gradually declined, although it was refurbished in the 1920s. In its final years, only the ground floors were utilized, housing a dance studio and a summer drama theater known as the Lake Placid Players. Long obsolete, a professional wrecking company tore down the sadly dilapidated structure in 1946, and the site was landscaped over.

It is obvious from the foregoing that the initial mushrooming of the Club stemmed from its successful introduction of winter sports and the consequent need to provide winter housing. That housing, of course, was also utilized in the warmer months and was the basis for the Club's overall expansion.

Theanoguen

Theanoguen clubhouse, also known as Iroquois Long House, started its career as the summer home of Bishop Henry Codman Potter. A letter dated May 6, 1884, and written by Bishop Potter's daughter Clara (later Mrs. Davidge), indicates that the house was in existence in that year. Therefore, its date of construction was probably early 1880s, making it one of the pioneer summer homes of the region. The letter also indicates the house was known as "Theanoguen" during Potter occupancy. (Theanoguen was the Iroquois name of King Hendrik, the great Mohawk war chief.) The Lake Placid Club did not christen it, but merely adopted a name already in use. The Club bought the estate, with its wonderful views, in 1901, whereupon Bishop Potter purchased Hawk Island in Lake Placid and built a summer home there.

Originally a moderate-sized building, Theanoguen immediately received additional improvements in the usual Club fashion. In 1911, it was trebled in size, and great plate glass picture windows were installed on three sides. There were kitchens, dining rooms, music, council, and smoking rooms on the first floor, with a total of eighteen bedrooms and ten baths on the second floor. Improvements continued over the years. Theanoguen clubhouse was popular with members who wished to spend the summer in a place of seclusion and quiet, somewhat removed from the more lively atmosphere of the main clubhouses.

In 1923, the Club winterized Theanoguen in order to accommodate the Lake Placid School for Boys (which later became Northwood School). It was utilized for school classrooms, library, and dining room for several years in the 1920s, when Club guests were not in residence, until the Club opened Northwood School in its present location in 1928.

Theanoguen was the nucleus of what the Club called its "Iroquois Group." A number of Club cottages with Indian names were close by—Oneota, Neoga, Iroquois Tower, Wabun, Wanika, Ononda, Cayuga, Seneca, and Tuscarora. The surrounding forest was called "Iroquois Wood," and it was here in 1904 that the Club had its first Indian Council Fire and ceremonials at the end of the summer, which became so great and famous a feature of its annual summer entertainments.

Mohawk (Thompson House and Placid Heights Inn)

The Theanoguen district has historical values beyond Lake Placid Club ownership. Three hundred feet east of Theanoguen, on the north side of Wilmington Road, once stood the Mohawk clubhouse of the Lake Placid Club. It has an interesting history dating back to the very early years of Lake Placid and North Elba.

In 1824, Roswell Thompson and his wife Jane came to North Elba, having purchased from the State of New York Great Lot 299, on which Theanoguen now stands. Roswell created a large farm occupying much of what is now Club land, and on the future site of Mohawk there stood for many years his string of log cabins, sheds, cooper shop, and blacksmith shop. About 1850, he and some of his sons built a fairly large farmhouse on the site.

Roswell Thompson had ten children: nine sons and a daughter. Six of the children were born in North Elba. The Thompsons became very closely allied with John Brown. Son Henry married John Brown's daughter Ruth. The one Thompson daughter, Belle, married John Brown's son, Watson, who was killed at Harper's Ferry. Two Thompson sons, William and Dauphin, went with John Brown to Harper's Ferry and met violent deaths in the raid. Descendants of Roswell Thompson still live at Lake Placid and represent the oldest pioneer family of our area.

After Roswell's death in 1874, the old Thompson farmhouse passed through several ownerships, and in the late 1890s was acquired by the Isham family, who enlarged it and for a time ran it as a hotel called Placid Heights Inn. (Wilmington Road hill just east of Theanoguen is still called "Isham Hill" by Lake Placid natives.)

In January 1906, Lake Placid Club purchased the old Thompson farmhouse or Placid Heights Inn and immediately began the work of rebuilding and remodeling, completely altering its architectural appearance with large additions. This clubhouse, Mohawk, with its considerable public rooms and bedrooms, was torn down many years ago. Like Theanoguen, the Lake Placid School for Boys occupied it in off-seasons—first in the early 1900s, and again in the 1920s. A historical marker at the site of the old Thompson farmhouse, later Mohawk, would not be amiss.

FORTY-SIX
South Meadow

Excerpt from an interview with Rollie Torrance on June 15, 1963. Rollie was a member of an old family in North Elba whose farm was—and still is—located near the South Meadow lumber camp. The Torrances were somewhat involved in the lumber camp's operation.

MM: Do you remember anything at all about the settlement at South Meadow? Is it true there was a school there?

RT: Yes, as I remember, father [Henman Torrance] built that schoolhouse. It was where you go down across the brook. There used to be a line of lots there. There was a fence up through there, and the schoolhouse was right inside that fence, and this settlement was over across the brook. There was quite a little settlement there. There were probably eight or ten houses. Some of them were log houses and some of them were frame. There was no post office up there. This was School District Number 4 before being centralized, and that was a branch district of Number 4. Father, Uncle Phin Taylor, Herb Taylor, and a fellow by the name of Grimes did practically all the carpenter work on the school. There were about twenty-one scholars. Lizzie Ames Leonard taught school up there. Horace Fenton also taught school up there. If I'm not mistaken, Ascha Jones, niece of Mrs. John North, also taught there.

MM: When was the first lumbering done here?

RT: The first I knew of anybody being in here was Cole and Lapham; I think they were from Au Sable Forks. John North lumbered in here. He was a foreman for Alice Falls Lumber Company. He did the territory in the South Meadow section. Hennessy lumbered in Indian Pass when the Rogers Company owned it. North had a number of different men in camps, and he was foreman over the whole thing.

* * *

[Found in MacKenzie's papers is this excerpt from a typewritten manuscript, *James Hennessy*, by Patrick Hennessy, September 1963.]

"One of the largest villages that sprang up around a lumber job was at South Meadow on the Adirondack Loj road, which was lumbered off under John North around the turn of the twentieth century. Whole families settled here to be with their men. There were many houses and other buildings, and also a schoolhouse. All trace of these buildings has long since vanished, except evidence of a few foundations."

FORTY-SEVEN
Newman
Date unknown

The lower section of Lake Placid village was known as Newman from 1891 until recent years. The name is seldom used today except by old-timers, but its origin is of interest.

By 1883, Lake Placid was a well-known summer resort expanding rapidly. In that year a village post office was established, located in Frank Stickney's store on Mirror Lake. It was a far cry to the lower end of the village, whose residents begrudged the long trip up Mill Hill by horse or foot for the daily mail. Soon it was decided to petition the Postmaster General in Washington, John Wanamaker, for a branch post office, and the petition went forward with a personal note from citizen Anna Newman. By a fortunate coincidence, Miss Newman was a childhood friend of Wanamaker; the two had attended Sunday school together in their native Philadelphia.

The response was immediate. By 1891, the lower end of the village had its own post office, bearing the name "Newman" in honor of Anne. It was only a matter of time before the entire area came to be called "Newman," as though it were a separate village.

Newman was, in fact, a fictitious kingdom. It had no official bounds set by the village fathers. The post office department itself found it unnecessary to define the area, for at that time no carrier service existed. Nevertheless, by common consent, "Newman" was understood to embrace all that section of the village below the Town Hall.

Miss Newman was, and remains in memory, the town's most colorful and legendary character. Spinster daughter of a prominent and prosperous Philadelphia family, she grew up with every social and cultural advantage. A visit to the Adirondacks changed the course of her life. Falling in love with the mountains, she purchased a large tract of land on the outskirts of Lake Placid, now known as Heaven Hill Farm, and proceeded to farm it on an immense scale. Reckless and haphazard in her practice of husbandry, she soon become the protagonist of many a North Country fable. In time, her fame as a do-gooder and generous community benefactor was exceeded only by her fame as a man-hater, horse lover, and eccentric. The strong personality and whimsical ways of Miss Anna Newman made her a legend in her own time, and the legend lives on in the many published stories mirroring her life.

Newman is steeped in the very early history of the village. Lake Placid's first settler, Elijah Bennet, came in 1800, maintaining a farm and home on Great Lot 280, in which Mill Pond is located.

Lake Placid's first industry, the Elba Iron Works, brought to the Newman section in 1809 a bustling and thriving settlement. In time, and about 1853, Mill Pond became the site of the area's first permanent sawmill and lumber industry.

Other early industries that flourished and died there around the turn of the twentieth century added many chapters to Lake Placid history, and it can be said that Placid's great winter sports program was born on Mill Pond.

A central post office serving the entire community was established near the Olympic Arena in 1936, bringing an end to the Newman post office. Nevertheless, the name Newman was long in dying and is still used occasionally today to denote that area of Lake Placid below the Town Hall.

Industries at Newman

In the section of Lake Placid known as Newman, several industries flourished in their time, dying out when the automobile was invented and the area changed its character.

Around the turn of the twentieth century, a blacksmith shop owned by Halsey Snow stood at the site of the present IGA building. There were two slaughterhouses: one on Power Street[46] near Mill Pond, and one operated by Norris Estes on the road leading to the new sewage disposal plant. The latter went out of business when the many farms in the area began to die out.

46 Now called Dow Road.

During the period between 1915 and 1920, a Tupper Lake firm operated an electric hardwood mill in the Sentinel Heights district, on the flats west of the Sentinel Road extension.[47] Much of the lumber milled came from the old Anna Newman farm.

George White's General Store

George G. White, born in Jay, Essex County, New York, in 1856, moved to Lake Placid as a young man and began working at the sawmills as a circular saw operator. In July 1886, he erected a building on the corner at Main[48] and Station Streets, at the bottom of Mill Hill. There for eight years he carried on a flourishing general merchandise trade. The village's first Newman post office was also located in the store, Mr. White having been appointed postmaster in 1893. In 1894, Mr. White sold his stock and rented the premises out as a general store to Durgan, Challis & Co., who later sold out to Walter Wood. The original building still stands and is presently occupied by The Handlebar, containing a bar and restaurant.[49]

George White's Opera House

In 1895, George White built the White Opera House block, at the time one of the handsomest buildings in town, three stories high and fitted with all the latest improvements, including steam heat. Approached by an outside staircase, the top story had a large hall with a stage and space for seating five hundred persons. There, wandering companies of actors, musicians, and vaudevillians once entertained the community, dances were held, and the first phonograph ever seen or heard by most Placidians was exhibited. Mr. White conducted a hardware store on the second level, later operated by Kennedy & Sons for many years. The ground story originally housed Morris Estes's butcher shop. The A&P and an antique store occupied the building in recent years. Still in excellent condition, it has now been refurbished as the Newman Opera House bar and restaurant, featuring rock and country music.[50]

---

47 Now called Newman Street.

48 That portion of South Main Street is now called Sentinel Road.

49 At the time this was being edited, The Handlebar had been recently replaced by the Station Street Grill.

50 The latest business to occupy George White's Opera House is a restaurant, Lisa G's. The owner occupies the building's second-floor apartment.

Newman Post Office

Prior to 1915, various stores near the Mill Pond housed the Newman Post Office (established in 1891)—George White's general store, Walter Wood's store, and Weston, Bull & Mihill.[51] From 1915 to its demise in December 1936, the Newman post office had its own separate building, previously occupied by Hattie Slater's millinery store. Once it played a prominent role as the bank in an early "wild west" bank robbery film shot in Lake Placid during the early 1920s. The town, at the time, was a favorite locale for silent movies filmed by the old Long Island studios antedating Hollywood. The building still stands and is now owned and occupied by the Raeoil Company.[52]

The American House

In August 1893, three brothers—James B., John, and Matthew Hurley, natives of Keene, New York—purchased for $2,000 a parcel of land on the Mill Pond side of Station Street, across from the railroad station. Shortly thereafter, they erected the American House, a substantial three-story hotel of thirty rooms. Catering to summer visitors, they often fed 180 guests at a time and lodged forty. A good livery was attached to the hotel. Although it never attained the popularity and fame of the great hostelries on Mirror and Placid Lakes in Lake Placid's "golden age of hotels," the American House was well patronized for decades. After a checkered career spanning half a century, it was gutted by fire in the early 1940s and was torn down. A warehouse of Mountain Paper Company now occupies the site.[53]

Lake Placid News Building

Built in the 1890s and for many of the early years the site of Pete McCollum's harness shop, an exemplar of the type of business carried on in the horse-and-buggy days. An addition was later tacked on the front. The *Lake Placid News* acquired it in 1975 and remodeled it, mainly by removing upper-story porches. Otherwise, the main structure is intact.

---

51 Weston, Bull & Mihill stood next to the building once occupied by the Raeoil Co. The lot is now occupied by a convenience store.

52 At this writing, the lower floor of the building is used as a restaurant called the Downhill Grill.

53 Hulbert Supply Co.'s Lake Placid store now occupies that sheet-metal building—but behind it still stands the American House's stables.

Old Jewish Synagogue

One lot down Mill Hill from the *Lake Placid News* building, the Jewish community of Lake Placid constructed the village's original synagogue in 1903. It remained in service as a place of worship for fifty-six years until the new synagogue on Saranac Avenue was completed in 1959. It has lately been converted into a private home. It is substantially the same building as it was before, but new windows serve to disguise its original function. Eddie Cantor and Sophie Tucker gave a benefit in Lake Placid in 1930 to help this synagogue financially.

Old Residences

Going down Mill Hill, on the left are three old houses, all built no later than the 1890s. In their day, they were handsome structures and more elaborate than the usual Newman home. In order of appearance:

1) House built by Frank and Kate Wilkins, in good condition.

2) House built by Charles N. Davis, a prosperous contractor. Renovations have been attempted.

3) Old Crowningshield house, with renovations in progress at this writing.

Two other old houses in this district are of interest:

1) The old Dwyer house, perched on the hill above Station Street, overlooking Mill Pond. This house was built before 1900 and, again, was a fine house for the place and period. It is still an eye-catching landmark, completely renovated inside just before the 1980 Winter Olympics and outwardly intact.

2) The old Charles Wood house, 6048 Sentinel Road, now the Prague Inn. Built in a hybrid Edwardian-Victorian style, with turret and encircling veranda, it is the last of this architectural type left in Lake Placid. It was built at the turn of the twentieth century.

Other old houses on Sentinel Road are said to have been built in the early 1900s.

Hurley Building

On Station Street, this was built in 1909 by three Hurley brothers for their grain, hay, wood, and coal business. Carter Pierce was the contractor. It is still owned by third-generation Hurleys and is now predominantly a gas and oil business. The original building is still intact and unchanged, an outstanding example of an early 1900s industry devoted to horse and cattle feed and community heating needs. The construction details of the great storage room and its lofty ceiling must be seen to be appreciated. The enormous coal and grain silos and chutes, erected in 1916, that once stood adjacent to the main building, were razed in 1975.

The Railroad Station

The first railroad station at Lake Placid was a two-story wooden building, apparently converted from a private home. The next, and present, station building was built circa 1904. The local historical society now owns it and operates it as a museum. Only minor face-liftings have occurred through the years—the removal of a long outdoor canopy over the boarding platform, a pillared portico at the front entrance, and balustrade decoration.

The railroad arrived at Lake Placid by degrees, the Chateaugay Railroad Company and its successors having built extensions from Plattsburgh to Dannemora, Lyon Mountain, Loon Lake, and Saranac Lake over a period of years. On June 13, 1890, the Saranac Lake & Lake Placid Railroad Company was chartered to lay standard-gauge track from Saranac Lake to Lake Placid. The first train to Placid, with fare at 10¢ a mile, rolled in on August 1, 1893. Passenger service came to an abrupt halt on April 24, 1965, after seventy-two years.

The Anna Newman Farmhouse

The farmhouse that became famous as the home of Miss Anna Newman still stands (with many structural changes and additions) on Bear Cub Road,[54] on the present Heaven Hill Farm owned by Henry Uihlein.[55] The central section is probably the second-oldest standing house in North Elba, built in the early 1840s by Horatio Hinckley, a prosperous farmer from Lewis, New York. In this house Hinckley's daughter, Abigail, was married to John Brown's son Salmon; the couple later migrated to California with John Brown's widow.

---

54 Now called Bear Cub Lane, County Route 26.

55 Henry Uihlein died in 1997.

Boozing in Newman

[The remainder of this chapter consists of several fragments found in MacKenzie's files. These "pre-composition" notes focused on moonshining in the Newman neighborhood.]

There was a constitutional amendment that went into effect in January 1920, popularly known as the Volstead Act, and Americans were forbidden to sell, manufacture, or transport intoxicating liquors. It was in effect for fourteen years. Those fourteen years were a short period in the life of a nation, but a momentous one in the social history of the American people. And in those fourteen years, a great many Americans, of course, proceeded to sell, manufacture, and transport intoxicating liquors—one jump ahead of the sheriff.

Nowhere did the law irk its citizens more than in Newman, that stronghold of fierce independence, although I must confess that almost all of them who fought it wound up over in the Elizabethtown jail. There were then in the Town of North Elba even more illicit moonshine stills than there are today. They were largely concentrated in that section of Newman then known as the "Hollow"—the area beyond the Chubb River bridge. The whole section began to have overtones of Li'l Abner.

The seizing of stills and contraband beverages in the Hollow made the front page of the *Lake Placid News* all during the [19]20s. Strangely, the uptowners were rarely mentioned—they either had a better working understanding with the law, or were somewhat cagier.

The Prohibition story in the Hollow is a very large subject and probably deserves a thorough study by somebody someday, but I have time to give just a couple of examples.

* * *

There were in this era but two policemen to serve the entire village. One was Bill Boyd, Chester Boyd's father. The other was Tom Black. Both are remembered as hot-tempered and rather excitable gentlemen. Bill Boyd was himself a Newmanite, but had little sympathy for his neighbors. Tom Black, on the other hand, was a ruddy-faced Irishman who was known to lift a glass or two, but his duty to uphold the law won out against his natural instincts. Bill Boyd generally covered Newman, but was treated so threateningly down there that he usually brought along with him Tom Black and ex-Sheriff Dashnaw to aid in arresting moonshiners. One day they found not one but two stills in the house of Louis Smith, a Polish man who had dwelt in Newman for only a few months but had made the most of his time there. Several, etc. … [Fragment ends.]

* * *

As for the town dump, who knows how many thousands and thousands of gallons of priceless booze were poured on its smoldering fires during this period.

FORTY-EIGHT
Ruisseaumont Hotel

From the Placid Pioneer, *Summer 1970 and from additional research in 1987.*

Perched on a tall hill overlooking the East Lake, the Ruisseaumont Hotel dominated the Lake Placid scene for years, from 1892 to 1909. Architecturally, the building was a perfect fright, a combination of Adirondack Victorian and Wuthering Heights Gothic. Nonetheless, it was an eye-catching edifice with gables, cupolas, piazzas, balconies, arches, and windows round, semicircle, square, and rectangular, topped by a soaring tower and a water reservoir that resembled a mushroom cap. As was the case with all Adirondack hotels, numerous additions were tacked on over the years.

The Lake Placid Improvement Company bought the land for the hotel on Lake Placid in May 1891. Alfred L. Donaldson (*A History of the Adirondacks,* Century Publishing Co., 1921, reprinted Purple Mountain Press, 1996) says the hotel was erected there in 1892, but apparently that is wrong. On January 1, 1892, the Lake Placid Improvement Company leased a cottage site on the land to William Z. Larned. The lease says the site was situated near "The Ruisseaumont." From that, it can be deduced the hotel was already there, and was built in 1891, but was probably not opened to the public until the summer of 1892. William Z. Larned was either the main or sole stockholder of the Lake Placid Improvement Company. The manager of the popular resort was Mr. T. E. Krumholz, an ardent promoter of water sports. (Ruisseaumont, incidentally, is from the French language: *ruisseau* for brook or stream, and *mont*(agne) for mountain.)

* * *

The first evil to befall the Ruisseaumont occurred on the evening of June 30, 1906, when a serious fire broke out in the launch slips, destroying almost all of them, plus several launches. A large, new, covered dock and slips were erected the following spring in expectation of the season's opening. But the Ruisseaumont was doomed. Some time in the night of July 2, 1909, the hotel took fire and burned to the ground. It was never rebuilt. Today Mrs. Frederick Heimerdinger's "Humdinger Hill" estate occupies the site.

Less is known of the Ruisseaumont than any other of the great hotels that flourished in Lake Placid's golden age of hotels. Who originated its name, which is still given to the colony in that lake area? What illustrious persons stopped there? What luxuries and entertainments were provided its guests? No record seems to have been left behind.

* * *

[Later, MacKenzie researched the history of the Ruisseaumont golf course, relating it in a letter dated September 16, 1987.]

The Ruisseaumont was never a "Jewish" hotel. It accommodated only Christians. And, as you will see in the next paragraphs, the Ruisseaumont golf course was never owned or built by the hotel. It came into existence after the hotel burned down; it was built for the members of the subsequent Jewish Ruisseaumont club and colony.

The hotel burned down on July 2, 1909. All the hotel-owned land on Lake Placid was then sold in 1910 to a Jewish syndicate, the Ruisseaumont Company, which maintained a clubhouse and colony on the land for so many years afterwards.

In October 1910, one Benjamin Wolf and his wife, Dora, of Philadelphia, Pennsylvania, bought all the lands that later became the Ruisseaumont golf links from Silas W. Prime and wife of Jay, New York, and from Ira H. Lyon and wife of North Elba. Almost all, if not all, of this land was originally a part of the old Ira Lyon farm. I would guess that Benjamin Wolf was acting as agent for the Ruisseaumont club and colony, although it was not until two years later, on September 14, 1912, when Benjamin Wolf and wife deeded all this golf links land to the Ruisseaumont Company.

The question now arises, who built the golf links: Benjamin Wolf or the Ruisseaumont Company? The most logical answer is the Ruisseaumont Company, and since it did not acquire the land until the fall of 1912, we might guess the course was built the following year, in 1913.

On May 25, 1939, the Ruisseaumont Company sold all the golf course lands to Fred Fortune.

FORTY-NINE
Searles House
January 1991

The story of the so-called Searles house on Signal Hill stems directly from the early history of Lake Placid village itself. The village of Lake Placid began to evolve in the 1880s when both Joseph Nash and Benjamin Brewster offered their large holdings for sale. On October 1, 1887, Brewster sold all of his land bordering Mirror Lake and Lake Placid—including Signal Hill—to John A. and George A. Stevens, with the exception of the future Mirror Lake Inn (then his home) and a few other small parcels previously deeded out.

Most city people looking for a site on which to build a summer home in the burgeoning village were first attracted to Joseph Nash's Grand View Hill. By the 1890s, though, the choicest sites on Grand View Hill had been taken, and summer people began to look toward Signal Hill as an excellent alternative.

John and George Stevens had divided the old Brewster lands on Signal Hill into cottage lots for sale. The Searles house was one of the first summer homes—and certainly one of the most beautiful and elaborate—to be built on a Stevens cottage lot. Its site, part of Lot 9, was purchased from the Stevens brothers on August 30, 1894, by Franklin H. Walker and his wife Mary of Detroit, Michigan, and went down to the shore of Mirror Lake. On the rear of this lot, bordering a lane now known as Norton Road, the Walkers immediately built the summer home that eventually would be best known locally as the Searles house. While it is possible the house was constructed in the fall of 1894, more likely it was the spring of 1895. Nothing is known of the Walkers beyond their names.

A photo believed to have been taken in 1896 by Chester D. Moses, later the official photographer of the Lake Placid Club, distinctly shows the Searles house in full frontal view, just to the right rear of the Brewster house (Mirror Lake Inn). The exterior appears to be precisely the same as today. The house to the rear, on the crest of Signal Hill, is the old MacDonald house, built in 1895. Still in existence, it is today owned and occupied by James La Fountain.[56]

A second photo, taken about 1900, shows the Searles house to the rear of the Brewster house and the right of a barn. Again, it presents the same appearance as today. Other summer homes have now appeared on Signal Hill: the Conlin house, today the residence of Mr. and Mrs. Edward Damp;[57] the Hadley house, now owned by Virginia Jackstadt;[58] and at the rear, on the crest of Signal Hill, the "silo house." The MacDonald house again shows up in the far background.

A third photo, probably taken in the winter of 1903–04, affords the best glimpse of the entire Searles house in the early days, presenting a side view. This appears to be, in all respects, the same building as today. Several more summer homes are now evident to the rear of the Searles house, most notably the imposing structure built by George H. Daniels, a New York Central Railroad executive, now the property of the E.L. Hart family.

The Walkers held the Searles house only until 1901. On May 1, 1901, the Walkers sold the house and lot to Lucy E. Norton, wife of Edwin Norton of Chicago, for $14,000, a handsome purchase price in those days. On June 24, 1901, Mrs. Norton, described as "of the city of New York," also purchased from the Stevens brothers for $1,000 adjoining Lot 5, directly in back of the Ben Brewster house (Mirror Lake Inn), then owned by Edward Brewster.

For reasons unknown, the house and lots went into a series of exchanges over the next few years. Mrs. Norton sold out to John Christopher Strauss of Hartsdale, New York, on December 22, 1904. Strauss sold the property to James Noble and Frederick Gauss on the same date, and on July 21, 1905, Noble and Gauss deeded the property back to Lucy E. Norton.

The Nortons continued to enjoy the property as their summer home until 1912. On August 16, 1912, Mrs. Norton deeded Lot 9 only, on

---

56 190 Stevens Road.

57 49 Norton Road.

58 20 Norton Road.

which the house stood, to her daughter, Mrs. Sylvia Norton Conway of Lawrence Park, Bronxville, New York. She excepted from the deed the part of the land lying between Mirror Lake Drive and the shore of Mirror Lake. There may have been a small cottage or boathouse on this latter parcel that she continued to use as a summer place.

Mrs. Norton, described as of "Paget West, Bermuda," gave a second deed to her daughter, Sylvia Conway, on March 24, 1916. This included all of her holdings—the Searles house, Lot 9, and Lot 5.

Mrs. Conway also later came into the ownership of the Brewster house (Mirror Lake Inn), apparently from Edward Brewster. She then sold it to her brother, Arthur W. Norton, in 1922. Arthur may have run the place as a small inn or boarding house before deeding it to Harvey Alford, the father of Climena Alford Wikoff, who founded the Mirror Lake Inn.

The Nortons were, of course, one of the pioneer summer families at Lake Placid, and their name has fittingly been perpetuated in Norton Road at the rear of the present Mirror Lake Inn and Searles house.

Sylvia Norton Conway was the wife of Carle Cotter Conway, president and chairman of the board of Continental Can Co. The Conways occupied the Searles house as their summer home until at least the mid-1920s, when they purchased Gull Rock Camp on Placid Lake. The Conway family became so prominent on Placid Lake for so many years that it has been completely forgotten locally that their summer abode was once the Searles house. Sylvia and Carle Conway were divorced soon after they purchased Gull Rock Camp, and Mr. Conway remarried. Sylvia acquired a large tract of land at Elizabethtown, New York, where she made her summer home for many years. Her brother, Arthur Norton, who died in Baltimore in 1938, also maintained a summer home in Elizabethtown after leaving Lake Placid.

On September 21, 1926, for reasons unknown, Sylvia Norton Conway conveyed the entire property, "including cottage, garage, boathouse and other outbuildings" down to Mirror Lake, to Adirondack Finance Corp. of Lake Placid, which almost immediately (October 1, 1926) deeded the beautiful summer place to Frederick C. Squier of Rahway, New Jersey. The Squiers are said to have occupied the Brewster house (Mirror Lake Inn) for several years previously, perhaps renting it from Arthur Norton. Mr. Squier was an executive of the New Jersey Zinc Company, and the family was very prominent in Rahway affairs. They made possible the Rahway library and gave generously to the Rahway Memorial Hospital and many other charities.

Mr. Squier died on August 29, 1937, willing the Lake Placid summer home to his widow, Minnie Scudder Squier, for life. Upon her death, the property was to go to their daughter, Marjorie S. Searles. Mrs. Squier died in Lake Placid the next year, 1938, and the property immediately passed to Mrs. Marjorie Squier Searles.

Mrs. Searles and her husband Harold (Harry) M. Searles added much to the life of the summer colony and the village in their long residence here. They were life members of the Lake Placid Club. Mr. Searles was an ardent horseman and a very active member of the Club's Saddle Club, as well as the local Lake Placid Riding Club, assisting in building a network of riding trails throughout the Town of North Elba. He was also a constant and generous subscriber to Lake Placid charitable organizations.

Members of the Searles family were leading citizens of Rahway, New Jersey, where they had extensive real estate holdings in the heart of the city. Mrs. Searles, a graduate of Vassar College, was very active in the Rahway Girl Scout Council as well as the library and hospital of Rahway.

Mr. and Mrs. Searles spent many happy years at their beautiful Lake Placid summer home with their daughter, Catherine, who became Mrs. Robert Doulton Stott. The Stotts were eventually divorced. Mr. Searles died in April 1953. Mrs. Searles died at Rahway on December 17, 1974, and was buried there. The Reverend William D. Hayes, rector of Lake Placid's St. Eustace Episcopal Church, conducted her funeral service.

Climena Wikoff acquired the house from the Searles family, and it became an annex of Mirror Lake Inn, used mostly to house figure skaters who trained at Lake Placid. When Mr. and Mrs. Edwin Weibrecht Jr. acquired the inn property in 1976, the Searles house came automatically into their ownership.

The original Mirror Lake Inn (Ben Brewster's house) was destroyed by fire the night of January 10, 1988, but most fortunately the adjacent Searles house escaped the flames. Now almost a century old, the beautiful former summer home still stands on Signal Hill, apparently outwardly unchanged from the day it was built. Inside, many of the unique and outstanding features of a pioneer Lake Placid summer home have been preserved. The Searles house is one of Lake Placid's architectural and historical treasures.

FIFTY
Northwoods Inn and Hotel Marcy
September 1, 1993

As we have seen, in the 1870s, Joe Nash gave up farming and the tourist trade and went into the real estate business, selling off lots from his great holdings. One of the first to acquire a slice of Joe's pie was Charles Wesley Kennedy, always known as "Wes." Wes Kennedy was born on October 30, 1844, presumably in our neighboring Keene, New York, to James Kennedy and his wife Eliza Parish. The family soon moved to nearby Wilmington; then, in 1870, they pulled up stakes again and came to North Elba, where they resided in a log cabin near the present Olympic ski jumps. Wes soon married Nancy Brewster of Lake Placid's pioneer Brewster family.

In 1880, Wes Kennedy bought from Joseph Nash a nice parcel of land overlooking Mirror Lake and bordering the west side of Main Street, which was originally Nash's cow path. In October, he started building a large house on the property and moved into it December 2, 1880. There is evidence he also conducted a general store on the premises, selling merchandise as diverse as dry goods, fishing tackle, stationery, shoes, and confectionary. The village post office was also located in the store for six years, for Wes was appointed Lake Placid postmaster on September 7, 1885, serving in that capacity until June 11, 1891.

Wes had been one of the first to build a house on Joe Nash's farmland. In the next twenty years, the growth of Lake Placid village was phenomenal. By 1900, it was an incorporated village and a nationally recognized summer resort, with seven major hotels and a number of smaller inns and boarding houses.

Wes Kennedy decided to get in on the action. According to an Essex County newspaper, in 1897 he erected "a large and handsome boarding home" on his property, which opened for business about July 15. He named it "Northwoods Inn." It is not known whether this was an enlargement of his original house or was an entirely new structure. From the start, Northwoods Inn attracted many summer guests.

In 1906, Wes Kennedy sold his inn at a good profit to Thomas A. Leahy, a former schoolteacher, born in Mineville, New York, in 1877 to Andrew and Margaret Heffernan Leahy. Mr. Leahy had come to Lake Placid in 1900 to work at the American House hotel, owned by the Hurley brothers. Over the next forty years, until his death in 1947, Leahy became one of the leading citizens of Lake Placid, serving as justice of the peace, member of the board of education, member of the New York State Assembly, president of the Adirondack Resorts Association and member of the III Olympic Winter Games committee. After operating the Northwoods Inn successfully for fourteen years, Leahy sold it to Frank W. Swift on October 1, 1920, and the next year bought Lakeside Inn, which he ran until his death.

Frank W. Swift, born in East Orange, New Jersey, on December 17, 1879, to Frank Cole and Mary Wing Swift, became one of the best known of Adirondack hotelmen. Early in the twentieth century, he managed the Tahawus House Hotel, in Keene Valley, and the Maplewood Inn, in Elizabethtown. Coming to Lake Placid about 1907, he briefly leased the Lakeside Inn with Harry Danforth, and then bought the old Lake Placid Inn, formerly Brewster's, the first hotel in Lake Placid. In 1920, he sold Lake Placid Inn and immediately purchased Northwoods Inn, which then could accommodate close to one hundred guests.

Lake Placid was a boomtown in the mid- to late 1920s, riding the crest of that roaring decade just before the disastrous Wall Street crash that led to the Great Depression. Frank Swift had to turn away many more people than he could accommodate. Swift had long harbored a dream of creating a great, modern, fireproof hotel in this resort village where the old wooden Victorian hostelries still predominated, and he proceeded to make that dream a reality. He started construction on his great brick Lake Placid-Marcy hotel in 1926, and completed it in less than a year. Swift partially financed the project by selling stock in the parent corporation, Northwoods Inn Hotel, Inc., of which he was president. Local residents also purchased a great many shares; in a sense, the new hotel was a community endeavor. However, its architecture, rooms, and furnishings were wholly conceived by Mr. and Mrs. Frank Swift.

The Lake Placid-Marcy—named for Mount Marcy, the highest mountain in the Adirondacks and New York State—opened on July 6, 1927, amid much fanfare. The *Lake Placid News* reported:

> The largest crowd to assemble in a hotel dining room in this section attended the opening to congratulate Mr. and Mrs. Frank Swift on the fine appointments of the house. On the lobby floor rich furniture and hangings, shaded lights, orchestra, and the buzz of conversation, made one rub his eyes and wonder whether this could be Lake Placid and not some great Metropolitan center. 325 diners thronged into the dining room to the music by the Marcy orchestra, Leo Dustin, leader, and the Stevens House orchestra under the direction of Jacques George. During the course of the banquet, favors were distributed to the guests, consisting of handsome bronze paper weights for the men and compacts for the ladies.

Swift also acquired several former summer homes behind the hotel for cottages. Most importantly, the old Northwoods Inn, beside which the Marcy had been built, was not demolished. It remained as an annex to the new hotel, serving as kitchen, guest storage, help's quarters, and the like. The entire complex had 160 guest rooms and 125 baths.

With its big city ways, the Marcy was a novel experience for Lake Placid, and the locals immediately patronized it. It provided an ideal setting for wedding and dinner parties, New Year's Eve celebrations, bridge clubs, ping-pong and backgammon championships, and billiard games. From the beginning, the Marcy also attracted a good share of the tourist trade, and especially winter sports fans, as it was one of the few winterized hotels in the area. Winter sports were rapidly becoming Lake Placid's trademark.

Drawn also to the sophisticated Marcy were celebrities from the entertainment world. In its early years, the Marcy hosted George Burns and Gracie Allen, musical comedy and radio star Harry Richman, and Anne Nichols, author of the famous play, *Abie's Irish Rose.* The most notorious guest in the early years was Mrs. Anna Hauptmann, widow of Bruno Hauptmann, kidnapper of the Lindbergh baby, who was en route to Canada with her lawyer.

But Frank Swift's fortunes and those of his backers were beginning to ebb. The Great Depression settled in, and the hotel was unable to meet its large obligations. Taken over by the mortgage holder, it was sold in 1931 to Fabian Securities Co. Swift stayed on as manager until 1932. In that year, the owners of the local Grand View Hotel leased the hotel. In 1934,

Charles L. Ornstein, manager of the Hotel Paramount in New York, took over the lease for a long term.

For one such as Frank Swift, for whom the breath of life was hotels, it was not the end of a career. He eventually purchased Alford Inn, next door to the Marcy, renamed it Lake Placid Inn, and ran it successfully until his death in 1944.

Beginning in 1940, the Marcy entered what was to be an unbroken thirty-year period of popularity and high repute. In July 1940, Fabian Theaters, today part of Time-Warner, leased the Marcy to Jack M. Davis and Gordon Ruiz, both of Palm Beach. Ruiz stayed but a year, and up through 1945 Davis was the sole lessee. In 1946, Davis bought the hotel outright under the name of Placid Marcy Company.

Jack M. Davis was born in New York City on August 24, 1914, to David and Jeanette Horowitz Davis. He attended New York University and City College. In 1930, Davis worked on Wall Street and then, interested in electronics, set up his own radio shop. He then joined the hotel business of his family, who owned the Mayflower in Palm Beach, and from there came to Lake Placid and the Marcy.

The decade of the 1940s was a propitious period for the new owner's initiation. Despite World War II, Lake Placid was thriving as a resort. War-weary Americans found it a restful and revitalizing haven, and swarms of European refugees discovered it as a nostalgic substitute for their own lost vacation resorts. The U.S. Army was occupying the Lake Placid Club as a rehabilitation and reassignment center, and the Army overflow occupied some of the rooms at the Marcy. The Marcy itself was very much involved in activities relating to the war. Davis had donated one of the stores in the Marcy to the local Victory Club for headquarters, and the club held dinners and fashion shows at the hotel as well as dances in the Fun Room, which eventually became the famous Driftwood Room.

During his long tenure, Jack Davis proved to be one of the most astute, innovative, and imaginative hotelmen ever to grace Lake Placid. His Marcy operation did much to keep Lake Placid alive and well from the 1940s until 1970. Plenty of entertainment was always provided. He advertised heavily in metropolitan papers, always emphasizing Lake Placid, and brought new faces into town. He was the first to bring package-deal busses into town, and the first to provide air conditioning. In the early days of TV, reception at Lake Placid was difficult at best. Only the Schenectady station could be contacted, and the Marcy had a virtual monopoly on it from 1947 until 1953 by erecting a tall reception tower on the hotel roof.

Sam and William Adler of New York City briefly owned the hotel from 1957 until October 1961, when Davis again assumed control.

During the Davis years, the Marcy expanded considerably. In 1953 Davis bought the Lake Placid Inn next door (now The Warehouse),[59] and in 1965 built the Thunderbird motel.[60] A swimming pool was installed at street level under the old Northwoods Inn. In 1962, a massive front extension brought the top four floors out to the fore of the two lower floors, greatly expanding the hotel's facilities. Davis also developed the hotel's Mirror Lake beach and installed an outdoor ice cream parlor on its Main Street deck above the beach. Radio star and songstress Kate Smith, who had a camp on Lake Placid, stopped by every day for her favorite ice cream soda.

The Marcy continued to attract luminaries of the entertainment world, among them Perry Como and the Andrews Sisters. Barbra Streisand and her family were guests before Barbra achieved stardom. Other notable guests were Governor Nelson Rockefeller, Eleanor Roosevelt, and symphony conductor Artur Rodzinski.

Amid all this prosperity and success, tragedy struck. In the early morning hours of December 28, 1966, fire broke out in the old Northwoods Inn annex, which housed the hotel kitchen, dining room, storage, offices, help's quarters, a few guest rooms, and the swimming pool at street level. By seven a.m. there was nothing left of Wes Kennedy's pioneer inn but a smoking ruin. Five employees died in the fire. It was the holiday season, and 475 guests were in the main hotel. All were safely evacuated into the street in below-zero (Fahrenheit) weather, most of them in nightclothes. The people of Lake Placid responded to the emergency generously. Merchants contributed clothes, gloves, food, and coffee, and all guests were given shelter at other hotels and even private homes. Most continued their holiday at Lake Placid.

"We like it here," one father said. "We want to stay."

The main hotel was spared major damage, and discouragement was not a word in Jack Davis's vocabulary. Only ten days later, the Marcy re-

---

59 See Chapter 56 on the Peacock Building.

60 At this editing, it is the Mountain View Inn.

opened, with 150 guests. The hotel was booked heavily for the months of January and February, and there were few cancellations.

Davis soon built the present two-story, steel-frame, concrete-block south wing on the site of the old Northwoods Inn.

In 1970, Jack Davis sold the Marcy complex to the Robert Case Bennet Corp.

The Marcy continued as a hotel. The hotel also housed the U.S. Olympic Training Center for a time after the XIII Olympic Winter Games, held in Lake Placid in 1980. In March 1986, the OTC moved into its own quarters on Old Military Road.

To date, the Robert Case Bennet Corp. has continued to own the Marcy in name, but under different principals. The principals today [1993] are contractor Gregory Ruppert and corporate lawyer Barry C. Maloney, who bought the hotel in the fall of 1986.

The Marcy entity now consists only of the hotel proper and the south wing. It is still mainly a hotel, but all accommodations are suites, each with a bedroom and a living room. The historic structure has a fresh look, and Ruppert and Maloney have interesting plans for its future. A mall is scheduled for the downstairs portion, and a pizza parlor and brewery will occupy the south wing.

Clearly, many more good years are in store for the sixty-six-year-old Marcy.[61]

FIFTY-ONE
Victor Herbert
July 31, 1980

Victor Herbert, whose brilliant operettas have thrilled the entire world, was this community's most distinguished and beloved summer resident of bygone days.

Victor discovered the beauty and peace of Lake Placid sometime in the late 1890s. For him it was the loveliest spot on earth, and he made it his summer home for over a quarter of a century. First staying as a guest at a Lake Placid Club cottage, he later built camps Joyland and Sunset on the

61 Written in 1993. The Lake Placid–Marcy was renamed the Northwoods Inn later in the 1990s.

east shore of Lake Placid, just above Paradox Bay, and bought adjoining Camp Woodland from Captain Cane.

His love for Lake Placid intensified as the years passed, and so did the town's regard for the genial and convivial celebrity. Even today, over fifty years removed from his death, stories of old-timers who remember him and his rare delight in life are told with deep affection.

Fame touched Victor at an early age. Born in Dublin, Ireland, on February 1, 1859, he was taken to Stuttgart, Germany, by his mother for schooling at the age of six. As he grew older, she felt he should be a doctor. But he played cello as a hobby, and it was soon apparent the boy had an extraordinary talent. Medicine was forgotten, and Victor received sound musical training in Germany, where he gained recognition as a composer and violoncello virtuoso.

In Vienna, he met his wife, the opera singer Therese Foerster, an ash blonde and rated the most beautiful girl of that city. The Metropolitan Opera Company brought the Herberts to the United States in 1886, she as a prima donna and he to play in the orchestra. The New York Philharmonic performed his early compositions, romantic and melodious. Mrs. Herbert soon gave up her own career to foster her husband's. Her sympathy and close companionship were to enrich Victor's whole life and work.

He won lasting renown in America, both as composer and orchestra conductor. Probably no other music created in this country, save Stephen Foster's, has become as familiar and precious a part of our heritage. It is played and sold as frequently today as when he lived. Many of his more than forty operettas have become classics, notably *Babes in Toyland, The Red Mill, Naughty Marietta, Eileen*, and *Sweethearts.*

It is known that Victor wrote at least *Babes in Toyland* at Lake Placid, and the greater portions of *Princess Pat, The Red Mill, Eileen*, and *Her Regiment.* Camp Joyland, designed by famed Great Camp architect William Coulter, was blissfully quiet and free of the disturbing sounds fatal to creative talent, and there he lived and worked. He composed in the morning, and sometimes at night until two a.m. One little room on the northeast corner of the second floor, bare except for piano and desk, was his workshop. He did all his own orchestrations, standing up and writing very fast. Sometimes he noted in the margin, "Dam hot here today" [sic].

One year his tranquility was marred by a music less dulcet than his own. His next-door neighbors, the McElroys, employed a family who kept a cow. The animal, staked out in the rough of the fifth hole of the old Stevens House golf course, produced a calf that was sold for veal in the summer. In her bereavement, the cow bawled heart-rendingly, day and night. The harassed Mrs. Herman, an extremely gentle woman, was finally driven to approach Hubert Stevens. "Hubert," she pleaded in her rich Viennese accent, "you have to do something, because that cow moos and moos, and my Victor can't make his moo-sic!"

Each summer he installed at camp the man who was writing lyrics for his score at the moment—Henry Blossom, Glen McDonough, or Joe Weber. The lyricist was banished to a boathouse room to delve for inspiration in solitary confinement. Blossom, a great favorite because of his gaiety and wit, used to cut clippings from papers and magazines for ideas. One day he had these spread out in the "inspiration room" when a gust of wind whisked them into the lake, much to Victor's amusement.

He spent three months of each year, from June to September, at Lake Placid with his wife and children. The family made the annual trip with car and chauffeur, bringing the New York servants with them. Camp caretakers over the years were local men Frank Pelkey and Bernard Farley.

Victor lent support to many local concerts and once gave a party for the Fire Department band. He was particularly interested in the singing career of a young girl who then summered here, Miss Irene See (later Mrs. Seymour Reed and mother of Grant Reed, of Lake Placid), and sponsored her concerts. She sang for a time with the Metropolitan Opera Company.

Victor loved living on Lake Placid and was a devoted trout fisherman. He began buying motor-driven speedboats for his son Clifford, who challenged the supremacy of other speedboat hot-rodders of the era. Clifford, a Cornell student, was a sunny and buoyant character, but his luck with boats was all bad.

By 1907, two speedboats had made their appearance on the lake, foretokening the doom of the old Adirondack guideboats. One was the *Victoria*, built like a racing shell and purchased by Victor for Clifford. Its clutch was installed to the rear of the motor, and on its trial run, a girl boarding the stern had her long and voluminous skirt caught in the clutch. Victor and Mrs. Herbert ordered Clifford to cover the clutch at once; they could not have that sort of thing on the lake.

William L. Supplee brought in the second speedboat, the *Theanogran.* Built for general passenger use, it was long, like the *Victoria.*

The question soon arose: Which one was the fastest?

A race was arranged in August and a course laid out, starting at the Yacht Club, going up the east lake through Sunset Strait, and thence around the lake. Both boats balked when they crossed the starting line, and they had to rev up again. *Theanogran* beat *Victoria* handily, and Clifford was disgusted. He sold his lemon to Eustis Seligman.

The next year his father bought a new boat, the *Rory,* the first all-mahogany craft on the lake. Clifford challenged Supplee and his *Theanogran* to a handicap race (it seemed likely *Rory* would win in a breeze). But again, Supplee triumphed.

Clifford was hard on boats. The *Rory* stayed around but one season, for it burned up very suddenly. One day Clifford could not get it started in the boathouse. He uncovered the top of the gasoline tank and, smoking a cigarette, went back to the engine and started tinkering around. He flipped his cigarette away, and it landed in the gasoline tank. The boat exploded, and Clifford was catapulted into the lake.

Victor bought yet another boat for his luckless son, telling him it would be the very last if he did not make good with it. It was the *Natoma,* a forty-footer and the most elaborate ever on the lake, with an enormous engine. Clifford never raced it. He claimed it had too many bugs—and, as forewarned, it was curtains for Clifford and his maritime machines.

Almost every evening, Victor boated around the lake and then returned to camp and started working. He swam every day, although he was not particularly interested in strenuous sports. A fluent linguist, he spoke perfect German, French, and Italian without an accent. Once the Lotus Club of New York gave a big bash in honor of the great Enrico Caruso. Victor, a close friend, was asked to give one of the speeches. He spoke in Italian; Caruso, the only one who could understand what he was saying, was vastly amused.

The composer was also a dedicated walker, climbing Mount Whitney often. His favorite woodland stroll was out West Valley Road[62] way,

62 Now called Wesvalley Road.

accompanied by his daughter Ella—later Mrs. Robert S. Bartlett—who summered here all her life. He always carried a little notebook and jotted down tunes as they lighted on his mind, often inspired by the songs of the Adirondack birds. Mrs. Bartlett presented this notebook, along with some of his original operetta scores, to the Library of Congress.

He was a frequent visitor at Main Street stores, where he was well-known and enthusiastically greeted on a first-name basis. Often on his walks to town, he would stop at the old Lakeside Inn, presided over by J. Vernon Lamb Sr. There he would invariably order a tot of Johnny Jameson Irish whiskey.

There was always wine at dinner in Lake Placid—he relished German Rhines and Moselles—and one martini before. But he would say to Mrs. Herbert, "Now, Mother, I just think we don't need this martini up here—the air is so wonderful!"

Even so, he was rumored to have a prodigious drinking capacity when the occasion demanded it. The story goes that when he was pleased with his orchestra's performance, he would invite the men out for drinks afterwards. Once, after a concert, he took them to a favorite tavern, where they raised glasses into the wee hours. Now and then, it was half-heartedly suggested that the party break up, and Victor would order another round. Everyone except the composer went home tipsy, and at rehearsal the next day suffered a collective hangover and played badly. Victor was indignant. "A fine bunch you are!" he grumbled. "I show you a good time, and this is the gratitude I get!"

Victor Herbert was kind, open, warm, and light-hearted. He was always available to anyone, incapable of discouraging those who thought they had musical talent or of sidestepping those who wanted a loan. His death on May 26, 1924, at age sixty-five, was sudden—and even in his final moments of life, that instinctive concern for others did not fail him.

He had lunched with friends in New York. Afterward, as they walked along 77th Street, Victor said he did not feel well. He must see a doctor, his friends urged, but he had never been ill and had no personal physician. There was a doctor's office nearby, and he went there, arriving just as the doctor's sister was coming out. She told Victor her brother was in conference with other physicians, and he replied, "Well, never mind, I will not disturb him"—whereupon he fell over and died.

It was a tragic loss to his family and the world, and no less to Lake Placid, for in this setting he loved so well, his work had intimate meaning. His magic melodies will live always. No musical fad of the moment can eclipse "Gypsy Love Song," "Kiss Me Again," "Ah, Sweet Mystery of Life," "Because You're You," "I'm Falling in Love with Someone," or the one that is surely a hymn to his beloved Adirondacks, the haunting "Indian Summer."

FIFTY-TWO
St. Moritz Hotel
July 1999

The period between 1880 and 1900 has become known historically as Lake Placid's "golden age of hotels." The St. Moritz Hotel fits into the category by a hair.

Albert Stickney, born in Michigan, and his wife Etta Littlejohn Stickney arrived in Lake Placid in 1899 and proceeded to build an inn called the Pines on the site of the present St. Moritz Hotel. It could accommodate twenty-five guests and opened the summer of 1900. An attractive, small, three-story building with ample porches, surrounded by trees and a spacious front lawn, it was a successful venture from the start.

The Stickneys operated the inn personally until 1920, when Robert B. Scott of Boston took it over, apparently on a lease. Scott was a hotelman of varied experience and had been with Lake Placid's Whiteface Inn and Stevens House for several years. Under his direction, the inn became a popular refuge for discriminating, well-to-do guests. It had bellboy service, and initially had an orchestra for musicales and dancing, led by Miss Bessie Spectre of the New England Conservatory of Music. Thomas Walinsby, formerly with the Carlton Hotel of London, England, was the chef. Bungalows and bungalow tents were also available. In 1922, semi-weekly dances were held in the spacious dining room, and the Pines Trio furnished music consisting of violin, piano, and cello. Music was also played during the luncheon and dinner hours, and concerts of sacred music were given on Sunday evenings.

The Stickneys sold the inn to Paul J. Augsberger in 1923 and soon passed into legend. Mrs. Stickney died the next year, 1924, and Albert Stickney died in March 1926 at age sixty-eight.

It was Augsberger who renamed the inn "St. Moritz Hotel" and soon defined the place for all time. Purportedly in 1926, a large, six-story addition swallowed up the original inn, and shortly the front of the hotel was faced with brick. No major changes were made in after years, and the hotel today substantially resembles the original addition. It is believed that Augsberger also built the Annex behind the hotel. Originally used as a storehouse and garage, it was later remodeled and enlarged to house an overflow of guests. The hotel was winterized and could stay open both summer and winter.

It is not clear when Augsberger ceased to operate the hotel. He seems to have been gone after 1930, probably a victim of the Great Depression. In any event, the St. Moritz received considerable publicity when, in January 1931, Helen Kane, the famous "boop-a-doop" girl of the period, vacationed there. In the summer of 1931, the hotel was advertising "nude sun bathing on the roof" and "private sun bath cabinets on the roof."

The years of the Great Depression set in. Frank Swift, well-known Lake Placid hotelier, managed the St. Moritz in 1933 and 1934. During the remainder of the 1930s, Edgar V.M. Gilbert ran the hotel as an adjunct to his famous Grand View Hotel. In the late 1930s, the capacity of the hotel was listed as 150.

J.R. Grossman took over the hotel in 1940. He had extremely ambitious plans for improvements, and by December had created an atmosphere entirely new to Lake Placid. The grill was transformed into the "Swiss Room," which would become a popular and unusual rendezvous for not only hotel guests but also the people of Lake Placid. It opened on December 21, 1940, just in time for the holiday crowd, to the music of Cy Norton and his versatile trio. The walls were of knotty pine and provided an attractive background for antique lighting fixtures. The bar itself was enclosed in a rustic ski hut, a room within a room. Huge blown-up photos of skiers and mountain views not only adorned the walls of the Swiss Room but were hung throughout the first floor and at the entrance to the lobby. The Swiss Room, in fact, was similar to a room in the St. Moritz Hotel in Switzerland.

Famous people visited the St. Moritz during the Grossman occupancy. In the summer of 1940, the internationally esteemed pianist Vladimir Horowitz and his wife, the daughter of Arturo Toscanini, stayed at the hotel. In the summer of 1941, Albert Einstein, who summered in the Saranac Lake area in the 1940s, was guest of honor at a hotel gathering and addressed the guests and their friends.

Despite renowned guests and the fabulous Swiss Room, Grossman failed financially and was soon gone. He had done nothing to refurbish the hotel beyond the Swiss Room. The hotel had fallen into the hands of the town and village for non-payment of taxes and was now owned by a consortium of bondholders, with town Supervisor Willis Wells as trustee.

In April 1943, Goodman Kelleher of Lake Placid, who himself owned a small bond interest, purchased the St. Moritz. Kelleher, a great and colorful character locally, had helped to brighten the Lake Placid scene and indeed had become a legend in the resort business. Starting out as a poor boy, he had achieved considerable financial success. At the time he purchased the St. Moritz he was also owner of the Majestic Restaurant in Lake Placid and the Clearwater Beach Hotel in Clearwater Beach, Florida. His fame reached beyond Lake Placid. Ripley's "Believe It or Not" column had featured him on January 10, 1936, as "The Cook's Cook," as he had been cooking his help's breakfast every morning for twenty years. Kelleher had a post card made of the cartoon and handed one out to each of his customers.

Given his track record, Kelleher soon put the St. Moritz Hotel back on its feet. The place was very much run down and immediately received a thorough cleaning. Barrel after barrel of rubbish was hauled to the village dump. Much of the furniture needed replacement, but new furniture was difficult to obtain during those war years. Kelleher solved the problem in his unique fashion. He bought a hotel in neighboring Wilmington and moved all the furniture up to the St. Moritz. He also put together an excellent staff. After many years of neglect, the St. Moritz was now a hotel to be reckoned with. Kelleher made many major improvements to the inside of the hotel. He kept the Swiss Room but removed most of the decorations in which Grossman had taken such pride.

Kelleher increased the capacity of the hotel by twenty rooms in another expression of his lively imagination and marketing skills. He purchased the old village barn on Greenwood Street, at the rear of the St. Moritz, and, in July 1947, at considerable expense, remodeled it into a most attractive twenty-room guesthouse that came to be known as Pine Lodge. All the rooms were finished in knotty pine, and most had connecting baths. This proved to be a very popular and lucrative feature of the St. Moritz.

During Kelleher's ownership, capacity was listed in 1947 as 175, in 1949 as 200, and in 1952 as 250.

Kelleher's nephew, William L. Rascoe, managed the hotel, having received his training at Gordon Kelleher's famous Majestic Restaurant, across from the high school on Main Street. When Kelleher died in 1953, Rascoe continued to manage the hotel for Mrs. Kelleher, and then purchased it in 1956. It was under the guidance of William Rascoe and his wife Joan Dixon Rascoe that the hotel experienced its greatest success.

The Rascoes were very civic-minded and attracted local organizations for dinners, luncheons, and meetings.

The hotel was also favored by bobsled groups. In 1960, Eugenio Monti and his championship Italian team were quartered there, and when the World Bobsled Championships were held here in 1961, the St. Moritz was headquarters for the Italian and Swiss teams. The St. Moritz was also the scene of the opening and closing banquets, and Governor Nelson Rockefeller of New York presided as the guest speaker.

In the 1960s, Lake Placid had developed a famous junior ski-jumping team, known throughout the nation. Many events were held in Lake Placid, and the St. Moritz provided housing and feeding for visiting junior jumpers.

The Rascoes also established the first ski-package plan in Lake Placid in cooperation with the Whiteface Mountain Ski Center, and ski-bus tours became the major part of its winter business. This program would sustain the hotel for many years to come.

The Schaefer Brewing Company became sponsors of Lake Placid's North American Winter Festivals, and the St. Moritz became headquarters for President Rudolph Schaefer and other company officers.

Many conventions were held in Lake Placid during the Rascoe regime, and the St. Moritz was headquarters for the New York State Lions, Veterans of Foreign Wars, New York State Fire and Police Association, and others.

There was always an orchestra at the hotel, in season, during the Kelleher and Rascoe years. The Swiss Room was kept open by the Rascoes, as well as a second bar and recreation room.

The Rascoes were also staunch Republicans, and many Essex County party officials and organizations chose the hotel for luncheons, dinners, and meetings. It was the headquarters of New York State Assemblyman Grant Johnson in his campaigns.

The St. Moritz was also the scene of at least one Democratic affair. In the fall of 1960, Robert F. Kennedy, presidential campaign manager for his brother, John F. Kennedy, was barnstorming the country. He flew to Lake Placid in his twin-engine Beechcraft on October 9, 1960. A large contingent of Democratic officials and supporters from Essex County met him at the Lake Placid Airport. A caravan of about fifty cars, with horns blaring, then proceeded up Main Street to the St. Moritz Hotel for a coffee hour and an inspiring talk by RFK.

In January 1964, William Rascoe sold the St. Moritz Hotel, containing sixty sleeping rooms, together with Pine Lodge, to Charles Vosburgh, of Cortland, New York. Vosburgh was a man who specialized in auction sales of hotels, and he promptly auctioned off the St. Moritz. Pine Lodge was severed from the hotel complex and was sold separately. The hotel was purchased, purportedly for the sum of $34,000, by a trio of local businessmen: Fred Dennin, Robert Reiss, and Jack Davis. Davis had brought the Hotel Marcy to fame.

In 1964, the hotel was leased to Zig Zag Inc. and was managed that summer by Lake Placid's famous bobsledder, Stan Benham. In May 1965, the trio of Dennin, Reiss, and Davis sold the St. Moritz to Diversified Hotels Inc., of New York City, which planned a year-around operation.

Since that time, the hotel has had a number of owners. A rather long-time owner was Stephen Reisinger, who operated the place from the late 1960s until 1980. Again, the ski-bus tours were the major part of the winter business. Directly after the 1980 Olympic Winter Games here, Reisinger sold out to Alfred and Frieda Dornacher, from Germany.

In 1985, while the hotel was still in Dornacher ownership, the Annex on Greenwood Street, a twenty-five-room, three-story building directly behind the St. Moritz, was destroyed by fire in the frigid, early-morning hours of January 18. The fire was determined to have been caused by arson. The Dornachers had been receiving threatening phone calls, probably from the arsonist, who was never apprehended.

The hotel of late years has been in the ownership of James LaFountain and Glenn Cameron.[63]

---

63 The St. Moritz Hotel was sold in 2004. The new owners renamed it The Pines.

Many hotels have come and gone in Lake Placid over its long history as a resort. The St. Moritz, now a century old by virtue of its inner core, the Pines, endures. The old landmark still dominates the crest of Saranac Avenue. It is the last survivor of Lake Placid's "golden age of hotels."

PART THREE

Lake Placid

FIFTY-THREE

Ice-trotting Races

In a letter dated March 11, 1983, Mary MacKenzie answers an inquiry about the history of ice-trotting races.

I have a lot of material on ice-trotting races on Mirror Lake in the early days. It is a bit difficult to get it all together, as there are three separate periods involved, but I shall try to put the whole story in chronological order for you.

One difficulty is that many printed news accounts are missing. The *Lake Placid News* began publication in 1905, but the paper has lost its files from 1905 to 1914. I have only scattered copies for those years in my historical collections. It is, therefore, necessary to guess at some aspects of the story. From 1914 on, the *News* is on microfilm and there is no problem.

Two Lake Placid newspapers antedated the *News*, the *Mountain Mirror*, and *The Adirondack*, both covering the 1890s. Very few issues of these papers exist, but from the random copies I have, it appears that ice harness racing was in vogue here as early as the 1890s. For instance, the *Mirror* of December 28, 1894, says, "Melvin Kennedy may be seen on the ice with some of the best trotting stock in Lake Placid, most any day."

A Keeseville paper reports Kennedy racing with his stallion Baronet in Plattsburgh in 1903.

The Adirondack of January 28, 1898, says, "John Stevens' trotters Clay Lambert and John McGregor went to Tupper Lake Saturday."

It seems that in the 1890s there was a North Country circuit for ice racing, with good purses. Events are reported at Tupper Lake, at Plattsburgh ("held under the auspices of the Gentlemen's Driving Club") and at places on Lake Champlain. One is readily drawn to the conclusion, and it is my opinion, that Lake Placid was a member of this circuit, and races were held on Mirror Lake. Since almost every one of the few existing newspapers mention ice harness activity, it must have been widespread and a main feature of Lake Placid life from the early 1890s into the first decade of the 1900s.

Apparently, there was a lapse of a few years, because two lone 1911 papers I have say:

> *December 10*: That the good old sport of ice trotting may be revived in town is foreshadowed by the purchase by John Stevens

> at the Old Glory sale at Madison Square Garden, New York, of the four-year-old mare Maycliffe. We have many lovers of this form of sport but none more consistently enthusiastic than John, who in past years has been known to keep a track open on Mirror Lake all winter long, mostly at his own expense, for the sake of indulging in his favorite amusement. His work with numerous horses in the past is well known to all the fraternity in northern New York, and coupled with his expert reputation in this line stands out prominently the fact that when John races a horse, he is handled absolutely on the square.
>
> *December 15*: John Stevens was the first horseman[1] to try out the ice on Mirror Lake. Mr. Stevens' recent purchase of Maycliffe, a four-year-old mare, showed good form and took kindly to the ice track.

Whether this 1911 revival was continuous up to 1914, I have no way of knowing, for few copies of the *News* of this period have come to light. I would judge, however, that it was continuous, because the ensuing microfilm shows that races were in full swing in 1914. Lake Placid's Mid-Winter Festival in February 1914 featured ice-trotting races. Many news accounts attest that the sport was very popular on Mirror Lake from 1914 through the year 1917. Names of numerous owners and drivers are reported. All of these were Lake Placid residents except for two prominent outsiders, Mart A. Drury and Willard Boyce. All the racing seems to have been done on an intramural basis, with only members of the Lake Placid Trotting Association competing, save Drury and Boyce. It must have been a large association since more than thirty local participants are mentioned—an awful lot for such a small village. There was great and enthusiastic rivalry.

The sport died out after 1917—why, I don't know. Perhaps it was the advent of World War I. In any event, I find no accounts from 1918 to 1933, except a report of the revival of the Saranac Lake Racing Association in 1922. In January of that year, some Lake Placid horses were entered in trotting races on Lake Flower in Saranac Lake. Perhaps the sport continued in our neighboring village for a while.

---

1 MacKenzie's note: The word "first" implies that there were other horsemen in Lake Placid addicted to the sport at that time.

In 1933, ice trotting was revitalized on Mirror Lake in no small measure. From 1933 through 1937 a long series of matinee races are reported, under the auspices of the Lake Placid Driving Club. This time, many horsemen came from all over Essex County, New York, and a few from neighboring Franklin County. It is interesting to note that three horsemen of the 1911–17 era were still racing in the 1930s: Fred Gladd, Fred Fortune (who owned a riding academy here), and Mart Drury, formerly of Saranac Lake and later of Malone.

On December 28, 1934, many of the county horsemen arrived in town to race on Mirror Lake the next day, stabling their horses in the Fortune barn. In the early morning hours of December 29, the barn caught fire and was totally destroyed. The thermometer stood at forty-below-zero Fahrenheit. Thirty-seven horses were in the building, and as men struggled to untie them, they pitched and reared, terrified by the smoke and flame. Some refused to leave their stalls, and it was necessary to throw them to the floor and drag them from the burning building. Only three animals were lost: two saddle horses owned by Fortune, and a racing horse of seventeen-year-old Miss Vergie Carson of Lewis, New York.

There are no accounts of ice harness racing after 1937.

You will note that Patrick J. Hennessy, who raced in the early 1900s, did not do so in the 1930s. He did, however, continue to help organize races, was an officer of the Driving Club, and often acted as a judge. He and Fred Fortune were really the leading promoters of the sport in Lake Placid. Pat, who was a good friend of mine before his death some years ago, told me many a tale of the old ice races.

The course in the 1911–17 period was a kite-shaped, one-mile track. In the 1930s, it was half a mile.

The Center for Music, Drama, and Art[2] here at Lake Placid has a collection of thousands of old glass photo plates of our era 1900–17. Among them are some splendid shots of ice-trotting races on Mirror Lake.

---

2 Now called the Lake Placid Center for the Arts.

FIFTY-FOUR

Home of the Hickories

Adirondack Life *magazine, Winter 1972.*

On the roof of New York State, in the winter of 1904–1905, ten men and women met to share a suicidal mission: a winter vacation in the Adirondacks. They had asked Dr. Melvil Dewey, owner of the Lake Placid Club, to keep his hostelry open while they experimented in a cold-weather outing. The good doctor amiably agreed, turned the water back on, ordered forty pairs of hickory skis from Norway (not a pair could be purchased in America), and sat back to tally the results of this incredible folly.

No one thought to engrave the names of those ten hardy pioneers on Adirondack granite. It is not yet too late. They were the author Irving Bacheller, whose books, including *Eben Holden* and *Keeping Up With Lizzie*, hit the best seller lists; his wife, Anna Schultz Bacheller; Mrs. Ackerman; Dr. and Mrs. Edgar VanderVerr of Albany; the latter's sister, Miss Wooster; Mrs. Ella B. Dana and her son, Ted (Edward C.), of Metuchen, New Jersey; Godfrey Dewey, son of Melvil; and lastly, Henry Van Hoevenberg of Adirondack Lodge fame, one of the more outré characters of local history. Also joining in some of the festivities were Mr. and Mrs. Asa O. Gallup and John C. Jubin of the Club staff.

The ten skied, skated, tobogganed, snowshoed, and otherwise gamboled in the snow, the women's petticoats sweeping the drifts. The experiment was a smashing success! The next winter, more visitors came than the Club could provide for. A brief two years later, a new, year-round clubhouse had to be built. By 1908, outdoor teas, camp dinners, climbing, and even all-night camping parties were on the winter agenda.

Dr. and Mrs. Dewey had started the Club as a private summer resort in 1895 with thirty members, five acres of land, and one building. In 1923, they had ninety-six hundred acres and 356 buildings. No small part of the phenomenal growth was due to winter sport buffs—in the winter of 1923, there were one thousand bookings! It was then Dr. Dewey declared with parental pride that Lake Placid was first in America for winter sports. The Lake Placid Club served up ice and snow to the continent, and the continent found them both palatable and healthful.

As a Club member wrote in the *Boston Transcript* in 1911:

> Very few wallflowers or all-day sitters will you find in the winter colony. You are here on purpose to get outdoors, snub the thermometer and try everything in sight. Untaught, you strike out on skis and find what it is to be unable either to stand up, sit down, move ahead or turn around. Almost nobody takes cold. I do not remember to have heard a solitary sneeze in ten days.

By 1922, a waggish newspaper in Switzerland was referring to St. Moritz as "The Lake Placid of Europe."

The idea of skiing in America was so new, however, it was some time before the sport was officially recognized to any extent. The National Ski Association did organize in 1904 to steer the Midwestern meets. Yet it was 1921 before the U.S. Eastern Amateur Ski Association came into being as the result of informal meetings held at Saranac Lake and the Lake Placid Club. The Federation International du Ski itself was not formed until 1924.

In 1920, the Sno Birds of Lake Placid were born. Their most outstanding member, the late Harry Wade Hicks of Lake Placid, became a legend in the history of organized skiing. It is impossible to assess fully the impetus this group has given skiing in North America. By 1922, there were five hundred members, wholly dedicated through direct participation or interest. Adopting the motto that every child "be born shod with skis," as in Norway, each pledged himself a one-man task force to foster it. Their emblem has become world famous: a snow-white bird in full flight over a field of blue. The raising and lowering of their flag at the start and close of the winter season became a stirring tradition.

The programs the Birds began to stage at the Club drew the eyes of the world to the lusty, stripling resort. It was nothing for them to conduct eighty formal competitions a winter, with 280 trophies and prizes awarded. Seasonal events with two highlights were sponsored: During Christmas Week, various colleges competed in winter sports, featuring cross country and jump skiing for the Marshal Foch bronze Winged Victory and President Harding trophies. The mammoth sterling silver cup presented by President Warren G. Harding carried the proviso that all competitions must be held at the Lake Placid Club. In January, there was a week of fancy, figure, and free skating; and then a week for curling. House parties and dances enlivened the days and nights. Throughout the winter, there were also large beginners' classes, races for women, skijoring parties, and "hare and hounds." Many celebrities took their first spills at Placid, Douglas Fairbanks Sr. among them.

Near the main clubhouse were six small ski jumps and three coasting towers, connected via ski run with another clubhouse at Valley Farm on the Au Sable River. The latter, equipped with stone fireplace, furnace, running hot and cold water, dining room, and chef, made an ideal rendezvous for rest, refreshment, and camaraderie. It was probably the forerunner of all ski slope lodges in the land.

During the late Teens and early Twenties, a glittering array of instructors enhanced the scene. One, sports director Marquis Nicholas degli Albizzi, was a skillful skier and mean banjo player, whose Mediterranean charm and wit are still remembered. Member of a military ski corps in the Italian Alps in World War I, he was to become a pioneer ski developer in Canada. And there were Ornulf Poulsen, a gentleman sportsman from Norway, reputedly one of the best skiers in the world; and Michael G. Malicheff, scion of a Russian family high in official circles before the October Revolution.

In 1921, the Club built a championship-caliber jump at Intervales (now the Olympic jump), and in February, with some misgivings about the outcome, ran its first annual ski tournament—to include the international amateur jumping and cross country contests. Success was instantaneous! Repeated in February 1922, the tournament had a true international flavor, with Canada, Sweden, Norway, and Switzerland vying with the United States.

By 1924, the competition had swelled to such dimensions that a crowd of thirty-five hundred spectators descended on Placid. Every room on Club grounds and in the village was snapped up. The second U.S. Eastern Amateur Ski jump and ten-mile run championships and the Sno Birds' second annual twenty-five mile run were featured. Special trains from New York brought hundreds from the metropolis, bearing banners that read, "We are bound for Lake Placid and the ski jump!"

The event evoked such passion among aficionados that, in 1925, a New Haven man, Earle Spencer Brinsmade, trekked all the way to Placid on skis, roughly three hundred miles. Using a pair of American-made hickories, this gentleman accomplished the entire journey from New

Haven under his own steam, save for two or three occasions when he skijored behind a sleigh for short runs. Leaving the morning of January 28 and spending nights at farmhouses, he crossed four states and arrived at the Mapledale cottage in Placid on February 13. Actual traveling time: one hundred hours.

Meanwhile, from across Mirror Lake, villagers watched the winter activities at the Club with some awe. True, they were also contributing, with speed skating, to Placid's spiraling fame, but ski fever had not yet infected them. By 1921, the disease reached the proletariat, and thirty citizens formed the Lake Placid Ski Club. Unfortunately, when the first flakes fell the following winter, several livewire members had left town and the Club was allowed to lapse. But in January 1925, the organization was renewed under the name of Lake Placid Ski and Snowshoe Club, with membership in the U.S. Eastern Amateur Ski Association.

First officers of the revived club were W.R. Wikoff, president; Carl A. Thornton, vice president; and Ralph Jabbott, treasurer. Secretary was Ronald MacKenzie,[3] for whom skiing was to become a way of life. Now universally proclaimed "Mr. Ski" of the east, Ron was elected to the Skiing Hall of Fame last winter.[4]

The members had a fine time together. There were outdoor winter picnics, hayrides, and weekly ski and snowshoe safaris. In December 1925, fifty new members invaded the club. Surface skiing became so popular that an annual Lake Placid-Saranac Lake cross-country race was inaugurated, leading from Saranac to Placid or vice versa (ten miles).

By 1929, winter ascents of Whiteface, Marcy, and MacIntyre on skis were rather commonplace. Even more ambitious climbs were made annually by members of the Appalachian Mountain Club. However, in 1925 the sport of mountain skiing was still a novelty, although experimental runs into the High Peak region, through Avalanche and Indian Passes, had been made for several years.

The first known winter ascent of Marcy had occurred in March 1893, but it was made on snowshoes. The first known winter ascent on skis of an Adirondack peak was in 1912, when Fridtjof Nansen, the famous Norwegian

---

3 Mary MacKenzie's brother-in-law.

4 This essay was published in 1972. Ron MacKenzie, who spearheaded the organizing committee for the second Olympic Winter Games in Lake Placid, died in 1978.

scientist, explorer and author, conquered Whiteface. His feat was astounding—even more so because he was then fifty-one years of age. The popularity of skiing in the Alps today is largely due to the fabulous Nansen—a great athlete in his youth, his polar expeditions a sensation in the 1890s, his later League of Nations activities earning him the Nobel Peace Prize.

On a 1925 trip to Lake Colden from Adirondack Lodge, H. Smith Johannsen, also some fifty years old at the time, showed the same mettle. Seven in his party had proceeded to the Lodge by car, where they donned skis and set out for the mountains. Leaving the Club at the same time, Mr. Johannsen skied all the way to the Lodge, a distance of ten miles. The party had not made more than a mile and a quarter on the trail before he came abreast of them. This grand old man, one of the immortals of early skiing, is still alive and well in Canada. Incredibly, he is still skiing at the advanced age of ninety-six.[5]

Those were the early years. Experience in cross-country and jump skiing was to weigh heavily in awarding the 1932 Winter Olympic Games to Lake Placid, and the Games were to touch off the great explosion in downhill skiing of the 1930s and 1940s.[6] Today, millions of Americans actively enjoy the sport. They may not know it, but their enjoyment stems directly from the frosty dream of ten men and women sixty-seven years ago[7] in the winter woods of Lake Placid.

FIFTY-FIVE
Winter Sports in Lake Placid
1985

Lake Placid, the only complete winter sports resort in America, and one of only a handful in the world, got off to an early start at the turn of the century. Its pioneer role, and its staging of the III Olympic Winter Games in 1932, made the nation winter-sports conscious.

The 1930s and 1940s saw great advancement in enthusiasm and development of all resources at Lake Placid—hockey, speed and figure

5 H. Smith "Jack Rabbit" Johanssen died in 1987 at the age of 111.

6 Note, however, that Alpine events—specifically, the slalom and downhill—were not part of the Winter Olympics until the 1948 Games in St. Moritz.

7 Written in 1972.

skating, ice harness and dog-team racing, tobogganing, winter carnivals, bobsledding, and luge.

Skiing was also a major concern. In the pioneer years, skiing meant touring and jumping (downhill and slalom were not even on the agenda of the III Games). Two hundred fifty miles of excellent cross-country trails, an Olympic sixty-meter jumping hill and a number of smaller jumps at Placid were spawned in that era, and the community has never lost its leadership in these fields. But immediately following the 1932 Olympics, the trend changed sharply and the public began to demand downhill runs and open slopes with uphill transportation. Ski resorts of this type mushroomed, but because of its peculiar geographic position, Lake Placid for some years was to lag behind the competition.

First, Placid strove against a natural handicap of heavily wooded terrain, lacking the treeless slopes of other sections. More significantly, it was hemmed in by the New York State Forest Preserve, which, according the state constitution, "shall forever be wild forest land." Not a tree could be cut without a constitutional amendment approved by the voters. It would be some years before the problem was overcome and a major ski center was constructed on state land in nearby Wilmington.

Meanwhile, in the rope-tow and ski-train era of the 1930s, the community did what was possible on available private lands. A few small ski centers sprang up in or near the village. In 1938, a larger center, Scott's Cobble, with a vertical drop of five hundred feet, was opened. This was a system of open slopes and downhill trails designed by Otto Schneibs, with a rope tow installed by Fred Pabst's Ski Tow Inc., eventually replaced by a Poma lift. Two other larger centers, Fawn Ridge and Mount Whitney, followed. All three were enormously popular. Scott's persisted until 1973, Fawn Ridge until 1977, and Mount Whitney is still in existence.[8]

A half dozen downhill and racing trails were also built in the 1930s. In 1938, with the completion of a Class A racing trail on a privately owned spur of Whiteface Mountain, major competitions followed. The run, made possible through funds donated by Lake Placid citizens, was the nation's finest, and eventually had a vertical descent of twenty-seven hundred feet and a length of two miles. It is now part of the vast Whiteface Mountain Ski Center.

---

8 The Lake Placid Club, operator of the Mount Whitney ski hill, ceased operations in the 1980s.

In November 1941, the voters of New York State, by a slim margin of less than ten thousand votes out of two million cast, passed a constitutional amendment allowing the state to build a major ski center on Whiteface Mountain. Actual construction was postponed because of World War II. Opened in 1949 on a shoulder of Whiteface called Marble Mountain, the center consisted of a T-bar with four trails and a log lodge. Lake Placid had now entered fully into the alpine skiing picture. But Marble Mountain was plagued by unfavorable wind exposures and lasted only until 1958.

When ski enthusiast Averill Harriman became governor of New York in 1954, he used his influence to win support for an entirely state-owned center on the main body of Whiteface. Upon voter approval of still another amendment, construction of the present great Whiteface Mountain Ski Center was completed in January 1958. The first snowmaking equipment was installed in 1961. In 1965, a major expansion resulted in the longest racing trail and the greatest vertical drop (3,216 feet) in the east. Further improvements were made for the World University Games in 1972, and with the awarding of the 1980 Winter Olympics, a complete renovation of trails and lodges began. All alpine events of 1980 were held on Whiteface, which stands alone at the head of Placid Lake amid thousands of acres of "forever wild" forest. The center is valued at $23 million, and its snowmaking systems are ranked among the largest in the world.

Even before 1980, the existing cross country trail system at the state's Mount Van Hoevenberg Recreation Center, with more than twenty kilometers of competitive-class trails, was one of the best in the country. Additional trails were built to meet the full fifty-kilometer Olympic network required. There are many other forest and mountain trails available for recreational ski touring.

The village's love affair with ski jumping has lasted for well over sixty-five years. Olympic teams and athletes from many nations have trained here and competed in the annual events sponsored by and synonymous with the name of Lake Placid: the Washington's Birthday, the New Year's, and the Masters jumps. In 1948, the Junior Chamber of Commerce inaugurated a unique Fourth of July jump held on real snow created from forty tons of ice. It continues to this day, but a new era of summer ski jumping has begun at Placid with the substitution of plastic matting for packed ice. Six major national and international competitions were successfully staged on plastic in the summer of 1983.

The famous Intervale jump, first used in 1918, was a sixty-meter jump at the time of the 1932 Olympics. Two new Intervale jumps were constructed of concrete for the 1980 Olympics, seventy and ninety meters. The ninety-meter tower is 262 feet tall, has a glassed-in elevator to the top, and an adjustable start platform. A snowmaking system capable of covering the hill in twenty-four hours saved the day in the 1980 Olympics, when there was a complete lack of natural snow. The hill is now known as the MacKenzie ski jump complex, in honor of the late Ron MacKenzie.

Whiteface Mountain, the ski jumps, and the cross country complex are now under the jurisdiction of New York State's Olympic Regional Development Authority, and the village itself is the official eastern Olympic Training Center. Competitions are flourishing, and the facilities are in constant use by Olympic hopefuls as well as vacationists.

If there is anything in which Lake Placid has excelled, it has been as a host town for major competitions covering the entire spectrum of winter sports. Its success has been largely due to the tremendous volunteer effort and contributions of its citizens. Over a period of more than sixty years, the small mountain community has gained worldwide prestige and has developed winter facilities unequalled as the host of untold local, regional, state, national, and world events. It has staged two Olympic Winter Games, the seventh World University Winter Games, national and world championships, many Olympic trials, the annual North American Winter Festival, Empire State Winter Games, and the Kennedy International Memorial Winter Games.

The list of additional skiing competitions held at Lake Placid is endless. Among the hundreds are:

- World Cup ski races, women's giant slalom, men's downhill and ski jump.
- World Biathlon Championships.
- International Ski Jump Championships.
- FIS World Jumping Championships.

- Pre-Olympic Nordic Competitions.
- North American cross country, junior jumping, trophy series slalom, and giant slalom championships.
- Canadian-American Slalom.
- National senior ski, giant slalom, junior Nordic, alpine, Junior Olympic Nordic, and biathlon championships.
- U.S. Eastern interscholastic, junior downhill and slalom, and jumping championships.
- U.S. Deaf Skiers Eastern Championships.

Lake Placid has also led the field in the encouragement and training of young skiers of all ages and the holding of many regional, state, and national junior events. As early as 1928, schoolboys were being trained in jumping, and in 1930 a ski jump was built near the Lake Placid Central School for their use. Several well-known national jumpers came out of this early program, among them: Jay Rand; Crosby Perry-Smith, U.S. Olympic team member; and Art Devlin, four-time national champion, twice North American champion, member of four Olympic teams and three world FIS teams.

The jumping program came to full flower in the late 1950s and the 1960s when, under the superior volunteer coaching of Bud Colby and John Viscome, Lake Placid's junior jumping teams became a national phenomenon. The boys swept all the eastern championships many times, winning as well a number of national junior jumping championships. In 1967 alone, four of five members of the National Junior Jumping Squad were Lake Placid boys. Many went on to star on college ski teams.

Out of this period came Jay Rand Jr., U.S. Olympic team member; Jim Speck, who competed for the U.S. in the first World University Games; Jim Page, one of the top skiers in the country while at Dartmouth, U.S. Olympic team member, and director of the 1984 Olympic Nordic Ski Team; and Joe Lamb, member of the 1972 Olympic Nordic Team and coach of the 1984 Olympic Nordic Team.

The program is still in full force and continues to produce champions like Jeff Volmrich, member of the 1984 U.S. Olympic Ski Jumping Team.

The town, for over half a century, has also sponsored and trained junior alpine skiers. Boys and girls in this program have been outstanding on the northeastern and national circuit. Five have been members of U.S. Olympic teams.

All in all, some fifty Lake Placid men and women have been named to U.S. Olympic teams since 1924, ten of them skiers.

A ski patrol was organized at Lake Placid several years before the National Ski Patrol, developing a special sled used by the Army in Alaska as a model during World War II. The Army and Lake Placid have always had a special affinity for one another. Companies of the 26th and 28th Infantries were brought to Placid in 1939, 1940, and 1941 to learn to maneuver on skis. No other sport contributed so gallantly to the U.S. Army in World War II. An entire division, the 10th Mountain Division, was made up of men who had skied for recreation, a number of them Lake Placid boys. The U.S. Army occupied the Lake Placid Club as a rehabilitation center in 1944–45. Local instructors introduced thousands of soldiers returning from overseas duty to the sport of skiing.

Lake Placid, as a major summer and winter resort, has always been a magnet for celebrities. Such entertainers as Douglas Fairbanks, Rudy Vallee, Judy Garland, Sammy Kaye, Arthur Godfrey, and Pat Boone have skied here, as well as such notables as Gene Tunney, Averill Harriman, Admiral Richard Byrd, and New York's colorful mayor, Jimmy Walker. It has been the favorite haunt of some of the best friends of American skiing. Lowell Thomas, best known for his long-running radio news program, learned to ski at Lake Placid in 1932. For the next fifty years, Thomas returned almost every winter for a skiing holiday at Placid, calling it "the world's magical place." This village was the favorite resort of Frank Elkins, the dean of American ski writers, who also learned to ski here. Kate Smith, a summer resident for forty-five years, gave a great boost to women skiers, donating a trophy in 1937 for an annual invitational ski tournament for Canadian and U.S. women.[9] Almost every girl skier on the American and Canadian Olympic teams has competed in this event at one time or another.

The names of many Lake Placid residents stand high on the roster of enthusiastic promoters and organizers of skiing in America. Foremost

---

9 The event was the "Annual Invitation Ski Tournament for Women for the Kate Smith Trophy." It was sponsored by the Lake Placid Club Sno Birds.

among them are the pioneer Melvil Dewey, founding father of winter sports resorts; his son Godfrey Dewey, a Lake Placid Hall of Famer, whose vision led to the holding of the first Winter Olympics in America; the indefatigable Ron MacKenzie, "Mr. Ski" of the east, also immortalized in the Lake Placid Hall of Fame; and Harry Wade Hicks, who participated for a lifetime in every aspect of skiing in the U.S. A founder and president of the U.S. Eastern Amateur Ski Association and a mainstay of the Lake Placid Sno Birds, Harry Wade Hicks once said, "Skiing is and should be the universal winter sport. Everyone under seventy-five years of age who can walk vigorously can and should ski."

H. Smith Johannsen, one of the early volunteer ski instructors at Lake Placid, would not have set the limit at seventy-five years. Now living in Canada, the famed "Jack Rabbit" Johannsen still gets out on a pair of skis each winter at the age of 108.[10]

Harry Hicks's greatest love, the Sno Birds of Lake Placid, organized in 1920, was a mainstay of sponsorship and promotion of winter sports athletes and competition in the U.S. for half a century. While still officially in existence, the Sno Birds have been inactive for a dozen years. Many of their functions have been taken over by that grand old gal, the Lake Placid Ski Club, founded in 1921 and still going strong at the age of sixty-three years.

One of the greatest contributions of the Sno Birds was the annual College Week at the Lake Placid Club, begun in 1921 and lasting until 1951, which gave great impetus to intercollegiate competition in skiing and other winter sports. The major event of its kind in the country, it was the forerunner of the College Winter Carnival as it exists today, and certainly the granddaddy of the present NCAA winter sports program.

Many sterling instructors grace the slopes of Lake Placid, carrying on the tradition of those who have come before. The pioneers Johannsen, Marquis Nicholas degli Albizzi, Ornolf Poulsen, and Michael G. Melicheff gave the sport its early glamour. They were followed by such notables as Erling Strom of Mount McKinley fame; George Martin; Olympic competitor Rolf Monsen, who had the first jumping school in America at Intervale; and the immortal Otto Schneibs, unquestionably the greatest ski teacher of all time. Founder of the American Ski School, he moved its headquarters to Lake Placid, where he resided for thirty-four years.

---

10 "Jack Rabbit" Johannsen died in 1987 at the age of 111.

His Lake Placid Hall of Fame dossier describes eloquently his enormous contribution to the mastery and love of skiing in the United States. And his famous saying is well understood by all who step into a pair of skis and *schuss* down a sparkling slope:

"Ach, skiing is not just a sport—it is a way of life."

[In May 1985, Mary MacKenzie prepared daily "interviews" on North Elba and Lake Placid history for broadcast on WIRD, Radio Lake Placid. Each day for three weeks, Susan Folta read a question Mary had prepared, and Mary read her response script. This is a "transcript" of one of those "interviews."]

Why was Lake Placid selected as the site for the 1932 Winter Olympics?
If I were allowed only one answer to this question, I would say very quickly, "Godfrey Dewey."

There are other answers, of course. First of all, usually but not always, a place is selected for the Winter Olympics because it has the necessary sports facilities. There have been exceptions. Squaw Valley is a good example of a place that really had nothing to begin with but a lot of snow. They provided facilities after they were awarded the Games (1960), but they never did build a bob run.

Secondly, experience in staging competitions carried a great deal of weight, and Lake Placid had plenty of that.

But most important, the International Olympic Committee does not seek out a community. There is lively, competitive bidding, especially in modern times, and a lot of work and time has to be devoted to preparing a bid and getting some sort of promise of financial backing. The bid is really a basic feature in being awarded the Olympics, and that's where Godfrey Dewey comes in.

Godfrey Dewey was the son of Melvil Dewey, who founded the Lake Placid Club. He grew up at the Club, participated in all the pioneer winter sports, and became acquainted with many people active and influential in winter sports. Godfrey was a brilliant, imaginative man who also had a great deal of shrewd practicality in his make-up. As early as 1927, he began to think that Lake Placid was perfectly capable of hosting a Winter Olympics. In 1928, he went to the Winter Olympics at St. Moritz as manager of the U.S. ski team, inspected all the facilities over there, and cultivated friendships with the right people.

In 1929, he approached the local Chamber of Commerce and the village fathers and convinced them that Lake Placid had a chance for the 1932 Olympics. As a result, he sailed for Europe, a committee of one, to present a bid to the International Olympic Committee. Six other sites in the United States were also contenders.

I think often of that solitary figure boarding the Ile de France on an errand that was less than hopeful, carrying a hastily drawn-up bid and a few sketches. A great contrast to the sixteen-man team on hand in Vienna for the 1980 bid, armed with crates of material. Godfrey Dewey nailed down the 1932 Olympics for Lake Placid single-handedly.

So there were three things that really led to the awarding of the 1932 Games to Lake Placid: our existing facilities, our experience in staging competitions, and Godfrey Dewey. I like to think that Godfrey Dewey was the key. It seems to me that, above all, it was his vision, his persistence, and his know-how that won the day.

FIFTY-SIX
Peacock Building (Formerly the Alford Inn and the Lake Placid Inn)
August 30, 2001

As we have seen, in the late 1870s, Joseph V. Nash began selling off his great farmlands. On February 27, 1880, he sold to Marshall Lamoy a lot containing one acre and twenty rods of land. The purchase price was $56.25. Lamoy later sold a parcel on the rear of the lot to Mary L. Mauran, who built a fine summer home there.

Marshall Lamoy, born in 1847, presumably in Wilmington, New York, came to Lake Placid from Wilmington. He was a Civil War veteran, having served with the 96th Infantry, Adirondack Regiment. On October 14, 1874, he married Melvina Kennedy of Wilmington, whose parents came to North Elba in 1880 and lived on the old Parkhurst farm near the present Olympic ski jumps. Marshall died in New York City on June 28, 1921. His wife died in 1924. Both are buried in North Elba Cemetery. They had a son Harold and two daughters, Effie and Frances.

According to the *Essex County Republican* of Keeseville, Marshall Lamoy built a large and handsome house on his premises in the fall of 1880. It was located directly on Joe Nash's old cow path, soon to become Main Street.[11] The house still exists as part of the present Peacock Building, which, therefore, is the oldest extant building on Main Street. In time, the Lamoys ran the place as a boarding house, both summer and winter, and sometimes rented it out for the summer.

On October 15, 1900, the Lamoys sold the house to Reverend William Wilmerding Moir for $5,550. Moir, a wealthy retired businessman, was the first rector of the recently established Episcopal church in Lake Placid, St. Eustace-by-the-Lakes, situated near the head of Mirror Lake. He remodeled and refurnished the house, using it as the Episcopal rectory. He died suddenly on May 13, 1902, and the house passed into the ownership of his brother, Arthur Moir of Saranac Lake. The little settlement on the west shore of Mirror Lake by now had seen phenomenal growth and had become an incorporated village.

In April 1906, Arthur Moir sold the house to Charles W. Kennedy of Lake Placid for $5,500. Kennedy was a brother-in-law of Marshall Lamoy and had established a small hotel known as Northwoods Inn, just a couple of lots to the south. Kennedy probably used the old Lamoy house for overflow.

On September 16, 1919, Kennedy sold the old Lamoy house to Harvey Alford, a North Elba farmer. Alford put a large addition on the south end of the house in 1925, and it became known as Alford Inn. Harvey did not run the inn himself. At this time, his daughter, Climena Wikoff, and her husband, W.R. Wikoff, took over the operation not only of Alford Inn but also of Mirror Lake Inn, near the head of Mirror Lake. W.R. Wikoff was manager of the Alford, and Climena was manager of the Mirror Lake. In 1927, the Alford could accommodate twenty-five people. It was one of the few local hostelries open in the winter months and was well patronized by those who came to take part in Lake Placid's rapidly growing winter sports program. An orchestra was on hand for weekly dances. W.R. Wikoff ran the Alford Inn throughout the late 1920s and early 1930s. It was the first hotel in Lake Placid (in December 1933) to be issued a liquor license after the repeal of Prohibition.

11 At 2512 Main Street.

In 1930, Frank Swift purchased the Alford Inn.

Frank W. Swift was born in East Orange, New Jersey, in 1879. He was a well-known and respected Adirondack hotelman. He came to Lake Placid about 1907. He bought the old Lake Placid Inn near the head of Mirror Lake and ran it for thirteen years. He was the driving force behind the building of the Hotel Marcy in 1927, situated on the lot between the Alford and Northwoods Inns, and managed the Marcy until 1932.

In 1937, Swift gave a new name to the Alford. It became the Lake Placid Inn to commemorate his old hotel, which had become so successful under his management but had burned down in 1920. Swift set out to make his new Lake Placid Inn a place where both tourists and local people would find good meals and entertainment. With renovations, the inn could now accommodate fifty people by the late 1930s. The bar and grill, affectionately known as "LPI," became one of the most popular spots in town for dancing and as a general meeting place.

Frank Swift died suddenly of a heart attack in 1944. His widow, Helene Swift, took over management of the inn. In April 1948, Jack T. Brown of Miami, an Army Air Corps pilot in the war, bought the place. In 1953, the owners of the Hotel Marcy purchased it for use as an annex. Until this period, the building, with its three stories, occupied a slight hill, or rise, above Main Street. The Marcy excavated the hill, probably in the 1960s, and the basement story opened onto Main Street.

In the 1970s, the Marcy sold its Lake Placid Inn annex to Eastern Mountain Sports and, after its many years of accommodating the public, the old inn became a commercial establishment.

In 1986, the building again came into ownership of the Hotel Marcy. The Marcy's new owners, Gregory Ruppert and Barry C. Maloney, acquired it from Eastern Mountain Sports.

Shortly, in 1989, Ruppert and Maloney sold the old inn to Gregory Peacock and Tylor Kehoe. About 1993, Peacock bought Kehoe out and has been sole owner since that time. Occupied in late years by the Warehouse, the building now houses Peacock's Adirondack Decorative Arts and Crafts.

Peacock has made many changes in the interior. The exterior certainly bears no resemblance to the original dwelling—but the north end, with its gable roof and dormer, does give evidence of the old Lamoy house nestled within.

Containing, as it does, the original Lamoy house built in 1880, the Peacock Building is historically significant and, as we have pointed out, the oldest extant structure on Main Street, Lake Placid.

FIFTY-SEVEN
St. Eustace Church and St. Hubert's Church
1980 and 1993

St. Eustace-by-the-Lakes

St. Eustace Church had its beginnings in 1894. In that year, the first Episcopal service at Lake Placid was held in the parlors of the famous old Stevens House, as part of the mission of Rev. Walter W. Larom of Saranac Lake. Summer services continued for several years at various hotels.

With initial contributions of $7,000, the construction of a little Gothic church, St. Eustace-by-the-Lakes, was begun on a spur of Signal Hill, overlooking Placid and Mirror Lakes. It was finished in the early spring of 1900, mainly due to the efforts of a remarkable man, Rev. William Wilmerding Moir.

Rev. William W. Moir

Rev. Moir, born in Manchester, England, became a prosperous and successful merchant in New York City. He forsook business and society for the ministry, and was ordained in 1891.

Coming to Lake Placid in the summer of 1899 for a rest, he promptly threw his energies into raising an additional $8,000 for the completion of the church. Lake Placid and its people were now so dear to him that he resigned from his New York City church, the Church of the Holy Communion, and became rector of St. Eustace.

On September 9, 1900, St. Eustace-by-the-Lakes was consecrated in a beautiful and inspiring service. Bishop Doane and visiting clergy vested at the Billings Boathouse, now Holiday Harbor. Framed by the romantic Placid Lake and Whiteface Mountain, the processional marched up the roadway to the little brown church, the cross gleaming in the brilliant sunlight. The bishop knocked upon the door, and Rev. Moir admitted him. A boys' choir from New York, friends of Rev. Moir, joined the local choir in the hymnody.

A scant two years later, Rev. Moir was dead at the age of forty-six, a victim of acute appendicitis. In his three years at Lake Placid, he had wrought miracles. Starting with but three persons, he brought over 250 into the parish. He guided the consummation of St. Eustace, and he raised the foundations of a second church, St. Hubert's, at the lower end of the village. He remodeled and refurnished the rectory. He built a parish house. He formed an industrial school, and numerous clubs and guilds within the church. Always dedicated to the physical as well as spiritual nourishment of young men, he provided a camp on Lake Placid for their recreation, and he organized the first local hockey team for boys in 1901.

Thousands of boys had affectionately known Rev. Moir as "Our Uncle Will." Young Upton Sinclair, soon to become a noted author, spoke for all of them when he said, "He was the noblest man I have ever known. If it ever be my fate to have talent and to be a force for righteousness among men, I shall feel in my deepest heart I owe it to my 'Uncle Will.'" St. Eustace Church itself was to flourish on his deeds and devotion for the next generation.

The Parish House

Conceived and financed by Rev. Moir, the parish house on Main Street, of Southern Colonial architecture, was completed in 1901. Rev. Moir was far ahead of his time in offering recreation along with religious rites. The main floor housed a gymnasium as well as chancel and altar, and also served as lecture and meeting hall. On a lower floor were locker and bathrooms, and a game room for bowling, pool, and billiards. A boathouse and skiffs occupied the ground floor. The Masons and Eastern Stars used the upper story. Scheduled regularly were cooking and dancing classes and basketball games.

The parish house was a popular social center until it was sold to private interests during World War I. The building still stands at 2515 Main Street and now houses the Village Emporium.[12]

St. Hubert's Church

St. Eustace-by-the-Lakes was a summer church. In winter, services were held at the rectory (now the home of Eastern Mountain Sports),[13] at the Stevens

12 At this editing, the building now houses a store called the Imagination Station.

13 At this editing, the former Episcopal rectory at 2512 Main Street now houses a store called Adirondack Decorative Arts and Crafts.

House annex, the Parish House, Slater's Hall (the present Raeoil building), and the Newman Opera House.[14] It was decided to build a winter place of worship on Sentinel Road. Planned by architect William G. Distin of Saranac Lake, a charming Swiss-style church named St. Hubert's was completed in 1902.

For close to a quarter century, St. Eustace-by-the-Lakes and St. Hubert's served the parish well. St. Hubert's was sold to the Pilgrim Holiness Church in the summer of 1924. The building eventually burned to the ground and was replaced by the present Pilgrim Holiness Church, of somewhat similar design.

Rev. Sidney Thomas Ruck

Following Rev. Moir's death, the church made do with a series of transient rectors, until the arrival of one who was to remain for forty years.

Rev. Sidney Thomas Ruck came to Lake Placid in the fall of 1916 from St. John's Church in Williamsport, Pennsylvania, and took up residence in the rectory then located on Parkside Drive. Two years later, the John Stevens home on Main Street was acquired for $12,000 and became the present rectory.[15]

Rev. Ruck retired in December 1956. During his long tenure, he endeared himself to the townspeople and took an active role in civic affairs as member of the school board and the Speed Skating Association, chaplain of the Volunteer Fire Department, and master of the Lake Placid Masonic Lodge.

The New St. Eustace Church

Two Episcopal churches in a village of twenty-five hundred proved a financial burden. Neither was practical, since each was at an extreme end of the village. While the parishioners sought a solution, they closed both St. Eustace-by-the-Lakes and St. Hubert's in 1922, and rented the Adirondack Baptist Church, directly across Main Street from the library, for services.

St. Hubert's was sold in 1924. In July 1926, the vestry voted to tear down St. Eustace-by-the-Lakes and rebuild the structure on the rectory lot at 2450 Main Street.

14 According to Dr. George Hart, who was a member of that congregation as a boy, St. Eustace also held services in the basement community room of the Happy Hour Theater on Main Street.

15 The rectory, situated high on the hill above the present Main Street site of St. Eustace Church, now has a Hayes Street address.

Ground for a new and larger church was broken on February 16, 1927. Under architect William G. Distin and contractor Leo A. Malone, the work proceeded rapidly. All the windows and timbers of St. Eustace-by-the-Lakes were salvaged and moved to the new site.

Bishop G. Ashton Oldham of the Albany Diocese laid the cornerstone on March 17, 1927, a day of glorious sunshine and unseasonably warm weather. Encased in the cornerstone were a Bible, a Book of Common Prayer, a copy of the *Lake Placid News*, and a statement by Bishop Oldham.

By June 1927, St. Eustace Church was ready for occupancy. The speed of construction was possible because all sections of the old church were numbered during dismantling.

On the memorable day of June 19, 1927, the first service was held, conducted by Rev. Ruck. Frank S. Leonard and Harold R. Thompson gave the early and later histories of the parish, and Mrs. Homer Lockwood spoke on "The Parish and Its Women." Soloist Mrs. Frank H. Philburt sang "I Heard The Voice Of Jesus Say."

The lot, the re-erection of the church, and the purchase of an organ represented a total cost of some $55,000. On August 15, 1943, completely out of debt, Bishop Oldham consecrated St. Eustace Church.

Special Features of St. Eustace

The present church is very similar in concept to St. Eustace-by-the-Lakes, with the addition of a stone tower sixty feet high and several innovations in interior arrangements. The siding is of stained cedar, and the roof of twenty-four-inch, one-inch butt heart cedar, rare in the North Country.

Guild Memorial Hall, contributed by the Women's Guild, occupies the lower floor and is used for Guild, Sunday school, and social purposes.

The sanctuary is modeled after that of St. Eustace-by-the-Lakes, but is larger in dimensions. The altar is the original one, as is the baptismal font, unique in that it is completely constructed of wood, restored to its original beauty.

The unusual wrought-iron lamps, hung on long chains, are rustic in design, and consist of iron bands with copper cups and saucers, both hand-hammered. Guy Slater and Mrs. Homer Lockwood designed them all, and Mr. Slater worked them at his Au Sable Forks blacksmith shop.

Mrs. John Gregson of Woodstock, Vermont, patterned the exquisite needlepoint kneelers at the altar rail and throughout the sanctuary. She also patterned the needlepoint frontal at the baptismal font. The women of the church crafted them, led by Mrs. W. Carter Lockwood, in a labor of love that took two years to complete. The motifs of native deer, fish, and flowers are in harmony with the Adirondack environment.

The three-manual church organ, built by the Estey Organ Company of Brattleboro, Vermont, is one of the finest in northern New York. It has twenty-four speaking stops and 944 pipes. Used for the first time on Christmas Eve 1929, it was formally dedicated on January 12, 1930, by an organ recital given by Wallace A. Van Lier, organist at the Lake Placid Club. A memorial to Mrs. Clara Leggo, devoted member of the church for many years, it was purchased for $10,000 through funds left by Mrs. Leggo and a contribution of over $8,000 by the Women's Guild.

From the steps of St. Eustace Church, the view is one not easily forgotten. Passing through the church doors on the triumphal strains of the recessional, one looks out over the quiet waters of Mirror Lake to the superb mountains beyond: Whiteface, Whitney, Cobble, and the Sentinels. They are lovely in all seasons—in the soft greens of spring and summer, the jewel-like tones of autumn, the dazzling white of winter.

Surely here, as in no other place, the heart can cry out in gratitude, "I will lift up mine eyes unto the hills, from whence cometh my help."

St. Eustace Window

The beautiful Tiffany-style "St. Eustace Window" was especially designed for the original St. Eustace-by-the-Lakes, and was the gift of Rev. William W. Moir in memory of his father James Moir. Our Placid Lake and Whiteface Mountain appear in the background of the middle panel.

St. Eustace, patron of woodsmen, was once captain of the guard to the Roman Emperor Trajan, his heathen name being Placidus. A great hunter, he killed only for the pleasure of sport. One day in his rambles, he encountered a white stag and pursued it far into the mountains. At last, the stag turned and spoke to him: "Placidus, Placidus, why persecutest thou me?" and a flaming cross appeared between its antlers.

Awestruck, Placidus cried out, "Who art thou?"

The stag replied, "I am Jesus, Whom thou persecutest, inasmuch as wantonly and for thy pleasure thou slayest these animals who are My children."

Placidus asked what he was to do, and the stag answered, "Arise and be baptized."

Placidus obeyed, and was baptized under the name of Eustace. He was deposed by Trajan, and after many sorrows, wanderings, and trials, was recalled by the Emperor Hadrian. Refusing to sacrifice to the Roman gods, he was roasted to death in a brazen bull with his wife and two sons in A.D. 129.

The window serves a dual purpose in commemorating Lake Placid's former Episcopal church of St. Hubert's. A similar legend surrounds Hubert, patron saint of huntsmen, dogs, and the chase, born in A.D. 652. A nobleman of Aquitaine, and son of Bertrand, Duke of Guienne, he, too, in a dark age, gave himself to the pleasures of hunting and slaying. On one occasion, in the forest of Ardennes on Good Friday, he heard a warning voice, and a white stag appeared before him with a cross between its antlers, surrounded by rays of light. This vision was the cause of his conversion.

After many years in the woods as a hermit, Hubert became a disciple of Bishop Lambert. In time, he was ordained Bishop of Liege, and it is said an angel delivered the stole with which he was invested. He died November 3, 727, and was buried in the Church of St. Peter at Liege. In 825, his remains were removed to a Benedictine cloister that now bears his name in the Belgian Ardennes.

The Women's Guild

The story of St. Eustace Church is not complete without mention of its loyal and industrious Women's Guild.

The guild's predecessor was the Women's Auxiliary and Altar Guild, organized by Rev. Moir in 1900, and active in missionary work. In 1910, the name was changed to Women's Guild when the group resolved to work for the church proper. First officers were Mrs. Edwin Kennedy, president; Mrs. Wesley Kennedy, treasurer; and Miss Isobel MacPherson, secretary. In 1912, a vice president, Mrs. E. L. Ware, was added. Mrs. Edwin Kennedy served as president for fourteen years, and was succeeded by Mrs. Joseph B. Williams in 1924. In the first twenty-nine years of its history, the guild had but four presidents.

The Guild held its first fair in 1912. In the early years, it raised substantial sums, and from 1917 to 1927 alone, the guild turned over $14,000 to the church treasurer. The guild has always played an important part in the life of the church. Over a period of seventy years, through food, craft and rummage sales, fairs, oyster suppers and church dinners, card and box parties, fashion shows, dances and motion pictures, it has made very large contributions to the building fund and the general work of the church.

Father Hayes

Father William D. Hayes came to St. Eustace as rector in 1969 from St. George's Church in Schenectady, New York. Father Hayes graduated from Union College in Schenectady and went on to Albany Law School. Unfulfilled in secular life, he turned to the ministry and graduated from General Theological Seminary of New York City in 1968.

In keeping with the tradition fostered by Rev. Moir and Rev. Ruck, Father Hayes has sought involvement in his community as well as his parish. He is [in 1980] chaplain of the Volunteer Fire Department and of Camp Adirondack, a minimum-security prison at Ray Brook, president of the Senior Citizens Housing Corporation, and a member of the Advisory Board of Uihlein Mercy Center.

[In a letter dated November 11, 1993, MacKenzie wrote that she had learned the name of the architect of the original St. Eustace-by-the-Lakes. She also found out who had designed and executed "our beautiful St. Eustace window." She had not known either of these facts when she wrote her history of St. Eustace Church in 1980.]

St. Eustace-by-the-Lakes, completed in 1900, was designed by William L. Coulter of Saranac Lake, New York. Coulter was also the architect of a number of early camps on Lake Placid and summer cottages on Signal Hill. William Distin of Saranac Lake became his successor and oversaw the reconstruction of the church on its present site.

In the almost hundred years since the St. Eustace window was presented to the church by our first rector, Rev. William W. Moir, the name of the firm that designed it has remained unknown. It is unsigned, but many have felt it could be a Tiffany because it has many Tiffany characteristics. I have now received information that a firm known as Calvert & Kimberly listed our St. Eustace window in a brochure of their work, also labeling it as

"The Moir Memorial." Interestingly, Mr. Calvert had first worked for the Tiffany studio, from 1889 to 1899, which could account for the Tiffany ambience of the St. Eustace window. The firm was variously known as Calvert & Kimberly, Duffner & Kimberly, and O.S. Kimberly Co.

In their brochure, the firm also claimed to have done a second window for our St. Eustace church, known as "The Lee Memorial." I am completely baffled by this reference. Could anyone shed light on what this window might have been, and if it could still be in the church? Rev. Moir did have a sister Mrs. Henry Lee, who might well have been the donor of a window originally installed in St. Eustace-by-the-Lakes.

Parishioners may also be interested in knowing that our rectory is one of the oldest buildings within the village still in existence. It was built in 1884 as a summer home by Mr. J. B. Crosby, said to have been a Chicago banker, and has received few, if any, external alterations.

FIFTY-EIGHT
The WCTU Horse Fountain
August 2, 1979

It was just an ordinary, black, cast-iron fountain—the fountain that chuckles and gushes and gurgles in the village parking lot.

It is nothing like the great Prometheus fountain at Rockefeller Center. It has none of the baroque splendor of the fountain of Trevi at Rome. And it cannot hold a candle to the famous little Manniken Pis fountain in Brussels. Still, it is Lake Placid's own, and it has a curious history harking back to the horse-and-buggy days.

At the turn of the twentieth century, the Women's Christian Temperance Union was a vital force in Lake Placid politics. Largely due to its efforts, the town had been voted a Prohibition town. Demon Rum, it is true, was still lurking in a few dark corners of the community, but not in public places.

If Demon Rum was not in evidence along Main Street, the horse was. For some years, an old wooden trough squatted at the top of Mill Hill, dispensing cool mountain water to the many beasts of burden that clopped between the upper and lower reaches of the village. In 1905, a horse fountain presented to the people of Lake Placid by the Women's Christian Temperance Union replaced the trough.

The fountain was dedicated in September 1905, on one of those rare, benign days heralding the last of summer. Save for a few guzzlers at illicit bars, the town turned out en masse for the celebration. The speaker was none other than James R. Day, chancellor of Syracuse University, who maintained a summer home here. His words ringing out to the misty hills, he delivered a lengthy and stirring temperance lecture.

> There is nothing good in drinking rum or selling rum—not one solitary thing," said Chancellor Day. "I am immensely proud of this village, and others are proud of this village. Bye and bye, you will see lots of people who are sorry they did not cast the first vote that made this village and its borders clean.
>
> But this very day, while you and I are here assembled to dedicate this fountain, forces are being amassed and will conspire on this little town in the Adirondacks, and they will lead their money in here as they are putting their liquors in here from time to time, and you will have to fight that whole traffic.

With that, the fountain was in business. No one knows today why the good ladies of the WCTU chose to provide a fountain for equines. It may be that, having fallen short of their goal of leading each and every citizen to water, they had shifted their sights to the horse. In any case, the fountain was evidently a success, although no report has come down to us directly from the horse's mouth. Located at the edge of the lot now occupied by Ray Preston's service station at the top of Mill Hill,[16] it long served as an equine watering hole.

The WCTU had not reckoned with the automobile. That snorting, fiery beast suddenly took over the roads, relegating the horse to a minor role in human affairs. Gasoline was now the liquid in demand. A filling station made an appearance at the top of Mill Hill, and the fountain was turned off.

Several years passed. Stored in the village barn, delicate cobwebs festooned the fountain. Finally earmarked for the dump, it was rescued in the nick of time by Louis Berg, who owned an apartment house on Parkside Drive.

16 This is at the intersection of Main and Sentinel Roads.

Louis asked the village if he might have it for his front lawn. Permission was granted, and the fountain was moved to its new home in 1924.

Louis Berg was a man who loved flowers. He painted the fountain white and filled it with earth and annual plants. Petunias, geraniums, live-forever, and the like bloomed there every summer, a pleasant sight for strollers on Parkside Drive. The original members of the WCTU, many of whom had by then gone to their reward, would probably have approved, were it not for the fact that Louis Berg ran a liquor store on Main Street.

The years rolled by, Louis Berg passed on, and his widow sold the apartment house in the early 1940s. His daughter, Johanna Berg Conway, returned the fountain to the village for safekeeping.

What to do with the old relic? Did nobody want it? Yes, Roy Conoboy, superintendent of the village electric department, did. Ever one to brighten the corner where he was, Roy moved the fountain down to the powerhouse, repainted it black, and set it amongst a planting of shrubs and flowers. Water was piped in. The fountain began to ring again, but it sang a lonesome tune. Only the few people who came and went at the powerhouse could hear it.

Now it was 1965. The village fathers had lately cut off a segment of Grand View Hill and installed a fine parking lot opposite the post office. The lot filled a definite need, certainly, but it lacked class. A decorative touch, a focal point, was wanting. The local Garden Club was consulted and came up with the perfect solution: Why not make use of the old fountain, wasting its song on the desert air down at the powerhouse?

In 1966, the fountain made what may have been its last voyage up Main Street, and was duly installed in the parking lot. There, despite the fact that pranksters occasionally feed it detergents and cake dye for special effects, it leads a happy life and is much admired.

Of course, it is nothing like the Prometheus fountain, or the fountain of Trevi in Rome, or the little Manniken Pis fountain in Brussels. It is just our old, black, iron horse fountain. But it has the nostalgic charm of a cracker barrel in a country store, it is part of our history, and we love it.

FIFTY-NINE
Camp Minnow Brook

In a letter dated September 15, 1988, Mary Mackenzie answered an inquiry into the history of Camp Minnow Brook.

The history of the Camp Minnow Brook land properly begins in the early 1870s, when William Fox Leggett, a Shakespearean actor of some renown, purchased Great Lot 273, Township 11, Old Military Tract, on Lake Placid. Camp Minnow Brook land is located in 273. Leggett built a summer home, a small log structure, just south of and next door to the later Camp Minnow Brook site. He soon enlarged it to become a three-storied log building he named Castle Rustico.

In his last years, Leggett became an invalid, spending most of the year at Lake Placid. In order to sustain himself, he began selling off lots from his large Castle Rustico holdings. One of the first camp sites he sold went to W. G. Leland, owner of the Grand Hotel in New York City. Arthur Hayes, a Lake Placid contractor, in 1898 built a camp for Leland out of logs from trees felled on the property. Leland occupied the camp but a short time and then sold it to Benjamin I. Ward of Passaic, New Jersey, who was in the bleaching business and had a factory at Fairview, New Jersey. This camp had several names through the years—Idilio, Beechward, Grenwolde—before most recently being christened Camp Solitude.

Christian Bahnsen, also of Passaic, visited the Wards shortly after their purchase and fell in love with Lake Placid. Soon he bought from Leggett the camp site just south of and contiguous to the Wards. You mention that Solitude and Minnow Brook were built by a brother and sister. I find no mention of this anywhere, and various facts seem to preclude the possibility. Mrs. Bahnsen's maiden name was Halterman, so she would not have been sister to either Leland or Ward, and it is very doubtful that Bahnsen had a sister in the United States. The Wards and Bahnsens, though, were apparently closely acquainted, and both families came from Passaic.

Mr. Bahnsen built Camp Minnow Brook in 1908. The contractor was again Arthur Hayes. Minnow Brook was larger than the Ward camp and was also built of logs taken from the property.

The Bahnsens were valued members of Lake Placid's summer colony for many years. Mr. Bahnsen was interested in local affairs and did much to assure completion of our present Methodist church, the Adirondack Community Church, also donating a beautiful memorial stained-glass window for the back of the chancel. He was a member of the Lake Placid Shore Owners Association, serving for a time as treasurer.

Christian Bahnsen was a self-made man. Born in Denmark, he emigrated to Germany as a young man and went to work for a manufacturer of woolen goods. He learned the business thoroughly and became proficient in every branch. When only twenty-four, he was sent to the United States as selling agent for the manufacturer. Finding American life and business to his liking, he made this country his home, organized his own wool manufacturing company, and became a recognized power in the industry. He was president of his New Jersey Worsted Mills, which eventually operated large plants at both Passaic and Garfield, New Jersey, and employed about eight thousand workers.

Mr. Bahnsen suffered a stroke in 1925, leading to a heart condition. He died at Camp Minnow Brook in August 1927. Mrs. Bahnsen continued to occupy the luxurious camp until her death in October 1933 at the home of her daughter, Viscountess Downs, at Wyksham Abbey, Yorkshire, England.

The Bahnsens had three daughters and one son: Marguerite Christine, wife of the Honorable Richard Downs, who was a member of a family residing in Yorkshire since the reign of Edward III, and who inherited the family title; Gertrude, who married Major Jack Shelley of the British Army; Mary Louise, who married Morrie McKim Pryor; and Henry Bahnsen of Passaic. Henry took over Camp Minnow Brook after his mother's death but does not seem to have occupied it regularly each year.

Camp Minnow Brook was renamed the Music Trail in 1951, and it was probably then, or possibly in the late 1940s, that Mr. Epstein purchased the place and thereafter, for many years, conducted on the premises a summer camp for children, specializing in instrumental music. I have no information in my files on the various owners of Minnow Brook land since the demise of the Music Trail.

SIXTY

Bank of Lake Placid

Date Unknown

The nearest bank during the years of Lake Placid's enormous growth from 1871 to the village's incorporation in 1900 was in Saranac Lake. In 1909, a group of forward-looking businessmen resolved to establish a local bank to fill the needs of Lake Placid's citizens and visitors. The superintendent of banks of New York State granted a charter for the Bank of Lake Placid on May 3, 1909, and the bank opened for business the following day, May 4, at the Noble Block on Main Street in premises now occupied by the Continental Shoppe.[17]

Capital was $25,000 and surplus was $2,500. The original issue of stock was oversubscribed and allotments were made to subscribers on a proportionate basis.

The original board of directors was comprised mainly of Lake Placid residents: George A. Stevens, proprietor of the Stevens House; Myron T. Brewster, real estate and contracting; Asa O. Gallup, manager of the Lake Placid Club; Clarence H. Watson, bookkeeper at the Stevens House; Forrest B. Guild, merchant; James B. Hurley, proprietor of the American House; James Shea, merchant; and Fred C. Day, dentist. It also included James W. Fleming, capitalist, of Troy, New York, and Clifford S. Sims, vice president and general manager of the Delaware & Hudson Railroad Co.

The first president was George A. Stevens, who served in that capacity until his death on September 17, 1920. Mr. Stevens and his brother, John, born in Black Brook, New York, had brought the noble old Stevens House to national fame. Vice president was Asa O. Gallup, a local civic leader who, aside from acting as manager of the Lake Placid Club, was a school trustee, a director of the Board of Trade, and president of the Lake Placid section of the Anti-Saloon League. He left Lake Placid in 1912 and died at Bronxville, New York, in 1918. The first cashier was Clarence N. Watson.

In a *Lake Placid News* article of April 30, 1909, the officers and directors called upon the citizenry to open accounts and thus help in a substantial way to make the new enterprise a success. "Several of Lake Placid's summer

---

17 Today the address is 2533 Main Street, occupied by Beglin's Jewelry and Gifts.

residents have promised accounts," went the plea. "We trust you will find it convenient to send to the cashier your first deposit in time to reach him for the opening day, May 4." The public responded gallantly. Deposits on the first day of business totaled $10,802.52.

It is interesting to note from the minutes of the first executive committee meeting that they had approved three loans. The borrowers were the Adirondack Baptist Church, St. Agnes Church, and the Village of Lake Placid.

The Bank of Lake Placid flourished, and by 1915, it was decided to construct a formal bank building. Ground was broken on the Green lot just south of the Lake Placid Pharmacy, now the Urfirer building, in May 1919. Through the earnest suggestions of President George A. Stevens, who took a keen pride in everything local, native rock was selected for the base and trimmings of the structure. Floyd E. Brewster, of pioneer Lake Placid stock, was the architect, and B.B. Lantry of Tupper Lake the contractor. Upon the death of Mr. Lantry the following winter, his son took up the completion of the building.

A year later, on May 10, 1916, the Bank of Lake Placid moved into its new and modernly equipped home. The top floor was devoted to offices occupied by the law firm of Isham & Isham and dentist Fred C. Day. The *Lake Placid News* said, "The building has an impressive and distinctive appearance, is handsomely finished within, and conveniently furnished."

The individuals then in active charge were vice president and manager John McGuckin, Clarence H. Watson, cashier, W.F. Archer, assistant cashier, and William Morrison, bookkeeper. Mr. McGuckin, born in New York City, had come to the Adirondacks as a young man for his health, and had previously been manager of the local Western Union office and village treasurer. He died suddenly in 1917 at the age of forty-four, serving the bank for only a year.

Upon the death of George Stevens in 1920, Forrest B. Guild became president and filled that office until 1944, when he was elected chairman of the board of directors. He retired from the board in 1964. A Vermonter by birth, Mr. Guild came to Lake Placid in 1897 and established the leading men's clothing store, the Hub. He was one of the founders of the bank, and at his death on December 29, 1972, at the age of ninety-eight, had been for a long time the last surviving member of the original organization committee and board of directors.

In the fall of 1930, the bank moved to temporary quarters in the Applied Arts store, now the law offices of Urfirer & Brooks, while a rear addition to the building and major remodeling proceeded by Hoggson Brothers of New York.[18] On December 29, 1930, the bank moved back to a building of many improvements, equipped with every modern device. Operating facilities were doubled, with more than one thousand square feet added to the main floor. An attractive feature was the lobby, with a large window in the rear revealing a splendid view of Mirror Lake. A counterscreen separated the lobby from the working area. Other innovations were a night depository, the second of its kind to be installed, and a concrete safe deposit vault, heavily reinforced with steel.

The officers at that time were Mr. Guild, president; James B. Hurley, Fred C. Day, and Frank H. Philburt, vice presidents; Clarence H. Watson, cashier; Sylvester R. O'Haire and William Morrison, assistant cashiers. Directors were Mr. Guild, James B. Hurley, Fred C. Day, J. Chester Jubin, F. Paul Stevens, and Frank H. Philburt. In celebration of its fiftieth anniversary, the Bank of Lake Placid held an open house on May 7, 1959. Its assets were now over $5 million, and capital funds over $450,000. An interesting feature of the open house was a currency and coin exhibit, loaned by the Federal Reserve Bank of New York.

Service of long duration has been a tradition among bank officers and employees. Clarence H. Watson was cashier for twenty-eight years, from organization in 1909 until his passing in 1937. Even on the day of his death, he had reported for work, suffering a heart attack in the evening. Born in Wilmington, New York, he was the son of Thomas Watson, one of the early ministers in this area, who preached at North Elba's White Church on Old Military Road and was the first librarian at the local library.

Sylvester R. O'Haire, teller and cashier for forty-four years, was born in Watervliet. He attended Holy Cross College and came to the bank shortly before World War I, during which he served with the Army in France. He married Odette Chagnaud in France in 1919 and then returned to Lake Placid and his position at the bank. "Syl" died in 1962 at sixty-nine.

William A. Morrison, assistant cashier, was born at Haverstraw, New York, in 1886. He came to the bank in 1917 and worked there for thirty-two years. He died in 1950 at the age of sixty-three.

---

18 The address today is 2477 Main Street.

Frank H. Philburt came from Vermont in 1924 and served as vice president and manager, and as a director, until 1941, when he retired. Mr. Philburt died at Lake Placid in 1954 at the age of seventy-three.

George Weaver, teller and cashier for forty-four years, and a native of Lake Placid, came to the bank after graduating from high school, and retired in 1974.

Frederick G. Mader's career with the bank spanned more than thirty years. Born at Albany, New York, he came to Lake Placid in 1941 and assumed the office of vice president and manager upon Frank Philburt's retirement. He became president in 1944, maintaining that position until 1970, when he was elected chairman of the board. He retired from active participation in 1974 and died in 1982.

His son, Paul K. Mader, succeeded Mr. Mader as president.

[A branch of NBT Bank has occupied the former Bank of Lake Placid building since September 30, 1989.]

SIXTY-ONE
National Hotel
Late 1995

Patti Reiss Brooks, author of the historical novel Mountain Shadows *(Pinto Press, 2004), wrote Mary MacKenzie while researching her book, asking for information on the National Hotel. Brooks was interested in the New York State Troopers Zone Station No. 1, and she had information that it was based at the hotel in the mid-1920s.*

On September 19, 1995, Mary's response contained the following history, with the caveat that she did not know of the troopers using the hotel as a base:

I am completely baffled by your statement that New York State Troopers Zone Station #1 was based in the National Hotel. In all my research, I have never come across this, either recorded or anecdotal.

Old editions of the *Lake Placid News* scarcely ever mentioned the National Hotel, but this is what I have been able to piece together about it:

Our famous hotelier, Henry Allen, built the National Hotel in 1909 after he sold the Grand View. It was a four-story structure, very plain but well built. It had a capacity of sixty, steam heat, private baths, and hot and cold running water.

It was directly across from the railroad station. It was never, of course, one of our grand hotels designed for wealthy summer guests. It was a commercial hotel, and its clientele was probably mainly business and sales people.

Henry Allen died in 1916, and Thomas A. Leahy acquired the hotel. During the great influenza epidemic of 1918, when so many townspeople came down with this dread affliction, Leahy donated the use of the National Hotel as a hospital, and doctors and nurses were stationed there.

Frank W. Swift bought the hotel in 1920. He managed it until 1924, when Raymond C. Prime purchased it.

In 1925, the [Lake Placid] Club contracted to purchase it, converting it into apartments for their help. When the Club reorganized in 1941, they surrendered their contract, and ownership was transferred to R.C. Prime Co. I gather that the building continued to be used for apartment living during Prime's ownership, but I think it may have been vacant during its last years.

In 1954, Prime gave the building to the Lake Placid Junior Chamber of Commerce for a civic center. The building was torn down, and a Veterans of Foreign Wars clubhouse was built on the site. This was short-lived. A private house now stands on the site.

I am mighty curious about this state troopers occupation. Where did you find this, and will you please send me your documentation so I can add it to my hotel file?

[On September 25, 1995, Brooks wrote MacKenzie with her source for the information on the state police troop stationed at the hotel.]

I gleaned some decent insight into the New York State Police Troop B from a small booklet published by the Franklin County Historical Society in Malone in 1967. In a chapter titled "The Black Horse Troop," compiled by Elizabeth Donovan, I read the following on page six:

In a report sent to the superintendent of the state police, February 8, 1925, Captain Broadfield listed the location of the various patrols working out of the Troop B headquarters. For instance, Zone Station No. 1 was located at Lake Placid, with Sgt. R.J. McDowell in charge:

LAKE PLACID
(National Hotel - tel. 239)
Sgt. R.J. McDowell, car 963
Tpr. H. L. Deming, Horse 43
Tpr. J. H. Ireland, Horse 28

Obviously, the horseman in me enjoys getting horses into my book. With this in mind, do you suppose the National Hotel had a barn for their guests' animals? Or would they have been stabled at the Parkside stable? I'm assuming that stable was there in 1925–26, but I don't know who operated it. Or, perhaps there was another public stable?

[MacKenzie replied on November 4, 1995:]

Strangely enough, right after receiving your September letter about the patrol stationed at the National Hotel, I was doing some research in old *Franklin Historical Reviews* and, lo and behold, I happened upon that article about the Black Horse Troop by Elizabeth Donovan. I probably had never read it when it came out in 1967, and so never noted the bit about the National Hotel. Anyway, I am glad to add this to my hotel history.

It would be my guess, though, that Station No. 1 was located in the National for only a short time, and probably the troopers got out of there in 1925 when the Lake Placid Club took over.

There is no evidence that the National Hotel had a barn to house their guests' animals. Besides, most of the hotel guests by the 1920s would have arrived by car or train. However, there was ample accommodation for the troopers' horses at another hotel just down the street, the American House, on Mill Pond. Here is what I have in my American House file:

> The headquarters for the Lake Placid Trotting Association was at the hotel, and owners of horses racing on the ice of Mirror Lake made a gala occasion of their trips here. The hotel had the only stables ample enough to house the visiting racers. The proprietors also conducted a livery in connection with the hotel, the 17 horses being engaged to take the 'drummers' uptown.

In view of the above, certainly the troopers' horses must have been kept in the American House barn rather than the Parkside Drive stable.

SIXTY-TWO

George and Bliss Marina

In a letter dated September 19, 1995, Mary MacKenzie describes the history of the George and Bliss Marina and the sightseeing boat, the Doris.

Albert Billings started Billings Landing, the boat livery that became George & Bliss in 1897. He enlarged the boathouse in 1899 and 1902. Albert Billings died in 1903, and in 1904 Thomas H. George and C. Herman Bliss, two of his employees, purchased the business and renamed it George & Bliss. This was a marina that not only made boats but serviced all the boats owned by camps on the lake. In February 1919, fire destroyed the entire, greatly expanded marina, but it was quickly replaced with the buildings we all knew so well for many years.

Herman Bliss died in 1927, and I believe his son Kenneth continued to have an interest in the business. Thomas George died in 1949, and his son Thomas George Jr. then headed the firm.

In 1962, George & Bliss merged with Grotes' Boat Landing, which had a competing marina in the old Stevens House boathouse on the Paradox [Bay]. There were a number of owners after that. The old George & Bliss buildings were torn down beginning in 1985, and there is nothing much there today but docks.

George & Bliss did not originally own the *Doris I*, the famous old sightseeing boat. Henry C. Stevens, father of Arthur Stevens, built her in 1898 on the shore of Lake Placid. Henry Stevens had an excursion service on Lake Placid, with docking facilities at his Brewster's Landing, immediately adjacent to George & Bliss. Brewster's Landing was totally destroyed in 1919 by the same fire that consumed George & Bliss. It was then that Henry Stevens sold to George & Bliss, and *Doris I* came into their ownership in 1919.

Arthur Stevens became co-captain of the *Doris* in 1903 when he was nineteen years old. He continued as *Doris I's* sole captain under George & Bliss ownership until she was retired in 1950.

The *Doris* was a wonderful old boat and very much a prominent feature of Placid Lake. Steam powered her until 1907, when a gasoline engine was installed. The *Doris* was dismantled soon after her retirement. I have some photos of her.

The *Doris*, of course, was an excursion boat, and also delivered the mail to campers on the lake.

I doubt very much that the *Doris* passengers were treated to a commentary back in the 1920s. There is such a commentary today, of course, but I don't believe such a practice was adopted until about the 1960s—for a number of reasons (about which I won't elaborate). I am pretty sure of this. Such tour commentaries are more or less a modern invention.

SIXTY-THREE
Interlaken Lodge
January 4, 1988

On October 1, 1887, Benjamin Brewster deeded a large section of his holdings in Lot 278 on Signal Hill to John and George Stevens, proprietors of the Stevens House hotel on adjacent lands. Utilizing some of the purchase for a hotel golf links, the Stevens brothers divided the rest into cottage lots for sale, including the present Interlaken Lodge parcel. The golf links never extended as far as Interlaken Lodge.

On June 8, 1897, for $2,750, the Stevenses sold to George W. Baldwin of Saranac Lake, New York, and Milton L. French of Malone, New York, quite a number of cottage lots, including the Interlaken Lodge parcel. Baldwin and French immediately deeded the tract to George W. Cushman of Malone, taking back a mortgage. Cushman defaulted on the mortgage, resulting in foreclosure, and the tract was subsequently transferred by referee's deed dated November 21, 1902, to Michael J. Callanan of Keeseville, New York. Callanan deeded the properties on April 1, 1908, to Branch & Callanan, lumber dealers of Saranac Lake.

It was undoubtedly the firm of Branch & Callanan that instituted a survey of the properties by B.E. McLeod, who prepared a map entitled "Map of Lake Placid Inn Property" dated July 1, 1909, still on file in the Essex County Clerk's Office in Elizabethtown, New York. Cottage Lots 7 and 8, having to do with Interlaken Lodge history, are clearly shown.

Branch & Callanan proceeded to sell their cottage lots. On August 22, 1911, Forrest B. Guild of Lake Placid purchased Lots 7 and 8 on Interlaken Avenue. Immediately, in the fall of 1911, Guild built on Lot 7 an imposing house, garage, and tennis court, designed by architect Max Westhoff of Saranac Lake. The house, still standing, is the present Interlaken Lodge. An interesting account of the building and furnishing of the house appeared in the *Lake Placid News* of January 7, 1912. Never occupying the place himself, Mr. Guild rented it out profitably to summer people over the next five years.

Forrest B. Guild was a leading citizen of Lake Placid. He was born near Rutland, Vermont, in October 1874 and grew up in that area. Migrating to the Lake Placid region as a salesman, he met Cora Leonard of Malone and married her in 1897. On April 1, 1897, he opened a men's clothing store in the Clifford Block, 2407 Main Street, Lake Placid, a building that is still standing.

In 1915, Mr. Guild erected his own business block at 2495 Main Street, moving into it in 1916, and until 1944 operated an exclusive store known as the Hub, specializing in men's clothing, shoes, and sporting goods. This building is now occupied by Julia's and With Pipe and Book.[19] On the second floor, Mr. Guild maintained a large apartment from 1916 until his death on December 29, 1972, at the age of ninety-eight.

Mr. Guild was also one of the founders of the Bank of Lake Placid in 1909. He was president of the bank from 1921 until 1944, and was on the board of directors from 1909 until 1964, when he retired, also serving as chairman of the board for twenty years.

On November 15, 1917, Mr. Guild sold Lots 7 and 8, along with his new house, to Vermont Trading Company of 568 Broadway, New York City, for the then very substantial sum of $24,000. Vermont Trading Company owned a chain of retail clothing stores in New York State. Robert Kamber of New York City, president and majority stockholder of Vermont Trading, had been a frequent visitor to Lake Placid in previous years and was, in effect, the real owner of the Interlaken property. He

19 At the time this was edited, the entire building had been taken over by With Pipe and Book.

occupied the present Interlaken Lodge as a beautiful and spacious summer home from 1918 until his death in the early 1940s. The property was then passed to his sons, Lawrence L. Kamber and Robert L. K. Weenolsen (formerly Robert Kamber Jr.).

The Kamber sons on December 29, 1944, deeded Lots 7 and 8 to Peter Blum of New York City. Now, for the first time, the house became a place of public accommodation. It is reported that during the summer of 1945, Mr. Blum converted it into a summer boarding house for well-to-do Jewish refugees from Hitler's Germany. It should be noted that during World War II, and for some years afterward, Lake Placid was a popular haven for Jewish refugees from Europe who had managed to escape with assets. For them, our village had the flavor and nostalgia of their native lake and mountain resorts. A number of boarding houses and hotels catered to them exclusively during this era, and Lake Placid's Main Street took on a distinctly cosmopolitan air in the summer months.

Peter Blum did not remain long at 39 Interlaken Avenue. On April 9, 1946, he sold out to E & P Realty Company, owned by Ezna and John W. Newton, its president and secretary. In 1955, John W. Newton became sole proprietor of the real estate. In 1956, he sold Lot 8, the vacant land on Interlaken Avenue just below the house, to Raymond F. Schack and wife, with the express restriction that no building in excess of two stories could be erected on Lot 8, and no swimming pool of any kind could be installed.

John Newton, as had Peter Blum, operated the main building as a boarding house for German Jewish refugees from 1946 until 1969, using the name of Newton's Homewood Farm. He was himself of German or Austrian birth, spoke with a distinct German accent, and had presumably Americanized his name. At Newton's Homewood Inn, he offered what he termed a "continental cuisine." Rumor has it that he possessed several different wives during his Lake Placid sojourn, all purportedly German girls skilled in continental cooking. It is said that when he became divested of one wife, he would travel to Germany and seek out another who could cook to his specifications. Evidently, after each arrived at Lake Placid and learned that her major role was not wife, but chief cook and bottlewasher for Newton's Homewood Inn, she would in time rebel and make an escape.

On May 1, 1969, John W. Newton sold the main house in part of Lot 7 to Gideon and Ruth Hawley (Mrs. Hawley was originally from Lake Placid), and within two years also sold to Hawley the "annex house" and garage on the remainder of Lot 7. The Hawleys operated the place until recent years under the name of Interlaken Lodge, catering to figure skaters in the summer and to various tourist groups from Canada and the United States in other seasons. Someone named Merchant was the next owner, but remained just a short time.

Roy and Carol Johnson now own and operate the Interlaken Lodge as an inn.[20]

SIXTY-FOUR
Lake Placid and the Silent Film Industry
Date Unknown

They alighted from the New York Central train on a May morning in 1913—a star-spangled troupe of movie people. It was enough to bring out the Fire Department Band.

The actors and staff of the great Pathe Freres had come to shoot adventure films (silent, of course) on location among the rugged mountains. With that, Lake Placid embarked on a brief but lively career as an outdoor studio for moving picture shows. It all lasted fifteen years.

The amazing movies burst upon a receptive America around the turn of the century. The early films were fundamental, but fun. In theaters like Lake Placid's old Happy Hour, the dirty heavies were roundly booed and hissed, the hero and heroine cheered on, and the triumph of justice wildly applauded.

In 1913, most pictures were being made in the New York City area, and producers were casting about for sierra, snow, and scenic views. They soon discovered the Adirondacks. Nobody knows how many scenarios were acted out in Lake Placid, Plattsburgh, Westport, Port Henry, Saranac Lake, and the Au Sable Valley, but the meager clues suggest they were legion.

The Lake Placid landscape was pure gold, said Harry Handworth, Pathe's live-wire manager and director. He found it ready-made for epics

20 Mary Learey now owns the Interlaken Lodge.

of Siberia, Canada, Alaska, the Poles, European icebox countries, and America's rowdy western frontier. Besides, said Handworth, the natives were friendly.

Handworth leased the John Stevens house (later the Mon Amour Hotel) on Paradox Bay, and the Pathe company settled in. More than seven movies were completed that first summer of 1913, the known ones being *The Boy Who Couldn't Go Wrong, The Haunted House, The Call of the Blood, The Climax*, and *The Second Shot.*

Hometown thespians, hired for walk-ons, were atwitter when the latter premiered at the Happy Hour in July. Mason Hathaway, a popular local handyman and Pathe's caretaker, had a part in nearly every picture made.

Handworth's wife Octavia, a toothsome young woman, usually starred, as did Morris McGee, Edna Langdon, Harry Woods, Hamish Ingram, and Burt Gudgeon, a daredevil stuntman. But the real celebrity was Crane Wilbur. Macho, romantic, iron-jawed, sheep's eyed—and lots more—Crane was already a national heartthrob. He became a superstar in 1914, along with serial queen Pearl White, when that most cherished of all cliffhangers was released, Pathe's *Perils of Pauline.*

Segments of *Pauline* may have been shot at Placid in 1913, but it is definite that the fourteenth episode (Crane and Pearl jumped off a cliff) was filmed on Bluff Island in Lower Saranac Lake the summer of 1914. Crane and Pearl were hounded by Saranac Lake paparazzi, who scented a spicy story. The two had shared some fishing dalliances at Hatch Brook, and a Saranac Hotel room as "Mr. and Mrs. C. White." Crane's wife Edna had just sued him for divorce, naming as correspondent "a young woman who played a part in one of his pictures."

Even so, at Lake Placid in 1913, Crane and his wife were still a twosome, fraternizing with local society. In fact, all the Pathe players were lionized, endearing themselves by staging one-act plays at the Opera House. Big-city hits were dished up to the populace for a small admission charge. As an added treat, the Lake Placid band, stationed on the Upper Porch of the Opera House, made mood music.

With the arrival of snow, the company happily contrived winter tales. In February 1914, Handworth announced he had severed relations with Pathe and formed a company of his own, Excelsior Feature Films.

The Pathe players departed and were replaced by twenty handpicked Handworth artists, including some Broadway notables.

Local talent again served as extra and bit players. Baby Anna Maynard (later Mrs. Joe Lawrence) was recruited for a role. One picture called for an elderly gentleman to pose as Father Time. Benjamin Brewster, a prominent citizen, was selected as eminently right for the part (he was eighty-four and had a long, white beard). When told he would shortly be viewed all over the country, Mr. Brewster was not surprised.

"Well, I'm known all over the country anyhow," said he.

In June 1914, the Eclair Picture Co. came to the Stevens House and made two unnamed movies. Harry Handworth was then filming his most ambitious photoplay, *The Toll of Mammon*, a four-reeler starring wife Octavia. Special scenery and furniture costing $2,000 arrived, and Elmer Marshall, a Lake Placid Club employee, built still more. The serialization of the blood and thunder *Mammon* story in the *Lake Placid News* whetted local appetites.

In late June, *The Toll of Mammon* was about to come to a climactic conclusion on Lake Placid before a large audience of villagers assembled on shore. The script called for the good boat *Mary Ann*, manned by desperados and pursued by a police boat, to be blown up. Forty sticks of dynamite with a long fuse were already aboard. But first, a rehearsal of a gun battle was ordered by Director Handworth from the camera boat. Somehow a spark from a .45 ignited the fuse prematurely. One of the villains on the *Mary Ann* spotted the danger and yelled a warning to his shipmates. All leaped into the water and made with dog-strokes for shore.

Harry gave rapid-fire orders to his driver to overtake the *Mary Ann.* A lot of money had gone into her funeral and he did not propose to lose her before the denouement was safely on film. *Mary Ann* was on a course of her own, zig-zagging for the base of Whiteface. She tacked to starboard and then came about completely, heading straight for the dock where the spectators watched with slack-jawed horror. There was a wild scramble. Old ladies who had not sprinted since youth reached higher ground in nothing flat, and a gentleman with only one good leg outdistanced them in kangaroo leaps.

Meanwhile, back on the *Mary Ann*, the fuse sputtered in the finest cliffhanger tradition. At last, the camera boat ran her down and Harry sprang aboard. In the nick of time he yanked out the fuse, boards, and dynamite, flinging them into the ice-cold waters of Lake Placid.

The grand finale was filmed without further incident, and *The Toll of Mammon* had rave reviews in New York. Harry let it be known he would build a permanent studio on the John Stevens lot. It would be glass—eight thousand square feet of it—and the most up-to-date in the land. But wait—it would cost a healthy $10,000. Excelsior must let go some of its stock. Would the citizens of Lake Placid like to get in on the ground floor? Ten solid businessmen came forward to help Harry out. Noel Feldstein, Laster Cautin, W. F. Cheeseman, James Shea, Arthur Adams, Frank Leonard, Rufus Walton, Doctors Potter and Proctor, and Edwin B. Ersing all bought stock at $1,000 dollars a share.

In October 1914, work started on the forty-by-eighty-five-foot basement. It halted abruptly a month later. The entire company, Harry announced, must leave posthaste for New York for the filming of a famous Broadway play. The erection of the studio must be postponed until spring, when they would all return.

Spring came, and summer, but still no word from Harry. The stockholders became uneasy. Harry surprised everyone by showing up in September 1915, but this time with the Vitagraph Company, a producer of higher art photo-dramas. With him were some polished stars of filmdom for the making of *Ansello Lee*, a gypsy bedtime story. Handsome Tony Moreno, black-eyed, swashbuckling, and impetuous, had the title part. Stunt girl Manone Childers, a willowy blonde, played the white girl whose perils were plural. Temptress Frankie Mann had the female lead.

A second gypsy opus, *The Painted Lady*, starring Billy Billings, a statuesque ingénue, was also completed.

Harry, glib as ever in his praise of Lake Placid, again vowed to return and get on with the studio. But he and his glass house were heard of no more. The local Excelsior stockholders were left holding the bag.

In January 1917 came the B. M. Moss Company, housed at the Lakeside Inn. Their film, *His Hour*, featured Zena Keefe of wolf-whistle glamour, mustachioed Allan Hale, a bit on the chubby side but dashing enough in a tooled leather coat, and the Butterfield (later Catchings) camp. Said Hale with a whiff of prophecy, "New Yorkers don't know yet what Lake Placid is. In ten years it will be the Switzerland of America." At the same time, actor Carlysle Blackwell's company made a movie at the Benson camp with Blackwell, June Eldridge, Archie Ashley, and Pina Nesbit.

The Selig Company, also quartered at Lakeside Inn, in March 1917 filmed *The Danger Trail* on Placid Lake, directed by Frederick A. Thompson. The leads were well known: H.B. Warner, Violet Hemming, and Lawson Butt. "Caribou Bill" of the moving picture camp in Saranac Lake added a dash of the far north with his Alaskan dogs and sleds.

Doris Kenyon, one of the silver screen's great beauties, arrived in March 1918 with her own company, Deluxe Pictures, to play in the Mary Roberts Rinehart story, *Street of the Seven Stars*, set in Switzerland. The company stayed at the exclusive Lake Placid Club, which, for the first time, permitted a movie to be made on its six thousand acres. More than two hundred club members—millionaire tycoons and decorous dowagers—donned skiing, skating, and coasting costumes and kicked up their heels in a mob scene. Director John O'Brien, formerly with Mary Pickford, declared the sequences "the most beautiful ever filmed."

Doris Kenyon was a frequent visitor at Lake Placid in the 1920s. Her brother, Raymond Kenyon, an Au Sable Forks dentist and state assemblyman for Essex County, had a camp at Silver Lake, where Doris often vacationed with her equally famous actor spouse Milton Sills.

Another celluloid doll, Billie Burke, wife of Florenz Ziegfield of Follies fame, stayed the entire summer of 1918 for the filming of *The Make-believe Wife*. The scenario would not play anywhere today: a charming society girl, lost while mountain climbing with a young man not her fiancé, must face the consequences of the scandal. Applauded in New York, the film was booked into the Happy Hour in January 1919 by the Lake Placid Winter Sports Committee, with the proceeds donated to the maintenance of the Mirror Lake skating rink.

At Lake Placid Club's Birchrock cottage in May 1919, the Lasky Famous Players found the ideal setting for *The Turmoil*, starring Mrs. Tremane, formerly Mrs. Vernon Castle.

During the winter of 1919–1920, the Ralph Ince Company spent weeks at Placid waiting for snow and finally shot an Alaskan film. Ince came again in December 1921 with no less than Eugene O'Brien and Norma Sheerer for *Channing of the Royal Mounted*, a Canadian Northwest saga. On December 9, the Happy Hour was stacked to the rafters for the personal appearance of O'Brien onstage, after showing his latest success, *Is Life Worth Living? Channing* was filmed at Fortune's camp near Tableland Farm. For the traditional bank heist, the Newman Post Office was the bank, and a number of town boys were the outlaws.

In February 1920, the Selznick Company shot *Out of the Snows* on Lake Placid in the lee of Pulpit Rock, with Whiteface as a backdrop. In this dramatic framework, the ship *Pole Star* lay marooned in "Arctic" ice. The cast is unknown except for the female lead, our old friend Zena Keefe, and one who would lend a good deal of substance to Placid's in after years, the inimitable Jacques Suzanne. Zena was sensational as an Eskimo darling, bedecked in scrumptious sealskin coat and boots. *The Avalanche* was in progress on a nearby mountain slope, and it starred two of the very greats of moviedom, Adolphe Menjou and Norma Talmadge. Jacques Suzanne assisted in creating the avalanche that was the piece de resistance of the show.

Suzanne, Arctic explorer, painter, dog team expert, animal trainer, friend of both Admiral Robert E. Peary and the Russian czar, was then under contract to Selznick and living at Fort Montgomery. Selznick soon engineered his permanent move to Lake Placid. Then began the years of cine-melodrama at Suzanne's Movie Ranch on Bear Cub Road.[21] All through the 1920s, film crews and stars milled about that primitive place where malamute dogs, wolves, coyotes, wild cats, palomino horses, rustic buildings, evergreens, and snow—and Suzanne himself—combined to provide trappings for tales of daring-do. Among the scores filmed were *The Trapper's Wife* with Kitty Gordon (in private life Lady Beresford), *The Broken Silence* with Zena Keefe, *The Man From Beyond* with the great magician Harry Houdini, and *Far From the Beaten Track* with King Baggot.

By far the most legendary film made at Placid was *Janice Meredith.* A famous Revolutionary War tale, it starred the delectable Marion Davies, close companion of William Randolph Hearst, and was produced by Cosmopolitan to the tune of a million dollars.

The Battle of Trenton and Washington's Delaware crossing were filmed at Plattsburgh. But when it came to choosing a habitat for Washington's ordeal at Valley Forge in the cruel bite of winter, Placid won hands down. In March 1924, an advance guard of technicians and carpenters moved

21 Now called Bear Cub Lane, County Route 26.

in and erected a village on part of Lake Placid Club's Highland Farm (later owned by Gus Lussi). A cast of one hundred, with Joseph Kilgore as Washington, followed by special train, augmented by two hundred of Lake Placid's manliest to fill the boots of Colonial soldiers.

Placidian Albert Gardner became an expert maker of snowstorms.

The company's trick horse, Red, tethered at Suzanne's camp, ran away during the height of production and was finally captured by horse trainer William Daley. He had, said Daley, caught up with Red "near the top of Mount Marcy."

Another farm, Heaven Hill, with its grand vistas, was the site of First National's *Wilderness Woman* in February 1926. Aileen Pringle and Lowell Sherman came with a cast of twenty, not the least important member of which was a black bear cub, Sonny. On location the first day, Sonny balked and refused to act in the unfamiliar polar chill. The proffer of condensed milk and blankets moved him not. But the day was carried when a resident bear cub, bred in the Adirondack deep freeze, was borrowed from Paul Stevens.

Sixty actors and staff of the comic Fox Films rolled in by special train in August 1926 for *Summer Bachelors*. The director was Allan Dwan, famous for his work with Douglas Fairbanks in *Robin Hood*, and the stars were Madge Bellamy, Matt Moore, Charles Wininger, and Walter Catlett, erstwhile Follies funnyman. The company, housed at both Northwoods Inn and Alford Inn, was whisked in fast motorboats to location on the big lake.

Lake Placid's storybook camps furnished a front for an Adirondack summer house party. The plot line was provocative: A group of wealthy New York businessmen generously send their wives and girlfriends away to European resorts for the summer. This accomplished, the men rush to phones and line up companions to help while away the interval. One of the summer bachelors throws a house party at his sumptuous lodge on Lake Placid, and scenes of romantic hide-and-seek ensue.

Great stars of Paramount arrived with Director Malcolm St. Clair in January 1927 to make *Knockout Riley*. The headliners were virile Richard Dix and wistful Mary Brian, with an assist from local skiers and skaters. One enchanted evening the entire cast of forty came down to Mirror Lake Rink and skated gregariously with the town folk to the strains of "The Skater's Waltz."

The last silent made at Lake Placid—and, for that matter, in the Adirondacks—was Fox Films' *The News Parade*, with stars Nick Stuart and

Sally Phipps, in February 1928. All the action centered about Lake Placid's winter sports competitions—the Gold Cup skate, the Washington's Birthday ski jump, sled dog races, and the Baldwin cup cross country ski.

It was over in a twinkling. Hollywood was now the nucleus of production, and its own scenic surroundings ruled out the need for the Adirondacks. Into the bargain, moving pictures began to talk. But, as any old-timer can tell you, nothing can ever top those grand old silent movie days.

SIXTY-FIVE
William Benson and Camp Majano
Date Unknown

William Sumner Benson was born in Titusville, Pennsylvania, in 1863. He was the son of Byron David Benson, a founder of the Tide Water Pipe Company Ltd., operators of one of the first pipelines for transporting petroleum in the United States, and a direct descendant of John Benson, a Puritan, who came to the Massachusetts Colony in 1638.

William Benson became associated with the family company, Tide Water Oil Company, and retired as its treasurer and vice president in 1925.

Mr. Benson suffered poor health for most of his life, and because of this left public school to go to the lumber fields his family owned in St. Lawrence County, New York. A few years later, he formed the Benson Mines there, working an iron deposit that he and some friends had discovered on the property. The mines were closed in 1913, but they were reopened in the 1930s and were worked for some time afterward.

Mr. Benson was a resident of Passaic, New Jersey, for many years up until his death at Passaic on May 31, 1942, in his seventy-ninth year.

Mr. Benson started to come to Lake Placid as early as 1912, and was a member of the Lake Placid Club. He probably at first stayed at the Club. His later permanent summer home, Camp Majano (meaning Rocky Point) on the point of Cape Marie on Buck Island in Placid Lake, was built in 1915, according to various Shore Owners' Association booklets. According to Arthur Hayes in his little book, *Lake Placid: The Switzerland of America*, Mr. Benson built the camp. Mr. Hayes says that William S. Benson, his brother Robert D. Benson, and his sister Mrs. Charles F.

Emerson all "spent large sums of money in building their camps on Buck Island on Lake Placid." While the Hayes book contains many errors and generally cannot be relied upon, Mr. Hayes was probably correct in this particular regard, as he lived in Lake Placid all his life and was familiar with the history of most of the camps on the lake.

William Benson also owned Camp Canadohts on the north side of Buck Island, just west of Camp Majano and facing Shelter Strait. Formerly called Unterwalden, it was probably built by the Rev. W. E. Schell in 1912; Schell had been the previous owner. Mr. Benson never occupied this camp but no doubt used it for guests or rented it out. During all his years on the lake, he occupied only Camp Majano.

William Benson's brother, Robert, president of Tide Water Oil Company and also a resident of Passaic, New Jersey, had Camp Schonoe, built in 1910, just below William on the east side of Buck Island. Robert died at Camp Schonoe in September 1931.

The sister, Mrs. Charles F. Emerson of Titusville, Pennsylvania, had Camp High Well (formerly Camp Kiwanis), built in 1915, just south of Robert Benson. According to Hayes, Mrs. Emerson's camp was sold to Judge Proskauer after her death.

William Benson took a great interest in the village of Lake Placid and its improvement. For some time he was chairman of the Village Park Committee, which also included Harry Wade Hicks and Henry Uihlein, and was for years on the board of directors of the Garden Club of Lake Placid. He was a trustee of the Shore Owners' Association of Lake Placid from August 1916 until his death, and was vice president of the organization from August 1930 to August 1936.

He took a very special interest in our local Adirondack Community Church, and was one of the prime movers in the building of the present stone Gothic church that replaced the old wooden building. He was an active member of the advisory board on all architectural details and contributed generously to the building fund. He also initiated and provided the funds for the attractive monument on the church grounds honoring the Lake Placid men who died in World War I service.

After William Benson's death, his son-in-law and daughter, Mr. and Mrs. David G. Ackerman, took over Camp Majano.

SIXTY-SIX

Montemare School

On September 15, 1998, Mary MacKenzie answered a letter asking her about the Montemare School.

Here is the history of Montemare School at Lake Placid:

In 1905, John M. Hopkins founded his preparatory school for boys, the Hopkins School, at Lake Placid. For the first few years, cottages at the Lake Placid Club were leased for classrooms and housing. By 1912, the school had grown to such proportions that the Club cottages were no longer sufficient, and Hopkins purchased a tract of twenty-one acres adjacent to Club lands and constructed his own school buildings. These were substantial, and included a gymnasium. They eventually became, as you will see, the Montemare buildings pictured in the sheet you sent me. An initial investment of over $75,000 produced what was then one of the finest school plants in our North Country. All the great facilities of the Lake Placid Club were open to the students.

The school was unusual in that it was migratory. Classes were held at Lake Placid from September to January and from April to June, and in Florida from January to April.

The Hopkins School became one of the better preparatory schools in America. It was so successful that in 1920, Miss Anna A. Ryan (A. B., Smith College) decided to establish a girl's school at Lake Placid to be run along identical lines. Miss Ryan was formerly head of Villa duPont School in Paris, and for four years was associate headmistress of Rosemary Hall, Greenwich, Connecticut.

The school was named Montemare (translated, "mountain/sea") and conducted its fall and spring sessions at Lake Placid and its winter session, after Christmas, at Miami Beach, Florida. For its first year, 1920–21, the school leased a cottage, Fernwood, at the Lake Placid Club. By June 1921, Mr. Hopkins was ready for retirement. Miss Ryan immediately purchased his extensive school property for her Montemare School. It is evident that the number of students was greatly on the increase, requiring buildings and grounds as extensive as the Hopkins property. The Hopkins School continued in other facilities, including the Lake Placid Club, as the Malcolm School, which eventually was taken over by the Lake Placid

Club Education Foundation and became known as the Lake Placid Club School for Boys.

Several articles from the *Lake Placid News* of 1921 and 1923 give considerable information about the Montemare curriculum. According to those articles, quite some emphasis was placed on physical recreation and competition "to attune the physical to the mental."

The Montemare School continued at Lake Placid and Florida until 1927. In November 1926, the Lake Placid Club Education Foundation bought from Miss Ryan the entire plant of Montemare School, consisting of twenty-one acres and facilities for fifty students, for its Lake Placid Club School for Boys. Montemare held its session in Florida that winter, and its spring 1927 session in the Lake Placid building. In June, it turned the property over to the Foundation. Apparently, Montemare School then came to the end of its existence. It certainly did not continue at Lake Placid, and I have found no evidence that it continued elsewhere. In the fall of 1927, the Foundation held its first classes in the building, renaming their school Northwood School. Northwood School is still there with its original buildings, augmented by a number of additions.

As I mentioned, students of the Hopkins School had full access to the Lake Placid Club's great sports and other facilities. It is my guess that the students of Montemare School were probably granted similar access. Although neither school was under Lake Placid Club ownership or direction, the Club took an interest in both as convenient and excellent schools for the children of their members.

It is very difficult to find published material about Montemare, but what I am sending should give you a pretty good idea of its character. I have no information at all about the Florida branch.

SIXTY-SEVEN
Homestead

Marjorie A. Erickson, granddaughter of Calvin W. and Lettie Cora Dake, former occupants of the Homestead, wrote Mary MacKenzie in March of 1995 asking for the Homestead's history. Ms. Erickson wondered if the Homestead was a rooming/boarding house or a hotel. She also understood that it was razed prior to the 1980 Olympics to make way for a new hotel. Mary's answer contained what she knew of the property, along with a request of Ms. Erickson to enlighten her on Mr. and Mrs. Dake and their part in the history of the Homestead.

The Homestead started out in the 1880s as a private home. In 1900, E.D. Viall owned it; I believe it was he who put on the first big addition. It was being operated in 1909 by Mrs. Martin Ryan. I have not as yet traced the title completely since that year, but I do know that it was sold to Thomas Roland in 1922 by Charles Green, who apparently had been the owner for several years, at least. The Roland family owned it continuously up to 1979, when it was torn down to make way for a Hilton complex.

I have not yet come across the name of Dake in the chain of title, but I do need to do more research in our County Clerk's Office. Are you sure that your grandparents Dake actually owned the Homestead, and were not simply leasing it? All my references indicate Charles Green owned it for some years prior to 1922, but I still need to make a thorough investigation.

[Ms. Erickson replied with the following history.]

I have just returned from a vacation, part of which was spent with an elderly cousin who grew up in Middle Grove, New York, and visited my family in Lake Placid. She seems to think that my grandparents owned the Homestead, or at least they leased with an option to buy.

My grandfather was Calvin Wesley Dake. He was born September 6, 1864, someplace in New York State, probably in Greenfield.

My grandmother was Lettie Cora Lewis. She was born March 7, 1867, in Greenfield, New York.

They were married October 17, 1883, and lived for a short while in South Greenfield, where their first child was born, before moving to the family farm in Middle Grove. While on the farm, two more children were born. All three children were girls, and the last one, Clara Estella Dake, became my mother forty years later. While they lived there they farmed, and my grandfather worked at Mr. Belkamp's sawmill.

In 1916, they left the farm and moved to Lake Placid, where they managed and possibly (not sure) owned the Homestead until 1922, when they moved to Asbury Park, New Jersey, and bought the Dake House at 303 Third Avenue. My grandfather died in Asbury Park on September 15, 1929. My grandmother continued to operate the Dake House until 1941, when she sold the property and went to live with her daughter in Tiffin, Ohio, and later to Saratoga Springs, New York. She died July 27, 1957, and is buried in Middle Grove beside my grandfather.

[In 1995, when MacKenzie responded to Marjorie Erickson's inquiries about the Dake tenure at the Homestead, she did not have access to a resource first made available in 2005: an electronic, searchable, online archive of the *Lake Placid News* dating back to 1914. The following information, culled from that archive early in the fall of 2006, confirms the family stories communicated to Ms. Erickson about her grandparents.

According to the *Lake Placid News* of February 4, 1916, Mr. and Mrs. C. W. Dake, of Middle Grove, NewYork—seven miles west of Saratoga Springs—leased the Homestead from Mr. and Mrs. C. H. Green with the intention of taking possession April 1 of that year.

Perhaps coincidentally, one of the Dakes' three daughters was married to Howard Cline, cashier of the new Lake Placid National Bank, which had opened the previous summer as a competitor to the Bank of Lake Placid. Cline, whose parents lived in Newark, New Jersey, had previously worked for the Fulton Trust Co. in New York City.

Calvin and Lettie Dake took possession of the Homestead on Tuesday, April 4, 1916. By the end of that month, the Dakes were ready to issue an announcement that "the Homestead will open under new management May 1, 1916. C. W. Dake, Proprietor."

Business was good. The *Lake Placid News'* July 28, 1916 "News of the Hotels" column reported that "the Homestead, under the efficient management of Mr. and Mrs. C. W. Dake, is enjoying an excellent season." The article went on to list the names of twenty-four "recent arrivals."

In October 1918, the *News* reported that "Mr. and Mrs. Calvin Dake and family have closed the Homestead for the season to go to Westfield, N.J. for the winter." (Westfield is about twelve miles WSW of Newark.)

The following spring (May 1919), the *News* noted that "C. W. Dake and family have returned to open the Homestead for the summer."

With that report, however, the Dakes passed out of the newspapers.

The *News* archives confirmed their proprietorship of the Homestead beginning in 1916 and continuing at least through 1919. According to their granddaughter, the Dakes left Lake Placid for the seaside resort of Asbury Park, New Jersey, where they bought a small hotel in time to open for the 1922 season.

The Greens, who apparently maintained ownership of the Homestead throughout the Dake tenancy, sold the small hotel to Thomas F. Roland in March 1922. According to the front-page newspaper story reporting that transaction, the Homestead had "17 sleeping rooms and seven baths, besides a dining room which will accommodate 40, a living room and a parlor."]

SIXTY-EIGHT
The Pratts: 144 Years on the Road
September 4, 1975

Back in 1879, William E. Pratt was highway superintendent of the Town of North Elba. Today, just about a hundred years later, his great-grandson, Kent Pratt, is highway superintendent of the Town of North Elba.

Remarkable? Yes. But that is not the whole story. For from 1909 until his death in July 1923, William E.'s son William D. was town highway superintendent. And from July 1923 through 1967, an unbroken period of forty-four years, still another Pratt, Gordon L., son of William D. and grandson of the original William, was town highway superintendent. Gordon's total hitch on the highways was actually forty-nine years. He died in 1972 after only four years of retirement. His nephew Kent may yet duplicate his unprecedented term. It is not improbable that young Kent Pratt, already in the department twenty years, may still be there in the year 2004. And, in the natural course of events, another Pratt will almost surely succeed him as "King of the Roads."

Then, too, additional descendants of William E. Pratt have served the highway department in various capacities over the years: Horace A. and Cecil, to name two of recent vintage, as well as William C. and Raymond Sr. In fact, the total tally of Pratt service to date is, as near as can be determined, an astronomical 144 years. How much greater it may be, no one knows. Still other Pratts may have served.

For a Pratt, working on the town highways is not just another job. It is a profession, and a proud tradition. That so many members of one family have been elected to the same office so many times over the span of a century is ample proof that Pratt efficiency, technical know-how, and devotion to duty have more than earned the public trust.

The Pratt family became rooted in America before the Revolution. In 1800, 175 years ago, the first Pratt came to live in Essex County, New York. Elijah Pratt removed from New England and settled in Willsboro. There he died in 1808, leaving behind five children, among them Daniel Pratt, born in 1806.

A successful farmer until his death in 1862, Daniel was prominent in public affairs and a class leader and steward of the Willsboro Methodist Church. In 1829, he married Philomena Freeman, a native of Utica, New York, who bore him seven children, including our William E. Pratt.

William E., destined to become North Elba's first Pratt highway superintendent, was born in Willsboro in 1830. Educated in district schools, he began to assist his father on the family farm at an early age. In 1862, two major events highlighted his life. He married Mary Glatt, rhymically uniting the bloodlines of Pratt and Glatt. (Mary, the widow of Christian Miner, was a native of Germany who emigrated to Philadelphia with her parents in 1845.) He also enlisted as a private in Company C, 62nd Regiment, New York Volunteer Infantry, and served in the Civil War. His brother Horace, a second lieutenant in the Civil War, was mortally wounded in front of Richmond and died at the age of twenty-seven.

Moving to North Elba in 1870, William E. settled upon a good farm of thirty acres on the Old Military Road and later acquired another fifty acres of detached land. His first home was fashioned of logs and stood east of the new elementary school on Old Military Road. Several years later, he built a substantial wooden farmhouse directly across the road from the old log house. The farm is gone, but the house still stands, in color a soft gold with white shutters, one of the most attractive properties in town. William D. Pratt took over the house when his father died in 1902 and all of his children—including Gordon, Horace, and Cecil—grew up there. It saw a number of owners after its sale by the widowed Mrs. William D. Pratt and is now in the hands of Mrs. Betty Stedman. Of interest is the fact that

Kent Pratt's brother, Horace D. Pratt, repurchased his great-grandfather's home in 1966 and lived there until 1973.

William E. Pratt prospered as a general farmer and stock dealer in North Elba, and besides acting as highway commissioner (as the job was then labeled) in 1879 and 1880, was a trustee of the School Fund. He and Mary Glatt produced eight children.

What is it like to be town highway superintendent? For the various Pratts, it has meant various things. For William E., the job was not that demanding, because in 1879 winter roads were better left unplowed. The automobile had yet to be invented, and sleds and sleighs required a good snow base for navigation. In fact, in that era, there were often two roads leading to a destination: a winter road, and a summer road. Winter roads invariably wound through deep woods where the snow was less likely to melt.

William E.'s big job was to keep the pikes in good repair in the snowless months. Highways were earth-surfaced with a road machine drawn by four to six horses. The main idea each year was to rake stones out of the dirt top, and that took all summer. In the very early days, long before William E., landowners did not pay a highway tax in cold cash but worked it out on the roads. At one time, the town had a man called a "pathmaster" who scraped down roads or dragged a particular stretch with equipment borrowed from resident farmers.

William E. Pratt's son, Superintendent William D. Pratt, had problems, and they did not go away. During his reign, the automobile appeared on the roads of North Elba, and in ever-increasing numbers. With the coming of the automobile, the job of highway superintendent underwent a vast sea change. Dirt roads no longer sufficed in summer, and in winter the snow had to be packed down in some fashion. Out of the latter need evolved the heavy wooden snow roller drawn by as many as eight horses. Then William D. Pratt dreamed up a plow. Called a "butterfly" plow, it was made of wood and was horse-drawn. Next came the tractor-drawn plow, which took all day to get to Saranac Lake and back. There was then a uniquely constructed "hoe" tractor plow that smacked of a Rube Goldberg invention. The first real truck plow did not come along until the late 1920s.

William D. put North Elba's first hardtop road, made of "water-bound macadam," into the Cascade region in 1920. Crushed stone was spread, dirt scattered and wet down with a sprinkler, and the compound pressed with a steamroller. "It was quite a road," Superintendent Gordon Pratt once recalled. "It lasted a long time, 'til traffic got too heavy."

For Gordon Pratt, the job meant forty-nine winters of erratic sleep, and for Kent Pratt it has come to have a similar meaning. In the wee hours of a frigid night, when the good people of North Elba are snugged down in their beds, the highway boss and his men are often rousted out to battle an Adirondack blizzard. All night, in howling winds and driving snow, the town trucks cruise the country roads, the roar of motors, clank of plows and staccato red lights giving comfort to the housebound. It is pleasant to awaken at night in a wailing storm and hear the plows plying the roads. They bring a sense of security, such as the old town criers must have done in the youth of America. One knows, sure as death and taxes, that the roads will be open by daybreak, and North Elbans can properly go about their business—unless, that is, a storm of alarming proportions and duration has descended upon the Elba plateau.

We asked Cecil Pratt, who worked under his brother Gordon for over thirty-six years, what the worst snowstorm he remembered was. There were so many bad ones, Cecil says, he can't pick a winner. Those snows of yesteryear, he maintains, are a rarity today. In his recollection, the worst storm was not a big snow, but a big blow—the brutal hurricane of November 25, 1950, that devastated the entire Adirondack Park. After twenty-five years, its destructive blow-down effects still mar the Adirondack woods. Curiously, despite the hundred-mile-an-hour gales and a four-inch rainfall inside an hour, the nearby Whiteface Mountain Ski Center escaped harm. The worst damage in North Elba, as far as highways were concerned, befell the Whiteface Inn road and the road around Mirror Lake. Trees snapped like matchsticks and toppled like dominoes, plugging the highways.

Gordon and his crew worked most of the night, trying to clear the road around Mirror Lake. They started cutting through while trees were still crashing down. With chain saws unknown then, the men had to use cross-cut saws. They also had to work in the dark, without benefit of streetlights, for the village had cut off electric power due to falling wires. Finally, they received instructions to get out of the dangerous area. Turning back, they found the road they had just cleared was choked again, and literally sawed their way back to the village.

Cecil cites one memorable snowstorm of the early 1930s. Bobsled races had been in progress at Mount Van Hoevenberg during the day. At noon, snow came. As darkness fell, it was blanketing Cascade Road with a vengeance, and cars emerging from the bobrun road bogged down in heavy drifts. The occupants took refuge at neighboring houses for the night. Gordon had but one snowplow then, and by the time it reached the hill above the bobrun road, everything was plugged up. It was not until the next day that the cars could be dug out, one by one.

In that time slot, digging cars out after an all-night rendezvous with a snowdrift was not uncommon, especially in Cascade Lakes Pass, which acts as a natural funnel for wind and drift. The town would plow up to the cars, and then shovel them out by manpower. "A lot of times, the plow would hit the cars before we knew they were there," said Cecil.

There was one time when even the town plow was snowbound. Horace Pratt, with Lou Strack, and Fred Darrah, spent the night in Cascade Pass in the big Walters plow truck. The Town of Keene plow came along at daybreak and dug them out.

The most notorious trouble spot in snowstorms has always been the Adirondack Lodge Road, where the wind has full sweep across open fields. There have been times when the wind-stacked snow has almost touched the cross arms of telephone poles.

There is not, and never has been, a special night crew for plowing. The regulars stay on the job until all roads are cleared, often working all night. Cecil remembers the time when the men would work forty hours at a stretch without sleep, stopping only to get a bite to eat along the road.

All the town dirt roads were paved during Gordon Pratt's term. When he first took charge, twenty-five men (working at $1.75 a day) were needed to maintain the highways. Sweat and horses were what did the job. By the time he retired, improved and heavy-duty trucks, loaders, scrapers, and what-have-you had reduced the force to about nine men.

Horace Pratt worked under his brother Gordon from 1923 until 1942. He recalls a time in the early 1920s when the village had just laid a beautiful brick pavement on Main Street (now concealed under blacktop). Then, as now, the village and town moguls did not always see eye to eye, and the village refused to allow the ponderous and potentially destructive town plow to follow their red brick road in passing Placid. Came a big snow of thirty-six inches and the village, lacking the town's snow-fighting equipment, was in trouble. It sent an SOS to Gordon, pleading with him to plow Main Street. "No soap," said Gordon. "I won't personally take the risk of breaking up your red brick road. You'll have to call the town supervisor." The village called Supervisor Wells. "No soap," said Willis Wells. Meantime, the wind blew stronger and the drifts grew longer. Willis said no for quite a spell. When the village had begged long enough and strong enough to satisfy the town, Gordon and his men were dispatched to disinter Main Street.

Cecil Pratt retired from the Highway Department in 1969. He lives in an inviting little house on Hurley Avenue, overlooking a superb view of Whiteface and the Sentinel Range. A veteran hunter and fisherman, he owns two snowmobiles, one for himself and one for any friend who wants to keep him company on his forest excursions. He also raises prize dahlias.

Horace Pratt, on the other hand, in retirement after his many years with the Highway Department, Fire Department, and Raeoil Corporation, raises pigs, chickens, and beef cattle on River Road (now bearing the haughty name of Riverside Drive, to the indignation of old-timers). Son Kent helps out when he has the time. Both Horace and Kent have neat homes perched on top of precipitous "P Hill" just off the Drive.

The Pratts have always been an outgoing, industrious clan, walking in the footprints of their pioneer forebears. And they have always been staunch North Country Republicans. Have they ever been opposed at the polls? Well, yes, but not very strenuously. Anyone who has ever run against a Pratt has been headed for a pratfall.

In 1967, when Gordon Pratt decided to retire, the Town Board looked to Kent Pratt as the man to succeed him. Not knowing how Kent might fare at the polls, they suggested that Gordon run again, resume the office in January 1968, and then resign, leaving the way open for Kent to fill the vacancy. But Kent would have none of that. "Let the voters decide whether they want me," he said, and ran for office that fall. The voters wanted Kent, and have wanted him ever since. He has yet to meet competition at the polls.[22]

---

22 Kent Pratt became North Elba Highway Superintendent in January 1968. He retired at the end of 2003.

Kent Pratt takes to the job like the proverbial duck to water. He, as did his father and uncles before him, started hitching rides on town equipment with his father as a toddler. Highway work is streamlined and motorized now, and a far cry from the back-breaking labor of his great-grandfather's day. Modern trucks and equipment have brought improved service, great efficiency, and a reduction in manpower. Only nine men work in the department now, and there is probably no other town in the state whose roads are plowed as quickly and as well.

Stated simply, the job of the Highway Department is one of maintaining, plowing, building, repairing, and resurfacing town roads and bridges. The town also does most of the work on the county roads within the Town of North Elba, and plows both state and county roads, with due compensation. Kent presently has three Ford and two GMC dump trucks and two large snowplows besides road-building equipment. Plows are also put on two of the smaller trucks.

There is a network today of many miles of road to maintain—west to Saranac Lake, north to the narrows in Wilmington Notch, east to Cascade Lakes, and south to Averyville and Adirondack Lodge. That network has evolved over a period of 175 years. In 1800, there was but one road from the outside world into and through North Elba: the Old Military Road. It still survives, from the Old Mountain Road on the north side of Pitchoff to the end of the McKenzie Pond Road into Saranac Lake. About 1801 a wagon track was opened into Averyville, and about 1814 another was constructed from Lower Mill Pond over the Sentinel Range to Wilmington. It was not until 1854 that Bill Nye, Bob Scott, and Peter Comstock laid out the Wilmington Road along its present track, and it entered the North Elba settlement via the present Riverside Drive. The Cascade Lakes stretch of state Route 73 was built in 1858.

Today there are not too many complaints from taxpayers about the town highways. To be sure, Kent Pratt's telephone begins to jangle when a storm is in progress. Everyone wants his road plowed first. About the only real thorny issue in the last decade has been the poisoning of roadsides to eliminate brush and evergreens, a practice frowned upon by environmentalists. For the first couple of years, dead and dying foliage on many roads was a sorry sight. The picture is brighter now. The chemical has done its work, the tangle of brush is gone, and the town can neatly and economically mow its roadsides in the modern way. There has been no apparent damage to the ecology.

Soon it will be time to put the snowplows on. This is done about the first of November. It takes half a day to ready all the trucks. Kent hopes there will be plenty of snow for Lake Placid's winter sports this year, but he doesn't want another storm like the one just before Christmas in 1970. That was a pretty bad one, as Adirondack storms go, and the Lodge road was closed for three days. The early part of last April, he was busy for a while, too. It snowed for over a hundred hours, five days straight, and about thirty-six inches fell in that one storm.

If there were room in the Highway Department, the rest of the North Elban fourth-generation Pratts might be there, but they have followed a different drummer. Gordon Pratt's son Gordon W. is in the real estate and insurance business. His daughter Beverley married James E. Reid. Raymond Jr. is a schoolteacher. Horace has two daughters, Sandra (Mrs. Dale Daby) and Mrs. Joan Ormsby. His son Horace D. is Lake Placid's chief of police, posing this intriguing question: Is there another Pratt dynasty in the making?

Nonetheless, there is a reservoir of future Pratt highway superintendents in North Elba to draw upon. All members of the fourth generation have children.

We asked Kent Pratt if he had ever considered any other career besides the town Highway Department. He thought that over for a second or two.

"What else *is* there?" said the great-grandson of William E. Pratt.

SIXTY-NINE
The Lake Placid Airport Before World War II
Date Unknown

The Lake Placid Company (Lake Placid Club) originally owned the field. It was completely undeveloped, but it appears that in the late 1920s airplanes were using it—probably including Club guests. For instance, in August 1927, a big eight-passenger tri-motor plane brought a party of four up from New York, landing on the field. And the *Lake Placid News* of

August 5, 1927, mentioned, "Summer guests at various hotels continue to favor the airplane as a speedy way to reach Lake Placid."

From the winter of 1926 on, through the late 1920s, the Curtiss Flying Service provided air flights from New York to Lake Placid in the wintertime, but always landing on Mirror Lake.

In the summer of 1929, the Lake Placid Club leased the airport (198 acres) to Aviation Consolidated Inc., of New York City. This organization was a consolidation of several well-known air companies. Lake Placid was a principal stop on the New York-Lake Placid-Montreal air route. The company, in addition, gave flying lessons and kept several planes at the local airport for the use of student fliers. Walter J. Watson, of New York, was manager of the airport. Meanwhile, in April 1929, a Lake Placid Aviation Club was formed to study and promote aviation. Quite a number of locals joined up. George Denton and George Campbell sponsored this club.

It appears Aviation Consolidated introduced a number of improvements at the airport, including the building of some sort of hangar. There was also fuel equipment and telephone service.

Roosevelt Flying Corporation was maintaining transport service between New York and Lake Placid. Over the Labor Day 1929 weekend, an Adirondack Air Meet took place at Lake Placid. A number of famous aviators took part. The airport seems to have been quite a busy place in the summers of 1929 and 1930. Aviation Consolidated was still operating the airport in 1930. To guide aviators, weather conditions at Lake Placid were wired daily from the weather station at Lake Placid Club to Radio Station WGY in Schenectady.

One man who figured in the Placid airport story is Fred McLane. The earliest mention found of him was December 1930, when he is called "Lieutenant McLane, former Navy flier." He was apparently an instructor for the Adirondack Flying Club. Fred C. McLane is referred to as manager of the local airport in November 1932. In that same year McLane, who had a cabin monoplane, instituted an airline between Lake Placid and Albany, where passengers changed for New York City. He operated as Adirondack Airways Inc.

Just when the Town of North Elba first leased the airport from the Club has not been determined; town records will have to be searched. The *Lake Placid News* makes no mention of the airport until 1932. The town probably took control in 1931.

Fred McLane continued as manager for a number of years until the state Conservation Commission hired him as a pilot.

In 1933, the town built new runways with a $3,000 appropriation for airport improvement from the Emergency Relief Administration. It accomplished a number of improvements, including leveling of the field, in the spring of 1934 with funds from the Federal Civil Works Administration. The town also applied at this time for additional funds for a steel hangar, administration building, lighting, and extension of village water, but quite certainly never received same.

An $80,000 Works Progress Administration grant was available for the airport in 1935, but only if the town received title to the land. The town did not receive the grant, as it did not own the land. A *Lake Placid News* article of December 13, 1935, said that 139 acres had been leased by the town from the Lake Placid Club, with an option to buy, expiring 1939.

In 1940, local officials attempted to create a commercial airport in concert with Canadian Colonial Airline, but the Civil Aeronautics Administration refused the application of Canadian for service here because the field was inadequate for large commercial planes. North Elba funds could not be used to develop the land until title to the land was secured.

SEVENTY
The Craig Wood Golf and Country Club
Date Unknown

Construction of a nine-hole golf course, to be known as the Lake Placid Golf and Country Club, on the pioneer Cyrus Taylor farm in the Town of North Elba, was apparently begun in 1924. The owner of the land and sponsor of the project was a corporation known as the Lake Placid Holding Corporation. The names of its officers and stockholders have not been determined. There were several other golf courses in Lake Placid at this time, but all were connected with hotels or private interests and were generally not open to the public. The corporate owners and sponsors felt that a public golf course available to the broad field of local people, summer cottage residents, and guests of the many boarding houses and hotels without links facilities was a must if Lake Placid was to compete successfully with other resorts.

Seymour Dunn, internationally known golf architect and the golf pro at the Lake Placid Club, personally supervised the layout and completion of the course. The Lake Placid Golf and Country Club opened in 1925. Buildings on the premises included an old farmhouse, barn, shed, garage, clubhouse, and shelter cabins. A tearoom was operated in the clubhouse. Scott North was the first golf pro. The second, Pat Doyle, was appointed in 1927; Doyle was one of the leading professionals in the country. The third pro, Dave Stevens, served in 1928.

The Holding Corporation began work on a second nine holes as early as 1927, and this work continued sporadically over the next few years. By 1931, close to $100,000 had been invested in the project, and in that year the Holding Corporation offered the course for sale to the Town of North Elba. The Town Board was amenable to the purchase, and on July 30, 1931, a proposition was put to a taxpayer vote at a special election for the acquisition of the country club golf course, its improvement, and completion to eighteen holes, for a total sum of $122,000. At the same special election, a proposition to build the Olympic Arena was also put to a taxpayer vote. The arena proposition was approved, but the golf course proposition was turned down.

In August 1932, the North Elba Park Commission entered into a lease with the Lake Placid Holding Corporation for town operation of the golf course beginning September 15, 1932. The lease stipulated an annual rent of $2,400, which covered a period of fifteen years, and the town was given the privilege of purchase within a period of ten years for the sum of $25,000.

The town immediately decided to complete the additional nine holes. It was felt not only that an eighteen-hole course was an absolute necessity, but that the work of completion would aid in the unemployment situation of that period of the Great Depression. The town accepted the plans of architect John R. VanKleek, who personally supervised the work. He had also that year laid out the new eighteen-hole course at Whiteface Inn.

The work of completing the additional nine holes proceeded rapidly, with the employment of anywhere from forty to 140 men under the Temporary Emergency Relief Administration. The course was built according to championship specifications. The damming of the stream running through the property created two small lakes. Improvements were also made to the original nine holes, and an addition was put on the clubhouse. New machinery and equipment were purchased, and new furniture was acquired for the clubhouse. Total cost of new construction and improvements was $43,285.04.

On April 8, 1935, the Town of North Elba purchased this great scenic golf course, and it has been in the ownership of the people of North Elba ever since.

On Monday, July 19, 1948, the name of the Lake Placid Golf and Country Club was changed to Craig Wood Golf and Country Club when the community honored its native son Craig Wood, one of the nation's all-time topflight golfers. Craig had started out as a local caddy, and over the years, he had become a star in golfdom's rugged big-time competition. Winner of many minor titles, Craig won the Masters in 1941 and went on to win the U.S. Open that same year, a feat seldom accomplished. A one-time runner-up in the British Open, he was known as "the golfer who finished second more times than any other man alive." He had almost won the Masters in 1935, but lost to Gene Sarazen in a playoff. Craig was elected to the PGA Golf Hall of Fame in 1956.

Craig was present at the official dedication ceremonies at the golf course in 1948. He thanked the officials and the crowd of about four hundred present, saying he was "deeply honored by such a gesture on the part of the Town of North Elba." He then teamed with Jim Searles, golf director at Lake Placid Club, to take second honors in a golf exhibition match against Claude Harmon, 1948 Masters champion, and Marshall Trusttum, pro at the local club.

Craig Wood died at Palm Beach, Florida, on May 14, 1968, at the age of sixty-seven. He is buried in our North Elba Cemetery.

SEVENTY-ONE

Garden Club of Lake Placid 1933 to 1953

Date Unknown

The Garden Club of Lake Placid was formed on September 18, 1933, at the home of Mrs. Milton L. (Edna) Bernstein, at Red Gables on Placid Lake.

The Club elected the following officers at the organization meeting: Mrs. Milton L. Bernstein, president; Mrs. George C. Owens, vice president; Mrs. H.H. Epstein, secretary; and Mrs. Henry Uihlein, treasurer. Mrs. Raymond C. Prime was named membership chairwoman, and Mrs. Louis Hammer horticultural chairwoman.

The object of the club was the general improvement of village and lakeshore property, and the members planned to concentrate on the improvement of property barren of shrubbery or flowers.

In 1934, the Club sponsored a competition among merchants to beautify their business properties on Main Street, and awarded prizes.

By 1935, the Club was in full swing. At a meeting on July l, 1935, plans were formulated for annual garden competitions to be sponsored and judged by the Garden Club. These competitions were to be open to all-year residents only, and those employing gardeners were not allowed to compete. Prizes were to be awarded for: the store making the best appearance through the use of plants and shrubs; the garden showing the greatest improvement over the previous year; best perennial garden; best annual garden; best rock garden; best vegetable garden; and best garden on the shore of Mirror Lake. There was also a junior class, and subsequently Mrs. Robert Isham gave a trophy each year for the best junior garden.

The Club held its first competition in August 1935, and it continued the event every year through 1942.

For two days in August 1935, the Club staged its first annual flower show. It was a very elaborate production and occupied the main floor of the Olympic Arena. Settings of a palatial Grecian country estate formed the background, with arbors and sundials interspersing the flower displays arranged around a large colonial pillared pagoda. A log cabin housed a display of Currier & Ives prints of Adirondack scenes and Redoute flower prints published about 1810. Mrs. Bernstein also displayed her own paintings. On Saturday evening, there was a program of entertainment including tap and ballroom dancing and solos by outstanding vocal artists of the summer colony. The Stevens House orchestra provided the music. There were numerous classes of competition and entries. The show netted $1,000, which the Club donated to the Lake Placid Hospital.

At the annual meeting on September 23, 1935, Mrs. Milton L. Bernstein was re-elected president. Other officers elected were Mrs. James

Shea, vice president; Mrs. Carl Thornton, secretary; and Mrs. Henry Uihlein, treasurer. On the board of directors were William Benson, Mrs. Robert T. Benson, Mrs. Louie Hammer, Mrs. Raymond C. Prime, Mrs. George Lattimer, Mrs. Melvil Dewey, Mrs. Lutcher Brown, Mrs. Constance Dixon, Mrs. Hunter Platt, and Mrs. Robert Isham. Mrs. Bernstein reported the membership had increased over the past year from fifty to 150.

The same officers continued in 1936. Membership was reported at 199. A second annual flower show was held, filling the entire Olympic Arena. Again, there were many classes of competition and many entries. The annual yearbook of the Federated Garden Clubs of New York cited this flower show as having two exhibits worthy of national competition. The Garden Club's own display consisted of a Cape Cod cottage and garage set in a lawn and flower garden, all enclosed by a picket fence. The local Civilian Conservation Corps had an exhibit. Again, the proceeds went to the Lake Placid Hospital. The garden competitions were also held that summer.

In 1937, the Club became a member of the Federated Garden Clubs of New York State. It staged a third elaborate annual flower show, with proceeds of $915 going to the Lake Placid Hospital. Unfortunately, no account can be given of the show's decorations, as all copies of the *Lake Placid News* for August 1937 are missing. The Club also painted the library in 1937, planted its grounds, and installed window boxes and shutters.

Membership in 1937 was sixty-one contributing and 144 active. At the annual meeting, in September, all officers elected in 1935 were continued. Mrs. Henry Marcy, Mrs. John W. Paris, and Mrs. Moritz Rosenthal were added to the board of directors, and the resignation of Mrs. Constance Dixon was announced. Others directors were Mrs. J.M. Proskauer, Mrs. R.D. Benson, W.S. Benson, Mrs. Louis Hammer, Mrs. George Lattimer, Mrs. Lutcher Brown, Mrs. Raymond C. Prime, Mrs. Melvil Dewey, and Mrs. Robert F. Isham. The Club voted that the civic project they would undertake in 1938 would be planting the Olympic Arena grounds with shrubs and flowers. They started work in the fall of 1937.

In 1938, the gardens of a number of members on Placid Lake were open for inspection during the entire summer. A three-day annual flower show was held at the Olympic Arena, again a magnificent production.

The center of the arena was arranged as a formal garden in a thirty-by-forty-eight-foot plot. Real flagstone steps and walks led from a terrace to the garden plot planted in blue and yellow. Two summer houses were provided by Lamb Lumber Co. and local contractor George Hole. The Lake Placid Club had a wild garden about a running stream and an Adirondack lean-to. The Stevens House, Marcy Hotel, Grand View, and St. Moritz furnished orchestras. The show culminated in a concert Saturday night by the thirty-piece orchestra of the Adirondack Music Camp at Chateaugay. There were a great many classes and entries. Gross receipts were $1,024, and the net proceeds were divided between the Lake Placid Hospital and the Garden Club's fund for civic improvement.

The flower and vegetable garden competitions were again held, and the planting of the Olympic Arena grounds was continued. The Club had developed since its organization in 1933 into one of the largest and strongest of its kind in the state. There were now sixty-nine contributing and 211 active members.

At the annual meeting, all officers and directors were re-elected. Mrs. Henry G. Rogers was made honorary vice president.

In June 1939, the Club sponsored and paid for the planting of large trees around the sides of the Olympic Arena. They did not hold the annual flower show because the ice season at the Olympic Arena had been extended and there was no extra space. Only the flower and vegetable garden competitions were held. At the annual meeting in September, all officers and directors were re-elected.

The annual flower show was again cancelled in 1940 because there was no space at the Olympic Arena, but the vegetable and flower garden competitions were continued. Mrs. Luke L. Perkins was made a director. The annual meeting was postponed to the summer of 1941. During the winter of 1940–41, the Club filled twenty-eight window boxes to be tended by the children at school.

The gardens of members on Lake Placid were again open for inspection in the summer of 1941, and courses in flower arranging were sponsored. The Club held the usual flower and vegetable garden competitions.

In August 1941, the Club staged the annual flower show in the Lake Placid Central School gymnasium. There were eighty-eight classes in twenty-one groups. Royal Scott of Morrisonville set up a miniature fish hatchery, consisting of live trout in a pool beside a garden and flower house. There was a display of vases and containers, and flower and garden films were shown. Five tri-colors were awarded. The children's class had one hundred exhibits. Started three years before to develop the interest of Lake Placid children in flowers, the class had phenomenal growth. The Club contributed $125 out of the show's proceeds toward the purchase of the new Main Street village park on Mirror Lake, and the Club planned to spend the balance of the proceeds on landscaping the park. Club members made personal visits to property owners along Main Street to encourage them to improve the land at the rear of their places.

At the 1941 annual meeting, the Club reported membership at 250. The same officers were re-elected. Kathleen MacConnell was elected a director to succeed Mrs. Henry Marcy, who had resigned. The other directors were re-elected.

In 1941, the Club made plantings at the library, and they planted small evergreens purchased by the Club from the Conservation Department around the village pumping station and on the Chubb River near the village electric plant.

The usual garden competitions were held in 1942, but there was no annual flower show because of the war. The Club did stage a small flower and vegetable Victory Show at the clubhouse of the Shore Owners Association. The price of admission was the purchase of a 25¢ war savings stamp. Apparently, they had no annual meeting and election of officers, as no account has been found.

Save for the encouragement and judging of victory vegetable gardens in 1943, the Club was inactive completely during the war years of 1943, 1944, and 1945. The Club remained completely inactive from 1945 through 1951.

The Garden Club of Lake Placid was reorganized on October 16, 1952, at a meeting held in the Town Hall. Officers elected were: Mrs. Luke L. Perkins, president; Mrs. H. Lutcher Brown, vice president; Mrs. Robert Isham, corresponding secretary; Mrs. Silas Donvan, recording secretary; Mrs. Henry Uihlein, treasurer. Mrs. Kenneth Stevens was named program chairwoman. They set membership dues at $1 for adults, 50¢ for juniors under 16, and $5 for associate memberships.

Beginning in 1953, meetings were held all year round. Mrs. Carl Ortloff and Mrs. James Campbell were co-chairwomen of the membership committee, and membership was reported at 110. The opening and showing of gardens at Placid Lake camps was renewed. The Club replanted the library yard, which had been ripped up for building operations, and also planted shrubs in the rear.

An informal flower show was held in August at the Signal Hill Club, limited to arrangement classes. Mrs. James R. Campbell and Mrs. Robert F. Isham were co-chairwomen.

At the annual meeting on October 15, 1953, Mrs. Luke L. Perkins was re-elected president; Mrs. Robert F. Isham, corresponding secretary; and Mrs. Silas Donvan, recording secretary. New officers elected were Mrs. Gilbert J. Scofield, vice president, succeeding Mrs. H. Lutcher Brown, and Mrs. Fred Abbott, treasurer, succeeding Mrs. Henry Uihlein.

SEVENTY-TWO
Garden Club History Talk

Mary MacKenzie gave this talk on September 26, 1962. Mary's praise for the Garden Club of Lake Placid is a fitting end to this collection of her historical writings. As she thanked the members of the Club for their dedication to Lake Placid, we thank Mary for her labor of love, the history of the Plains of Abraham.

We're going to have a birthday cake with our tea today because we're ten years old. That doesn't mean to say, of course, that we've had a garden club in Lake Placid only ten years. It seems there has always been a garden club or some sort of women's community club ever since Lake Placid first hacked its way out of the wilderness. Unfortunately, as much as we'd like to, we can't take credit for all the wonderful work done by the grand women of these old organizations. We reactivated a former garden club that had become dormant, and with very few exceptions, our membership was entirely new.

We're going to take just a very few minutes and review our brief history and incidentally give ourselves a few pats on the back. It's really amazing, when you think back, how much we've actually done. We've had a lot of fun, too, and a lot of enjoyable social functions, but I think we can also say with due pride that we have earned an accolade for our community service.

We have sponsored annual anti-litter and clean-up campaigns, house and garden contests, and these efforts have borne fruit.

We have provided counsel to the village on park plantings and Christmas decorations.

We have added to the cultural and social life of the town with our outstanding house and garden tours and Christmas teas.

We have staged annual flower shows of a professional caliber as an attraction for our summer visitors.

We have added to the beauty of the village with our tulip signs, our plantings at the veteran's monument, the library and railroad station, and the very artistic winter displays in the empty store windows. And now, of course, we are engaged in our most ambitious project to date: the landscaping of the Mill Pond.

We vigorously fought for the Adirondack Thruway with time, effort, and money, and we courageously opposed almost every other garden club in the state of New York—and thereby earned the dubious epithet from the state group of "those devils."[23]

With a great variety of stimulating programs, each of us has become better educated in the fields of conservation, bird lore, horticulture, the world of nature, flower arranging as an art, and village improvement.

All these are tangible things. But I think our greatest contribution to Lake Placid has been an intangible one. We have given to our community an awareness of the need for home and village beautification, and we have never failed to keep that awareness alive, and in so doing we have won almost unanimous respect. Now, we all know that men are very foolish creatures in their scornful and ignorant attitude toward women's clubs—and especially garden clubs, which they think, like gardens themselves, are literally for the birds. But not a month goes by now but what the men of Lake Placid, in some way, show their approval and gratitude for our efforts, and today our public relations are at an all-time high.

We have one hundred active members, and in a small community of only three thousand souls, this is a very amazing fact in itself. And don't forget that these members are really active. I don't believe there is one single member but who has contributed something of value, not once but many times. We are a united, congenial, well-integrated group, and

23 Here MacKenzie is referring to I-87, the Adirondack Northway. In 1959, the Federated Garden Clubs of New York came out against the construction of the Northway; the Garden Club of Lake Placid was the only member of the federation to support it.

many new, enduring, delightful friendships have been formed among our members.

Of course, we have been most fortunate in our leadership. What other club could boast of having a roster of presidents such as this: Dorothy Perkins, Jane Connelly, Lane Jurgens, Eunice Soden, and Ruth Hart? Very fine women, every one of them, an asset to us and to all of Lake Placid. We owe them a very large vote of thanks for their wonderful work—and let's not forget Mrs. Kenneth Stevens, too, who has always functioned as a sort of Jane-of-all-trades, guide, and general factotum for us.

To all of them present today, a very warm thank-you on our tenth birthday.

APPENDIX

Chronology of the History of North Elba and Lake Placid

July 1989

Prehistoric	A Mohawk Indian summer village exists on the "Plains of Abraham" in North Elba for a long period of time.
1800	First settlers Elijah and Rebecca Bennet arrive in North Elba (then part of the Town of Elizabethtown; after 1808, part of the new Town of Keene) from Vermont and establish a farm on the outskirts of the present Lake Placid village.
1800–1810	Many other Yankee farmers arrive in North Elba. By 1810, two hundred people are residing in the colony, known as the Plains of Abraham, sometimes called Keene Plains or simply The Plains.
1809–1810	Archibald McIntyre, state comptroller, establishes the Elba Iron Works on the Chubb River, creating the present Lower Mill Pond or Power Pond. More people move in to work at the forges. The local farmers begin manufacturing charcoal for the works.
1815	The prosperous colony now numbers about three hundred people, and is generally referred to as Elba, although the name Plains of Abraham for the great plateau east of the later site of John Brown's farm lingers on.
1816	The infamous "year without a summer" in the northern hemisphere. It snows every month of the year, and ice forms on the ponds even in July. In Essex County, and North Elba especially, the crops are ruined, and near starvation follows in the winter of 1816–17.
1817	The Elba Iron Works fails financially and is shut down, leaving many without work. There is a general exodus from Elba due to the "year without a summer" and the closing of the iron works. Only the Iddo Osgood family remains permanently.

1819	The Simeon Avery family arrives and settles in what later became known as the Averyville section of North Elba. The Jacob Moody family arrives and is the first to settle in the Saranac Lake end of North Elba.
1820–1840	By 1820, only ten families are living in North Elba. Elba becomes virtually a ghost town for the next twenty years, with no more than a dozen families in residence at one time. In 1824, the Roswell Thompson family arrives and establishes a farm near present Theanoguen on Wilmington Road. (Thompson descendants still reside in Lake Placid and are our oldest pioneer family.) Iddo Osgood establishes Osgood's Inn on Old Military Road in the early 1830s.
1840–1849	The Remembrance Nash family arrives in North Elba in 1840, and the Thomas Brewster family arrives in 1841. A new migration to North Elba begins. By 1846 the abolitionist and philanthropist, Gerrit Smith of Peterboro, New York, has accumulated large land holdings in North Elba and offers them for sale. He also gives away many of his lots to free Negroes of New York State, establishing North Elba's famous black colony. The late 1840s bring the first signs of the tourist trade. Sportsmen, mountain climbers, writers, and artists begin to trickle in. The only places of accommodation are Osgood's Inn and a few farmhouses.
1849	In June 1849 the abolitionist John Brown, whose name will soon ring around the world, arrives at North Elba to take up farming and assist the black colony to become good, practical farmers. In October, Elba gets its first U.S. post office, known as "North Elba." The "North" had to be tacked on to Elba to distinguish it from another Elba in Genesee County. In December, the Legislature forms a new North Elba township, taken from Keene.

1850	North Elba officially becomes a separate township on January 1. The census shows two hundred people living in the town, the same as in 1810. Joseph V. Nash, son of Remembrance Nash of North Elba, purchases land from Gerrit Smith on the west side of Mirror Lake (then Bennet's Pond), builds a log shanty on the lake shore, and begins to carve a large farm from the wilderness. He is the first to settle in what is now the village of Lake Placid.
1851	Nash's brother-in-law, Benjamin Brewster, son of Thomas Brewster of North Elba, purchases from Gerrit Smith land to the north of Nash, also bordering Mirror Lake, and is the second settler in what will become Lake Placid village. Both men make further purchases in following years, and their two farms eventually encompass the area from Placid Lake down to the present high school, including what is now Main Street, and all of Grand View and Signal hills—what is now the upper village.
1852–1855	Joseph Nash builds a frame farmhouse where the Lakeside Motel of the Hilton complex now stands. Tourists begin to knock at his door, seeking a place to stay. He puts an addition on his house, creating a small inn, Nash's Red House. This is the first and only place of accommodation for tourists in what is now Lake Placid village for the next sixteen years.
1859	John Brown, who has been involved in abolitionist activities for several years, goes to Harper's Ferry, Virginia, with his little band, seizes the U.S. Army arsenal there, is captured, and is hung. His body is brought back to North Elba and buried on his farm on December 8.

1860–1870	More settlers arrive in town, on the outskirts of the present village. The tourist trade increases there. In 1864, Martin Lyon establishes his Lyon's Inn, or North Elba House, on Old Military Road. Robert Scott expands his farmhouse on Cascade Road and creates the Mountain View House. The site of the present village is occupied only by the Nash and Brewster farms and a saw mill on Mill Pond.
1871	Benjamin Brewster builds the first hotel (a rather small, primitive structure) in what will become Lake Placid, just north of the present Mirror Lake Inn. First called Brewster's, it is greatly enlarged over the years and comes to be known as Lake Placid Inn.
1872	The first summer camps are built on Placid Lake.
1876	Joseph Nash builds a second hotel at Lake Placid, on Signal Hill, called the Excelsior House. It is sold in 1878 to John Stevens and becomes the Stevens House. Destroyed by fire in 1885, the Stevens House is rebuilt in the spring of 1886, is expanded over the years, and becomes one of the most famous hotels in the Adirondacks.
1877–1895	The great Lake Placid land rush is on. Joseph Nash and Benjamin Brewster realize the potential of their land holdings and begin to sell off lots. The first store, Stickney's, is built on Mirror Lake in 1878, and Main Street takes shape along Joe Nash's old cow path. A U.S. post office called Lake Placid appears. There is phenomenal growth. Homes, stores, churches, and major hotels are built—the Grand View, Allen House, Mirror Lake House, Lakeside Inn, Westside (later Whiteface Inn), Ruisseaumont, Castle Rustico, and Adirondack Lodge—and Lake Placid enters into its "golden age of hotels." Railroad service arrives in 1893.

1895	Melvil Dewey, state librarian and inventor of the Dewey Decimal System for libraries, establishes the Lake Placid Club on the east side of Mirror Lake, in a former farmhouse known as Bonnyblink. It has the first golf course at Lake Placid.
1900	Lake Placid becomes an incorporated village after an evolutionary period of only thirty years. It is now a nationally recognized summer resort. Elaborate summer homes begin to appear on Signal Hill, and the building of summer camps on Placid Lake continues.
Winter of 1904–05	Lake Placid's image is changed for all time when Melvil Dewey keeps his Lake Placid Club open for the winter season. Ten hardy members participate in skiing, skating, and tobogganing, entitling us to the claim of pioneer winter sports resort of America. So many Club members sign up for the next winter season that Melvil Dewey builds a winter clubhouse.
1905–1913	The Lake Placid Club builds more winterized clubhouses and provides many winter sports facilities—skating rinks, toboggan runs, ski trails, and small ski jumps on the golf links.
1913–1914	The village itself gets into the winter sports act. The Village Board of Trade (later called the Chamber of Commerce, which in turn was later incorporated into the Lake Placid-Essex County Visitors Bureau) begins to actively promote winter sports in the village. The village builds and maintains a municipal skating rink, and major speed-skating races begin. Lake Placid holds its first winter carnival in 1914. The entire village is lavishly decorated, many events are staged, and much newspaper publicity is received.

1913–1928	In 1913, Lake Placid becomes an outdoor studio for the making of silent movies. Hundreds of such movies are shot here for the next fifteen years. This is the heyday of the great speed-skating years. Many national and international races are awarded to Lake Placid, which receives great publicity throughout the U.S. and Canada. By 1920, Lake Placid is a world-famous winter resort, and probably reaches its zenith as a summer resort in the 1920s, attracting as summer residents many famous individuals from the fields of music, literature, and the performing arts. By 1928, the Lake Placid Club has become a huge complex. In 1921, it established a competition-caliber ski jump at Intervales and began to host national and international jumping events.
1929	The III Olympic Winter Games are awarded to Lake Placid, mainly through the insight and efforts of Godfrey Dewey, Melvil's son, and also because of Lake Placid's facilities and experience in staging major competitions.
1929–1932	There are great preparations in these three years, including the building of the Olympic Arena, the bob run, and the speed-skating oval. In 1930, the first annual Horse Show is held. It continues until the war years.
1932	The III Olympic Winter Games are held successfully, in spite of the worldwide Great Depression.

1933–1941	The value of the Olympic Arena, built at great cost to the taxpayers, becomes evident in these Depression years. It is the center of activity—great figure-skating shows, major hockey games, and conventions. In 1934, the first summer ice season is inaugurated. The famous Lake Placid figure skating training program begins. It still continues today and has added much to the economy as well as the renown of Lake Placid for over half a century. Downhill skiing comes into vogue, fired by the III Olympics. Small ski centers spring up—Scott's Cobble, Fawn Ridge, Mount Whitney—but a major ski center is lacking due to Lake Placid's location amidst the state Forest Preserve. In 1941, the voters of the state (by a slim margin) approve a constitutional amendment permitting the state to build a major ski center on Whiteface Mountain. Construction is postponed because of the advent of World War II. Downhill racing trails are built. The bob run, the only one on the North American continent, is the scene of important competitions.
1941–1945	The war years. Lake Placid is a favored summer and winter resort for war-weary Americans and European refugees. The U. S. Army takes over the Lake Placid Club as a rest and rehabilitation center.
1949	State ski center opens on a shoulder of Whiteface called Marble Mountain. Trails are plagued by unfavorable wind exposures, and it becomes evident that a new center must be built in a different location.

1950–1974	The publicity value of the III Olympics has faded, but Lake Placid retains its reputation as an important summer and winter resort and growth continues. With the aid and patronage of Governor Averill Harriman, the great new Whiteface Mountain Ski Center opens in 1958, and Lake Placid can at last compete with the well-known U.S. ski resorts. During this period, Lake Placid hosts prestigious competitions, including world championships, the Kennedy Memorial International Games, the Empire State Winter Games, the Washington's Birthday Ski Jumps, topped by the World University Games in 1972, actually a much larger event than the 1932 Olympics. Many Lake Placid athletes compete in various Olympic Winter Games in this time slot. Local coaches John Viscome and Bud Colby produce an incredible Lake Placid junior ski-jumping team, rated the top junior athletic team in the nation, which wins all of the eastern—and some of the national—championships over a period of fifteen years. In 1970, Mrs. Ruth Newberry reincarnates the Lake Placid Horse Show. It has continued to the present and has grown to be one of the top-rated horse shows in the U.S.
1974	Lake Placid is awarded the XIII Olympic Winter Games for 1980.
1974–1980	Preparation and construction of facilities for XIII Winter Olympics.
1980	Lake Placid hosts the XIII Olympic Winter Games.

1980–1989	Lake Placid is named official Olympic Training Center, and construction of Center complex is in progress. Major sports competitions continue. Enormous building boom in the village and town.

ABOUT THE EDITOR

Lee Manchester was born in 1956 in Minneapolis. He attended Geneva College in Beaver Falls, Pennsylvania, and the University of North Carolina at Charlotte.

Lee's introduction to publishing came while he worked for Narcotics Anonymous World Services in Los Angeles, first as a clerk typist for the organization's membership magazine, then as feature writer, editor, and communications director. He edited the *Lemoore Advance,* a community newspaper in Central California, for two years before coming to the Adirondacks in 2000. Lee was a staff writer at the *Lake Placid* (N.Y.) *News* until 2006, when he joined the administrative staff of Wagner College on Staten Island in New York City.

In 2004, Adirondack Architectural Heritage gave Lee its special recognition award for raising public awareness of regional preservation issues. The previous winners of that award had been the Preservation League of New York State and the New York State Department of Environmental Conservation.

Lee co-authored and edited *The Lake Placid Club: 1890 to 2002* (Saranac Lake, N.Y.: Adirondack Publishing Co., 2002).

Following Lake Placid historian Mary MacKenzie's death in 2003, Lee compiled and edited a collection of nearly 150 poems she had written as a young woman, which were found in her desk. *Blueline,* the literary magazine of the Adirondacks, published the collection as a book-length supplement in 2005. It was titled *Collected Poetry: 1931 to 1937, by Mary Landon MacKenzie.*

Lee currently lives with his wife Jody Leavens on Grymes Hill, Staten Island, and in Jay, New York.